Privatised Law Reform: A History of Patent Law through Private Legislation, 1620–1907

T0270788

In the history of British patent law, the role of Parliament is often side-lined. This is largely due to the raft of failed or timid attempts at patent law reform. Yet there was another way of seeking change. By the end of the nineteenth century, private legislation had become a mechanism or testing ground for more general law reforms. The evolution of the law had essentially been privatised and was handled in the committee rooms in Westminster. This is known in relation to many great industrial movements such as the creating of railways, canals and roads, or political movements such as the powers and duties of local authorities, but it has thus far been largely ignored in the development of patent law. This book addresses this shortfall and examines how private legislation played an important role in the birth of modern patent law.

Phillip Johnson is the Professor of Commercial Law at Cardiff University. His research interests include patent law, public law, and legal history. His publications include a leading practitioner text, the *Modern Law of Patents* (LexisNexis), and *Parliament, Inventions and Patents: A Research Guide and Bibliography* (Routledge).

Privatised Law Reform

A History of Patent Law through
Private Legislation, 1620–1907

Phillip Johnson

Routledge
Taylor & Francis Group

LONDON AND NEW YORK

First published 2018 by Routledge

2 Park Square, Milton Park, Abingdon, Oxfordshire OX14 4RN
52 Vanderbilt Avenue, New York, NY 10017

Routledge is an imprint of the Taylor & Francis Group, an informa business

First issued in paperback 2020

British Library Cataloguing-in-Publication Data
A catalogue record for this book is available from the British Library

Library of Congress Cataloging-in-Publication Data
A catalog record for this book has been requested

ISBN: 978-1-138-56555-5 (hbk)
ISBN: 978-0-367-59398-8 (pbk)

Typeset in ITC Galliard Std
by Swales & Willis Ltd, Exeter, Devon, UK

Contents

Acknowledgements

There are a number of people whom I would like to thank. The many archivists and librarians who helped with the research for this book and for *Parliament, Inventions and Patents: A Research Guide and Bibliography*, which was written at the same time. I would particularly like to thank Philip Baker who kindly sent me copies of his working documents for *Proceedings in Parliament 1624: The House of Commons* which helped greatly. Thanks also to Robert Burrell and the anonymous referees for their comments on earlier drafts of the manuscript. My interest in history began many years ago at school, largely because of Hugh Gregor my enthusiastic teacher. I have long wanted to thank him.

I would like to thank Alison Kirk my commissioning editor at Routledge for her support and George Warburton my production editor at Swales & Willis and Jane Olorenshaw my copy editor. Most importantly, thanks go to Jo for her endless support.

Notes on sources

This monograph was produced at the same time as *Parliament, Inventions and Patents: A Research Guide and Bibliography*. That guide was an attempt to record every official document relating to patents and inventions and Parliament over the period 1600–1976. Any reader seeking a detailed bibliography in relation to any of the patent Acts and Bills, rewards or other patent-related material referred to in this text will hopefully find that the Research Guide is a useful starting point. Its existence has also limited the need to provide wider bibliographic information in this text.

Private Bills were not always published, and many of the reports and materials connected to them have been lost or destroyed. The best source for private Bills materials is, unsurprisingly, the Parliamentary Archives. A document reference in the text is, unless otherwise stated, for that archive (such references begin HL/ or HC/). Another vital source for details of petitions and committee reports are the journals of the House of Commons (CJ) and House of Lords (LJ), and references to these journals includes the date of the entry as well as the volume and page number.

For the 1830s, the best record of Parliamentary debates can be found in the *Mirror of Parliament*, rather than Hansard. The volume numbers of this publication have been included although different versions of the publication have different break points for each volume. However, the page numbers are continuous through the volumes and consistent between the versions.

Where an Act is referred to in the text the short title is used. If this was not assigned by the Act or Bill, the name given in the Chronological List of Statutes or, in relation to Bills, that given in the Commons or Lords Journals, has been used. Private Bills all had preambles albeit of differing lengths. During the relevant period recitals were unnumbered. However, to make it easier to navigate the bills recital numbers have been assigned in this text based incrementally on each "Whereas".

Where a reference to a *Gazette* notice is made in the text, it is to the first such notice that appeared (in the earlier period, there would be three notices) and it is a reference to the *London Gazette* (although notices would usually be published in the *Edinburgh Gazette* and *Dublin Gazette* as well). The *Research Guide* provides details of all the notices related to a particular Bill if these are required.

Throughout the text the various editions of *Erskine May's Treatise on the Law, Privileges, Proceedings and Usage of Parliament* have been used as a source for the rules of Parliamentary procedure and practice. The source used is the edition of that text which was being used at the time the event in question took place. However, the first edition of the work (published 1844) was more comprehensive and useful than any other text which came before. It has therefore been used as a source of the rules of procedure before 1844 where there is no better source.

Finally, before 1852 patents were not assigned numbers. Bennet Woodcroft produced various indexes of patents between 1617 and 1852 and assigned the patents numbers. The year of grant has also been added. In "The History of the Patent System under the Prerogative and at Common Law" (1896) 12 *LQR* 141 and (1900) 16 LQR 44, Wyndham Hulme summarised and assigned patent numbers (using Roman numerals) to certain Elizabethan grants. His numbering has been used in relation to such grants here.

In relation to material connected to the old Scottish Parliaments, the reference used is that which has been assigned by the Records of the Parliaments of Scotland to 1707 (RPS) project conducted by St Andrew's University. The project provides an online version of both the English and old Scots version of the text. Those seeking references to the printed *Acts of the Parliament of Scotland* can find them in the *Research Guide*. Finally, where the old Year Books have been referred to they have been given their SEIPP code which was given to them by David Seipp for his online resource *Legal History: The Year Books* which is hosted by Boston University.

Table of cases

Tables of legislation

References in curly brackets are to the code used in *Parliament, Inventions and Patents: A Research Guide and Bibliography*

Public Acts

Public Bills

Private Acts

Private Bills

Statutory Instruments

Scottish Acts

Irish legislation

International conventions

1   A history of patents

Introduction

The law of patents is a modern invention. This does not mean, however, that the history of patents is short or uneventful. It is history which could still begin at many points and provide fruitful and original debate. This is because "patent history is a subject that is still largely waiting to be written".[1] Where the expanse of uncharted territory is so vast it might seem strange to begin with the role of private legislation: a relatively esoteric area which even when a common part of the legal landscape was described as something of which the public were "profoundly ignorant, and possibly, if they knew, they would be callously indifferent".[2] Yet the role of private legislation in the development of patent law has been largely unexplored or overlooked. Indeed, it has often been dismissed with a few notable highlights being used to demonstrate matters which are often beyond their scope. The history so far presents numerous accounts relating to the passage of the Statute of Monopolies in 1624[3] and there are notable studies of the economic history of patents from the late seventeenth century to the nineteenth.[4] In addition there are studies which were attempting to use history to address the (then) present day issues with the patent system[5] or deal with particular issues, such as Parliamentary rewards[6] or the movement for the abolition of the patent system.[7]

---

1 Brad Sherman, "Towards a History of Patent Law" in *Intellectual Property in Common Law and Civil Law* (Ed Toshiko Takenaka) (Edward Elgar 2013), p 3.
2 See John H Balfour Browne, *Forty Years at the Bar* (Herbert Jenkins 1916), p 13 (the memoirs of a leading member of the Parliamentary bar in the latter part of the nineteenth century).
3 Harold G Fox, *Monopolies and Patents: A Study of the History of Future of the Patent Monopoly* (Toronto 1947); Chris R Kyle, "But a New Button to an Old Coat: The Enactment of the Statute of Monopolies 21 James I cap 3" (1998) 19 J *Legal History* 203; Elizabeth Read Foster, "The Procedure of the House of Commons Against Patents and Monopolies, 1621–1624" in *Conflict in Stuart England: Essays in Honour of Wallace Notestein* (ed William Appleton Aiken and Basil Duke Henning) (Jonathan Cape 1960), p 57; Edward C Walterscheid, "The Early Evolution of the United States Patent Law: Antecedents" (Part 3) (1995) 77 J *Patent and Trademark Office Society* 847 (this is part of a series of articles).
4 Harry Dutton, *The Patent System and Inventive Activity during the Industrial Revolution 1750–1852* (Manchester 1984); Christine MacLeod, *Inventing the Industrial Revolution: The English Patent System 1660–1800* (Cambridge 1988); Sean Bottomley, *The British Patent System during the Industrial Revolution 1700–1852* (Cambridge 2014).
5 In particular, Harold G Fox, *Monopolies and Patents: A Study of the History of Future of the Patent Monopoly* (Toronto 1947); John W Gordon, *Monopolies by Patents and the Statutory Remedies available to the public* (Stevens 1897); and Klaus Boehm and Aubrey Silberston, *The British Patent System: I. Administration* (Cambridge 1967).
6 Robert Burrell and Catherine Kelly, "Parliamentary Rewards and the Evolution of the Patent System" (2015) 74 *Cam LJ* 423; Robert Burrell and Catherine Kelly, "Public Rewards and Innovation Policy: Lessons from the Eighteenth and Nineteenth Centuries" (2014) 77 *MLR* 858.
7 Fritz Machlup and Edith Penrose, "The Patent Controversy in the Nineteenth Century" (1950) 10 *Journal of Economic History* 1; Moureen Coulter, *Property in Ideas: The Patent Question in mid-Victorian Britain* (Thomas Jefferson University Press 1991), Ch 3 to 5 (although she deals with some other topics as well).

The history of patents, however, is noted by its periods of silence. It remains a patchwork of discussions, often about similar matters. It is also littered with simplification. This discussion will attempt to challenge one of the commonly held views, typified by Boehm and Silberston's statement:[8]

> After the Statute of Monopolies there was no important patent statute for over two hundred years.

This statement, at one level, is true. But it misses the rich tapestry of activity where Parliamentarians considered patents and inventions. Indeed, in one sense, it is just plain wrong as there were numerous patent statutes during the seventeenth and eighteenth century – but they were private legislation. While the form and nature of private legislation will be discussed below, in summary, it is an Act of Parliament which creates a special rule for an individual – an exception to general regulation. This discussion will consider whether, and the extent to which, those exceptions became the general rule.

The exception becomes the rule

In the simplest terms, each and every person has the right to petition Parliament and ask for a statute to help just them. If something was prohibited by an Act of Parliament (any Act) you could ask Parliament to exclude you from its application.[9] Similarly, if you wanted to override another person's rights you could ask Parliament to let you (and just you) do it. Just because you could ask Parliament to make a special law for you, it does not mean it will do so or where it does it might impose certain conditions upon you. As one successful private Act would usually, although not always, lead others to petitioning Parliament for the same thing or something similar, so there was a process of evolution and with it a development of law. Put simply, private legislation, as it could relate to anything, became a testing ground for policy. As Clifford puts it in his seminal work[10] on the history of private legislation published in 1885:

> Year by year the records of Parliament show that nearly every great industrial and social movement during the present century has stood in need of private legislation. As one subject of legislation becomes obsolete, or the necessity for it was avoided by general legislation, a successor was never wanting. . . . In dealing with. . .private Bills, Parliament accumulated an experience of the utmost value, and was able from time to time to modify and correct local provisions upon proof of their failure, and at last found them on a safe basis for general legislation.[11]

---

8 Klaus Boehm and Aubrey Silberston, *The British Patent System: I. Administration* (Cambridge 1967), 18.

9 As to non obstante clauses see Chapter 5.

10 A work described acerbically as one which "all have praised and few have read": John H Balfour Browne, *Forty Years at the Bar* (Herbert Jenkins 1916), pp 86–87.

11 Fredrick Clifford, *A History of Private Bill Legislation* (1885) (Frank Cass 1968), Vol 1, pp 266*–266**; Erskine May gives a list of general Acts which had replaced private Acts in 1883: Sir Thomas Erskine May, *A Treatise upon the Law Privileges, Proceedings and Usage of Parliament* (8th Ed, Butterworths 1883), pp 759–767 (the section was truncated in subsequent editions).

In relation to local Acts relating to local government a similar point was made by Frederick Spencer in 1911:

> As regards the constitutional structure of governing bodies, the local Acts of the period 1700–1835 formed probably the largest mass political experiment which has ever been carried out in a particular period of time within the limits of a single State. No one who wishes to create a fancy constitution could find better material for suggestion than the eighteenth century local Acts would afford. At first sight the variety of experiment is bewildering. But, though there is little cause for believing that Parliament consciously followed any defined principles in the construction of the bodies it created, or that those who desired their creation had any views of political architecture based on anything firmer than temporary or local expediency, yet, on analysis, the apparent incoherency can be made to yield some kind of order.[12]

It is possible to go further than Clifford and Spencer, however, as sometimes individuals sought special exemptions from rules and Parliament considered why a rule existed and then decided whether the Bill should be passed or not. Thus, private legislation not only provides a testing ground for laws which were later relaxed, but also for laws which Parliament refused to loosen. Indeed, where Parliament spoke on an issue the judges often followed. Just as the common law went through an "evolution" or, as the Solicitor General (the future Lord Mansfield) suggested in *Omychund v Barker*,[13] "the common law. . . works itself pure"[14] so did legislation through a prism of private Bills.

The role of private legislation in patent history

This discussion looks at private legislation, or more precisely individual private petitions, Bills and Acts, and to the extent possible it seeks to establish whether, or at least the extent to which, private legislation shaped the general law of patents. It will also look at the significance, if any, the courts placed on private Acts when they began interpreting the general rules Parliament finally enacted. In other words, it will seek to establish the extent to which Clifford's general statement about private legislation applies to the development of patent law. In contrast to other histories of patent law, it will put private legislation centre stage. This is not to suggest that private legislation has been ignored in other histories of patent law. But usually it has given little or no weight.[15] Typical is a statement by Christine MacLeod:

> Parliament occasionally discussed individual patents, when the patentee sought an extension of his term or a private Act to give him stronger powers. . .[16]

---

12 Frederick Spencer, *Municipal Origins: An Account of English Private Bill Legislation Relating to Local Government 1740–1835* (Constable & Co 1911), p 115.

13 (1744) 1 Atk 21 (26 ER 15).

14 (1744) 1 Atk 21, 23 (26 ER 15).

15 Even contemporary discussions of reform give it little weight in Thomas Turner, *Remarks on the Amendment of The Law of Patents for Inventions* (Frederic Elsworth 1851), p 5 the sources of reform ideas are presented by private Bills are not included.

16 Christine MacLeod, *Inventing the Industrial Revolution: The English Patent System 1660–1800* (Cambridge 1988), p 3; MacLeod also mentions private Acts being passed in Scotland: p 8.

Accordingly, while MacLeod[17] and others[18] make reference to private legislation it is only occasionally that commentators[19] have seen those Acts as demonstrating Parliament's role in developing wider patent policy.[20] The histories that have been written have concentrated on the grant of patents, and the practice of the law officers, as well as the number or type of patent being granted rather than the legislation governing practice. In this story, the theatre is firmly Parliament and the actors who directed patent policy are shown to be both within the Houses of Parliament and without in the form of petitioners. It is a story which involves men of influence, power and money. Yet, as with many Parliamentary stories, and particularly those which often were played out in committee rooms rather than on the floor of the Houses we have a canvas with many gaps – often gaps which can never be properly filled. It starts in the session of Parliament in 1621 where the Bill of Monopolies passed in the Commons, but was defeated by the Lords as this was also the year in which two private Bills relating to patent law were promoted albeit one was of a very strange nature as will be seen. Our story reaches its conclusion in the final session of Parliament where a private Act relating to patent law was enacted (or indeed, sought), namely in 1907. Over most of the first two hundred years of this period, patents went from being a rare exclusive privilege granted to the few (in fact, the very few) to being available on equal terms to everyone who met clear rules. There are difficulties however, over this same near three-hundred-year period, when the records of Parliament were developing with some periods having detailed Parliamentary diaries and others having few records beyond that recorded in the journals of Parliament.[21]

A series of stories

The role of private legislation in the development of patent law is not part of a generally progressive history towards a new enlightened era, rather it is how particular problems or shortfalls led to changes in patent law sometimes quickly, sometimes after much debate, and sometimes after taking backward steps. It is a series of stories and those stories when read together provide a new picture of how patent law developed. Before the stories begin, in Chapter 2, the nature of private legislation, and the process for enacting it, are examined as it was the process which often led to changes in substance. Readers who are aware of the process of enacting private Bills may wish to pass over this chapter. The process for

---

17 Christine MacLeod, *Inventing the Industrial Revolution: The English Patent System 1660–1800* (Cambridge 1988), p 17 (statement by supporter of Lombe's Silk Engines Act 1731), p 33 (Royal Lustring Company's private Act to extend their patent), p 49 (Howard and Watson's invention), p 73 (Walcot's patent term extension); Christine MacLeod, *Heroes of Invention: Technology, Liberalism and British Identity, 1750–1914* (Cambridge 2007), p 84 (Watt's Act).

18 See for example. Sean Bottomley, *The British Patent System during the Industrial Revolution 1700–1852* (Cambridge 2014) (references to individual petitions: Christopher Le Blon (pp 48–49); Thomas Lombe (p 122); James Watt (p 260) and Hornblower's Bill 1792 (p 260); Harry Dutton, *The Patent System and Inventive Activity During the Industrial Revolution 1750–182* (Manchester 1984) (private Acts for patent extensions mentioned in passing: p 28, 48 and 155).

19 The most notable exception being: Robert Burrell and Catherine Kelly, "Parliamentary Rewards and the Evolution of the Patent System" (2015) 74 *Cam LJ* 423; Robert Burrell and Catherine Kelly, "Public Rewards and Innovation Policy: Lessons from the Eighteenth and Nineteenth Centuries" (2014) 77 *MLR* 858.

20 Most commonly this is a reliance on the significance of Lombe's Silk Engines Act 1731 in developing the specification: Christine MacLeod, *Inventing the Industrial Revolution: The English Patent System 1660–1800* (Cambridge 1988), 49 and Robert Burrell and Catherine Kelly, "Parliamentary Rewards and the Evolution of the Patent System" (2015) 74 *Cam LJ* 423 at 428.

21 See Chapter 2, p 29–30.

prosecuting private legislation became more regimented over the period as the standing orders went from a patchwork of rules to an entire code: a code which included special rules for patents some of which were later adopted in general legislation.

The journey begins in earnest in Chapter 3 with an exploration of the failure of the Bill of Monopolies and the passing of the Statute of Monopolies, both of which would now be termed hybrid legislation (that is a mixture between private and public legislation) and two related private Acts. This pivotal legislation[22] influenced many of the fields of private legislation that followed as it set the rules from which exceptions were sought. Chapter 4 explores private Acts which actually protected the invention itself, in other words, where the person went to Parliament (rather than to the Crown) to protect his or her invention. Indeed, as will be discussed, the Scottish Parliament before the Union with England developed an extensive (if flawed) economic policy to encourage manufacturing by enacting legislation to give special rights to individuals so as to encourage them to practise their trade or introduce new industries to Scotland.

This will be followed in Chapter 5 by an examination of the classic example of individuals being given exemptions to general laws by way of a non obstante clause – that is the clause included in patents to enable the patentee to practise his or her invention notwithstanding general prohibitions. It will be shown how the Statute of Monopolies itself meant that a non obstante clause in a patent for an invention was probably unenforceable. Yet, it will go further, and explain how the Statute of Monopolies probably precluded the grant of such patents in the first place so that non obstante clauses never got out of the starting blocks.

From this false start, the story will move in Chapter 6 to the granting of exclusive rights to regulate companies and later how patents became embroiled in the prohibition under the Bubble Act[23] yet how the restriction on companies owning patents continued long after the Bubble Act was repealed.[24] This led promoters of companies to seek private Acts to transfer patents to their newly formed companies. Yet, surprisingly, those connected to patents strongly resisted allowing companies to own patents and early attempts to lift the restriction were quashed.

The story then turns, in Chapter 7, to the disclosure of the invention in the specification and show that Parliament should, in one respect, be given more credit for its role in introducing a disclosure requirement. But, on the other hand, it was content to allow certain inventors to be excused from the requirement. It is here that the conflicting impulses of legislators can be explored to see how close the law came to an altogether different approach to disclosure of the invention.

The prolongation (or extension) of patents is the most well-trodden topic when it comes to private Acts of Parliament. The role of Parliament is routinely mentioned by some patent historians although usually only with a few comments.[25] Chapter 8 will look at how these laws developed and how the views taken of these laws, in particular their protection of improvements, mean that the picture is often not as clear as might be expected. It will be shown how standing orders managed to effectively end the practice of granting private Acts

---

22 Which is sometimes said to have be seen as significant only since the modern era: Brad Sherman and Lionel Bently, *Making of Modern Intellectual Property Law* (Cambridge 1999), pp 208–209.

23 Royal Exchange and London Assurance Corporation Act 1719.

24 Bubble Companies, etc Act 1825.

25 The major exception is Burrell and Kelly, who provide a detailed treatment: Robert Burrell and Catherine Kelly, "Public Rewards and Innovation Policy: Lessons from the Eighteenth and Nineteenth Centuries" (2014) 77 *MLR* 858.

to prolong patents. Yet ironically it was also one of the first areas where general legislation replaced private Bills. Chapter 9 looks at the closely related areas of Parliamentary rewards. These rewards were at the time (and still are) seen as an alternative incentive to the patent system. Like private Acts they were usually, although not always, started by a person petitioning Parliament and, it has been suggested, they have contributed to the development of patent law in their own right.[26]

In Chapter 10, the story is one of fees and renewals. The need to pay a renewal fee was a way of reducing the cost of obtaining a patent in the first place and whittling out useless patents, but with renewal fees came the failure to pay those fees and the loss of valuable patents. Private Acts stepped in to allow patentees to save their valuable invention from oblivion and as time went on the right of restoration was introduced into the general law. What is so significant about this particularly technical issue is that the number of private Acts enacted and Bills sought was much greater than any other area and enabled the clearest picture to be formed of the connection between private legislation and the development of general patent policy.

In the final part of the story, Chapter 11, the issue is more technical still. With the birth of the international patent system under the Paris Convention for the Protection of Industrial Property[27] came a system of priority: a mechanism whereby an individual could file in one country and claim that date of filing in another for the purposes of assessing novelty. Foreign applications could, for the first time, save domestic ones. But with a new system came a short and sharp test of when applications could be re-dated to claim unclaimed priority. With this came a role for private Acts albeit the answer was fixed almost as soon as the question was asked.

Once the storytelling is complete, the journey will go full circle and return to evaluate the extent to which private Acts have enabled patent law to develop and to show how the highly individualised system of patents and private legislation led to law reform.

---

26 See for example, Robert Burrell and Catherine Kelly, "Parliamentary Rewards and the Evolution of the Patent System" (2015) 74 *Cam LJ* 423.
27 Signed in March 1883.

2 Private Bill procedure

Introduction

Private legislation is probably as old as Parliament itself. It is possible to say that the House of Commons elected a Committee of Grievances and the House of Lords Receivers of Petitions from the earliest times.[1] These receivers became triers of the petitions by the fourteenth century[2] and the receivers and triers of petitions created a mechanism for private legislation to be sought. Private Bills provided a mixture of court and Parliamentary proceedings. Thus, the procedure involved the examination of witnesses by Counsel during the same stages of proceedings as were (and are) undertaken for a public Bill: it must come before the Houses of Parliament for a First Reading, a Second Reading and a Third Reading[3] and the same question is put to the House, as for public Bills, whether they should be granted these readings, with the same rules of debate and discussion applying.[4] Importantly, an Act of Parliament whether private or public had the full power of Parliamentary sovereignty; it could repeal a public Bill expressly and so, naturally, it could do so by implication.[5] This dual role was expertly explained by Erskine May:

> This union of the judicial and legislative functions is not confined to the forms of procedure, but is an important principle in the inquiries and decisions of Parliament upon the merits of private bills. As a court, it inquires and adjudicates upon the interests of private parties; as a legislature, it is watchful over the interests of the public.[6]

1 Fredrick Clifford, *A History of Private Bill Legislation* (1885) (Frank Cass 1968), Vol 1, p 271 (he refers to a Lords election of receivers in 1278).

2 Fredrick Clifford, *A History of Private Bill Legislation* (1885) (Frank Cass 1968), Vol 1, p 272.

3 The convention of three readings of a Bill appears to have firmed up during the Elizabethan era, before that time some Bills had up to eight readings: see Sir John Neale, *The Elizabethan House of Commons* (Penguin 1949), pp 356–357.

4 Thomas Erskine May, *A Treatise upon the Law Privileges, Proceedings and Usage of Parliament* (1st Ed, Charles Knight & Co 1844), p 386. In general, throughout the text, the references will be to the closest contemporary version of Erskine May. However, where references are to periods before 1844 reference will either be made to other sources or to the first edition.

5 For over a century various editions of Erskine May have said this basic proposition has been "questioned", but it remains the law: see Sir Malcolm Jack (ed), *Erskine May's Treatise on The Law, Privileges, Proceedings and Usage of Parliament* (24th Ed, LexisNexis 2011), p 929.

6 Thomas Erskine May, *A Treatise upon the Law Privileges, Proceedings and Usage of Parliament* (1st Ed, Charles Knight & Co 1844), p 385; this basic statement has remained in every subsequent edition: see the latest edition: Sir Malcolm Jack, *Erskine May's Treatise on The Law, Privileges, Proceedings and Usage of Parliament* (24th Ed, LexisNexis 2011), p 923.

Private or public?

Before the development of the modern classification of Bill as private, local or public[7] there was ambiguity over whether a particular Bill should be properly seen as private or public.[8] This arose largely because most Acts which had followed the private procedure would include a section declaring the Act to be a public Act so that it could be judicially noticed by the court.[9] This meant that during the eighteenth century many Acts were enrolled as public Acts while they had followed the private Bill procedure before Parliament.[10] As this story is concerned with the role of the private Bill procedure in the development of the general public law, the term "private Bill" or "private Act" will be used throughout notwithstanding the Act in question might have be classified differently at the time (and in particular, in the later period, as a local Act). Before continuing on to look at the process for enacting private Bills it is important to understand a few basic principles.

Structure of private Bills

Preamble

The preamble of a Bill is used to set out why particular legislation is expedient, that is, why Parliament should enact it (and if it was not expedient, it should not be enacted). Preambles were once common in public Bills, for example the Statute of Monopolies includes the following:

> Forasmuch as your most excellent majesty in your royal judgment, and of your blessed disposition to the weal and quiet of your subjects, did in the year of our Lord God 1610 publish in print to the whole realm, and to all posterity, that all grants of monopolies, and of the benefit of any penal laws, or of power to dispense with the law, or to compound for the forfeiture, are contrary to your majesty's laws, which your majesty's declaration is truly consonant, and agreeable to the ancient and fundamental laws of this your realm:
>
> and whereas your majesty was further graciously pleased expressly to command that no suitor should presume to move your majesty for matters of that nature;
>
> yet, nevertheless, upon misinformations and untrue pretences of public good many such grants have been unduly obtained and unlawfully put in execution, to the great grievance and inconvenience of your majesty's subjects, contrary to the laws of this your realm, and contrary to your majesty's royal and blessed intention, so published as aforesaid:" for avoiding whereof and preventing of the like in time to come,

---

7 For a view at the turn of the twenty century see Courtenay Ilbert, "The English Statute Book" (1900) 2 *Journal of the Society of Comparative Legislation* 75 at 79–84.

8 So some authors avoid this classification: Robert Burrell and Catherine Kelly, "Parliamentary Rewards and the Evolution of the Patent System" (2015) 74 *Cam LJ* 423 at 425, n 4; and also J Innes, "The Local Acts of a National Parliament: Parliament's Role in Sanctioning Local Action in Eighteenth-Century Britain" (1998) 17 *Parliamentary History* 23. As to the modern classification see: Sir Malcolm Jack, *Erskine May's Treatise on The Law, Privileges, Proceedings and Usage of Parliament* (24th Ed, LexisNexis 2011), pp 924–925.

9 Before the commencement of the Interpretation of Acts, Act 1850, s 7, a private Act had to be specifically pleaded and proved: *Greswolde v Kemp* (1842) Car & M 63 (174 ER 668).

10 Indeed, the difficulty of following the numbering of Acts is a reflection of this. As to numbering see: Robert W Perceval, "Chapter Six, VI, vi, 6 or 6: The Classification and Recording of Acts" (1949) 13 *Parliamentary Affairs* 506.

The role of preambles in public Bills diminished[11] as it became the case that the general expediency of a Bill was agreed following the Second Reading debate.[12] However, the preamble's role in relation to private Bills remains pivotal:

> In private Bills. . .which from their very nature are exceptions to the general law, a preamble must explain, however shortly, the reasons why the legislation is expedient on each of the more important subjects dealt with, and must show. . .that promoters have complied with Standing Orders or with general legislation. . . But the several statements thus made that legislation is expedient go to the root of each Bill.[13]

In other words, the preamble sets out the facts which must be proved to justify the Bill being passed.[14] The preamble comprises a series of recitals each beginning with "Whereas" and the promoter had to prove each recital to make their case. In the early period, recitals were often quite short but as time went on, the stories they tell became more detailed. As the promoter choses the facts they thought they needed to support the expediency of the Bill, the things pleaded could vary greatly between Bills with similar purposes. Furthermore, as expediency involved Parliament giving a judgment on the merits of the preamble (a policy decision as it were) it may be that even if every fact is proven in the preamble, Parliament decides that it is not expedient to pass the Bill.

If the preamble was approved, consideration moved on to the operative part (that is the clauses of the Bill). These clauses had to achieve the purpose of the Bill as set out in the preamble. By about 1840, the House authorities started circulating "Model Bills" to the Parliamentary agents to improve the quality and consistency of the Bills.[15] This meant that where a promoter of a Bill wanted to depart from a model clause they would need to have good reason to do so and explain it in the preamble.[16] However, until required by Standing Orders in the late nineteenth century there were no model clauses for patent Bills.[17]

---

11 There are some instances where judges have lamented the end of preambles: *LCC v Bermondsey Bioscope* [1911] 1 KB 445 at 451; for a modern perspective see, Daniel Greenberg (ed), *Craies on Legislation* (11th Ed, Sweet and Maxwell 2017), [2.5.10]; Baroness Jay (Leader of the House), HL Deb, 26 October 1999, Vol 606 (5th), cols 275–276.

12 Thomas Erskine May, *A Treatise upon the Law Privileges, Proceedings and Usage of Parliament* (1st Ed, Charles Knight & Co 1844), p 408.

13 Fredrick Clifford, *A History of Private Bill Legislation* (1885) (Frank Cass 1968), Vol 2, p 865.

14 As to the subsequent evidential value of these assertions see *Wyld v Silver* [1963] Ch 243 at 261.

15 Orlo Williams, *The Historical Development of Private Bill Procedure and Standing Orders in the House of Commons* (HMSO 1948), Vol 1, 105; there was an extensive discussion of the value of Model Bills (Clauses Consolidation Bills) in the *Report of Select Committee to Examine Applications for Local Acts* (1846 HC Papers 556), Vol 12, p 1, Q 557 (p 63); Q 569 (p 65); QQ 716–718 (p 18); QQ 730–731 (p 82); and QQ 781–785 (p 88).

16 Orlo Williams, *The Historical Development of Private Bill Procedure and Standing Orders in the House of Commons* (HMSO 1948), Vol 1, p 105.

17 Indeed, when an approved (private) book of precedents for private Acts was published in 1829 (*Private Acts of Parliament selected and approved by a Committee of the House of Lords* (Stevens & Sons 1829)), the precedent for Class H (Bills for Confirming or Prolonging Letters Patent) was actually for the licensing of a playhouse (p 658) the reason stated as "Bills of this description rarely occur in practice. The above form, which, perhaps, in strictness, belongs to Class G, has been selected with a view to utility." Although, Parliamentary Agent, *Practical Instructions on the Passing of Private Bills through Both Houses of Parliament* (Stevens and Son 1825) included precedents for notices and petitions connected with such Bills: see pp 111–115 and Appendix H (pp 240–241).

Standing order

The regulation of business before the Houses of Parliament was made more certain by the adoption of standing orders. In relation to private Bills, Standing Orders began to be passed during the seventeenth century, but they covered a few very limited aspects of procedure. Over time the number increased until by the end of the period in 1907 there was a code of nearly three hundred orders governing private Bills.[18] These orders regulated procedure (such as what must be lodged and when) but they could also, indirectly, regulate substance (Third Reading will not be given to a Bill where it is not promoted by the inventor[19]). In any event, it has always been possible for either the Commons or Lords to dispense with their own Standing Orders in a particular case and, eventually, committees were established for the purpose of considering whether such dispensation was appropriate.

Parliamentary agents

The shepherding of private Bills through Parliament was originally undertaken by officers of the Houses who would help petitioners with the process – for a fee – and as the volume of private legislation grew certain offices in the House became lucrative.[20] Without the help of these officials the Bill would stall and usually fail. Over time Parliamentary agents began to work outside Parliament (so-called "outdoor agents") originally at the same time as the House officials continued to provide the service (so-called "indoor agents"). However, as the nineteenth century progressed, House officials were forbidden to act as agents.[21] This led to a full cadre of professional Parliamentary agents[22] and only such agents were permitted to promote or oppose a Bill before Parliament. Indeed, the role of agents meant that in some instances towards the end of this history they had some role in the development of procedural and substantive law.

Private Bills: early period

All Parliamentary legislation developed from the petitioning of the King, through petitioning the King in Council and, finally, the King in Parliament.[23] The distinction between public general legislation and private legislation was not originally important. All legislation

---

18 *Standing Orders of the House of Lords relative to Bringing in and Proceeding on Private Bills* (1907 HL Papers 28 and 194), Vol 1, 41; *Standing Orders of the House of Commons. Part I.--Public business. Part II.--Private business* (1907 HC Papers 329), Vol 66, p 307.

19 See Chapter 8, p 132–3.

20 The Clerk to Parliament made between £4,500 and £10,500 annually from private Bills between 1790 and 1799 (and the Assistant Clerk between £350 and nearly £800 during the same period – Appendix VI) although later the fees were lower but more generally shared (Appendix X): see Orlo Williams, *The Clerical Organization of the House of Commons* (Oxford 1954); and David L Rydz, *The Parliamentary Agents: A History* (Royal Historical Society 1979), Chapter 2.

21 New entrants were banned from outside agency from 1835 and all such work had to cease by 1840: Orlo Williams, *The Historical Development of Private Bill Procedure and Standing Orders in the House of Commons* (HMSO 1948), Vol 1, pp 52–53.

22 These were governed by rules imposed by the Speaker originally in 1837 and the modern basis of agency started in 1838: David L Rydz, *The Parliamentary Agents: A History* (Royal Historical Society 1979), 1837 Rules, 210 and 1838 Rules, p 212.

23 Orlo Williams, *The Historical Development of Private Bill Procedure and Standing Orders in the House of Commons* (HMSO 1948), Vol 1, p 23.

could be begun by petition[24] as well as by motion.[25] Thus, public and private legislation were not distinguished in principle or in form.[26] Indeed, as mentioned above, it was possible for a Bill to follow some or all of the procedure for private legislation and then be printed as a public Act.[27]

The story of private patent legislation begins during James I's reign,[28] a period when the procedural distinction between private and public remained unclear and when the King was actively discouraging legislation and had a particular disdain for private legislation.[29] Henry Scobell, who gave an account of the procedure of the House of Commons[30] in the mid-seventeenth century, describes only a few specific details on the procedure for private Bills.[31] Thus, we know that private Bills were read in the morning before the House was full[32] and were read after public Bills on report and which Counsel should be heard first and whether witnesses should be heard before the House or in committee.[33]

Private business begins to develop

The first recorded Standing Order on private business was made by the House of Commons in 1685. It ended the possibility of starting private legislation by motion and required all such legislation to begin by petition.[34] The second Standing Order on private Bills, passed in 1690, required a copy of Letters Patent be annexed to any Bill for confirming the same.[35] These obligations were very limited and so the procedure for private Bills was still very much like that for public business, particularly in the House of Commons.

---

24 Josef Redlich (trans Ernest Steinhal), *The Procedure of the House of Commons: A Study of its History and Present Form* (Archibald & Constable 1903), p 13.

25 This was still possible in relation to private legislation in Scobell's time: Henry Scobell, *Memorials of the Method and Manner of Proceedings in Parliament on Passing Bills* (1656) (1670), p 41.

26 Thomas Erskine May, *A Treatise upon the Law Privileges, Proceedings and Usage of Parliament* (1st Ed, Charles Knight & Co 1844), p 384.

27 Sheila Lambert, *Bills and Acts: Legislative Procedure in Eighteenth-Century England* (Cambridge 1971), 84.

28 Both in England and Scotland (albeit his reign as James VI in Scotland began on 24 July 1567).

29 Elizabeth Read Foster, *The House of Lords 1603–1649: Structure, Procedure, and the Nature of Its Business* (North Carolina Press 1983), p 189.

30 Henry Scobell, *Memorials of the Method and Manner of Proceedings in Parliament on Passing Bills* (1656) (references to the republished 1670 edition). He also discusses procedure in the Lords: Henry Scobell, *Remembrances of Some Methods, Orders and Proceedings of the House of Lords* (Henry Hill 1689) but the discussion is much more limited.

31 There remain controversies over the period of the Interregnum (from 1640 to 1649) where Ordinances were initially passed instead of Acts of Parliament (as they lacked Royal Assent) and subsequently (from 1649 to 1660) Acts were passed by the House of Commons alone: for a discussion of this period see: Elizabeth Read Foster, "The House of Lords and Ordinances 1641–1649" (1977) *Am J Legal History* 158; Michael Mendle, "The Great Council of Parliament and the First Ordinances: The Constitutional Theory of the Civil War" (1992) 31 *Journal of British Studies* 133; Charles H Firth and Robert S Rait, *Acts and Ordinances of the Interregnum, 1642–1660* (London 1911), p iii.

32 Henry Scobell, *Memorials of the Method and Manner of Proceedings in Parliament on Passing Bills* (1656) (1670), p 41.

33 Henry Scobell, *Memorials of the Method and Manner of Proceedings in Parliament on Passing Bills* (1656) (1670), p 51.

34 9 CJ 719 (26 May 1685); a similar order was passed by the House of Lords on 7 December 1699 (No 95) and requiring the petition to be signed 16 February 1705 (No 103): the Standing Orders numbers are based on those given in Historical Manuscript Commissions, *House of Lords Manuscripts 1712–1714* (HMSO 1953), Vol 10, *Roll of Standing Orders of the House of Lords* (No 2923), p 1 ('HL SO 1664–1715').

35 10 CJ 412 (13 May 1690).

Indeed, the distinction between public and private business in the earliest periods was unclear as fees could be paid on Bills which might be considered public as well as those that would later be seen as private. Accordingly, the decision of whether to proceed with the Bill as a private Bill or a public Bill was originally solved by the officials of the House asking the simple question: "Could they extract fees from someone? If so, it was a private Bill,"[36] the fees being paid to the officials in question. The regulation of fee collection was eventually resolved by the introduction of a Table of Fees and so the distinction was formalised on that basis in 1751:

> every bill for the for the particular interest of any person or persons, whether the same be brought in upon petition, or motion, or report from a Committee, or brought from the Lords, hath been and ought to be, deemed a private bill, within the meaning of the table of fees[37]

The so-called *Liverpool Tractate*[38] which was written in about 1762[39] does not refer to private Bills as such, but rather to Bills upon which fees must be paid and so those which are required to go through the private Bill procedure.[40] It is the *Tractate* along with a Memorandum from the papers of a leading Parliamentary Counsel of the day (Robert Harper)[41] that provide the best evidence of how the procedure worked at this time; sometimes called the pre-Standing Orders period.[42]

The petition

House of Commons

A person seeking a private Bill in the House of Commons would need to find an individual member to propose it. This meant that those with influence or power were far more likely to have a private Bill proceed. The member would stand and speak to the nature of the petition and then go and present it at the bar.[43] He was then asked formal questions and the clerk would read the petition to the House[44] after which a question was put whether the petition

36 Sir John Neale, *The Elizabethan House of Commons* (Penguin 1949), p 323.
37 26 CJ 277 (4 June 1751).
38 Catherine Strateman (ed), *The Liverpool Tractate: An Eighteenth Century Manual on the Procedure of the House of Commons* (Columbia 1937).
39 Catherine Strateman (ed), *The Liverpool Tractate: An Eighteenth Century Manual on the Procedure of the House of Commons* (Columbia 1937), p xxii.
40 Sheila Lambert, *Bills and Acts: Legislative Procedure in Eighteenth-Century England* (Cambridge 1971), p 85.
41 See Sheila Lambert, *Bills and Acts: Legislative Procedure in Eighteenth-Century England* (Cambridge 1971), Ch 5.
42 This is the title of Chapter 3 in Orlo Williams, *The Historical Development of Private Bill Procedure and Standing Orders in the House of Commons* (HMSO 1948), Vol 1.
43 Catherine Strateman (ed), *The Liverpool Tractate: An Eighteenth Century Manual on the Procedure of the House of Commons* (Columbia 1937), p 21 (in accordance with Standing Order of 10 December 1692 – misreported in Liverpool). Special rules apply to the City of London, but no patent legislation in this period ever involved the City.
44 Catherine Strateman (ed), *The Liverpool Tractate: An Eighteenth Century Manual on the Procedure of the House of Commons* (Columbia 1937), p 21; this may be why so much detail from petitions are included in the Commons Journal during this period.

be referred to a committee. At this time, referring it to a committee was not yet a formality and there are examples of petitions for patent Bills where this did not happen.[45]

If and when the petition was referred to a committee, the House would indicate who may attend that meeting (or indicate that "all voices" may attend); or, occasionally, it may be referred to a Committee of the Whole House (which essentially means it was heard on the floor of the House of Commons, rather than in a committee room). The members stood to indicate their desire to serve on the committee although additional members with expertise, such as lawyers or merchants, might be added.[46] In contrast to later practice, there was a perception that those with a knowledge or interest in the Bill should speak on it.[47] In general, the committees hearing petitions were small where the Bill was unopposed or not contentious, but could become large where a Bill was interesting or opposed.[48]

Committee examination of petition

The date of the committee was not published during the early period and so it was probably fixed by consultation unless the Bill was opposed in which case a more formal procedure was adopted. Opponents of a Bill could lodge their own petitions to argue that the allegations in the petition were ill-founded; alternatively, they could pray for different provisions to be included in the Bill or, of course, they could support it. In practice, Counsel appearing to oppose the petition was rare as it was too early for the policy of the Bill to have been properly formed.[49] Nevertheless, stalling tactics by sympathetic members could be an effective way of delaying a Bill – adjourning repeatedly so that the petition never left committee[50]– and there could be votes and intensive debate on the petition. This meant an opponent might brief a receptive Member of Parliament as to the questions which could be asked to undermine any proposed Bill so as to show that Standing Orders were not complied with or that there was no *prima facie* case that the passage of a Bill would be expedient.[51]

The Chair would report back to the House what the committee found and then read the report before a motion was put to bring in a Bill. The report on these petition committees were lengthy and, as they were read out to the House, they were reported at length in the Commons Journal.[52] This means that we have an indication of the evidence heard against a Bill and some idea of why a petition was, or was not, successful.[53] This is particularly valuable as the Parliamentary copies of the minutes and records of these committees were almost

---

45 E.g. Le Blon's Petition 1734 (22 CJ 259; 27 February 1734).

46 Catherine Strateman (ed), *The Liverpool Tractate: An Eighteenth Century Manual on the Procedure of the House of Commons* (Columbia 1937), p 28.

47 Orlo Williams, *The Historical Development of Private Bill Procedure and Standing Orders in the House of Commons* (HMSO 1948), Vol 1, p 30.

48 Orlo Williams, *The Historical Development of Private Bill Procedure and Standing Orders in the House of Commons* (HMSO 1948), Vol 1, p 29.

49 Catherine Strateman (ed), *The Liverpool Tractate: An Eighteenth Century Manual on the Procedure of the House of Commons* (Columbia 1937), pp 42–43.

50 Or sometimes the committee never get around to meeting.

51 Thomas Sherwood, *A Treatise upon the Proceedings to be Adopted by Members in Conducting Private Bills* (Private 1828), p 7.

52 Many of the committee reports which were not printed in the journal were later published by Luke Hansard: *Reports from the Committees of the House of Commons 1715–1801* (Hansard 1802).

53 See Lydells' Ballast Engine Petition 1775 (27 CJ 66; 8 January 1775); the lengthy report is at 27 CJ 235 (17 March 1755).

entirely lost in the fire of 1834 and all that remains are some notes in private collections.[54] If the committee found in favour of a petition then leave would be given to introduce the Bill usually by the person who chaired the committee.

House of Lords

The approach was different in the House of Lords. One of their Lordships must propose the petition, as in the Commons,[55] but instead of referring it to a committee the petition would be referred to two judges.[56] These two judges would hear witnesses on oath[57] and they would be presented with a copy of the Bill. Assuming the judges approved the Bill as something which can pass into law, it would be taken to the Lord Chancellor for First Reading. Thus, the procedure on petition in the House of Lords was, at this time, far more judicial than administrative or legislative.

First Reading

Once the Bill could be presented it needed to be printed[58] and a summary of the Bill (called a breviate) produced.[59] The Bill was presented in the same fashion as a public Bill with a summary read out then it was put to First Reading (in the House of Commons by a member supporting the Bill; and in the House of Lords by the Lord Chancellor). By this time, it was already well established that the First Reading of the Bill was not a time to oppose the legislation, but a mere formality. George Bramwell explained the process in the Commons which remained the same well into the nineteenth century:[60]

> The member, intending to present the bill, seats himself at the bar of the House, with the written copy and two prints of the bill, the order of leave, and brief of the bill in his hand; and upon being called to by the Speaker, he answers 'a bill', upon which the Speaker without putting the question, desires him 'to bring it up'. The member then carries up the bill (making three obeisances to the chair) and delivers it to the clerk at the table.

Second Reading

In the House of Commons, the Second Reading of the Bill could be heard anytime after three days had elapsed from the day fixed (i.e. the First Reading)[61]; in the Lords it was

---

54 See for example, Minutes of Re-Commitment of Mr Watt's Engine Bill (11 April 1775): Eric Robinson and Albert Musson (ed), *James Watt and the Steam Revolution: A Documentary History* (Adam & Dart 1969), (Document 16), p 69–76.

55 Harper's Memorandum: Sheila Lambert, *Bills and Acts: Legislative Procedure in Eighteenth-Century England* (Cambridge 1971), p 88.

56 HL SO 1664–1715, No 104.

57 Any oath had to be taken at the Bar of the House of Lords, and a certificate was issued that the oath had been taken: see Harper's Memorandum in Sheila Lambert, *Bills and Acts: Legislative Procedure in Eighteenth-Century England* (Cambridge 1971), p 88.

58 Following a SO introduced on 12 November 1705: 15 CJ 18; also see HL SO 1664–1715, No 101.

59 Harper's Memorandum in Sheila Lambert, *Bills and Acts: Legislative Procedure in Eighteenth-Century England* (Cambridge 1971), p 88.

60 George Bramwell, *The Manner of Proceedings on Bills in the House of Commons* (Hansard 1823), p 58.

61 A rule introduced by SO on 24 November 1699 (13 CJ 5–6).

less formal and it would often take place within a day or two after the First Reading.[62] Until the late 1820s, it was on Second Reading that any objection to the principle of the Bill should be taken.[63] Accordingly, Counsel and witnesses could be heard at the bar of the House and the basic form of this examination was similar to that in court: the witnesses would be called and Counsel would examine them after which any member of the House could present his questions.[64] Thus, at this point, one of the major hurdles for a Bill was Second Reading as it could be defeated entirely.[65] It followed that if it passed Second Reading it was not appropriate to oppose the expediency of the Bill in committee, but merely to amend the Bill's text.[66] Nevertheless, it was rare for Bills to be defeated at Second Reading in the House of Commons and, in relation to private Bills on patents, there are only one or two clear examples.[67] Importantly, in the latter part of the eighteenth century there are some newspaper reports detailing Second Reading debates on private Bills providing some indication of the points made.[68] The Bill would then be committed.[69]

Committee

The approach in committee depended on whether the Bill was opposed or not. Once the Bill had been committed, notice of the meeting was given in the Lobby.[70] During the meeting, committee members (but not other members of the House) could raise issues with the Bill themselves or they could question witnesses.[71] When the Bill was unopposed it appears that "very tender Proof serves to support the Preamble"[72] and the remaining records of the House of Lords suggest that unopposed or at least uncontentious Bills had only a few lines

---

62 Harper's Memorandum in Sheila Lambert, *Bills and Acts: Legislative Procedure in Eighteenth-Century England* (Cambridge 1971), p 88.

63 Charles Ellis, *Practical Remarks and Precedents of Proceedings in Parliament* (Butterworths 1802), p 33 (Lords); p 39 (Commons); Anthony Hammond, *A Summary Treatise on the Practice and Proceedings in Parliament* (Butterworth 1825), p 59 suggests this was still the view as late as 1825.

64 This is evidenced by the Minutes of the Second Reading of Hornblower's Patent Bill 1792: Birmingham Library: MS3147/2/35/23.

65 A motion to delay Second Reading until after prorogation (e.g. for three or six months), rather than refusing it a reading entirely, was the usual way of rejecting a Bill: Thomas Erskine May, *A Treatise upon the Law Privileges, Proceedings and Usage of Parliament* (1st Ed, Charles Knight & Co 1844), pp 277–278.

66 Anthony Hammond, *A Summary Treatise on the Practice and Proceedings in Parliament* (Butterworth 1825), p 59.

67 Hornblower's Patent Bill 1792 (Birmingham Library: MS 3147/2/36/1) and much later the Anti-Dry Rot Bill 1838 (no copy remains) (this also regulated a company and so was not a pure patent Bill as it were); it was more common in the Lords: see James Turner Dye Invention Bill 1791 (Ingrossment: HL/PO/JO/10/2/65A); Kendrew and Porthouse's Bill 1794 (Ingrossment: HL/PO/JO/10/2/67); Dr Bancroft's Patent Bill 1799 (Ingrossment: HL/PO/JO/10/2/70); Bradbury's Bill 1818 (1818 HL Papers 100), Vol 88, p 485.

68 E.g. Lord Dundonald's Patent (Tar, Pitch etc) Act 1785; see *Morning Chronicle and London Advertiser*, 30 April 1785.

69 In theory it was possible to move straight to Third Reading: while this happened in relation to public Bills after the seventeenth century it did not happen for private Bills.

70 Catherine Strateman (ed), *The Liverpool Tractate: An Eighteenth Century Manual on the Procedure of the House of Commons* (Columbia 1937), p 47.

71 Orlo Williams, *The Historical Development of Private Bill Procedure and Standing Orders in the House of Commons* (HMSO 1948), Vol 1, p 33.

72 Catherine Strateman (ed), *The Liverpool Tractate: An Eighteenth Century Manual on the Procedure of the House of Commons* (Columbia 1937), p 47; The *Tractate* also reports how sometimes they were satisfied without any proof.

of minutes,[73] although some might run to a few pages.[74] In either case, it was little more than reciting the preamble.[75] According, passing through this stage was largely a formality for an unopposed Bill. However, where the Bill was opposed the *Liverpool Tractate* explains what happened:

> when your committee meets, the first thing to be done is to read the Preamble and then proceed to examine evidence to prove it: if the Point is litigated, this Examination may probably be very tedious, especially if the parties have money enough to throw away in feeing counsel.[76]

The committee went through each allegation in the preamble and decided whether they were proved or not. It would then go to each clause of the Bill and determine whether it should stand as part of the Bill.[77] The role of the committee was to recommend amendments and report on the allegations (i.e. the preamble) of the Bill.[78] Its powers did not extend to rejecting the principle of the Bill as such[79] although it could omit all the operative clauses – which is much the same thing.[80] The evidence heard by the committee was not reported to the House, only the fact that the Bill had been examined.[81] Accordingly, unlike petition committees, there is no record in the Commons Journal of what happened during these committees.

Report and Third Reading

On report the Chair would state whether the preamble was proven and any amendments made to the Bill.[82] There would be a vote in the House on the amendments made during committee[83] and, once approved, the Bill would be ingrossed. Where there were substantial concerns about the amendments the committee made (or did not make) to the Bill, it could be re-committed for further consideration.[84] The Bill was then read for a third time

---

73 E.g. Byrom's Shorthand Act 1741; see House of Lords Committee Books (HL/PO/CO/1/12), 19 May 1742, p 31.

74 E.g. Elizabeth Taylor's Patent Act 1776; see House of Lords Committee Books (HL/PO/CO/1/21), 22 March 1776, pp 311–315.

75 As the fees of the clerks was based on the time to write up notes, there was an incentive to write longer notes.

76 Catherine Strateman (ed), *The Liverpool Tractate: An Eighteenth Century Manual on the Procedure of the House of Commons* (Columbia 1937), p 47.

77 Catherine Strateman (ed), *The Liverpool Tractate: An Eighteenth Century Manual on the Procedure of the House of Commons* (Columbia 1937), p 47 and 48.

78 Catherine Strateman (ed), *The Liverpool Tractate: An Eighteenth Century Manual on the Procedure of the House of Commons* (Columbia 1937), p 47.

79 See Charles Manners-Sutton (Speaker), *Mirror of Parliament*, Vol 2, 7 April 1829, p 1142 (in relation to Crossley's Petition (Gas Lights) Bill 1829 which was to extend a patent).

80 See discussion of Nicholas Facio's Petition to extend his patent (Watches, Inventions and Extension of Patent Bill 1704), where this appears to have happened, in Edward Wood, *Curiosities of Clocks and Watches: From the Earliest Times* (Richard Bently 1866), pp 307–308.

81 Catherine Strateman (ed), *The Liverpool Tractate: An Eighteenth Century Manual on the Procedure of the House of Commons* (Columbia 1937), p 48; Resolution of 4 June 1607 (1 CJ 378).

82 The amendments made by private Bill committees were only recorded on occasion in the Commons Journal and this ceased by the middle of the nineteenth century. In the Lords the amendments were recorded until 1873.

83 E.g. Porcelain Patent Act 1775; see 35 CJ 382 (15 May 1775).

84 As happened with James Watt's Fire Engine Patent Act 1775: see 35 CJ 280 (7 April 1775).

when any further amendments were added to the Ingrossment by hand. It was possible for a petition to be lodged at the Third Reading even when an opponent had been unsuccessful in committee. Once it passed Third Reading, it was carried to the other House where the procedure started again at First Reading (although, in the House of Lords, the judges would still consider the text of the Bill). Any amendments made by the second House would be returned to the first to be approved and thereafter it would be given Royal Assent.

The early codes

In the half century following the production of the *Liverpool Tractate* in 1762, the private business of the House increased substantially with enclosure, turnpikes, canals and, later, railways and so the business needed to be managed. This led to it becoming increasingly formalised with Standing Orders and business moving away from the floor of the House into committee rooms. While the number of private Bills and petitions relating to patents during this period was quite low, they too attracted particular rules.[85] The evolution of Standing Orders more generally is not part of this story, but an important stage was the creation of the Private Bill Office in 1810 which became the channel between the Houses of Parliament and the Parliamentary agents[86] and where everything had to be lodged. The procedure began to develop and formalise more rapidly from the mid-1830s and so an explanation of the procedure at the time of the enactment of the Letters Patent for Inventions Act 1835 provides an indication of how business was conducted at one of the busiest times for private patent Bills.

Notices

Where a person wanted to apply to the House for leave to bring a Bill for confirming or prolonging the term of a letter patent[87] it was necessary to give notice of the same.[88] This notice had to be inserted three times in the *London Gazette* in the four months preceding the session of Parliament when the Bill would be lodged (and the same number of times in the *Edinburgh* or *Dublin Gazette* where it extended to Scotland or Ireland).[89] It had to include the name of the invention, a distinct description of it as well as the patent term. This requirement of posting notices in the *Gazette* means that from the end of the eighteenth century, it is possible to discover who *intended* to petition Parliament for a Bill to prolong their patent but did not do so. However, there was no notice requirement for other many other classes of private Bills (including those relating to Letters Patent) until the requirement to post notices became more or less general in 1838.[90] The purpose of the notice was to enable persons to object either before the petition was lodged or during the Bill's passage through Parliament.

---

85 See Chapter 8.

86 Orlo Williams, *The Historical Development of Private Bill Procedure and Standing Orders in the House of Commons* (HMSO 1948), Vol 1, p 47.

87 See Chapter 8.

88 SO (1830), Part XVI, r 1; this rule originated 53 CJ 524 (1 May 1798).

89 SO (1830), Part XVI, r 2.

90 The House of Commons Standing Orders were amended in 1837 so that notices had to be given for a wide range of Bills (see General Order I – 92 CJ 638; 15 July 1837). It was not until the following year they were required for incorporation Bills however.

Lodging a petition

As before, a private Bill could only be brought in the House of Commons upon a signed petition, which had to be lodged within fourteen days after the first Friday[91] in every session of Parliament.[92] A printed copy of the proposed Bill had to be annexed to the petition[93] as did a copy of the Letters Patent.[94] The petition was referred to the Select Committee on Petitions for private Bills who determined[95] whether Standing Orders had been complied with[96] but there was no longer a requirement for it to consider whether there was a *prima facie* case for expediency.[97]

Passage of the Bill to Second Reading

Once the petition was found to comply with standing orders, the Bill still had to be presented by a member of the House. This meant that a member of the Commons had to be found to support the Bill.[98] As Parliamentary agents became responsible for prosecuting Bills, it was no longer the case that influence was required – only money to pay fees. Once printed copies had been distributed[99] the Bill would be read for the first time which, at this point, still had the formal processes described by Bramwell.[100] In addition to the pre-existing rule that there must be three clear days between the First and Second Reading[101] it was also necessary for at least two months to have elapsed since the notice was published before the Bill could be read a second time.[102] This was to give opponents time to lodge petitions against the Bill. In the three-day period, the clerk at the Private Bill Office would check the Bill to see if it complied with Standing Orders and other requirements as to form (if it did not, the order for First Reading was discharged and a new Bill had to be presented)[103] and finally all the fees had to be paid.[104]

Second Reading was still the time when the general expediency of the measure was approved,[105] but over the course of the century it became the practice to challenge a Bill at this stage only where it was against the general public policy (rather than over concerns with the

---

91 Where lodging by this date was not possible it was necessary to account for explain the delay in presenting the petition: Thomas Erskine May, *A Treatise upon the Law Privileges, Proceedings and Usage of Parliament* (1st Ed, Charles Knight & Co 1844), p 401.

92 SO (1830), Part I, r 1; the eighteenth century included various resolutions for a Parliamentary Session as to the date upon which petitions could be lodged; a permanent rule was passed on 18 June 1811 (66 CJ 440).

93 SO (1830), Part I, r 10.

94 SO (1830), Part XVI, r 4 (this originated in 1690).

95 Unfortunately, there are no records of the House of Commons Standing Order Committee, but those of the House of Lords remain: The House of Lords Committee Books (in HL/CO/1) eventually include one volume for Standing Orders every session.

96 SO (1830), Part I, r 9.

97 See "Private Business of House of Commons" (1843) *Law Magazine, or, Quarterly Review of Jurisprudence* 129 at 132.

98 Thomas Erskine May, *A Treatise upon the Law Privileges, Proceedings and Usage of Parliament* (1st Ed, Charles Knight & Co 1844), p 400.

99 The breviate (which was now prepared with the assistance of Speaker's Counsel) had to be lodged at least three days before Second Reading: See SO (1830), Part XVIII, r 8; Thomas Erskine May, *A Treatise upon the Law Privileges, Proceedings and Usage of Parliament* (1st Ed, Charles Knight & Co 1844), p 408.

100 See p 14.

101 SO (1830), Part I, r 11; and three days notice had to be given to the Private Bill Office by the agent: r 13.

102 SO (1830), Part I, r 12.

103 SO (1830), Part XVIII, r 6.

104 SO (1830), Part I, r 14.

105 Thomas Erskine May, *A Treatise upon the Law Privileges, Proceedings and Usage of Parliament* (1st Ed, Charles Knight & Co 1844), p 408.

expediency of the particular Bill).[106] This change in procedure meant that the expediency of the Bill was determined conditionally upon facts which would later be proved in committee.[107] In other words, by the mid-nineteenth century, Second Reading had become a formality for private Bills in much the same way First Reading had been for well over a century.

Committee on the private Bill

Where the Bill was unopposed it was referred to the Chairman of the Ways and Means (or, in the Lords, the Lord Chairman) and the proposing member would be the other member of the committee albeit in relation to unopposed Bills it was usually little more than a formality. Nevertheless, the Chairman could treat an unopposed Bill as opposed where the committee wanted to hear evidence,[108] although in such a case, only the promoter of the Bill would provide evidence. In general, however, the committee would simply report the Bill to the House with or without amendment. Unfortunately, where amendments are made there is little or no evidence of why this was done.[109]

Where the Bill was opposed it would be referred to an Opposed Bill Committee. The members of the Opposed Bill Committee were usually chosen on the basis of the local area the Bill concerned, but as patent Bills did not have any physical location they were usually assigned to a nominated committee.[110] The committee appointed the date of the hearing which had to be at least seven days after Second Reading.[111] The procedure on committee was said to be "regulated with a view to secure impartiality and due attention to the interests of the parties".[112] The Chairman of the committee could (where empowered to do so by the House[113]) make an order for the attendance of persons and documents so to facilitate the hearing of the Bill.[114] However, in reality, parties would usually be able to get their witnesses and evidence voluntarily so such a power would be rarely exercised (or even granted). All petitions both promoting and opposing the Bill would usually be referred to the committee, and an order would be made that the petitioners, their Counsel or their agents be heard.[115] Proceedings would begin by the petitions being read and then Counsel for and against the Bill presenting themselves (and where the party did not appear it was assumed that the petition was abandoned).[116]

---

106 See HC Deb, 21 July 1857, Vol 147 (3rd), col 133 (on the Mersey Conservancy Bill).

107 Sir Thomas Erskine May, *A Treatise upon the Law Privileges, Proceedings and Usage of Parliament* (8th Ed, Butterworths 1883), p 799.

108 See for example the *Report of Select Committee on Potters' Patent Bill; Skrivanow's Patent Bill and Gilbert and Sinclair's Patent Bill* (1887 HL Papers 100), Vol 9, p 469.

109 For example, when third party rights were introduced in Mills' Patent Act 1873 there is simply a statement that the clause (which included those rights) was agreed: see House of Lords Committee Books (HL/PO/CO/1/250), 14 March 1873, p 44.

110 Thomas Erskine May, *A Treatise upon the Law Privileges, Proceedings and Usage of Parliament* (1st Ed, Charles Knight & Co 1844), p 410; with a quorum of five: SO (1830), Part I, r 20.

111 SO (1830), Part I, r 15.

112 Thomas Erskine May, *A Treatise upon the Law Privileges, Proceedings and Usage of Parliament* (1st Ed, Charles Knight & Co 1844), p 411.

113 But not otherwise: see Thomas Erskine May, *A Treatise upon the Law Privileges, Proceedings and Usage of Parliament* (1st Ed, Charles Knight & Co 1844), p 428.

114 SO (1830), Part I, r 20.

115 Thomas Erskine May, *A Treatise upon the Law Privileges, Proceedings and Usage of Parliament* (1st Ed, Charles Knight & Co 1844), p 413.

116 Thomas Erskine May, *A Treatise upon the Law Privileges, Proceedings and Usage of Parliament* (1st Ed, Charles Knight & Co 1844), pp 423–424; also see Worm and Balé's Patent Act 1891; Opposed Bill, Evidence 1891, Vol 17: HL/PO/PB/5/57/17 (no witnesses appeared so treated as unopposed).

When it was challenged, the preamble was considered first and the promoter would call witnesses in support of the allegations recited therein.[117] These witnesses could be cross-examined by any party challenging the preamble (i.e. the policy of the Bill) but not by a party who challenged only a clause. Thereafter, the witness could be re-examined. Once all the promoter's witnesses had been called and examined by the parties, Counsel for the promoter summed up the case. Thereafter, Counsel for the petitioners against the Bill were heard in turn and witnesses examined and cross-examined in the same way.[118] Once the evidence had been heard, the room was cleared and the question put whether the preamble was approved.[119] Where it was not approved, this was reported to the House and the Bill failed. If it was approved, the committee reconvened and any petitions against clauses, or proposed amendments, were heard following a largely similar procedure.

While this was the official procedure before a committee it was not always as straight forward and where it was a contentious Bill, it may well have been somewhat chaotic. During the spate of company and railway formations in the 1830s and 1840s there were concerns about the independence of members[120] which led to Anthony Trollope's parody of a Parliamentary committee for a new bridge in *The Three Clerks*[121]:

> The member for Mile End was doubtless sharp, but Mr. Vigil was sharper. His object was, in fact, merely to do his duty to the country by preventing a profuse and useless expenditure of money. His anxiety was a perfectly honest one—to save the Exchequer namely. But the circumstances of the case required that he should fight the battle according to the tactics of the House, and he well understood how to do so.

After describing the presentation of the evidence of both sides, Trollope gives his verdict on how the decision was made[122]:

> At the close the members met to prepare their report. It was then the first week in August, and they were naturally in a hurry to finish their work. It was now their duty to decide on the merits of what they had heard, to form a judgement as to the veracity of the witnesses, and declare, on behalf of the country which they represented, whether or no this bridge should be built at the expense of the nation.
>
> With his decision each was ready enough; but not one of them dreamed of being influenced by anything which had been said before them. All the world—that is, all that

117 Thomas Erskine May, *A Treatise upon the Law Privileges, Proceedings and Usage of Parliament* (1st Ed, Charles Knight & Co 1844), p 424.

118 Thomas Erskine May, *A Treatise upon the Law Privileges, Proceedings and Usage of Parliament* (1st Ed, Charles Knight & Co 1844), p 425 (May explains that *locus standi* to challenge the preamble can be difficult, but in a patent case it will usually be a person with a genuine interest in working the invention and so it would not have been so difficult it is assumed).

119 Thomas Erskine May, *A Treatise upon the Law Privileges, Proceedings and Usage of Parliament* (1st Ed, Charles Knight & Co 1844), p 425.

120 The private Bill procedure, in relation to the formation of companies and particularly railway companies, was believed to be corrupt with members of Parliament having a personal interest in the Bills before them: James Taylor, *Creating Capitalism: Joint-Stock Enterprise in British Politics and Culture, 1800–1870* (Royal Historical Society 2006), p 140; as to attempts to address it see HC Deb, 28 February 1839, Vol 45 (3rd), cols 965–984 and HC Deb, 21 September 1841, Vol 59 (3rd), cols 679–685.

121 Anthony Trollope, *The Three Clerks* (1858) (Penguin 1993), Ch 32, p 396.

122 Anthony Trollope, *The Three Clerks* (1858) (Penguin 1993), Ch 32, pp 401–402.

were in any way concerned in the matter—knew that the witnesses for the bridge were anxious to have it built, and that the witnesses against the bridge were anxious to prevent the building. It would be the worst of ignorance, ignorance of the usage of the world we live in, to suppose that any member of Parliament could be influenced by such manoeuvres. Besides, was not the mind of each man fully known before the committee met?

Various propositions were made by the members among themselves, and various amendments moved. The balance of the different parties had been nearly preserved. A decided victory was not to be expected on either side. At last the resolution to which the committee came was this: 'That this committee is not prepared, under existing circumstances, to recommend a grant of public money for the purpose of erecting a bridge at Limehouse; but that the committee consider that the matter is still open to consideration should further evidence be adduced.'

The Bill, as amended by the committee, is signed by the Chairman and returned.[123] The minutes of the committee are also laid on the Table of the House[124] (but not the *evidence* heard by the committee).[125] After the committee hearings whether orderly or chaotic, the Chairman would reports back to the House as to findings on the allegations proven or otherwise[126] and a new printed copy of the amended Bill had to be provided by the Promoter three days before report.[127] Thereafter, an Ingrossed copy of the Bill would be produced.[128] Only once the Ingrossment had been produced could it have a Third Reading.[129] It was possible to propose further amendments on report or Third Reading (as with a public Bill) provided notice was given at least a day beforehand to the Private Bill Office.[130] However, such late amendments were not welcome and when they were made the Bill was usually referred back to committee.

The House of Lords

Once a Bill had had a Third Reading in the Commons, it would go to the Lords where it would be read for a first time.[131] Thereafter, it was referred to the Committee on Standing Orders to check it complied with the orders.[132] It was possible to petition the committee to challenge compliance with Standing Orders once more[133] and where this was done the parties and witnesses could be heard. Once the Bill had been reported as complying with Standing Orders it would go to its Second Reading[134] after which it would be committed. Where it

---

123 SO (1830), Part I, r 22.

124 SO (1830), Part I, r 27.

125 In relation to opposed Bills, there are Minutes of Evidence held in the Parliamentary Archive.

126 SO (1830), Part I, r 26.

127 SO (1830), Part I, r 29.

128 SO (1830), Part I, r 31; a certificate had to be issued that the paper Bill was the same as the Ingrossment.

129 SO (1830), Part I, r 32.

130 SO (1830), Part XVIII, r 17.

131 Or if it began in the Lords, it would go to the Commons for First Reading.

132 SO No 219 (inserted 16 August 1838: 70 LJ 751).

133 Thomas Erskine May, *A Treatise upon the Law Privileges, Proceedings and Usage of Parliament* (1st Ed, Charles Knight & Co 1844), p 436; although some SO only applied in one House so other it was just created for these orders not originally checked.

134 As in the Commons, a printed copy of the Bill is necessary: SO No 96 (18 LJ 20; 16 November 1705); this order was codified and numbered see *Standing Orders of the House of Lords* (HL Papers 1 of 1826–7), Vol 120, p 13.

was unopposed, it was committed to the whole House but essentially the Lord Chairman considered the Bill and confirmed compliance with Standing Orders and the general law. As in the Commons, the Chairman could require evidence to be heard on an unopposed Bill.

In relation to opposed Bills, five Lords would form the committee[135] and the procedure adopted in the Lords as to the parties appearing, calling evidence and so forth was similar to the Commons. The only notable difference was that witnesses in the Lords always gave evidence under oath.[136] As there were Standing Orders in the Lords relating to patents[137] additional proof might have been needed to that required by the Commons. Once the committee had heard the Bill, it reported back to the House whether it had been proven and if it had it could have its Third Reading. And any amendments required by the Lords would be sent back to the Commons for their concurrence before it passed for the formal Royal Assent.[138] Once more, the procedure for the private Bill was very similar to that for the public; however in contrast to earlier periods there was very little debate outside committee.

The procedure in the later period

By the time the Patents, Designs and Trade Marks Act 1883 was enacted, the procedure for private Bills had developed substantially. This represents the twilight of the private Bill[139] and, by this point, there was a clear process with little involvement from most members of the Houses of Parliament.

Standing Order compliance

The cost to promoters of proving compliance with Standing Orders became enormous as the Houses' requirements increased and a large number of witnesses needed to attend in case the matter was challenged.[140] This led to the Commons in 1846 appointing an examiner to check whether petitions complied with Standing Orders; and the Lords did the same in 1854.[141] The examination soon avoided the need for witnesses to stand around the House waiting to confirm they had received the relevant notices: rather the examiner could ask for affidavits or other evidence to show compliance.[142] The time it took for private Bills petitions to be examined halved.[143] Unfortunately, the only materials that remain in relation to the

---

135 Thomas Erskine May, *A Treatise upon the Law Privileges, Proceedings and Usage of Parliament* (1st Ed, Charles Knight & Co 1844), p 439.

136 Thomas Erskine May, *A Treatise upon the Law Privileges, Proceedings and Usage of Parliament* (1st Ed, Charles Knight & Co 1844), p 440.

137 See pp 132–5.

138 Thomas Erskine May, *A Treatise upon the Law Privileges, Proceedings and Usage of Parliament* (1st Ed, Charles Knight & Co 1844), p 454.

139 Both for patents and more generally.

140 For a good summary see Orlo Williams, *The Historical Development of Private Bill Procedure and Standing Orders in the House of Commons* (HMSO 1948), Vol 1, pp 72–74; also see *Report of Select Committee of House of Lords on Management of Railroads* (1846 HC Papers 489), Vol 13, p 217 at p 4.

141 The role was shared and eventually it was formally assimilated; Sir Thomas Erskine May, *A Treatise upon the Law Privileges, Proceedings and Usage of Parliament* (8th Ed, Butterworths 1883), p 771.

142 Orlo Williams, *The Historical Development of Private Bill Procedure and Standing Orders in the House of Commons* (HMSO 1948), p 75.

143 Orlo Williams, *The Historical Development of Private Bill Procedure and Standing Orders in the House of Commons* (HMSO 1948), p 75.

work of the examiners was where they heard evidence after a contest over proving Standard Orders or where a special report to the House following uncertainties about non-compliance with Standing Orders. Occasionally, the certificates they issued are included in the papers referred to the Standing Order Committee of the House of Lords. In most cases, the records have not been retained.

By the 1880s the procedure had become much quicker and more straightforward. Once the relevant petition and materials had been deposited (including with the relevant government department[144]) any person arguing the Standing Orders were not complied with could provide a memorial[145] to that effect and deposit it in the Private Bill Office. The objections were to matters of procedure only and it was not possible to challenge the merits at this stage.[146] Even without objection, a petition was still examined for non-compliance and, during this phase, patent Bills would routinely not comply with Standing Orders as the notice provisions were not suited to Bills for confirmation of a patent for the non-payment of fees.[147] After examination, whether it was opposed or not, the petition was returned to the Private Bill Office. If the examiner reported the petition did not comply with Standing Orders, it was referred to the Standing Orders Committee to decide whether they should be dispensed with in the particular case[148] and where this was not ordered, it was usually fatal to the Bill.[149] In relation to patent Bills, the failures were usually excused due to the nature of the legislation not fitting the standard Parliamentary timetable as the petition needed to be lodged as soon as possible after the failure to pay the renewal fees was noticed.

Motions

Once the petition had been examined, a motion could be made for the Bill to be read the first time. This could be made by any member, usually someone who had been approached by a Parliamentary agent;[150] after this followed Second Reading, after at least three days but not more than seven days after the First Reading.[151] Once the Bill had been approved on Second Reading, it was committed and the committee could not meet until six days had elapsed since Second Reading.[152]

---

144 For the roles of Government Departments and the need to deposit private Bills with them see: Orlo Williams, *The Historical Development of Private Bill Procedure and Standing Orders in the House of Commons* (HMSO 1948), p 111–117.

145 These had the same form as a petition.

146 There was an attempt to defeat Worm and Balé's Patent Act 1891 on its merits before the House of Lords Standing Orders Committee. A concession was made by the patentee and the opposition ended leading to the Standing Orders being dispensed with: House of Lords Committee Books (HL/PO/CO/1/324), 30 April 1891, pp 166–168 (there is a transcript of the proceedings in a 22 page booklet).

147 See Chapter 10.

148 Sir Thomas Erskine May, *A Treatise upon the Law Privileges, Proceedings and Usage of Parliament* (8th Ed, Butterworths 1883), p 790.

149 Sir Thomas Erskine May, *A Treatise upon the Law Privileges, Proceedings and Usage of Parliament* (8th Ed, Butterworths 1883), p 793.

150 Sir Thomas Erskine May, *A Treatise upon the Law Privileges, Proceedings and Usage of Parliament* (8th Ed, Butterworths 1883), p 785.

151 SO (1883), r 204 (see *Standing Orders of the House of Commons, 1883* (1883 HC Papers 345), Vol 54, p 165); See Sir Thomas Erskine May, *A Treatise upon the Law Privileges, Proceedings and Usage of Parliament* (8th Ed, Butterworths 1883), p 797.

152 SO (1883), r 211.

Committee

Where the Bill was unopposed it was referred to the Chairman of Ways and Means and three members[153] and he could treat it as an opposed Bill if he thought fit (i.e. requiring witnesses to prove the allegations). The promoter simply had to prove the preamble to the satisfaction of the committee by explanation and evidence.[154] The standard of proof would not have been very high where there was no opposition and, as the minutes indicate, in most cases the party turned up, made a statement and left, the Bill being approved.

Where the Bill was opposed, it was referred to a committee with three members[155] who had to give a declaration of impartiality.[156] Gone were the days of Trollope: once the declaration was given the member had to continue to attend[157] and if more than one member was absent the committee was not quorate.[158] The committee had any petition[159] filed not more than ten clear days after First Reading[160] read to them and the parties were heard as before.[161]

After 1865 petitioners had to print their petitions and provide them to members of committee before the first day of sittings.[162] As during the earlier period, the hearing of the Bill involved the calling of witnesses and their examination by the parties first on the preamble and then on the clauses, provided that an opponent could only question a witness on the preamble if they were challenging it.[163] The most significant change since the earlier period was that the witnesses before the Commons were heard on oath as they had been before the Lords[164] and costs could be awarded where a party was unreasonable or vexatious.[165] Otherwise the matter was heard as before with a hearing and then vote on the preamble and then a hearing on a vote on the clauses.

When the committee reported the matter it gave the report to the Private Bill Office with the amended Bill. Where it was not amended it moved onto the Third Reading, but where it was amended the report is ordered to lie on the table[166] and a new printed Bill, as amended in committee, had to be provided to the Private Bill Office.[167] There had to be three

153 Sir Thomas Erskine May, *A Treatise upon the Law Privileges, Proceedings and Usage of Parliament* (8th Ed, Butterworths 1883), p 803; SO (1883); r 137.

154 Sir Thomas Erskine May, *A Treatise upon the Law Privileges, Proceedings and Usage of Parliament* (8th Ed, Butterworths 1883), p 843.

155 SO (1883), r 117.

156 SO (1883), r 118.

157 SO (1883), r 120.

158 SO (1883), r 119.

159 It was possible to challenge a petitioner's *locus standi*. Where this happened referees heard the matter as a separate tribunal: SO (1883), rr 87 and 90 (it was the Chairman of Ways and Means, the Deputy Chairman and Counsel to the Speaker as well as seven elected members. The court required three to sit): Sir Thomas Erskine May, *A Treatise upon the Law Privileges, Proceedings and Usage of Parliament* (8th Ed, Butterworths 1883), pp 817–819.

160 SO (1883), r 129.

161 It was necessary to get a certificate of appearance from the Private Bill Office before the petition would be sent to the Committee: Sir Thomas Erskine May, *A Treatise upon the Law Privileges, Proceedings and Usage of Parliament* (8th Ed, Butterworths 1883), p 815.

162 Order of the House: see 120 CJ 69 (16 February 1865).

163 And as before, where they did not appear their opposition was deemed to be withdrawn: Sir Thomas Erskine May, *A Treatise upon the Law Privileges, Proceedings and Usage of Parliament* (8th Ed, Butterworths 1883), p 856.

164 Parliamentary Witnesses Act 1858.

165 Parliamentary Costs Act 1865.

166 SO (1883), r 213.

167 SO (1883), r 214.

clear days between the report lying on the table and the Third Reading. It was possible to propose an amendment to, or a clause for, the Bill so that it could be heard at Third Reading; although leave of the Chairman of Ways and Means was needed if it was offered by the promoter of the Bill.[168] Thus on the motion for Third Reading being approved the Bill would be printed fair[169] and then pass the Commons and proceed to the Lords.

The House of Lords

Assuming the Bill had obtained the approval of the Lord Chairman whilst it was in the Commons its progress through the Lords had become "easy and expeditious".[170] Once the House of Lords appointed its own examiners the process in the Commons and Lords was harmonised (although there were still some differences in Standing Orders).[171] But once something had been through the Commons, the Lord's examiners only considered the matter where the compliance with a particular Standing Order had not previously been considered by the Commons (thus, it was not considered again).[172]

The Bill would be read the first time once it had been certified by the examiner, and unless the Bill started in the Lords, it could proceed to First Reading straight away. A petition for additional provision was not allowed in the Lords, except with the Lord Chairman's permission, if the Bill had come up from the Commons.[173] Thus, it moved to Second Reading and it was committed. Where it was unopposed, it similarly passed out of committee once it had been seen and approved by the Lord Chairman.[174] Where a Bill was opposed it was remitted to a Committee of Selection which comprised the Lord Chairman and four other Lords. The petitions of opposition were heard in a similar way to the Commons and, unlike in earlier times, an oath could be taken in the committee rather than at the bar of the House.[175] Where the Bill was amended in committee it had to be reprinted before Third Reading unless the Lord Chairman ordered otherwise.[176] If it was given a Third Reading it was passed and, if amended, returned to the Commons for their approval. It was then given Royal Assent. The passage of private Acts had long become an administrative procedure with only occasionally public policy raising its head.[177]

---

168 SO (1883), rr 216 and 217.

169 SO (1883), r 221.

170 Sir Thomas Erskine May, *A Treatise upon the Law Privileges, Proceedings and Usage of Parliament* (8th Ed, Butterworths 1883), p 879.

171 And non-compliance with the Standing Orders in the House of Lords was not relevant to its passage in the Commons: see Charles Manners-Sutton (Speaker), *Mirror of Parliament*, 1 May 1829, Vol 2, pp 1359–1360.

172 Sir Thomas Erskine May, *A Treatise upon the Law Privileges, Proceedings and Usage of Parliament* (8th Ed, Butterworths 1883), p 880.

173 Sir Thomas Erskine May, *A Treatise upon the Law Privileges, Proceedings and Usage of Parliament* (8th Ed, Butterworths 1883), p 885.

174 Sir Thomas Erskine May, *A Treatise upon the Law Privileges, Proceedings and Usage of Parliament* (8th Ed, Butterworths 1883), p 885.

175 See Parliamentary Witnesses Act 1858.

176 Sir Thomas Erskine May, *A Treatise upon the Law Privileges, Proceedings and Usage of Parliament* (8th Ed, Butterworths 1883), p 890; Lords SO No 144 (1883) (*Standing Orders of the House of Lords Relative to the Bringing in and Proceedings on Private Bills 1883*) (1883 HL Papers 210), Vol 1, p 37.

177 *Report of Select Committee on Potters' Patent Bill; Skrivanow's Patent Bill and Gilbert and Sinclair's Patent Bill* (1887 HL Papers 100), Vol 9, p 469.

The Chairman of Committees

The House of Lords appointed a Lord Chairman of Committees from the 1730s[178] and he had a central role in relation to private Bills.[179] He was a permanent paid official (although a member of the House) who was originally concerned with the form of Bills rather than substance.[180] However, by the mid-1830s, the committee on unopposed Bills did not meet and it was left to the Lord Chairman to act as the sole judge of the public interest. Thus, as an agent described the Lord Chairman of that time:

> We all know in the House of Lords all unopposed bills go before one tribunal, namely Lord Shaftesbury; nobody else sits on them at all. . .he sees that the public are properly protected and private rights also[181]

Indeed, a treatise writer of the day describes how the Bill should be presented sooner so the clauses could be arranged with Lord Shaftesbury and he could add what he thought proper.[182] If an agent or promoter did not adopt the language requested by the Lord Chairman they would lose trust and this would make practice rather difficult.[183] Thus, if the Bill was unopposed and the Lord Chairman had given his approval by initialling it, a Bill could pass within a few minutes.[184] The Lord Chairman had immense power and shaped the acceptability of certain clauses and the drafting of certain Bills. Yet the history of how this happened – in conversations in offices or committee rooms – is lost to history, as the minutes of the committee itself are very restricted. Lord Shaftesbury's successor, Lord Redesdale, was appointed in 1851 and he continued in his post until his death thirty-five years later. It is reasonable to say that the shape of the unopposed Bills (i.e. the majority of them) passed between 1830 and 1885 were acceptable because Lord Shaftesbury and later Lord Redesdale said they were. Their word, it appears, was law.

This meant that for many years the role of the Commons in unopposed Bills was perfunctory. Where there was an unopposed Bill it went before a private Bills committee and usually one member would turn up and would be told it had been approved in the other House and so they simply signed the Bill.[185] In 1840, the situation in the Commons changed and the Chairman of the Committee of Supply became the Chair of all unopposed committees;[186]

178 Sheila Lambert, *Bills and Acts: Legislative Procedure in Eighteenth-Century England* (Cambridge 1971), p 91.
179 David L Rydz, *The Parliamentary Agents: A History* (Royal Historical Society 1979), p 52; even before Lord Shaftesbury this appears to be the case see Charles Ellis, *The Solicitor's Instructor in Parliament Concerning Estate Bills and Inclosure Bills* (London: John Rider 1799), pp 16–17 (suggesting that the Bill be shown to the Lord Chairman to see if he approves of it).
180 David L Rydz, *The Parliamentary Agents: A History* (Royal Historical Society 1979), p 53.
181 *Report from Select Committee on Private Business* (1837–8 HC Papers 679), Vol 3, p 405, Evidence of Sir George Burke (Q 106), p 8.
182 See Parliamentary Agent, *Practical Instructions on the Passing of Private Bills through Both Houses of Parliament* (Stevens and Son 1825) at p 24 (also see section headed "Wait on Lord Shaftesbury" at p 27).
183 *Report from Select Committee on Fees of Private Bills* (1826–7 HL Papers 114), Vol 219, p 1 at p 83, Evidence of Thomas Sherwood; *Report of the Select Committee on Establishment of the House of Commons* (1833 HC 648), Vol 12, p 179, Evidence of John Dorington (Q2361-2374), pp 155–156.
184 *Report from Select Committee on Private Business* (1837–8 HC Papers 679), Vol 3, p 405, Evidence of Sir George Burke (Q 106), p 8.
185 *Report from Select Committee on Private Business* (1837–8 HC Papers 679), Vol 3, p 405, Evidence of Sir George Burke (Q 106), p 8.
186 95 CJ 533 (17 July 1840).

this changed to the Chairman of Ways and Means in 1847. Yet the role played by these Chairmen was never, in practice, equivalent to that of the Lord Chairman (although the role was described in a similar way in 1851: so as to prevent injury to the public[187]). In contrast, it was Speaker's Counsel who had the greatest influence in the Commons. Agents describe how he would go through the Bill clause by clause with the corrections and amendments required pointed out to the agent. Counsel would check it again before it went into the committee.[188] Accordingly, from the 1830s onwards, the passage of (at least) unopposed private Bills was largely in the hands of one or two men in each House.

Fees

The cost of a private Bill was a varied and complicated thing. Put simply the costs of a private Bill involved two aspects. One was the administrative costs paid to various clerks and officials of the Houses of Parliament and the other was the fees paid to Parliamentary agents, Counsel and others who worked towards promoting the Bill. The first set of fees was prescribed by the so-called Table of Fees which set out the fee each official should be paid for each stage. There would be a multitude of fees payable to the Speaker, clerks, assistant clerks, door keepers and others at Second Reading[189] and to committee clerks and shorthand writers at committee stage before starting the whole process again in the other House. While the fees were meant to be fixed by the Table of Fees and no other charges were meant to be offered to House officials, it is clear that additional "tips" were paid to encourage business to move more swiftly.[190] There was an additional complexity and expense that arose from the practice of so-called cumulative fees.[191] This meant that where more than one set of interests were concerned in the Bill additional fees had to be paid for each such interest. This meant that Bills with eight interests would attract eight times the fees (called four-double Bills).

This uncertain *official* fee scale meant that the estimates for the cost of a particular Bill were somewhat difficult to predict and this is even more difficult to calculate now. For instance, it is generally thought that the fees for a simple immigration Bill in the mid-eighteenth century might be about £60 although varying a little around that sum.[192] To show the other end of the scale, Clifford cites the Littleport and Downham Drainage Bill which was enacted in the 1799–1800 session[193] with fees of £197 as one "area". In 1810, it was decided to subdivide the various districts and the official fees on the same basic policy with multiple

187 *Select Committee on Private Business: First Report* (1851 HC Papers 35), Vol 10, p 741, (Q 77), p 13, Evidence of James Booth.

188 *Report from the Select Committee on Second Report of Statute Law* (1857 Sess 1 HC Paper 99), Vol 2, p 773, Evidence of GK Richards (Q 186), p 22.

189 See Charles Ellis, *The Solicitor's Instructor in Parliament Concerning Estate Bills and Inclosure Bills* (London: John Rider 1799), p 36.

190 Usually called gratuities: see the table of gratuities in *Select Committee on Establishment of House of Commons, Report, Minutes of Evidence, Appendix* (1833 HC Papers 648), Vol 12, p 175 at p 25 (Evidence John Henry Ley); Charles Ellis, *The Solicitor's Instructor in Parliament concerning Estate Bills and Inclosure Bills* (London: John Rider 1799), p 48 refers to an "expedition" fee for Ingrossments; also see David L Rydz, *The Parliamentary Agents: A History* (Royal Historical Society 1979), pp 65–66.

191 See Fredrick Clifford, *A History of Private Bill Legislation* (1885) (Frank Cass 1968), Vol 2, pp 731–732.

192 See Sheila Lambert, *Bills and Acts: Legislative Procedure in Eighteenth-Century England* (Cambridge 1971), pp 37–38.

193 Enacted as the Bedford Level (Hundred Foot River and Ouse) Drainage Act 1800.

districts were £1,448.[194] Accordingly, the fees on Bills could vary greatly and one of the most substantial fees, the ingrossment fee which would be paid to the clerk to write out the Bill, would relate directly to the length of the Bill. As many patent Bills were quite short, ingrossing costs could be kept down, and usually included only one interest, and the official fees would be closer to those of a naturalisation Bill, rather than the drainage Bills mentioned above. It would be reasonable therefore to assume that most of the patent Bills would attract fees of between £60 and £100 to be passed in the eighteenth century (in 2016 money, it would between £4,446 and £7,410[195]).

However, once ingrossment ended in 1849[196] there is good evidence as to what the official fees in the Commons would have been. A report produced in 1856 sets out the fees paid in the Commons on all private Bills over the period between 1848 and 1855.[197] This means that the fees for *half* the process at least (as further fees were due in the House of Lords) are clear. At this stage, the fees appeared to be about £80 (in 2016 money, it would be £7,371[198]) for an uncontested Bill related to patents[199] but when the Bill was opposed the fees could rocket to hundreds of pounds.[200]

The second cost would be the professional fees of solicitors, Parliamentary agents, Parliamentary counsel and the paying of witness expenses and so forth. These costs, like today, would depend on whether the Bill was of a new sort (needing time for Counsel to settle) or following a precedent, the number of rival interests involved and the extent to which, if at all, the Bill was opposed. The extent of these fees is so variable (as they have always been in litigation) that examples are only of limited assistance. We know that James Watt paid his patent agent £119 8s 4d in relation to his Bill in 1775.[201] Otherwise the evidence is largely based on estimates of the probable cost.

194 Enacted as the Bedford Level Drainage Act 1810.

195 Based on a retail prices comparison since 1800: Lawrence H Officer and Samuel H Williamson, "Five Ways to Compute the Relative Value of a UK Pound Amount, 1270 to Present," MeasuringWorth, 2017.

196 104 CJ 52 (12 February 1849) and 625 (31 July 1849) (applies to private and local Bills); also see *Resolutions Relating to the Ingrossing and Inrolling of Bills* (1849 HC Papers 20), Vol 45, p 19; 81 LJ 18 (8 February 1849).

197 *Return of Amount of Fees Charged at House of Commons on Private Bills Presented to House, 1848–55* (1856 HC Papers 266), Vol 51, p 49.

198 Based on a retail price comparison since 1848: Lawrence H Officer and Samuel H Williamson, "Five Ways to Compute the Relative Value of a UK Pound Amount, 1270 to Present," MeasuringWorth, 2017.

199 The fees on Low's Patent Bill (eventually Low's Patent Copper Company Act 1848) were £81 (*House of Commons Fees on Every Private Bill Presented between 1848 to 1855* (1856 HC Papers 266), Vol 51, p 266 at p 7); Laird's Patent Bill 1851 were £81 (*ibid*, p 23); Claussen's Patent Bill 1852 were also £81 (*ibid*, p 29) and those for the North British Flax Company Bill 1852 were £87 (*ibid*, p 30). The variation can be greater, however, Westhead's Patent Bill 1849 had fees of £102 (p 15).

200 The companies set up to run telegraph companies and work the relevant patents were often contested and had high fees: Magnetic Telegraph Company Bill 1851 had fees of £361 (*ibid*, p 24); the European and American Electric Printing Telegraph Company's Act 1851 had fees of £280 (*ibid*, p 22). Similar fees appeared in other contested patent assignment Bills: Price's Patent Candle Company's Act 1848 had fees of £212 12s (*ibid*, p 8). However, some company Bills which were used to assign patents to companies had much lower fees when uncontested: United Kingdom Electric Telegraph Company's Act 1851 had fees of £97 (*ibid*, p 26) and the Patent Solid Sewage Manure Company's Bill 1852 had fees of £81 (*ibid*, p 29).

201 Account from Nathaniel Barwell (Abingdon St, London 9 May 1775); cited in Eric Robinson, "Matthew Boulton and the Art of Parliamentary Lobbying" (1964) 7 *Historical Journal* 209, fn 14. Barwell was, as most Parliamentary agents were at the time, a Parliamentary clerk and some biographic details are in in Orlo Williams, *The Clerical Organization of the House of Commons 1661–1850* (Oxford 1954), pp 73–75. Finally, Robinson suggests that the Barwell account is in the Doldowlod Archive which was an archive of Watt's papers held by his descendants. That collection has now been sold off and whilst much of it has been bought by the Birmingham library this account was not amongst those papers. It is therefore probably in unknown private hands.

The 1834 Select Committee, which considered fees, includes various accounts setting out the expenses in obtaining a Bill.[202] The total costs of the Caversham Inclosure Bill 1832 (unopposed)[203] was £310 15s 6d of which £122 13s 2d was official fees and the remaining £188 2s 4d was legal fees. While Godson's patent treatise discusses the process for obtaining a private Act of Parliament, it does not provide any indication of the probable fees.[204] In part, this was probably because so few private Acts had been passed at the time the text was written. Nevertheless, Samuel Morton indicated in 1829 that he believed the cost of obtaining a private patent Act to extend his patent would be about £300,[205] a few years later, Lord Brougham thought it would be more than twice that sum at £800.[206] It is reasonable to assume, therefore, that unopposed private Bills, or those which are only slightly opposed, would cost a patentee a few hundred pounds. Slightly more than a patent for England before 1852, but probably less than the three patents required for the United Kingdom.[207]

In contrast, a strongly opposed Bill could be very much more expensive. Before the 1835 Select Committee, the evidence on the Camberwell Poor Bill 1833[208] indicated the extent of the difference. That Bill had official fees of £416 16s 6d, Parliamentary agency fees of £210 10s 4d, solicitor's fee (including advertising) of £686 16s 10d, Counsel's fee of £333 13s 6d, and witness payments of £103 4s 9d. The total cost of the Bill was, therefore, £1,751 1s 11d (in 2016 money, £152,500).[209] There are no records in relation to an opposed Patents Bill.

Reporting

The history of Parliamentary reporting is very patchy.[210] In the seventeenth century and in much of the eighteenth century the best source of Parliamentary debates comes from the

---

202 A full fee note for the New Outfall Bill (enacted as the Nene Outfall Act 1827) with a detailed breakdown was included in the Evidence before the Select Committee: *Report from Select Committee on Private Bills Fees* (1834 HC Papers 540), Vol 11, p 333, at pp 98–111. The report includes many other fees for other Bills at this time.

203 Enacted as the Caversham (Oxfordshire) Inclosure Act 1832. *Report from Select Committee on Private Bills Fees* (1834 HC Papers 540), Vol 11, p 333, 35–36; this was probably on payment of double fees (also see Cheltenham Sewers Act 1833 (properly called the Cheltenham Sewerage, Cleansing and Draining Act 1833) (pp 12–13) which was unopposed and had a similar cost £326 19s 1d) albeit it is indicated to be a Bill attracting double fees.)

204 See Richard Godson, *A Practical Treatise on the Law of Patents for Inventions and of Copyright: With an Introductory Book on Monopolies* (London 1823), pp 148–150.

205 *Report from the Select Committee on the Law Relative to Patents for Invention* (1829 HC Papers 332), Vol 3, p 415 at 92; in 2016 money £300 would be £24,230 based on a retail prices comparison: calculated using Lawrence H Officer and Samuel H Williamson, "Five Ways to Compute the Relative Value of a UK Pound Amount, 1270 to Present," MeasuringWorth, 2017.

206 *Mirror of Parliament*, 1 September 1835, Vol 3, 2849; HL Deb, 1 September 1835, Vol 30 (3rd), col 1187; in 2016 money £800 would be £72,300 based on a retail prices comparison: Lawrence H Officer and Samuel H Williamson, "Five Ways to Compute the Relative Value of a UK Pound Amount, 1270 to Present," MeasuringWorth, 2017.

207 See discussion as to patent fees before the Patent Law Amendment Act 1852 at p 160–164.

208 Enacted as the St. Giles, Camberwell Rates Act 1833.

209 *Report from Select Committee on Private Bills Fees* (1834 HC Papers 540), Vol 11, p 333 at pp 60–1 and 62.

210 For a more detailed discussion see Arthur Aspinall, "The Reporting and Publishing of the House of Commons Debates 1771–1834" in Richard Pares and Alan (AJP) (ed), *Essays Presented to Lewis Namier* (London: Macmillan 1956) at, p 277; Peter Thomas, "The Beginning of Parliamentary Reporting in Newspapers 1768–1774" (1959) 74 *English Historical Review* 623; William Lowe, "Peers and Printers: The Beginnings of Sustained Press Coverage of the House of Lords in the 1770s" (1988) 7 *Parliamentary History* 241; Kathryn Rix, "'Whatever Passed in Parliament Ought to Be Communicated to the Public: Reporting the Proceedings of

diaries of members of Parliament or clerks' official notes. Indeed, Parliamentary diaries for the 1620s are quite extensive. Accordingly, we have diaries for the session in 1621[211] when the Bill of Monopolies failed to pass and also for 1624 when the Statute of Monopolies did pass.[212] These diaries are not, however, anything like a system of modern objective Parliamentary reporting and it is important to remember that diarists may have biases in what they record. It is not known how closely they were listening or whether they were capturing exact phrases or relaying what they heard from witnesses and so forth.[213] Aside from these diaries there are some limited reports in newspapers before 1770,[214] but it was from that date that newspapers began to routinely report Parliamentary proceedings. This was despite the fact it was still contrary to the rules of the House to report proceedings and so those who attended could not make notes and had to rely on their memory.[215] This meant that many reports were copied from each other and myths could be propagated between various newspapers.[216]

Nevertheless, in the early period, it was still the case that many private Bills were debated on the floor of the House at some length and so there are often much better records of what Parliament thought in relation to such Bills between 1770 and the early 1800s than there are again at any time later in our period. Hansard's records of private Bills usually only extended to noting that a particular stage had been passed as there was rarely any debate on the floor of the House. While there are exceptions, it is clear that in the 1830s when the much superior *Mirror of Parliament* was being published only a handful of private Bills were debated on the floor of either House.

This meant that much of what is recorded on a particular private Bill comes from the various committee books held in the Parliamentary Archive. The detail in these books can vary as what is retained depended to some degree on whether the Bill was contested or not. By way of example all that is recorded in the Minute Book for an uncontested Bill such as Hunt's Patent Bill in 1880 was: "Agents: Dyson. The Preamble was proved by Mr Bowyer. The Clauses and Schedule were agreed to without amendment. To Report."[217] Yet where something was contested and evidence heard, a significant amount of information about the background may be in the records, for example the pages of evidence and records on Price's Patent Act 1848 continue for well over a hundred pages.[218]

the Reformed Commons, 1833–1850" (2014) 33 *Parliamentary History* 453; JC Trewin and EM King, *Printer to the House: The Story of Hansard* (Methuen & Co 1952), Ch 1 and 10.

211 Wallace Notestein, Frances Relf and Hartley Simpson, *Commons Debates 1621* (Yale 1935); Samuel Gardiner (ed), *Notes of the Debates in the House of Lords officially taken by Henry Elsing, Clerk of the Parliaments*, 1621 (1871) 103 Camden Society (Old Series).

212 See Philip Baker (ed), *Proceedings in Parliament 1624: The House of Commons* (2015), British History Online; Samuel Gardiner (ed), *Notes on the Debates in the House of Lords: Officially taken by Henry Elsing, 1624–1626* (1879) 24 Camden Society (New Series).

213 As to these points see: Chris Kyle, "Introduction" to *Parliament, Politics and Elections 1604–1648* (2001) 17 Camden Society (Fifth Series) 1 at 4–7.

214 JC Trewin and EM King, *Printer to the House: The Story of Hansard* (Methuen & Co 1952), Ch 1.

215 The most famous being "Memory" Woodfall: see: JC Trewin and EM King, *Printer to the House: The Story of Hansard* (Methuen & Co 1952), pp 53–54.

216 See the discussion in relation to the reporting of proceedings in *Donaldson v Becket* (1774) 2 Bro PC 129 (1 ER 837) and the copying between reporters leading to myths developing: Tomas Gomez-Arostegui, "Copyright at Common Law in 1774" (2014) 47 *Connecticut Law Review* 1.

217 Unopposed Bill Committee Minutes, 1880 (HC/CL/WM/UB/1/33), 2 July 1880, p 59.

218 HC/CL/PB/2/15/12 (there were 19 witnesses).

Statutory confusion

There are two significant shifts that occurred during the period. The first is that date of the New Year moved from Lady Day (25 March) to 1 January in 1752 by reason of the Calendar (New Style) Act 1750. The second is that prior to the Acts of Parliament (Commencement) Act 1793, Acts of Parliament commenced at the *beginning* of the session in which they were passed.[219] This meant that the year attributed to them was based on the first day of the session and not the date of Royal Assent (as it has been since 8 April 1793). In practice, retroactive effect was avoided by including a commencement provision which usually meant a new obligation did not arise until 40 days after the end of the current session of Parliament.[220]

To take a well-known example, the Statute of Monopolies[221] is sometimes dated 1623 and sometimes 1624. The Parliamentary Session in which it was passed assembled on 12 February 1624 (using modern dating), but at the time this would have been 12 February 1623 (as it was before 25 March). It received Royal Assent on 29 May 1624. Accordingly, at the time it would have been said to be an Act passed in 1623, but using modern dating practice it would be 1624 either because a modern calendar is used or, mistakenly, it is dated from Royal Assent. In this story, the modern calendar will be used for all proper dates but the date of the statute on the Chronological List of Statutes (which usually follows the date given at the time of enactment) will be used.

Scotland

The old Scottish Parliament, which existed until the Act of Union in 1707, was far more active in granting individual inventors and industrialists rights than its English counterpart.[222] It must therefore be part of this story to examine how the Scottish Parliament worked from the late sixteenth century up until its abolition. It was always a mono-cameral legislature, but its constitution evolved slightly over the years. There were five estates (or groups)[223] who had attended, although these estates' access varied over its history; they were: Officers of State,[224] the higher Clergy,[225] the Nobility,[226] the Barons of the Shires,[227] and the Burgesses

---

219 *Partridge v Strange and Croker* (1553) 1 Plowd 77 (75 ER 123).

220 For example, see Statute of Monopolies, s 4.

221 Its short title is "The Statute of Monopolies Act": see Schedule 2 of Statute Law Revision Act 1948.

222 In contrast, the Old Irish Parliament had only three petitions for private Bills none of which received Royal Assent: Silk Crapes Bill 1725 (3 Irish Commons Journal ('ICJ') 418; 11 November 1725); Turner Cormac's Bill 1793 (15 ICJ 211; 22 June 1793); Thomas and William Blair's Bill 1795 (16 ICJ 143; 13 May 1795); as to the procedure see: James Kelly, "The Private Bill Legislation of the Irish Parliament 1692–1800" (2014) 33 *Parliamentary History* 73.

223 The Officers were clearly not an estate.

224 See Charles Terry, *The Scottish Parliament: Its Constitution and Procedure 1603–1707* (James MacLehose: Glasgow 1905), pp 4–9.

225 See Charles Terry, *The Scottish Parliament: Its Constitution and Procedure 1603–1707* (James MacLehose: Glasgow 1905), pp 10–11.

226 See Charles Terry, *The Scottish Parliament: Its Constitution and Procedure 1603–1707* (James MacLehose: Glasgow 1905), pp 12–19.

227 See Charles Terry, *The Scottish Parliament: Its Constitution and Procedure 1603–1707* (James MacLehose: Glasgow 1905), pp 19–46.

of the Royal Burghs.[228] The varying nature of the constitution of the Parliament will not be considered here, but the procedure is relevant.

This procedure can be divided into five phases. The first, where the Lords of the Articles (or Committee of the Articles) conducted the business of Parliament; the second, where the Conventors created the committee system; the third, its temporary abolition (and unification with the English Parliament) under Oliver Cromwell; the fourth stage was after the Restoration with the return of Committee of the Articles in a weakened form; and the final, and most active, the secular phase between the revolution of 1688 and the Parliament's abolition.

The Lords of the Articles originally date from the Parliament of 1347 where certain persons were chosen to hold the Parliament allowing the rest of the members to return home.[229] This procedure eventually became routine and, from about 1424, the nominated persons became the Lords of the Articles. Their role was to consider certain things nominated by the Crown and, essentially, to conduct all deliberative and legislative function of the Parliament.[230] Accordingly, the procedure of the Parliament itself was straightforward. The Parliament was summoned, the Lords of the Articles elected, the remaining members went home. At the end of the Parliament the whole Parliament met once more to ratify everything decided by the Lords of the Articles, often in a single day.[231] It had long been assumed that the Crown, through the Officers of State being appointed to the Committee of the Articles, was able to dominate their deliberations. However, more recent research suggests[232] that it was a much more independent body than originally thought. In any event, the Lords of the Articles were temporally abolished by an Act of 1640,[233] but reinstated with the Restoration[234] until the ousting of James VII (James II of England) at which point they were finally abolished upon the accession of William and Mary.[235] The utter dominance of the Lords of the Articles means that prior to 1640, the role of Parliament was nominal. Legislative decisions were taken by a single committee and then ratified by the whole Parliament. In many respects, therefore, it is impossible to consider the progress of private legislation before the Scottish Parliament in this period, rather all that can be done is acknowledge what was enacted.

The second period begins with the moves to oppose Charles I in 1637 and the attempt to force the King to change some unpopular policies (particularly, royal religious policies). A year later, his opponents demanded, in the National Covenant, a free Parliament and general assembly.[236] The failure of the King to address the grievances eventually led to the

---

228 See Charles Terry, *The Scottish Parliament: Its Constitution and Procedure 1603–1707* (James MacLehose: Glasgow 1905), pp 47–63.

229 Charles Terry, *The Scottish Parliament: Its Constitution and Procedure 1603–1707* (James MacLehose: Glasgow 1905), p 103.

230 Charles Terry, *The Scottish Parliament: Its Constitution and Procedure 1603–1707* (James MacLehose: Glasgow 1905), p 104.

231 Charles Terry, *The Scottish Parliament: Its Constitution and Procedure 1603–1707* (James MacLehose: Glasgow 1905), p 104.

232 Roland Tanner, 'The Lords of the Articles before 1540: A Reassessment' (2000) 79 *Scottish Historical Review* 189; and Alan R MacDonald, 'Deliberative Processes in Parliament, c.1567–1639: Multicameralism and the Lords of the Articles' (2002) 81 *Scottish Historical Review* 23.

233 Act Regarding the Choosing of Committees out of Every Estate [RPS: 1640/6/39]; also see David Stevenson (ed), *The Government of Scotland under the Covenanter 1637–1651* (Scottish History Society 1982), p xxiv.

234 Commission to the Lords of the Articles and Processes [RPS: 1661/1/13].

235 The Lords of the Articles were the first grievance listed in the Articles of Grievances [RPS: 1689/3/121]. They were abolished by the Act Concerning the Election of Committees of Parliament [RPS: 1690/4/22].

236 David Stevenson (ed), *The Government of Scotland under the Covenanter 1637–1651* (Scottish History Society 1982), p xi.

formation of a rival government to the King by the so-called Conventors[237] who eventually governed through a central Committee of Estates[238] with sub-committees dealing with particular aspects (such as the Committee of War). While the conflict with the King was largely a religious one, at least at first, it became a full blown constitutional challenge when they held a Parliament in defiance of the King in 1640.[239] When the Parliament met, it abolished the Lords of the Articles and required that all grievances had to be aired in open Parliament. Further, it permitted the full Parliament to delegate particular matters to committees. During this period, sessions of the full Parliament could last from a few days to months[240] (in contrast to a day or two under the Lords of the Articles). The committee system also led to the formation of the Committee of Bills, which dealt with petitions relating to private rights, and the Committee of Overtures which considered proposals for more general legislation.[241] Thus, by this stage, the deliberative functions of the Scottish Parliament separated out private and public legislation. The Orders of 1641 indicated that every overture (that is suggestion for public legislation) should be communicated to each Estate to be considered separately and, where a committee existed, to the committee for its consideration. The Estates and Committee then had a day to consider the overture.[242] It appears the same policy adopted in relation to petitions, supplications and ratifications of property transactions (i.e. private matters).[243]

After the defeat at the Battle of Worcester by English army, the Scottish Parliament was abolished and there was united Parliament under Cromwell. When it was revived in 1661, the role of Committees was greatly diminished and overtures could no longer be referred to them,[244] but where a committee existed, as for trade, it could consider aspects of policy. The final period, after the exile of James VII, saw the Scottish Parliament increasingly beginning to follow the procedures in Westminster with First and Second Readings of Bills, and matters being referred to and from committees.

Policy development

The records of the Scottish Parliament were very limited and the minutes before 1640 do not demonstrate how debates were (or if they were) conducted in the full Parliament.[245] Indeed, while the Lords of the Articles existed there was really little need to debate anything

---

237 David Stevenson (ed), *The Government of Scotland under the Covenanter 1637–1651* (Scottish History Society 1982), pp xii–xvi.
238 They were often called "Tables" rather than Committees, at least originally.
239 David Stevenson (ed), *The Government of Scotland under the Covenanter 1637–1651* (Scottish History Society 1982), pp xxi–xxii.
240 David Stevenson (ed), *The Government of Scotland under the Covenanter 1637–1651* (Scottish History Society 1982), p xxxiv.
241 David Stevenson (ed), *The Government of Scotland under the Covenanter 1637–1651* (Scottish History Society 1982), Appendix 6, p 186.
242 Charles Terry, *The Scottish Parliament: Its Constitution and Procedure 1603–1707* (James MacLehose: Glasgow 1905), p 143.
243 Charles Terry, *The Scottish Parliament: Its Constitution and Procedure 1603–1707* (James MacLehose: Glasgow 1905), p 144 appears to treat the two as the same in any event.
244 Charles Terry, *The Scottish Parliament: Its Constitution and Procedure 1603–1707* (James MacLehose: Glasgow 1905), p 147.
245 Charles Terry, *The Scottish Parliament: Its Constitution and Procedure 1603–1707* (James MacLehose: Glasgow 1905), p 139.

as the Parliament itself merely adopted the decisions presented to it.[246] The Articles would consider general public measures as well as private petitions such as supplications, petitions or requests for ratification.[247]

With the abolition of the Lords of the Articles in 1640, and the creation of the committees, the Parliament often held long sessions and matters could be debated at length.[248] Both public and private matters could be referred to committees, and the Committee of Bills was expressly set up to consider petitions and similar private business.[249] Some minutes of the period exist, but they do not demonstrate any idea of policy. After the Restoration of Charles II in 1660 and until 1689, Parliament could not initiate legislation in the conventional sense as that duty had returned to the Lords of the Articles. However, from the Restoration there was a privilege to debate a particular measure[250] and the Parliament now met once or twice a week during sessions to discuss public affairs rather than simply endorsing the decisions of the Lords of the Articles at the end of the session.[251] A measure might be sent down from the Articles to be considered and then approved and sometimes even amended[252] during this period and so there was clearly an active role and the Parliament record shows some evidence of this. It was also the case that Royal Assent (or the touching of the sceptre) could take place at any time during the session rather than just on the last day.

The Revolution of 1688 led to the abolition of the Lords of the Articles after which the Parliament was in charge of deciding what legislation should be initiated and considered. Indeed, in the last twenty years of its existence there are an increasing number of documents preserved indicating legislative proposals, petitions and so forth. In this period, the procedure of the Scottish Parliament appears increasingly like that of Westminster. Allowing an overture to proceed was like giving leave to introduce a Bill and a Bill once introduced could be read.[253] If the overture was not read it could be withdrawn and, where it needed consideration, it could be left on the table for others to consult.[254] Where a measure was complicated it might be remitted to a committee – in relation to inventions and manufactories that would be the Committee of Trade. The move towards two or three "readings" of a Bill was a late development in the Scottish Parliament as it is clear that during the early Restoration period a Bill could be approved in a single reading.[255]

246 Charles Terry, *The Scottish Parliament: Its Constitution and Procedure 1603–1707* (James MacLehose: Glasgow 1905), p 137.
247 Charles Terry, *The Scottish Parliament: Its Constitution and Procedure 1603–1707* (James MacLehose: Glasgow 1905), p 153.
248 Charles Terry, *The Scottish Parliament: Its Constitution and Procedure 1603–1707* (James MacLehose: Glasgow 1905), pp 138–139.
249 Charles Terry, *The Scottish Parliament: Its Constitution and Procedure 1603–1707* (James MacLehose: Glasgow 1905), p 153.
250 Charles Terry, *The Scottish Parliament: Its Constitution and Procedure 1603–1707* (James MacLehose: Glasgow 1905), pp 145–146.
251 Charles Terry, *The Scottish Parliament: Its Constitution and Procedure 1603–1707* (James MacLehose: Glasgow 1905), p 147.
252 Charles Terry, *The Scottish Parliament: Its Constitution and Procedure 1603–1707* (James MacLehose: Glasgow 1905), p 148.
253 Charles Terry, *The Scottish Parliament: Its Constitution and Procedure 1603–1707* (James MacLehose: Glasgow 1905), p 151.
254 Charles Terry, *The Scottish Parliament: Its Constitution and Procedure 1603–1707* (James MacLehose: Glasgow 1905), p 151.
255 Charles Terry, *The Scottish Parliament: Its Constitution and Procedure 1603–1707* (James MacLehose: Glasgow 1905), p 151.

To begin

This chapter explored the process for enacting private Bills: it provides not only an outline of the procedure but highlights how one or two individuals could have such profound influence on the development of law. More importantly, it sets a framework for understanding why some private Bills passed easily and others struggled to get off the ground. The system, like the early court system, was not one of merit alone but who you knew. It was, and is, an expensive system which precluded access for all but the most rich and powerful and it is hardly surprising therefore that what follows is the history of famous and successful inventors and not the small businesses. In the early period, the procedure excluded those without political influence and in the later period those without money. Yet this system, with its flaws, led to radical developments in patent law as will now be seen.

3　The beginnings

Introduction

Starting a history of the role of private legislation in patent law with the enactments in the two Parliaments of 1621 and 1624 may seem somewhat disingenuous. There were no "proper" private Bills relating to patent law enacted in either Parliament. There were two public Acts and one judgment which was enrolled as an enactment. One of the public Acts was the infamous Statute of Monopolies, the other Heron's Fish-curing Patent Void Act 1623. The judgment, which was enrolled as an enactment, will be called the Censure Act 1621. In addition, there were two public Bills which did not progress: the Welsh Butter Bill 1621 and the Bill to Confirm Patent Grants 1621.

Yet all is not as it seems. Heron's Fish-curing Patent Void Act 1623 would fall within most, including the modern, definitions of private legislation[1] and the fact that it might have been enacted by way of the public Bill procedure does not change its nature, particularly as the difference at that time was so slight. The Statute of Monopolies is arguably what would later be called a hybrid Bill that is "a public bill which affects a particular private interest in a manner different from the private interests of other persons or bodies of the same category or class".[2] The Statute prohibits patents for monopolies (with some exceptions, most notably including inventions), but specifically includes provisos for grants to certain named individuals – this last element making the Bill hybrid.

The Censure Act 1621 is different. It is not a conventional enactment, rather it was the result of what might later be called impeachment proceedings.[3] However, the House of Lords ordered it to be enrolled among the statutes as explained below.[4] Yet the proceedings against two of the defendants, Sir Giles Mompesson and Sir Francis Michell, related to patents and their conduct was a significant factor leading to the Bill of Monopolies being introduced in 1621.[5] Before looking at this groundbreaking session, the canvas needs to be drawn.

1　Malcom Jack (Ed), *Erskine May: Parliamentary Practice* (24th Edition LexisNexis 2011), p 921: "Private legislation is legislation of a special kind conferring particular powers or benefits on any person or body of person – including individuals, local authorities, companies or corporations – in addition to or in conflict with the general law."

2　See the modern definition: Speaker Hylton-Foster, HC Deb, 10 December 1962, Vol 669 (5th), col 45.

3　But see p 39 fn 31 below.

4　3 LJ 135 (26 May 1621).

5　Also the view taken by Chris R Kyle, "But a New Button to an Old Coat: The Enactment of the Statute of Monopolies 21 James I cap 3" (1998) 19 *J Legal History* 203 at 206.

The pre-history

The policy of James I and his son, Charles I, was largely an attempt to raise revenue and most of the tactics used were little more than continuation of earlier Tudor policy. If one steps away from monopolies for a moment and considers the more controversial customs farms this becomes clear. At the accession of James I, the policy of English monarchs had been to farm out the customs duties.[6] What this essentially meant was the right to collect customs was purchased by a private individual from the monarch and the farmers then took a share of the customs collected with the balance being paid to the Crown. The regulation of a trade or activity was part of this policy being extended (and Mompesson's grant for Inn's falls into this category). Thus, if there was a need to license something before it could trade then the right to grant licences could be sold to a patentee and the revenues split between the "patentee" and the Crown. Indeed, when the direct collection of customs (i.e. by Crown officials alone) was adopted at the end of the sixteenth century, the revenues to the Crown actually fell below what was realised when the right was farmed.[7] Therefore, if this is true for other industries,[8] then selling the right to regulate not only made more money for the Crown, but it also enabled vested interests to be maintained.

However, the dissatisfaction with this approach and the attendant grant of monopolies, in particular patents over entire industries, had been brewing since the latter part of Elizabeth I's reign: a time of economic depression as well as one where there was an increase in the number of patents granted.[9] The complaints against patents increased[10] which led the Parliament of 1597 to debate the issue and petition Elizabeth.[11] A more robust challenge followed in 1601 when a Bill was introduced on monopolies,[12] which was to ensure that a patent for a monopoly was only valid to the extent the common law permitted without the additional strength of the Royal Prerogative.[13] Elizabeth managed to put the issue into abeyance with her so-called "Golden Speech" where she said that patents had, she believed, only been granted where they were in the public good even though they might also provide a private benefit.[14]

The end of Elizabeth's reign was marked by *Darcy v Allin*[15] where the court invalidated the infamous playing card patent[16] albeit the reasons for it doing so are ambiguous. Stranger

---

6 See AP Newton, "The Establishment of the Great Farm of the English Customs" (1918) 1 *Transactions of Royal Historical Society* 129.

7 AP Newton, "The Establishment of the Great Farm of the English Customs" (1918) 1 *Transactions of Royal Historical Society* 129 at 146.

8 The nature of the regulation makes it difficult to undertake any comparison.

9 Chris R Kyle, "But a New Button to an Old Coat: The Enactment of the Statute of Monopolies 21 James I cap 3" (1998) 19 *J Legal History* 203 at 204–205.

10 A good summary is available in Chris Dent, "Generally Inconvenient: The 1624 Statute of Monopolies as Political Compromise" (2009) 33 *Melbourne LR* 415 at 427.

11 All that remains is the Queen's response: see Simon D'Ewes, *Journals of All the Parliaments during the Reign of Queen Elizabeth* (John Starkey 1682), p 547 (9 February 1598).

12 It was introduced on 20 November 1601: Bill to Explain Letters Patent 1601.

13 See Simon D'Ewes, *Journals of All the Parliaments during the Reign of Queen Elizabeth* (John Starkey 1682), p 649.

14 Simon D'Ewes, *Journals of All the Parliaments during the Reign of Queen Elizabeth* (John Starkey 1682), p 659 (30 November 1601).

15 (1601) 1 HPC 1; 11 Co Rep 84 (77 ER 1260); Noy 173 (74 ER 1131); Moore 671 (72 ER 830); 1 WPC 1; also see Matthew Fisher, "The Case That Launched a Thousand Writs, or All That Is Dross? Re-conceiving Darcy v Allen: the Case of Monopolies" (2010) *IPQ* 356; Jacob Corré, "The Argument, Decision, and Reports of Darcy v. Allen" (1996) 45 *Emory Law Journal* 1261.

16 Edward Darcye (1598) PR 40 Eliz, Pt 9, m 37 (Eliz Cal No 735) (National Archive: C66/1485).

still was that it was a judgment of the Queen's Bench (a common law court) and not a decision of the Privy Council. This was permitted during Elizabeth's reign by reason of her Proclamation allowing subjects to seek a remedy against a Royal grant in the common law courts,[17] but as the Act relating to Henry Heron's patent will show later, there was still doubt as to whether this applied during the reign of James I – until it was resolved by the Statute of Monopolies.[18]

Soon after his accession, on 7 May 1603, James I[19] issued a proclamation inhibiting the use of any Elizabethan grant or charter until it had been reviewed by the Privy Council.[20] Despite these earlier grants being reviewed, and a Bill passing the House of Commons in 1606 to restrict monopolies and penal rules,[21] the number of monopolies granted grew. The pressure mounted,[22] eventually James I issued his Book of Bounty in 1610.[23] The Book prohibited monopolies generally but permitted certain types to continue, including those for inventions.[24] As Kyle notes[25] this presents a simple dichotomy: (a) permitted monopolies and (b) those which were forbidden. Thus, in the *Clothworkers of Ipswich Case*[26] a charter granted to a local corporation gave it the right to determine who may be a cloth worker, but this was held to be an unlawful monopoly. The issue of monopolies, therefore, remained a continuing gripe until James I called a Parliament in 1621 when it reached a head.

The Parliament of 1621

When Parliament met for business on 5 February 1621, it was the first time it had done so for seven years.[27] One of the four issues on its agenda was addressing grievances.[28] These grievances included, but were not restricted to, monopolies granted by the King. One outcome was the Censure Act 1621, but as indicated already there were also four Bills

---

17 James Larkin and Paul Hughes, *Tudor Royal Proclamations* (New Haven 1969), Vol 3, p 235 (No 812) (dated 28 November 1601).

18 Statute of Monopolies, s 4.

19 This period is one of the most extensively explored in the literature: see for instance: Edward Wyndam Hulme, "The History of the Patent System under the Prerogative and at Common Law" (1896) 12 LQR 141; William Hyde Price, *The English Patents of Monopoly* (Houghton, Mifflin & Co 1906), Chapter 1 and 2; Arthur A Gomme, *Patents of Invention: Origin and Growth of the Patent System in Britain* (1946); Harold G Fox, *Monopolies and Patents: A Study of the History of Future of the Patent Monopoly* (Toronto 1947); William Letwin, "The English Common Law Concerning Monopolies" (1954) 21 *U Chicago LR* 355; Edward C Walterscheid, "The Early Evolution of the United States Patent Law: Antecedents" (Part 3) (1995) 77 *J Patent and Trademark Office Society* 847; Adam Mostoff, "Rethinking the Development of Patents: An Intellectual History, 1550–1800" (2001) 52 *Hastings LJ* 1255; Matthew Fisher, *Fundamentals of Patent Law: Interpretation and Scope of Protection* (Hart 2007), Ch 2.

20 A Proclamation Inhibiting the Use and Execution of Any Charter or Grant Made by the Late Queene Elizabeth, of Any Kind of Monopolies, &c: see James Larkin and Paul Hughes, *Stuart Royal Proclamations: Royal Proclamations of James I 1603–25* (Oxford 1973), Vol 1, p 11 (No 6).

21 Penal and Monopolies Bill 1606 (Ingrossment: HL/PO/JO/10/2/1E).

22 James I renounced a number of grants to try and stem the disquiet: 1 CJ 316–18 (19 November 1606).

23 It is included in Wallace Notestein, Frances Relf and Hartley Simpson, *Commons Debates 1621* (Yale 1935) ('CD 1621'), Vol 7, Appendix B, Part 2, p 491.

24 See *A Declaration of His Majesties Royall Pleasure, in What Sort He Thinketh Fit to Enlarge* (Robert Barker 1610) (Facsmile Reprint 1897) (this version also includes a short note on the Proclamation).

25 Chris R Kyle, "But a New Button to an Old Coat: The Enactment of the Statute of Monopolies 21 James I cap 3" (1998) 19 *J Legal History* 203 at 206.

26 (1614) 1 HPC 31; 11 Co R 53 (77 ER 1218); Godbolt 252 (78 ER 147).

27 The last Parliament was dissolved on 7 June 1614.

28 CD 1621, Vol 2, X's Journal, p 24 (5 February 1621); Book of Committees, Vol 6, p 249, fn 1.

which did not reach the statute book. The Bill of Monopolies, which was passed by the Commons, but not the Lords; the Welsh Butter Bill passed both Houses but failed because the Commons did not agree to the Lords' amendments; Henry Heron's Bill was passed by the Lords but fell at first reading in the Commons; and the Bill to Confirm Patent Grants failed at its first reading in the Commons.

The Parliaments of the 1620s are well documented in the political diaries of certain members of the House of Commons and, albeit in a more limited fashion, in Henry Elsyng's notes[29] of House of Lords debates. In 1621, and to a lesser extent in 1624, the diaries are replete with discussions of monopolies and patents (and other grievances) and they provide a rich background narrative which we do not see again until the middle of the nineteenth century. The story, as told by those diarists and the journal, takes us to the trial of Mompesson and Michell. It begins, however, by an explanation of how the judgment in this trial can be seen as a private Act and so part of this story.

The Censure Act as an Act of Parliament

The Censure Act 1621 was the enrolment of a judgment against four individuals: Sir Giles Mompesson, Sir Francis Michell, Francis Bacon the Lord Chancellor, and Edward Flood.[30] The first two censured were what would later be called "impeached"[31] for matters related to patents; Francis Bacon, the Lord Chancellor, for taking bribes and Edward Flood for improper statements about the King's daughter. The basis for it to be treated as an enactment is the House of Lords resolution of 26 May 1621:

> Whereas, by the Order of the Eighteenth of this Month, the Lords Sub-committees for Privileges, &c. are to peruse the Draught of the Judgments given here in Court; and, if they approve them, then to appoint them to be ingrossed in a Roll:
>   The said Lords Sub-committees did this Day (after the House was adjourned) deliver unto the Clerk the Judgment given here against Gyles Mompesson, drawn up at large by their Lordships Appointment, and perused by them, and commanded the Clerk to enter the same in the Roll amongst the Statutes.

The judgment was therefore enrolled, albeit it never made it to the roll on enactments now held by the House of Lords.[32] Accordingly, the question of whether it was really an Act of Parliament is a difficult one. Petyt in *Jus Parliamentarium*[33] defines an Act as "A final Resolution of particular original Cases, brought and given in full Parliament, upon publick Conference and solemn debate; and not upon a Writ of Error before the Lords".[34] In *R v Archbishop*

---

29 He was one of the Parliamentary clerks; for a biography of Elsyng see: Elizabeth Read Foster, "The Painful Labour of Mr. Elsyng" (1972) 62 *Transactions of the American Philosophical Society* 1.

30 In relation to the other defendants see: *Proceedings in Parliament against Francis Bacon, Lord Chancellor* (1620) 2 State Trials 1037; *Proceedings in Parliament against Edward Floyde* (1621) 2 *State Trials* 1134.

31 The term was not actually used in relation to the men at the time but it came later: Colin Tite, *Impeachment and Parliamentary Judicature in Early Stuart England* (Athlone Press 1974), p 41.

32 It is held at the National Archive: Chancery: Parliament Roll, Part 1 (National Archive: C65/186).

33 William Petyt, *Jus Parliamentarium: Or the Ancient Power, Jurisdiction, Rights and Liberties or the Most High Court of Parliament* (London: John Nourse 1739), Vol 1; also see Charles McIlwain, *The High Court of Parliament and its Supremacy* (Yale 1910), pp 216–229.

34 William Petyt, *Jus Parliamentarium: Or the Ancient Power, Jurisdiction, Rights and Liberties or the Most High Court of Parliament* (London: John Nourse 1739), Vol 1, p 32.

of York[35] it was suggested by Sergeant Parning that "an Award in Parliament is equal to an Act of Parliament"[36] and so a judgment of Parliament could therefore exempt an individual case from a general public Act[37] and so the Censure Act 1621 might not be an Act in the modern sense, but at the time it was probably considered as such and so warrants a place in this story. We now turn to look the proceedings against the two notorious patentees: Mompesson and Michell.

The nature of the proceedings

The judicature procedure that tried Mompesson and Michell is said by Foster to have evolved out of that for private Bills.[38] This, it is suggested, was probably the wrong way around.[39] It is not that the proceedings against the patentees evolved from the "old private Bill" procedure, but rather the private Bill procedure was a development of the existing judicial role of Parliament in response to petitions from individuals. In any event, the Parliament of 1621 and its successor in 1624 condemned many patentees either for the patent being void in origin or in execution (or both).[40] In the first case, the patent was granted contrary to the King's intentions – which he had expressed in his 1610 Book of Bounty – and therefore the grant must be attributed to the grantee's impropriety[41]: such patents were an improper monopoly and as such condemned.[42] The second type of condemnation arose where illegal acts were undertaken to enforce the patent,[43] such as improperly obtaining warrants of imprisonment. Michell and Mompesson's patents were condemned on both grounds.

The trial of Michell and Mompesson in the House of Commons

The trials of both Michell and Mompesson are widely discussed[44] as they are seen as part of the evolution of Parliamentary judicature.[45] The procedure is not material to this discussion

35 YB Hilary Term, 6 Ed III, plea 15 (Seipp 1332.015).

36 YB Hilary Term, 6 Ed III, plea 15 (Seipp 1332.015); translation in Petyt, *Jus Parliamentarium* (1739), p 41.

37 YB Hilary Term, 6 Ed III, plea 15 (Seipp 1332.015); based on translation in Petyt, *Jus Parliamentarium* (1739), p 41.

38 Elizabeth Read Foster, "The Procedure of the House of Commons against Patents and Monopolies, 1621–1624" in *Conflict in Stuart England: Essays in Honour of Wallace Notestein* (ed William Appleton Aiken and Basil Duke Henning) (Jonathan Cape 1960), p 57 at 75; she bases her reference on Charles McIlwain, *The High Court of Parliament and its Supremacy* (Yale 1910), pp 219–223; and Albert F Pollard, *The Evolution of Parliament* (Longmans 1920), p 118.

39 Indeed, both the sources she cites seem to put it the other way around.

40 1 CJ 566–68 (12 March 1621).

41 See for example, CD 1621, Vol 2, X's Journal, pp 145, 250, 253–254 (27 February 1621); Elizabeth Read Foster "The Procedure of the House of Commons against Patents and Monopolies, 1621–1624" in *Conflict in Stuart England: Essays in Honour of Wallace Notestein* (ed William Appleton Aiken and Basil Duke Henning) (Jonathan Cape 1960), p 57 at 74 and fn 90.

42 Elizabeth Read Foster, "The Procedure of the House of Commons against Patents and Monopolies, 1621–1624" in *Conflict in Stuart England: Essays in Honour of Wallace Notestein* (ed William Appleton Aiken and Basil Duke Henning) (Jonathan Cape 1960), p 57 at 74 and fn 91.

43 Elizabeth Read Foster "The Procedure of the House of Commons against Patents and Monopolies, 1621–1624" in *Conflict in Stuart England: Essays in Honour of Wallace Notestein* (ed William Appleton Aiken and Basil Duke Henning) (Jonathan Cape 1960), p 57 at 74.

44 For a detailed narrative account see: see Colin Tite, *Impeachment and Parliamentary Judicature in Early Stuart England* (Athlone Press 1974), Ch 4 and 5; they are included in Corbett's States Trials: *Proceedings in Parliament against Sir Giles Mompesson* (1621) 2 State Trials 1119; *Proceedings in Parliament against Sir Francis Michell* (1621) 2 State Trials 1131.

45 See Frances Relf "Lords Debates 1621" (1929) 42 Camden Society (Third Series) 1; more recently see J Stoddart Flemion "Slow Process, Due Process and the High Court of Parliament: A Reinterpretation of the Revival of Judicature in the House of Lords 1621" (1974) 17(1) *Historical Journal* 3.

and so it will not be explained in detail,[46] rather the significance for our purposes is how the trials of Michell and Mompesson set the scene for the Bill of Monopolies 1621.

The origin of proceedings against Mompesson, a sitting MP, was a discussion in the Committee of Grievances, chaired by Sir Edward Coke,[47] on 19 February 1621.[48] The first grievance against Mompesson was his patent on inns[49] and within a few days of it being discussed he was suspended from Parliament to allow his case to be investigated. The case against Michell mainly related to his alehouse patent, the underlying claim was that he had not only profited directly from the patent but that he received a steady income from Newgate jail from those he sent there for infringing the patent.[50] It was his case, rather than Mompesson's, which progressed first. He petitioned the Commons explaining himself,[51] but their response was short and swift: he was declared unworthy to be a Justice of the Peace and imprisoned in the Tower of London.[52] This sanction appears to have been for contempt of the House (by putting forward a "spurious" petition) as much as for his misdemeanours[53] in relation to the patent.[54]

In the following week, Mompesson was returned to be questioned by the Committee of Grievances where he faced questions not only about the patent for inns, but also his patent for gold and silver thread and the patent for investigating concealments of land. In contrast to Michell, the Commons were more circumspect in their dealings[55] with Mompesson and they spent some time trying to work out what powers of punishment they possessed. Thus in the last weeks of February 1621 and the first weeks in March, the Commons was occupied with how to deal with Mompesson. Events overtook them as on 3 March, he fled and a warrant was issued for his arrest.[56] While he was still at large the proceedings against him continued and, significantly, on 5 March 1621 the grounds to censure Mompesson were discussed along with the conduct of Michell. It was during this debate that Sir Dudley Diggs first proposed that a Bill might be drawn to deal with projectors, suitors and certifiers (i.e. a Bill of Monopolies)[57] so that they may be damned to posterity – a proposal which was said to be much applauded.[58] Later that day, a similar proposal was made by Sir John Walter[59] and

---

46 For a more detailed explanation see: Elizabeth Read Foster "The Procedure of the House of Commons against Patents and Monopolies, 1621–1624" in *Conflict in Stuart England: Essays in Honour of Wallace Notestein* (ed William Appleton Aiken and Basil Duke Henning) (Jonathan Cape 1960), p 57 at 67; Colin Tite, *Impeachment and Parliamentary Judicature in Early Stuart England* (Athlone Press 1974), pp 86–87.

47 Stephen D White, *Sir Edward Coke and "The Grievances of the Commonwealth": 1621–1628* (North Carolina Press 1979), p 117.

48 CD 1621, Vol 4, Pym, pp 78–81; CD 1621, Vol 5, Wentworth, pp 475–476 (19 February 1621); CD 1621, Vol 6, Book of Committees, pp 249–253.

49 At the time there was a complex set of regulations, for an introduction see James Brown "Alehouse Licensing and State Formation in Early Modern England" in *Intoxication and Society: Problematic Pleasures of Drugs and Alcohol* (ed J. Herring, C. Regan, D. Weinberg, P. Withington) (Palgrave 2012), p 110.

50 Colin Tite, *Impeachment and Parliamentary Judicature in Early Stuart England* (Athlone Press 1974), p 91.

51 CD 1621, Vol 2, X's Journal, pp 127–128 (23 February 1621).

52 Colin Tite, *Impeachment and Parliamentary Judicature in Early Stuart England* (Athlone Press 1974), p 91.

53 In the context of felonies and misdemeanours.

54 CD 1621, Vol 6, Book of Orders, p 453.

55 As for possible reasons see Colin Tite, *Impeachment and Parliamentary Judicature in Early Stuart England* (Athlone Press 1974), pp 93–94.

56 1 CJ 535; CD 1621, Vol 2, X's Journal, pp 157–162 (3 March 1621).

57 CD 1621, Vol 2, X's Journal, p 167; Vol 6, Holland, p 31; Member of the House, *Proceedings and Debates of the House of Commons in 1620 and 1621* (1766) ('Nicholas'), Vol 1, p 122 (5 March 1621).

58 CD 1621, Vol 5, Smyth's Diary, p 272 (5 March 1621).

59 CD 1621, Vol 5, Belasyse Diary, p 25 (5 March 1621).

a Bill to end the monopoly of selling and transporting Welsh butter[60] was read.[61] These calls were joined by Sir Edward Coke[62] and a few days later on 12 March by Sir Nathaniel Rich.[63]

In other words, the proceedings against Mompesson and Michell had spurred the House to legislate generally to deal with improper monopolies. While this shows a direct link between a quasi-private Bill and the Bill of Monopolies it should not be taken too far. The proceedings against Mompesson and Michell were some of the first against patentees, but there were others. The general sentiment of the 1621 Parliament was to break improper (but not all) monopolies, and so even without their malfeasance there would inevitably have been something to spur a call for a general prohibition. In other words, Mompesson and Michell were the pegs upon which to hang the policy, but there were other less prominent pegs available.

Bill of Monopolies 1621

In the months that followed, the Commons, and to a lesser extent, the Lords spent a considerable amount more time on the censure of Mompesson, Michell and others than it did on the Bill of Monopolies itself.[64] Yet the two matters continued to progress side by side with concerns about other individual patentees continuing to be raised. Accordingly, on the second reading of the Bill of Monopolies reference was made to Richard Mompesson's[65] grant for aniseed and cinnamon,[66] and also to the grant relating to the importation of stone pots.[67] Indeed, immediately after the Bill of Monopolies was committed, the House returned to Giles Mompesson's case.[68]

The first hand testimony and evidence of the conduct of the egregious patentees was likely to have been a direct cause for selecting the sanction in the Bill of Monopolies to be under the Statute of Praemunire[69] which was explained by Sir Edward Coke, the author of the Bill in his *Institutes*.[70]

> The judgement in a Praemunire is that the Defendant shalbe from thence forth out of the Kings protection, and his lands and tenements, goods and chattels forfeited to the King, and that his body shall remain in prison at the Kings pleasure. So odious was this offence of Praemunire, that a man that was attainted of the same might have bin slaine by any man without Danger of Law.

This exceptional punishment[71] was intended to ensure that few would ever dare run a monopoly contrary to the Act. The scope of a legitimate monopoly was therefore of the upmost importance which was why the provisos were so important.

---

60 Welsh Butter Bill 1621; a transcript is in CD 1621, Vol 7, p 108.
61 It is not clear why this particular trading monopoly was dealt with separately from other monopolies.
62 CD 1621, Vol 2, X's Journal, p 194 (8 March 1621).
63 CD 1621, Vol 6, Holland Debates, p 53 (12 March 1621).
64 A text of the Bill showing amendments is in Samuel Gardiner (ed), *Notes of the Debates in the House of Lords officially taken by Henry Elsing, Clerk of the Parliments, 1621* (1871) 103 Camden Society (Old Series), p 151.
65 He was from a different branch of the same family as Giles.
66 CD 1621, Vol 2, X's Journal, p 219 and fn (a) (14 March 1621).
67 This is probably the patent held by Thomas Browne and Tobie Steward; see Dennis Haselgrove "Steps towards English Stoneware Manufacture in the 17th Century Part 1 – 1600–1650" (1989) 6 *London Archaeologist* 132.
68 See CD 1621, Vol 6, Holland Diaries, p 62; CD 1621, Vol 2, X's Journal, p 220; 1 CJ 554 (which refers to Michell but not Mompesson) (14 March 1621).
69 Statute of Praemunire of 1393.
70 Sir Edward Coke, *The First Part of the Institutes of the Laws of England* (Flesher 1628), pp 129–130 (s 199).
71 For a full list of things punished in this way see William Blackstone, *Commentaries on the Laws of England: Book: Of Public Wrongs* (Ed Wilfred Priest) (Oxford 2016), Chapter 8, pp 116–118 (Oxford pp 77–78).

Origins of the proviso for patents for invention

The central proviso in this story is what became section 6[72] of the Statute of Monopolies, which allowed for patents for inventions.[73] The issue of inventors was raised by William Hakewill on second reading[74] as to whether the "sole working" (or "sole workers")[75] would be prejudicial to corporations,[76] and inventions.[77] Thereafter, others stated that the Bill should not extend to monopolies for new manufactures, but only to those relating to old trades.[78] While the Bill was still in committee, Sir Edward Coke explained to the house the basis of the Bill of Monopolies. He directly linked it back to the Book of Bounty and its proclamation that monopolies and dispensations of penal law were against the law.[79] He continued by listing precedents before that book where Royal grants had been withdrawn as monopolies;[80] demonstrating, he said, that monopolies were unlawful in law. In any event, when the Bill came out of committee there were provisos added for grants to cities and corporations[81] which would later become section 9 of the Statute of Monopolies.[82] It was then recommitted for further consideration.

When the Bill was reported again after being re-committed, there appeared the first of the savings for particular types of inventions – potentially making the Bill what would later be called hybrid. The first was a proviso to protect the patents for saltpetre[83], allum,[84] and iron ordnance[85] working.[86] It is not clear the extent to which the Commons wanted to save the patents or just to allow the King to obtain ordnance. The second proviso specifically excluded any grants to the Earl of Nottingham for selling wines.[87] It is unclear why Parliament saved the patent as there was no record of the debate: it may have been allowed due to his advanced age (he was 85)[88] and his role as Admiral of the British fleet which defeated the Spanish Armada.

72 Although, section 5 of the Statute of Monopolies deals with the same thing in relation to then existing patents.
73 Like the other provisos it probably was not included in the original Bill as introduced: see Chris R Kyle "But a New Button to an Old Coat: The Enactment of the Statute of Monopolies 21 James I cap 3" (1998) 19 *J Legal History* 203, who takes view it was added as there were only four clauses originally (at p 207) as does Stephen D White, *Sir Edward Coke and "The Grievances of the Commonwealth": 1621–1628* (North Carolina Press 1979), p 129, n 192.
74 1 CJ 553 (14 March 1621).
75 The words which were found in Clause 1.
76 CD 1621, Vol 2, X's Journal, p 218 (14 March 1621).
77 Not mentioned in CD 1621, Vol 2, X's Journal; but see 1 CJ 553 (14 March 1621).
78 CD 1621, Vol 2, X's Journal, p 219; Vol 4, Pym's Diary, p 153 (14 March 1621).
79 CD 1621, Vol 2, X's Journal, p 228 (15 March 1621).
80 CD 1621, Vol 2, X's Journal, pp 228–229 (14 March 1621) (they were: the grant that all sweet wines to go through Southampton; William Simpson for stone pots; Sir Thomas Wilkes for making salt; Sir John Packington for starch; Sir Edward Darcy for importing and exporting cork).
81 What was Bill of Monopolies 1621, cl 11 (and s 9 of the Statute of Monopolies).
82 See Chapter 6.
83 It is not clear there was a patentee at the relevant time. John Evelyn held the contract for making saltpetre (Lyle, *Acts of the Privy Council of England, 1619–1621* (HMSO 1939), Vo 37, pp 117–118), but when the patent was requested by the House of Commons in 1624, it transpires that he did not have one: 1 CJ 702 (10 May 1624).
84 The alum mines were held by the King, and not a patentee at this time.
85 The patent belonged to Sackville Crowe (1621) 18 Jac I, Pt 12, No 1 (National Archive: C66/2227).
86 See CD 1621, Vol 4, Pym's Diary, p 197; 1 CJ 575 (26 March 1621).
87 Bill of Monopolies 1621, cl 12; Kyle takes view this was added in Commons: Chris R Kyle "But a New Button to an Old Coat: The Enactment of the Statute of Monopolies 21 James I cap 3" (1998) 19 *J Legal History* 203 at 208; also see Stephen D White, *Sir Edward Coke and "The Grievances of the Commonwealth": 1621–1628* (North Carolina Press 1979), p 132.
88 The grant would not have survived him. He died on 14 December 1624, but he obtained no proviso in the Statute of Monopolies.

Later in the passage of the Bill, further provisos were found to have been improperly added.[89] One related to allowing the King to use non obstante clauses[90] a matter considered in detail in Chapter 5; and the other limited the application of the Act to a single session. The addition of these clauses may have had something to do with the iron ordnance proviso as the relevant patentees had provided the clauses to two members.[91] In any event, they were struck out.

The move to save certain patents was taken a step further by Sir Henry Poole who proposed a Bill[92] to confirm certain "good" Royal grants. Essentially, the enactment would have confirmed any patent under the Great Seal for money or service done with certain patents excluded from the saving.[93] The Bill did not even pass First Reading and was roundly criticised with Sir Dudley Digges going as far as to suggest that the Bill was dangerous[94] and he, along with Sir William Strode,[95] said that individuals who want to preserve their patent should present their own Bills. It is clear, therefore, that the Commons wanted to terminate patents in all but the most limited cases and that any exception would be hard won. Yet provisos were added to clarify and expand the exception for saltpetre and iron ordinance as well as adding a proviso to cover allum and allum mines. While rejecting the probity of the provisos themselves, Coke pragmatically accepted that they were necessary to enable the Bill to progress through Third Reading.[96] He, like others, may have been willing to accept them in the belief that patents were not "validated" by a proviso, but simply excepted from the Bill and governed by the common law.[97]

The debates through the early passage of the Bill in the Lords are largely unrecorded until the Bill of Monopolies was defeated at Third Reading.[98] This defeat led their Lordships to propose a new Bill with the same purpose.[99] The Commons and Lords struggled to reconcile over the following weeks; in the end however, the Bill lapsed at the end of the session. In contrast, the Welsh Butter Bill was passed by the Lords with amendments, which were never agreed by the Commons probably because it was not thought to be an important Bill[100] and was somewhat overtaken by the desire to get the Bill of Monopolies enacted.

The failure of the Bill of Monopolies left the Commons feeling slighted as they believed that monopolies did not affect their Lordships, and were within their peculiar province.[101] Kyle has put forward some reasons why the Lords rejected the Bill: its complexity meant there were genuine concerns about curbing the Royal Prerogative; a lack of communication

---

89 CD 1621, Vol 4, Pym's Diary, p 318 (8 May 1621); they were appended to the Bill (rather than textually amended).

90 CD 1621, Vol 4, Pym's Diary, p 318 (8 May 1621); this effect is more ambiguous in Barrington's Diary, Vol 3, p 198.

91 CD 1621, Vol 3, Barrington's Diary, p 198 (8 May 1621).

92 Bill to Confirm Patent Grants 1621 (1 CJ 590; 25 April 1621).

93 A summary of the Bill is in Nicholas, Vol 1, p 314 (no text of the Bill survives if it ever existed).

94 Nicholas, Vol 1, p 314 (25 April 1621).

95 CD 1621, Vol 3, Barrington's Diary, p 78 (25 April 1621).

96 1 CJ 619; Nicholas, Vol 2, p 62; CD 1621, Vol 3, Barrington's Diary, p 326 (12 May 1621).

97 Stephen D White, *Sir Edward Coke and "The Grievances of the Commonwealth": 1621–1628* (North Carolina Press 1979), p 132.

98 3 LJ 177 (3 December 1621).

99 See CD 1621, Vol 2, X's Journal, pp 508–509 (10 December 1621).

100 CD 1621, Vol 5, Belayse Diary, p 190 (31 May 1621).

101 Elizabeth Read Foster "The Procedure of the House of Commons against Patents and Monopolies, 1621–1624" in *Conflict in Stuart England: Essays in Honour of Wallace Notestein* (ed William Appleton Aiken and Basil Duke Henning) (Jonathan Cape 1960), p 57 at 77; Nicholas, Vol 2, pp 302–303; CD 1621, Vol 2, X's Journal, pp 508–9 and 521–2; CD 1621, Vol 6, Z's Diary, p 230 and 237.

between the two Houses;[102] its hasty and poor drafting[103] as well as being seen as a challenge to their Lordships' own chances of received patronage from Royal grants.[104] The drafting point is significant as the Lords, and in particular the judges, considered it to be their role to clarify drafting and legal points in Commons Bills.[105] Indeed, even with the improved drafting of the 1624 Bill, there were still significant queries as to its purpose and intent. Therefore, it is arguable that had the 1621 Bill been better drafted,[106] it may well have been enacted in the 1621 session. Nevertheless, the passage of this 1621 Bill made it clear that the Commons believed there should be a general rule – a prohibition on monopolies – which should not extend to inventions or, indeed, certain other specified monopolies. This demonstrated already how exceptions might be made for the private individual in legislation: albeit those limitations would be very restricted.

1624

The Bill of Monopolies was re-introduced by Coke on the first working day in the next Parliament.[107] It received its First Reading[108] and Second Reading[109] over the next few day. On its Second Reading, the Commons was reminded by Glanville that it was only declaratory.[110] The committee which considered the Bill made numerous amendments[111] such as clarifying which common law courts could hear the claim,[112] limiting the new treble damages provision[113] so that it was not retrospective, and extending the legislation to Wales. There was also an exemption introduced to exclude printing from the prohibition of monopolies.[114] It is apparent other provisos were considered by the committee, but not included. The Bill was re-committed, reported and then read a third time.[115]

Before moving on to consider the Bill's progress through the Lords, it is worth highlighting that there were still doubts over whether a court could revoke the King's Patent. Henry Heron had been granted a patent for the exclusive right to salt, dry and pack fish in Devon and Cornwall for 31 years.[116] The patent was challenged by a writ of *scire facias* in the Court of Chancery[117] and Heron was ordered to attend the court. He did not do so and so in a sort

---

102 There was no joint conference.
103 As Coke himself admitted, see Stephen D White, *Sir Edward Coke and "The Grievances of the Commonwealth": 1621–1628* (North Carolina Press 1979), p 130.
104 Chris R Kyle "But a New Button to an Old Coat: The Enactment of the Statute of Monopolies 21 James I cap 3" (1998) 19 *J Legal History* 203 at 211–212.
105 Elizabeth Foster, *The House of Lords 1603–1649: Structure, Procedure and the Nature of its Business* (University of North Carolina Press 1983), pp 72–73; Chris R Kyle "But a New Button to an Old Coat: The Enactment of the Statute of Monopolies 21 James I cap 3" (1998) 19 *J Legal History* 203 at 212.
106 So the Lords could change the drafting to give effect to the policy.
107 1 CJ 671 and 715 (23 February 1624).
108 1 CJ 672 and 716 (24 February 1624).
109 1 CJ 674 and 719 (26 February 1624).
110 Philip Baker (ed), *Proceedings in Parliament 1624: The House of Commons* (2015), British History Online ('CD 1624'), 23 February 1624: Spring, f 33; Nicholas, f 25; also see 1 CJ 674.
111 CD 1624, 9 March 1624: Pym's Diary, f 23 (the best summary of what was agreed).
112 What became section 2 of the Statute of Monopolies.
113 What became section 4 of the Statute of Monopolies.
114 What became section 10 of the Statute of Monopolies.
115 1 CJ 680 and 731 (9 March 1624) and 1 CJ 685 and 735 (13 March 1624).
116 See Preamble to Heron's Fish-curing Patent Void Act 1623; the text of the patent is at CD 1621, Vol 7, 359.
117 Not a common law court.

of default judgment the court revoked the patent. Yet the uncertainty[118] over whether the court had power to revoke the patent meant that a private Act had to be passed to validate the judgment.[119] Whether Henry Heron's case had any influence on the power to adjudicate patents being given to the common law courts by the Statute of Monopolies is unclear,[120] but after that power was granted no Act similar to Heron's would ever be required again (notwithstanding, it was usually the case that revocation cases were heard before the Privy Council for another century).

Returning to the Statute of Monopolies, the First Reading in the House of Lords took place immediately after it was brought from the Commons[121] and the Second Reading occurred on 18 March at which point it was committed to 32 peers with four senior lawyers in attendance.[122] The committee included most of the senior Privy Councillors; indicating how seriously the Bill was being taken by the Lords.[123] Two weeks later on report,[124] a joint conference with the Commons was proposed. By this stage numerous petitions had been received for special allowance: but they were put off until after the conference.[125]

The results of the conference were reported to the Commons on 19 April 1624.[126] The major objections of the Lords were set out by Montagu CJ. The first concerned the use of "savings" in a declaratory law. Coke said they were provisos and not savings and they just left the law as it was before the enactment. Indeed, the effect of this was clarified when the provisos for particular patents were introduced and the following words added[127]:

> But that the said several Letters Patents last mentioned shall be and remain of the like Force and Effect and as free from the Declarations, Provisions, Penalties and Forfeitures before-mentioned, as if this Act had never been had nor made, and not otherwise.

The second objection by Montagu CJ was the failure to define a monopoly, but Coke expressed concern[128] with trying to define a "monopoly" saying it was generally understood as "a claim to use that solely which of right is common free to many".[129] The third concern related to a court reaching a decision without knowing the King's pleasure regarding that monopoly; Coke simply said that such a case could be delayed until his pleasure was known.[130]

---

118 A similar Bill, in relation to the same action, had been before the 1621 Parliament.
119 Heron's Fish-curing Patent Void Act 1623; there was a practice of reversing decrees in Chancery by private Bill; see Elizabeth Read Foster, *The House of Lords 1603–1609: Structure, Procedure, and the Nature of Its Business* (University of North Carolina Press 1983), p 105; but confirming a decree was more unusual.
120 Statute of Monopolies, s 2.
121 3 LJ 261 (13 March 1624).
122 3 LJ 267 (18 March 1624).
123 Chris R Kyle "'But a New Button to an Old Coat": The Enactment of the Statute of Monopolies, 21 James I cap 3" (1998) 19 *J Legal History* 203 at 213.
124 3 LJ 287 (3 April 1624).
125 Samuel Gardiner (ed), *Notes and Debates in the House of Lords: Officially Taken by Henry Elsing, 1624-1626* (1879) 24 Camden Society (New Series) 50.
126 1 CJ 770; the most detailed account of what was said appears to be CD 1624, 19 April 1624: Pym, ff 71–73v.
127 See Statute of Monopolies, s 13 (similar, but slightly different wording, is used in ss 9, 10, 11 and 14).
128 A recurring problem: see comments on the meaning of an "invention" of Archibald Rosser in his Statement filed before the 1835 Select Committee: Phillip Johnson, "Minutes of Evidence of the Select Committee on the Letters Patent for Inventions Act 1835" (2017) 7 *Queen Mary Journal of Intellectual Property* 99 at 115.
129 CD 1624, 19 April 1624: Pym, f 71v; he resisted a definition in 1621: see Stephen D White, *Sir Edward Coke and "The Grievances of the Commonwealth": 1621–1628* (North Carolina Press 1979), pp 130–131.
130 CD 1624, 19 April 1624; Pym f. 71v and Earle, ff 149-149v; 1 LJ 770.

The fourth objection related to new inventions and it is worth setting out Pym's record of this objection and the response in full[131]:

> That the proviso for patents of privilege to exercise new inventions did not extend to those that were to be granted hereafter, but only to such as were in use, and that proviso is limited by too narrow words, "and such should not be inconvenient". That may be inconvenient for one time or place which is not for another, and a particular inconvenience may be accompanied with a greater good.
>
> Answer: it was yielded that the proviso should be extended for 14 years' privilege to be granted in the future, and that it should be enlarged thus, "generally inconvenient".

While not mentioned by Pym, the Lords also seemed concerned about improvement inventions. But Coke did not yield, the Commons Journal recording that his answer was: "An addition to an old invention, not new, but a new button to an old cloak."[132] The final objection related to corporate charters and the restriction of the Royal Prerogative. Coke simply replied that the Bill did not apply to these charters and so the Prerogative could not be restricted.[133]

After the general objections, the conference moved on to the exceptions for individuals,[134] and Sir Thomas Coventry (the Attorney-General) questioned how the Bill would affect particular grants: the private part of the Bill as it were. The existing provisos[135] for saltpetre, gunpowder and ordnance and shot were agreed as they were concerned with the defence of the realm.[136] Another existing proviso, for printing,[137] was amended to remove the restriction of 11 years.[138] A new proviso was added at the Lords' insistence for transporting coal from Newcastle.[139] Lord Arundel indicated that this privilege ensured that the river was dredged and so it should continue.[140] A proviso was added[141] to protect Maxwell's Royal grant to transport 18,000 calf skins and the Commons agreed the new law would not touch the grant.[142] Finally, a proviso was agreed to protect existing and future patent offices although this did not extend to offices to regulate taverns which had to be within the power of the King.[143]

The Commons then agreed to form a sub-committee to consider further patents: Sir Henry Vane's subpoena patent,[144] Sir Richard Young's patent ingrossing under the Great Seal,[145] Mansell's glass patent[146] and James Chambers' patent for sheriffs.[147] Coke reported

---

131 CD 1624, 19 April 1624: Pym, ff 71v and 72.

132 1 CJ 770 (19 April 1624).

133 CD 1624, 19 April 1624: Pym, f 72; Earle, ff 149–150v.

134 George Unwin, *The Gilds and Companies of London* (Methuen & Co 1908), p 317 says these exceptions were "without the slightest justification".

135 What would become Statute of Monopolies, s 10.

136 CD 1624, 19 April 1624: Pym, f 72.

137 What would become Statute of Monopolies, s 10.

138 CD 1624, 19 April 1624: Pym, f 72.

139 What would become Statute of Monopolies, s 12.

140 CD 1624, 19 April 1624: Pym, f 72.

141 What would become Statute of Monopolies, s 13.

142 CD 1624, 19 April 1624: Pym, f 72.

143 What would become Statute of Monopolies, s 10; CD 1624, 19 April 1624, Pym, f 72.

144 Henry Vane (1614) PR 11 Jac I, Pt 14, No 9 (National Archive: C66/1981).

145 (1618) PR 16 Jac I, Pt 12, No 8 (National Archive C66/2176); the warrant is mentioned in National Archive: State Papers Domestic (7 April 1618): SP 14/141 f.120.

146 Mansell's Patent and Extension (1624 No 33A).

147 1 CJ 771 (19 April 1624).

from the committee[148] on 1 May and indicated that the committee agreed that the first three patents should be allowed, but not renewed; and so the Lords could add a proviso.[149] It is generally said[150] that all three obtained provisos in the Bill, but the enacted text does not mention Vane and Young's patent, but only Mansell's.[151] This was despite the fact that Mansell's patent had been challenged during the 1621 Parliament.[152]

However, it appears that their Lordships decided that the earlier proviso for patent offices covered both Vane and Young. Thus, the patents were not condemned or specifically saved. Indeed, despite the Commons suggesting the patents should not last beyond the current holders they remained for centuries thereafter. Sir Richard Young and Robert Pye had been given the patent in 1618 and they surrendered it in 1625,[153] however the patent office for ingrossing under the Great Seal continued to provide a lucrative income from fees until it was made a salaried role in the Chancery re-organisation of 1833[154] before the office was finally abolished in 1874.[155] The rights of the patent holder for the Subpoena Office likewise continued into the nineteenth century being slated for abolition in 1833 after the death of the current patent holder.[156]

A further proviso was added by the Lords in relation to Lord Dudley's grant for making iron and sea coal.[157] Finally, there was ongoing concern that Privy Councillors could be convicted of Praemunire if a letter was sent by the Privy Council to stay an action before a court. Prince Charles (later Charles I) even supported an amendment[158] to protect Privy Councillors although there was also opposition from the Archbishop of Canterbury amongst others.[159] The Bill was recommitted to consider this aspect and an amendment was made[160] for that purpose as was another amendment to include a proviso for Abraham Baker's patent for making smalt.[161] The Bill was given a Third Reading and the Commons agreed the amendments including the new provisos.[162] It then received Royal Assent and a new era began.

---

148 As to the deliberations on Vane's patent see: CD 1624, 22 April 1624: Nicholas, f 168 and Dyott, f 74.

149 1 CJ 696; CD 1624, 1 May 1624: Nicholas, f, 188v; Holland, f 69v; Pym, f 86.

150 Stephen D White, *Sir Edward Coke and "The Grievances of the Commonwealth": 1621–1628* (North Carolina Press 1979), p 135; Chris R Kyle "'But a New Button to an Old Coat": The Enactment of the Statute of Monopolies, 21 James I cap 3" (1998) 19 *J Legal History* 203 at 214–215.

151 See Statute of Monopolies, s 13.

152 Stephen D White, *Sir Edward Coke and "The Grievances of the Commonwealth": 1621–1628* (North Carolina Press 1979), pp 125–126.

153 See National Archive: SP/16/2 f 186; and *Calendar of State Papers, Charles I*, Vol 2, No 103, 27 May 1625, p 29.

154 Lord Chancellor's Offices Act 1833, ss 3 and 4.

155 Great Seal (Offices) Act 1874, s 6; for a short summary of its history see Sir Henry Maxwell-Lyte, *Historical Notes on the Use of the Great Seal of England* (HMSO 1926), p 270.

156 Court of Chancery (England) Act 1833, s 12.

157 3 LJ 394 (20 May 1624); Samuel Gardiner (ed), *Notes on the Debates in the House of Lords: Officially taken by Henry Elsing, 1624–1626* (1879) 24 Camden Society (New Series) ('LD 1624–1626'), p 98; it became Statute of Monopolies, s 14.

158 Chris R Kyle "'But a New Button to an Old Coat": The Enactment of the Statute of Monopolies, 21 James I cap 3" (1998) 19 *J Legal History* 203 at 215; also see Chris R Kyle "Prince Charles in the Parliaments of 1621 and 1624" (1998) 41 *Historical Journal* 603 at 612.

159 LD 1624–6, p 98.

160 It appears Kyle takes this view no amendment was made: Chris R Kyle "'But a New Button to an Old Coat": The Enactment of the Statute of Monopolies, 21 James I cap 3" (1998) 19 *J Legal History* 203 at 215; although there is no record of an amendment being made in the Journal of the House of Lords it is clear one must have been made as a provision exists as Statute of Monopolies, s 8.

161 3 LJ 397 (21 May 1624).

162 1 CJ 711 and 794 (25 May 1624).

The role of the patent Parliaments

The Parliaments of 1621 and 1624 are clearly pivotal in the history of patent law. They substantially hindered the practice of giving patents and monopolies to favourites although not, yet, the practice of monopolising whole industries.[163] These earlier patents, however, had to be viewed as part of a wider policy of farming out government regulation, a policy which in essence lasted until well beyond the seventeenth century. The role the Statute of Monopolies played in the evolution of patent law is widely accepted but, as has been shown, that Statute (and the failed Bill of Monopolies three years earlier) already acknowledged that some patents were special or, more accurately, some patentees might be entitled to special treatment. Essentially, therefore, the Parliaments that first seriously considered patent legislation also realised that there would need to be exceptions from the general rules in certain cases. It was a precedent upon which the history of private patent Acts was built – although not a precedent that ever needed citing.

163 See p 81–83.

4   The protection of inventions by enactment

Introduction

The protection of a specific invention by a private Act of Parliament has rarely followed a pattern, at least in England. This is in stark contrast to other groups of private Acts, which have usually evolved from one or two individual Acts before falling into some sort of normalcy. It must be remembered that during the seventeenth century, the grant of a Royal patent was a rare occurrence.[1] The use of private Acts to obtain protection for an invention originally arose from the absence of the King during the Civil War. Yet after the Restoration of Charles II the practice continued where Parliament was seen as an option for inventors and companies alike. As the story moves into the eighteenth century, private Acts were sought (often unsuccessfully) where there were problems with subject matter or simply where it was cheaper than obtaining patents in England and Scotland separately. The story of England in this respect is nothing to that of its northern cousin. Before the Union of 1707, the Scottish Parliament adopted a vigorous, aggressive and ultimately doomed policy trying to promote Scottish industry both through granting exclusive rights and through the exclusion of foreign competition. It is to the first of these groups that the story now turns.

In place of the King

The direct grant of "patents" by Parliament during the Civil War is hardly surprising. The King was not accessible to (or an enemy of) many of his subjects. Accordingly, he was not able (or willing) to grant Royal patents to inventors during this time. This meant from about 1642 until the Restoration of the Monarchy in 1660 no patents were granted by the King. Initially, therefore, an inventor who wanted protection for an invention had to look else-where; and so they turned to Parliament. During the Civil War, this led to two ordinances being enacted to protect particular inventions, as well as a similar number of inventors failing to obtain an ordinance. These ordinances were laws which had been passed by both Houses, but not given Royal Assent. At the time, the Parliamentary government treated them as equivalent to an Act of Parliament.[2]

---

1 There were far fewer than 400 granted during this period; Woodcroft's Index suggests that there were 364 patents granted by 1700: see Bennet Woodcroft, *Titles of Patents of Invention: Chronologically Arranged from 1617 to 1852* (Eyre and Spottiswoode 1854). However, this ignores the period between 1600–1616 and the Interregnum.

2 Subsequently, it was deemed nothing done without Royal Assent during the interregnum was lawful: Sedition Act 1661, s 1.

The first of these ordinances was granted to Delicques and Fancault in 1643[3] protecting their "engine" for drawing up ships, lading and cannon. The ordinance was not an analogue for a prerogative patent as there were two major differences. First, it lasted only seven years (and not fourteen)[4] and, secondly, it was restricted to uses permitted by the Admiralty.[5] As it related to *military* technology different considerations might have been applied during the Civil War as it may have been seen to be desirable to restrict its use to those fighting on the "right" side. In contrast, Petty's Ordinance in 1648 granted the inventor fourteen years of exclusivity for his invention for multiple writing.[6] This ordinance required the Solicitor General to draw up a patent and to have the Great Seal applied.[7] This was a clear instance of Parliament acting in lieu of the King, rather than the inventor (Petty) going to Parliament because there was something which was outwith the scope of the "normal" patent law. In other words, Parliament appeared to be acting within the Statute of Monopolies.

As there were only two ordinances relating to patents passed, it is not possible to determine any pattern. Indeed, the two additional draft ordinances provide little further enlightenment. The text of the Draft Ordnance Ordinance in 1645, which passed the House of Lords, but not the Commons, must from its long title have sought an exclusive right. However, there was no indication of the length of time it was due to last or whether it too would have had the Great Seal applied (or indeed anything more about it).[8] Finally, Chamberlen's Draft Ordinance, which similarly passed the Lords but not the Commons, was to last fourteen years yet it was also not clear whether it was to get the seal.[9] It is plausible that both of these two ordinances were intended to be like Petty's and were simply the inventor having recourse to Parliament for privileges which would otherwise have been granted as a patent by the King.

Following the execution of Charles I on 30 January 1649 and the abolition of the House of Lords,[10] two further Acts[11] were passed by the Rump Parliament. The first granted protection to George Manby[12] and the second to Jeremy Buck.[13] These were simple grants for fourteen years[14] and appear, once more, to have been enacted in lieu of a grant from *a* King. Indeed, once Oliver Cromwell became Lord Protector he went back to granting patents in the same way as monarchs had before him[15] which meant that the necessity of petitioning

---

3   Delicques and Fancault's Ordinance 1643.
4   Delicques and Fancault's Ordinance 1643, ss 1 and 3.
5   Delicques and Fancault's Ordinance 1643, s 4.
6   Petty's Ordinance 1648, s 1.
7   Petty's Ordinance 1648, s 2.
8   The only remaining materials on this Ordinance is a petition and this just includes details of what is sought: Petition for Ordinance (26 September 1645): Sixth Report of the Royal Commission on Historical Manuscript (1877)(C 1745), p 78 (HL/PO/JO/10/1/193).
9   All that remains is the petition: *To the Honourable House of Commons Assembled in Parliament, the Humble Petition of Peter Chamberlen, Doctor in Physic* (1649) (Wing C1908).
10 An Act for Abolishing the House of Peers 1649.
11 As they were now called.
12 Manby's Patent Act 1650.
13 Buck's Patent Act 1651.
14 It is possible Buck's grant was for seven years. The version of the Act in *Acts and Ordinances of the Interregnum 1642–1660* (HMSO 1911), p 509 states it to last fourteen years. However, the Commons Journal record of the report stage gives the title of the Bill with a reference to the right lasting seven years (6 CJ 543; 27 February 1650) but no other text is available.
15 Rhys Jenkins, "The Protection of Inventions during the Commonwealth and Protectorate" (1913) 11 S-VII *Notes and Queries* 163 identifies twelve instances where a person applied to the Lord Protector for a patent

Parliament for private Acts or ordinances disappeared; and records show no further grants by Parliament before the Restoration of Charles II. Accordingly, Manby's and Buck's Acts demonstrate very little other than what is well known, namely that the Rump Parliament was standing in place of the King as the executive government of England.

Restoration to Glorious Revolution: Parliamentary patents

The return of Charles II to the throne in 1660 restored the conventional power for granting patents. Nevertheless, it was not long before two private Acts were passed and a number of petitions and Bills were read before Parliament. It began with Charles Howard, son of the Earl of Arundel. He had obtained a prerogative patent for tanning hides on 27 October 1660,[16] and within a few weeks a Bill received its First Reading in the House of Lords to grant him the same fourteen-year term.[17] It is not clear why Howard believed he needed to obtain a Bill for the same protection he had already been granted by a patent. MacLeod suggests[18] it was to avoid the laws on tanning leather invalidating his grant.[19] However, it is more likely that it was for the same reason that John Colnett repeatedly sought a private Act during 1662 and 1663.[20] Colnett had obtained a patent on 6 September 1661[21] but, like Howard, his invention lacked novelty[22] at the time of grant and so was revoked. The proposed legislation would, amongst other things, have deemed the invention novel despite it having been previously disclosed.[23] Both these petitioners were seeking to obtain protection for something where the patent was either invalid or of dubious validity.

Marquis of Worcester's Act 1663

The most famous private Act during this period is that passed in favour of the Marquis of Worcester – a prolific inventor. He was a prominent Royalist who had lost a substantial part of his fortune assisting the Royalist cause and he was banished in 1648 along with Charles II.[24] He returned to England a few years later and was, initially at least, imprisoned in the Tower

between 1654 and 1660 although not all were granted. As there were only one or two granted a year after the Restoration it is possible that these were the only twelve such instances notwithstanding the absence of some of the Cromwellian patent roll: see Ralph B Pugh, "The Patent Rolls of the Interregnum (1950) 23 *Historical Research* 178.

16 Patent No 130 (1660).

17 Leather Trade Bill 1660 (Ingrossment: HL/PO/JO/10/1/300); it reappeared again in the House of Commons in 1661: 8 CJ 262 (30 May 1661).

18 Christine MacLeod, *Inventing the Industrial Revolution: The English Patent System 1660–1800* (Cambridge 1988), p 82.

19 Probably those under the Leather Act 1603.

20 Colnett had three Bills considered during 1662–1663 (Colnett's Bill 1662 (HC) (8 CJ 373; 26 February 1662); Colnett's Bill 1662 (HL) (11 LJ 426; 10 April 1662) (HL/PO/JO/10/1/314); Colnett's Bill 1663 (11 LJ 493; 16 March 1663) (HL/PO/JO/10/1/316)); the furthest any got was Second Reading.

21 It is not included in Woodcroft's collection: John Colnett (1661) PR 13 Chas II, Pt 25, No 8 (National Archive: C66/2980).

22 It was revoked in favour of Kenelm Digby: see Roy Digby, *The Gunpowder Plotter's Legacy* (Janus 2001), p 187; T Longueville, *The Life of Sir Kenelm Digby* (Longman 1896), pp 255–256. It has been claimed that the patent was obtained with Colnett as a front man: Betty Jo Dobbs, "Studies in the Natural Philosophy of Sir Kenelm Digby: Part II: Digby and Alchemy" (1973) 20 *Ambix* 143 at 150.

23 Colnett's Patent Bill 1662 (HL), cl 1; see *Seventh Report of Royal Commission on Historical Manuscripts* (HMSO 1879) (C 2340), p 164 (HL/PO/JO/10/1/314).

24 6 CJ 165 (14 March 1649). His son sat in the Cromwellian Parliament however.

of London.[25] Soon after the return of Charles II he was granted a single patent[26] which covered a variety of inventions: a fast firing pistol, mechanism for the quick release of horses from a carriage, a long-running watch and a method of steering a boat.[27] However, he is probably most famous for inventing his "water commanding engine" which was protected by the Marquis of Worcester's Act 1663 rather than by a prerogative patent.

This Act was truly extraordinary in that it granted the Marquis the right to enjoy the invention for 99 years with a tenth of the profits[28] being paid to the King.[29] The Act was shepherded through the House of Lords by the Marquis himself and through the Commons by his son. The rationale for the Act was unique. While the invention was novel and would clearly have warranted a patent, the Act appears to have been granted by Parliament to replenish his lost fortune and not strictly to reward his invention. It was the term which needed exceptional Parliamentary approval and no more. Indeed, when the Marquis published his famous book *A Century of Invention*[30] his dedication included thanks to Parliament for the Act and seeing it as "sufficient" reward.[31] It appears however little money was actually received.

The remaining grants in the seventeenth century

Sir Philip Howard and Trevor Watson were granted a patent in 1668,[32] but it was challenged before the Privy Council by the Company of Painters Stainers of London. There appears to be two conflicting views of what happened in that challenge. On one version Howard and Watson had an absolute victory.[33] On the other, recorded by Pepys, the inventors had a partially invalid patent and at that point it was not possible to amend it to make it secure.[34] In any event, Howard and Watson sought a private Act to protect their invention for twenty-five years.[35] Had Pepys been right it would have been an instance of a private Act setting the (modified) extent of the invention[36] and extending the term of the patent.[37] This would be

---

25 Henry Dicks, *The Life, Times and Scientific Labours of the Second Marquis of Worcester* (London: Bernard Quaritch 1865), Ch 13.

26 Unity of invention only became a concern following the enactment of the Patent Law Amendment Act 1852: see Rules and Instructions to Be Observed in Applications Respecting Patents for Inventions, and by Persons Petitioning for Letters Patent for Inventions, and for Liberty to Enter Disclaimers and Alterations According to the Statutes 1852 (October 1852), 20 *Repertory of Patent Inventions* 263; it was included as a requirement in Patents, Designs and Trade Marks Act 1883, s 33; also see *Jones' Patent*, Griffin's PC 265.

27 Patent No 131 (1661).

28 This proviso was added in committee in the Lords: House of Lords Committee Books (HL/PO/CO/1/1), 28 March 1663, p 314–315. It is not clear why it was thought necessary. Possibly due to the extraordinary length of the grant.

29 Who in turn assigned these profits to the Marquis in lieu of certain lands promised: *Memoranda [by Williamson, Taken from the Signet Books,] of Warrant and Grants Passed during the Month*: National Archive: SP 29/93 f 116.

30 Charles Partington, *A Century of Invention from the Original MS* (John Murray, 1825).

31 Charles Partington, *A Century of Invention from the Original MS* (John Murray, 1825), p lxxv.

32 Patent No 158 (1668).

33 The version in Howard and Watson's Patent (1667) 11 HPC App (which is copied from Edward Wyndham Hulme, "Privy Council Law and Practice of Letters Patent for Inventions from the Restoration to 1794" (1917) 33 LQR 63 at 68). It is this version which is reflected in the Privy Council Register: see National Archive PC 2/61, ff 138 and 160–161).

34 Mentioned in *The Diary of Samuel Pepys*, 23 April 1669.

35 See National Archive: PC 2/61, f 138.

36 They had to file a description: see pp 108–110.

37 In fact, the method probably did not work: see JJ Wilkinson, "Historical Account of Wood Sheathing for Ships" (1842) 36 *Mechanics Magazine* 403.

a classic case of a private Act remedying a defect in the patent law (the absence of a right to amend), but one that did not raise its head again[38] until patents were regularly litigated in the courts in the early nineteenth century. [39] However, the records show that, by default, Howard and Watson's patent was found by the Privy Council to be new and valid.[40] The private Act was probably sought because Howard and Watson were worried about a more robust challenge and so they sought extra support from Parliament for their grant.

In the following decade, Sir Samuel Moreland unsuccessfully sought protection for his pumps and water engine through a private Bill[41]; however, for reasons unknown, he changed tack and subsequently obtained a prerogative patent to protect the invention.[42] Yet he returned to Parliament for further provision some three years later, which was largely to protect the improvements he had made to his invention.[43] Another example which cannot be elucidated further is Samuel Hutchinson, the inventor of convex lights, who was given leave to present a Bill in 1685,[44] but he never did so and no records remain of what he intended other than that he was seeking the benefit of his invention.[45] It may have been a patent term extension or ancillary rights.

The private Acts granted during the second half of the seventeenth century follow no real pattern. While they each granted protection, the English Parliament did not have a consistent or any policy in Parliamentary grants, the term of those grants or the rights it gave. As will be seen below, this is in stark contrast with the Scottish Parliament who had a developed policy to encourage new manufactures within the realm.

The formation of companies with exclusive rights

As discussed in more detail in Chapter 6, the old tradition of companies being given exclusive rights covered inventions as well as other matters. In the latter part of the seventeenth century these companies were smaller in number. One of the most notable example[46] was the White Paper Company which was formed and given the exclusive right to make white paper for fourteen years from 1690[47] confirming and extending a charter granted by James II in 1686.[48] After Samuel Hutchinson's aborted petition in 1685,[49] the Convex Light Bill

---

38 Thomas Brunton posted a notice for a private Act in 1823 (London Gazette, 7 September 1822 (Is: 17850, p 1464) to amend his patent following it being found to be void for being partially bad in *Brunton v Hawkes* (1821) 1 HPC 803; 4 B&Ald 541 (106 ER 1034).

39 It first became possible under the Letters Patent for Inventions Act 1835, s 1.

40 See Privy Council Register: National Archive: PC2/61, ff 160–161. The parties were ordered to set out in writing a description of their method and the Company of Painters refused.

41 Moreland's Pump Bill 1674 (no records exist of this Bill).

42 Patent No 175 (1674).

43 The text of the Bill is lost, but this was the suggestion of its opponent: Anon [James Ward], *Reasons Offered against Passing Sir Samuel Morland's Bill* (1677) (Wing R576).

44 Hutchinson's Lamp Petition 1685: 9 CJ 726 (3 June 1685).

45 Which had actually been granted to Edward Wyndus for financial reasons (Patent No 232 (1684)); see William Scott, *The Constitution and Finance of English, Scottish and Irish Joint Stock Companies* (Cambridge 1911), Vol 3, p 52.

46 There were certain saltpetre companies formed: see William Scotts, *The Constitution and Finance of English, Scottish and Irish Joint-Stock Companies to 1720* (Cambridge 1911), Vol 2, pp 471–474. This in turn led to a Bill being introduced into Parliament over the validity of the grant: see Making Saltpetre Bill 1691.

47 White Paper Company Act 1690, s 3 (the underlying patent was granted to Eustance Burneby in 1675: Patent No 178 (1675). It would have expired when Parliament was petitioned.

48 See State Papers Domestic (3 July 1686): National Archive: SP 44/337, ff 57–60 (Warrant for a Charter).

49 Hutchinson's Lamp Petition 1685: 9 CJ 726 (3 June 1685).

was rejected in 1692,[50] but the Convex Light Company was given the exclusive rights in the convex lights in 1694 for twenty-one years (essentially an additional seventeen years)[51] provided they paid £600 annually to London Orphans fund.[52] The final private Act granting exclusive rights to a company was the Lustrings Act 1697 which, once more, granted the company exclusivity over making alamodes for fourteen years.[53] Parliament's willingness to grant such rights waned through the eighteenth century as "stock-jobbing" became a pejorative term[54] and private Acts to incorporate for any purpose were passed very reluctantly.

When Parliament began to enact legislation to incorporate companies once more, it was no longer willing to grant monopolies and made this very clear as evidenced by the Gas Light and Coke Company Act 1810. While it did not protect an invention as such, the Act expressly states that no exclusive rights are granted to the company.[55] The views of Parliament had changed over the previous century. No longer was it appropriate to grant a monopoly of the whole industry. This was confirmed in 1837 when a Bill to establish the Birmingham Plate and Crown Glass Company was rejected because it would create a monopoly[56] over the industry and in the same year what became the London Caoutchouc Company Act 1838 faced similar objections and was robustly, but unsuccessfully, challenged on Third Reading in the House of Commons (although the final Act included no grant of exclusive rights).[57] The acceptability of companies being granted exclusive rights had clearly died in the early part of the eighteenth century and could not survive the moves towards free trade during the late eighteenth and early nineteenth century. This did not stop inventors continuing to try their luck by seeking private Acts throughout the long eighteenth century however.

The long eighteenth century

In 1712 John Hutchinson sought a private Act to protect his time movement invention. In his petition he gave his reasons as being that a patent would not be adequate as he would not be able to perfect his invention and make a return before it expired.[58] The Clockmakers Company opposed his Bill[59] on the grounds that many of its members had made improvements but none had sought an Act of Parliament to protect it (going on to point out the failure of the Watches, Inventions and Extension of Patent Bill 1704 (Facio and Debaufre's Bill) for term extension)[60] and this led to further papers being presented to Parliament by

---

50 Convex Light Bill 1692 (no records remain of this Bill).

51 The underlying patent behind the enterprise was granted in 1684 (No 232) to Edward Wyndus.

52 London, Orphans Act 1694, ss 5 and 28.

53 Lustrings Act 1697, s 14.

54 See pp 88–92.

55 Gas Light and Coke Company Act 1810, s 36.

56 The text of the Bill does not survive, but it is possible that this was a monopoly in the economic sense, rather than an exclusive right; however the reports talk about exclusive rights so it may be related to an invention: see John Hodgson Hinde, *Mirror of Parliament*, 28 June 1837, Vol 3, p 2024 (this comment was made during the debates on the London Caoutchouc Company Bill).

57 Third Reading was adjourned mid-debate a number of times: *Mirror of Parliament*, 7 June 1837, Vol 3, p 1733; *Mirror of Parliament*, 14 June 1837, Vol 3, p 1852–1854; *Mirror of Parliament*, 22 June 1837, Vol 3, p 1936; *Mirror of Parliament*, 23 June 1837, Vol 3, pp 1949–1950; *Mirror of Parliament*, 28 June 1987, Vol 3, pp 2024–2025.

58 Petition of John Hutchinson: London Metropolitan Archive: CLS/L/CD/E/004/MS03952.

59 See 14 CJ 462 (18 December 1704).

60 Reasons offered against the Bill by the Clockmakers Company: London Metropolitan Archive: CLS/L/CD/E/004/MS03952.

Hutchinson in which he claimed he was an inventor and the Clockmakers were not.[61] The Clockmakers Company submitted another paper[62] saying they were inventors and a conventional fourteen-year patent was the appropriate reward. Despite a further paper from Hutchinson,[63] his Bill never left committee and so died. It appears that this was the last time someone tried to protect an otherwise patentable invention by a private Act.[64]

Subject matter issues

There appear to have been very few private Acts or Bills specifically to address subject matter issues; although, as discussed in Chapter 9, it may be that Parliamentary rewards provided a more straightforward method of rewarding unpatentable inventions. The first case of an Act being granted for an "unpatentable" method was that of John Byrom. He had invented a method of shorthand which he wanted to be published, but his method was not protected under the Statute of Monopolies as it excluded printing,[65] nor under the Copyright Act 1709 (the Statute of Anne) as it only protected the making of copies.[66] His argument for the Bill included the fact a Mr X had started advertising to teach his method of shorthand and so he would soon lose everything.[67] Accordingly, Parliament granted him a twenty-one-year monopoly over his method of shorthand[68] and a further £100 penalty for anyone teaching the method before any explanation of the shorthand was published.[69] In any event, Byrom taught his shorthand as a way of earning a living and he only printed fifty copies of his method during his lifetime which he gave to select pupils,[70] a full explanation of his Universal Shorthand only being published until after his death.[71] This means the Act was unusual in that it gave an individual an income for teaching his craft, rather than promoting the dissemination of the art.

Failed attempts

Byrom's Act was followed by some attempts during the remainder of the eighteenth century to get protection by way of an Act of Parliament, but these were largely aborted at the stage of a petition being lodged or referred to a committee. Robert Hunter Morris petitioned Parliament for the exclusive right to make salt in the British Colonies in

---

61 Reasons for the Bill: London Metropolitan Archive: CLS/L/CD/E/004/MS03952.
62 The Clockmakers Father Reasons against Mr Hutchinson's Bill: London Metropolitan Archive: CLS/L/CD/E/004/MS03952.
63 Further Reasons for the Bill. . .in Answer to the Clockmakers: London Metropolitan Archive: CLS/L/CD/E/004/MS03952.
64 In addition there was Cox's Unloading Machine Petition 1757 (27 CJ 693; 10 February 1757), where the petition for protection was lodged with Parliament before the patent was granted but the report on that petition was after the grant of the patent. It is probable that it was an attempt to extend the length of the patent.
65 Byrom's Shorthand Act 1741, recital (2).
66 Byrom's Shorthand Act 1741, recital (3).
67 House of Lords Committee Books (HL/PO/CO/1/12), 19 May 1742, p 31.
68 Byrom's Shorthand Act 1741, s 1.
69 Byrom's Shorthand Act 1741, s 2.
70 James Lewis, *An Historical Account of the Rise and Progress of Short Hand* (London 1839), p 111.
71 John Byrom, *The Universal English Shorthand or the Way of Writing Invented by John Byrom* (Manchester: Joseph Harrop 1767).

North America.[72] He had made no invention, but rather was seeking a monopoly to fund the setting up of a marine salt works, using known methods, in the British Colonies; on the basis that a person who brings an invention to England (or the American colonies) is deemed to be the inventor[73] even where the invention is well known elsewhere. His petition was not therefore utterly hopeless (although it did not progress). In the following year, John Bindley petitioned[74] for the grant of an exclusive right to protect a green dye (verdigrease) which had previously only been made in France.[75] The committee heard evidence that he was the only person making good verdigrease in England as well as other evidence in support.[76] The matter was referred for consideration by a Committee of the Whole House, but it never appeared again. What remains unclear about Bindley's petition is why he did not seek a conventional patent. There is no suggestion that a fourteen-year term was inadequate and the evidence was that nobody in England knew how to make it before Bindley introduced it.[77] It may simply have been a case of self-collusion: he had introduced the invention before he thought of obtaining a patent.

A further aborted attempt for a grant was part of the saga relating to Dr Cuthbert Gordon's dyeing inventions. As discussed in Chapter 9, he was awarded £200 by the Privy Council (following a resolution of Parliament) upon certain proofs. After struggling to get his reward he petitioned Parliament once more in 1793 seeking a *Bill for ascertaining and establishing his Discoveries on a proper advantageous Footing for the Benefit of the Community and of the Petitioner*.[78] It is unclear what he was seeking in his Bill as all records are lost; although his struggles did eventually lead to his reward being paid.[79]

Langton's wood seasoning invention

The last invention protected under a private Act was that of John Langton. He invented a method of seasoning timber. His grant was essentially a way of extending his patent, but rather than petitioning Parliament for a private Act for that purpose he applied for an Act to obtain the profits from his invention.[80] The most likely reason why he elected to extend the protection in this way rather than extend his patent[81] was that extending his patent so early in its term would have been contrary to the House of Lords' Standing Orders.[82] What is more surprising is that the Lords did not see his Bill as an attempt to circumvent the Standing Orders. The reason might possibly be seen from how his pleaded his preamble. First, it suggests that it would take too long to prove that his method of preserving timber

---

72 28 CJ 85 (11 February 1758).

73 *Edgeberry v Stephens* (1691) 1 HPC 117; 1 WPC 35.

74 Petition of John Bindley: 28 CJ 1000 (19 December 1760).

75 See Report on Petition: 28 CJ 1039 (23 January 1761).

76 28 CJ 1039 (23 January 1761).

77 28 CJ 1039 (23 January 1761).

78 46 CJ 266 (25 February 1793).

79 See pp 150 and 152–4.

80 The difference between Langton and other people who extended their patent by having the protection protected by an Act of Parliament is that Langton did not recite his patent in the Act itself: he therefore was not relying on it directly.

81 Patent No 5,236 (1825).

82 See pp 132–3; in particular, he was too early as his patent was granted on 11 August 1825 and so he would have had to wait another eight years to apply to extend his patent.

was superior to other methods[83] and that the capital required to meet the outlay of proving the invention works was too great.[84] In other words, the invention could not yet be worked. Secondly, the Act recites:

> The said Invention relating to the Preparation for Use of a Material of such general Consumption may be immediately, laid open to all His Majesty's Subjects on fair and equitable Terms, so that the Public may reap the Advantages to be derived therefrom in their fullest Extent.

Thus, the Act involved Langton exchanging exclusivity under the patent for something less.

The Act provided a complicated mechanism for using the invention. There was a general ban on anyone using the invention for twenty-one years,[85] but a person who advertised seven days in advance that they were going to use the invention was entitled to do so upon payment of a 5% royalty (6 pence on twenty shillings of gross value of timber sold)[86]: a compulsory licence of sorts. Further, any person who made the vessel for carrying out the method had to keep it locked and secure except when being inspected by Langton[87] there was also an accounting requirement.[88] It was essentially meant to reflect what would have been in place if there had been a patent extension granted.[89] He was also obliged to make sure that within three years 500 tons of shipping was constructed using timber treated by his method.[90] Failure to treat this much timber led to the Act ceasing to have effect, although this last requirement was relaxed, by a subsequent private Act, when it was clear that the target could not be achieved.[91] There was clearly ambiguity about whether Langton's method (or someone else's) was being used and so the second Act deemed certain uses to be uses of his invention.[92]

Doubts about novelty – self-collusion

While it is possible that some private Bills were pursued after the Interregnum[93] because of fears about the novelty of the invention,[94] and this may have been Bindley's motivation,[95] there appears to be only one instance where a provision of an Act was clearly included to preserve the novelty of an invention. Even in this case it was a strange situation; the patentee, Charles Payne, had filed a specification in the Court of Chancery before the patent was granted and

83 Langton's Profits (Wood Seasoning Invention) Act 1829, recital (2).
84 Langton's Profits (Wood Seasoning Invention) Act 1829, recital (3).
85 Langton's Profits (Wood Seasoning Invention) Act 1829, s 1.
86 Langton's Profits (Wood Seasoning Invention) Act 1829, s 1.
87 Langton's Profits (Wood Seasoning Invention) Act 1829, s 2.
88 Langton's Profits (Wood Seasoning Invention) Act 1829, s 3.
89 At least according to representations made to the committee on the Bill in the House of Lords: House of Lords Committee Books: (HL/CO/PO/1/84), 3 June 1829, p 443. It should be noted that the *Minutes of Evidence Taken before Lords Committee to Whom Langton's Bill Was Referred* (1829 HL Papers 82), Vol 162, p 223 relate to the committee formed under SO 198 and not the committee on the Bill.
90 Langton's Profits (Wood Seasoning Invention) Act 1829, s 5.
91 Langton's Profit's Act 1831, ss 1 and 2.
92 Langton's Profit's Act 1831, s 3.
93 In this text, the term Interregnum will be used for the period between the outbreak of the Civil War and the Restoration of Charles II, references to institutions during this period will use the term Commonwealth.
94 See p 52.
95 Bindley's Verdigrease Manufacture Petition 1760: 28 CJ 1000 (19 December 1760).

so it was a case of self-collusion. This was remedied by section 20 of the Timber Preserving Company's Extension Act 1848 which specifically provided that the petition's publication would not count against the patent. This mistake demonstrates the last time when substantive issues of patentability were addressed by a private Act. However, the story returns to an earlier period when the clearest example of such issues arises – with improvement inventions.

Improvements

English patent law was slow to follow the reality of invention: that it is incremental. Instead the law made improvements unpatentable in a series of cases beginning with *Matthey's Patent*,[96] a patent on improved knife handles, which was revoked when the Cutler's Company said such an improvement would ruin them. In *Bircot's Case*[97] the Exchequer Chamber held that a mere improvement in the smelting of lead ore was unpatentable. This rule[98] was only overturned in 1776 by Lord Mansfield in *Morris v Branson*.[99] Yet the "new" rule was far from firmly established. In *Boulton & Watt v Bull*[100] the second argument raised by the defendant was that that Watt's Steam Engine was a "mere improvement"[101] and it was the judgment of Buller J which finally established the patentability of improvements:

> That a patent for an addition or improvement may be maintained, is a point which has never been directly decided; and Bircot's case, 3 Inst. 184, is an express authority against it, which case was decided in the Exchequer Chamber. What were the particular facts of that case we are not informed, and there seems to me to be more quaintness than solidity in the reason assigned, which is, that it was to put but a new button to an old coat, and it is much easier to add than to invent. If the button were new, I do not feel the weight of the objection that the coat on which the button was to be put, was old. But in truth arts and sciences at that period were at so low an ebb, in comparison with that point to which they have been since advanced, and the effect and utility of improvements so little known, that I do not think that case ought to preclude the question. In later times, whenever the point has arisen, the inclination of the court has been in favour of the patent for the improvement, and the parties have acquiesced, where the objection might have been brought directly before the court. In Morris v. Branson . . . Lord Mansfield said "after one of the former trials on this patent, I received a very sensible letter from one of the gentlemen who was upon the jury, on the subject whether on principles of public policy, there could be a patent for an addition only. I paid great attention to it, and mentioned it to all the judges. If the general point of law, viz. that there can be no patent for an addition, be with the Defendant, that is open upon the record, and he may move in arrest of judgment. But that objection would go to repeal almost every patent that was ever granted." . . .Since that time, it has been the generally received opinion in Westminster Hall, that a patent for an addition is good. But then it must be for the addition only, and not for the old machine too.

96 (1571) 1 HPC 1n; Noy 178; 1 WPC 6.
97 (1572) 1 HPC 71; 3 Co Inst 184 (Ex Ch, ET 15 Elizabeth).
98 Lord Mansfield's manuscripts confirm that the defendant tried to plead the rule in *Bircot's Case*: James Oldham, *English Common Law in the Age of Mansfield* (North Carolina Press 2004), p 201.
99 (1776) 1 HPC 181; 1 WPC 51.
100 (1795) 1 HPC 369; 2 Blackstone (H) 463 (126 ER 651).
101 (1795) 1 HPC 369; 2 Blackstone (H) 463 at 488 (126 ER 651 at 664).

The maintenance of the objection by the defendant that Watt's invention was an improvement clearly indicates that there were concerns over subject matter insofar as it relates to improvements, until late in the eighteenth century. Accordingly, during this period where a person made an improvement (either on their own invention or another's) it was unclear whether a patent could be granted. In the absence of the improvement being patentable subject matter, some other form of protection would be needed. This would suggest that an inventor of an improvement might seek a private Act of Parliament to secure the protection of their invention.

The patent term extension Acts

In the two decades beginning 1775[102] a cluster of private Acts was enacted to extend the term of the respective patents. Some of these Acts[103] included a requirement to file a specification.[104] Burrell and Kelly[105] suggest that this was the replacement of the adequate specification with a "new" specification and use this obligation as an indication that Parliament was requiring better disclosure of inventions. In other words, they suggest, to get an extension it was necessary to make a proper disclosure. However, a quite different view can be taken of this requirement. The private Acts were essentially granting protection to a new "improvement" invention which could not otherwise be protected under *Bircot's Case*.[106] Further, as was well established by the 1770s, if a new invention was being claimed in the Act then a new specification (disclosure) needed to be made. In other words, these extensions were not simply the extension of an existing patent but usually the grant of a new "Parliamentary" patent[107] which covers both the original invention and its improvement.[108] Parliament was endorsing the accepted practice of requiring a specification to describe the invention/improvement claimed ("the improvement view").

Support of new invention approach

The difficulty with substantiating this view of the requirement to file a specification, namely, that the invention claimed is actually an improvement, is that there are so few private Acts or petitions to examine during this period to reach any conclusion. This is compounded by the lack of contemporaneous materials. However, there are two reasons to think that this

---

102 An earlier attempt to use a private Act to protect an improvement was Samuel Morlands Bill 1677. Indeed, it appears that he needed to provide a model of the improvement at some point (without time limit). As the description of the Bill comes from an opponent it may not be accurate: see Anon [James Ward?], *Reasons Offered against Passing Sir Samuel Morland's Bill* (1677) (Wing R576).

103 It is erroneously suggested by Robert Burrell and Catherine Kelly, "Parliamentary Rewards and the Evolution of the Patent System" (2015) 74 *Cam LJ* 423 at 433 that such a requirement was included in Elwick's Patent Act 1742 and Meinzies' Patent Act 1750. However, the extract they include is from the preamble (and not the enacting part) and reflects the recitation of the Letters Patent being extended. In other words it was an existing (and past obligation) and not a future one imposed by Parliament.

104 Porcelain Patent Act 1775, s 2; Elizabeth Taylor's Patent Act 1776, s 2; Liardet's Cement Patent Act 1776, s 6; Bancroft's Patent Act 1785, s 4.

105 Robert Burrell and Catherine Kelly, "Parliamentary Rewards and the Evolution of the Patent System" (2015) 74 *Cam LJ* 423 at 435.

106 (1572) 1 HPC 71; 3 Co Inst 184.

107 Only Champion (Porcelain Patent Act 1775) and Taylor (Elizabeth Taylor's Patent Act 1776) had the underlying patent extended after 1775 all the others had the invention protected under the Act itself: see pp 126–7.

108 Not taking into account the rule introduced later in *Jessop's Case* (1795) 1 HPC 555; 2 Blackstone (H) 476.

view is correct. The first is that improvements are generally claimed where a private Act required a specification to be filed and during the passage of one such Act the additional novelty was claimed as a basis for supporting it. The second is that specifications were not generally required in such Acts – and in particular they were not required where no improvement was pleaded.

In the relevant period there are four private Acts which require a specification to be filed and four[109] that did not. In addition, eight other persons petitioned Parliament unsuccessfully for a Bill to extend their patent (some more than once); in two of those cases[110] an Ingrossment of the Bill survives and in another the Bill's First Reading text is available.

Requirement to file a specification

The improvement view is supported to some extent by Elizabeth Taylor's Patent Act 1776 where the preamble states:

> The said Elizabeth Taylor his Widow, and Walter Taylor their Son, have been at great Pain and Labour, and at a large Expence, in improving the same; and considerable Improvement have been made therein by the said Walter Taylor

Thus, the Act provides that the improvements have to be specified in an instrument in writing and the failure to so specify the improvements makes the Act void.[111] Strangely, however, the patent was extended without expressly including the newly specified improvements. It is probable that the Act would have been read to include both the original invention and improvement, but it is equally possible that the original patent is extended (on the base of invention) in exchange for disclosing unpatentable improvements.

The classic example of the requirement to file the specification is Liardet's Cement Patent Act 1776. The patent (and the improvement) which were central to this private Act were at the centre of the infamous *Liardet v Johnson*.[112] While the preamble pleaded no improvements, the Act granted Liardet the "sole Privilege and Advantage of exercising, and vending, the said Composition or Cement mentioned in the said Letters Patent. . . Additions and Improvement since made therein"[113] and with this extended privilege came the obligation to "particularly describe and ascertain the Nature of his said Invention in its present improved State" and to deposit a specification within four months or the Act would become void.[114] Indeed, during the debate on Liardet's Bill, the Earl of Cathcart specifically stated that the claim for the Bill was at least partially based on the fresh novelty of the improvements.[115]

109 It should be noted that Booth's Patent Act 1792 was not a term extension and so the requirement to file a specification is unrelated: see Chapter 7.

110 The Ingrossment of James Turners Dye Invention Bill 1791 survives (HL/PO/JO/10/2/65A), but it largely follows the Act he finally obtained.

111 Elizabeth Taylor's Patent Act 1776, s 2.

112 (1778) 1 HPC 195; 1 Carp PC 35; 1 WPC 52; (1780) 1 Y&C 527 (62 ER 1000); indeed, the defendant alleged that he infringed neither specification as both lacked novelty: *An Appeal to the Public on the Right of Using Oil Cement* (London: J Hand 1778), p 68–69.

113 Liardet's Cement Patent Act 1776, s 1.

114 Liardet's Cement Patent Act 1776, s 6.

115 *Middlesex Journal and Evening Advertiser*, 30 March to 2 April 1776; *Morning Post and Daily Advertiser*, 2 April 1776.

This clearly suggests that the specification is being filed to ensure that there has been an adequate disclosure of the improvements over which exclusive rights have been granted.

Similarly, Edward Bancroft claimed in his preamble that he had made "certain improvements" to his method of dyeing which he had claimed and specified in his 1775 patent.[116] Thus, part of the deal struck with Parliament was that he had to disclose those improvements within four months of the enactment or the Act would become void.[117] In contrast to the earlier example, the Act granted the "sole Privilege and Advantage of making using, exercising, using and vending the said Invention, mentioned in the said Letters Patent, with the Additions and Improvements since made therein"[118] Once more, the specification is being filed to require an adequate disclosure of the improvement also covered by the extension.

The final Act of the quartet, the Porcelain Patent Act 1775, is more difficult to fit within this neat picture. Its preamble sets out how William Cookworthy filed a specification to satisfy the proviso in the patent. It continues by explaining that Richard Champion (who bought the patent from Cookworthy) has:

> at very considerable Expence, and at great Pains and Labour, in prosecuting the said Invention; and by reason of the great Difficulty attending a Manufacture upon a new Principle, hath not been able to bring the same to Perfection until within this last Year; and it will require further Pain, Labour and Expensce, to render the said Invention publick Utility.

Thus, additional work is pleaded after the grant of the patent. So it could be said that the requirement for filing a specification[119] was in exchange for the protection of the "perfections" being granted. However, there are two alternative possibilities, the first being that in this case Burrell and Kelly are right. The second is that the provision is largely a result of the actions of Josiah Wedgwood (largely from behind the scenes) trying to kill the Bill.[120] In Champion's case the requirement to file a specification may actually have been a wrecking amendment of sorts. The Act required the specification to state "the Mixture and Proportions of the Raw Materials of which his Porcelain is composed" and a similar requirement of the glaze.[121] It is clear from the face of the provision that the specification related to the glaze already existing (as it was already with the Lord Chancellor). The difficulty may have been the proportions for the porcelain itself. Hard-paste porcelain is made from feldspathic rock (e.g. granite), kaolin and china stone.[122] The proportions of each depended on the particular sample adopted and so might require experimentation on the substance from a particular area. Indeed, the difficultly in working out the correct proportions has been attributed to Cookworthy's original failure.[123] Accordingly, making Champion file details of the proportions may actually have been a way of trying to negate the benefit of the Act.

116 Patent No 1,103 (1773).
117 Bancroft's Patent Act 1785, s 4.
118 Bancroft's Patent Act 1785, s 1.
119 Porcelain Patent Act 1775, s 2.
120 For a description of the proceedings and the various arguments raised see: Hugh Owen, *Two Centuries of Ceramic Art in Bristol* (Bell and Daldy 1873), Chapter 5.
121 Porcelain Patent Act 1775, s 2.
122 Petuntse.
123 Hugh Owen, *Two Centuries of Ceramic Art in Bristol* (Bell and Daldy 1873), p 148.

The Acts for which no specification was required

This main support of the improvement view is the fact that some Acts *did not* have a requirement to file a specification. The private Acts of David Hartley,[124] the Earl Dundonald,[125] James Turner[126] and Henry Conway,[127] and the Bills of Ann Wharam[128] Jonathan Hornblower[129] and John Kendrew and Thomas Porthouse[130] all sought extensions for the original patented invention without any improvement. And no specifications were required. One example which may fall into either category is James Watt. The preamble to his Act states that he was not able to put his invention into effect until 1774,[131] but it does not suggest any improvement as such. Indeed, Watt sought new patents to cover his improvements.[132] However, this may not be the end of the story as when Watt was considering whether to petition Parliament he believed he was choosing between surrendering his existing patent and getting a new one or applying to Parliament for a Bill. In early 1775, Watt had approached Alexander Wedderburn, then Solicitor General, and been informed he could surrender his patent and get a new one.[133] However, he had also been advised that extending his current patent by Private Act would be cheaper than getting a new patent.[134] While it may be Wedderburn advised that an existing patent could be simply started anew this seems very unlikely. It is more likely that he advised that an old patent could be surrendered to enable a new patent to be granted for an improved version of the invention. In other words, as with the other cases, the Act may have been to protect an improvement. In any event, in contrast to other private Acts, the preamble to his Act included a full description of his invention.

A grant for the whole of the Great Britain

The prolongation Acts also provided a mechanism to extend the geographical scope of a patentees protection.[135] Thus, James Watt held an English patent[136] but when he obtained his

---

124 Hartley's Patent (Fire Prevention) Act 1776.

125 Lord Dundonald's Patent (Tar, Pitch, etc.) Act 1785.

126 Turner's Patent Act 1792.

127 Conway's Patent Kiln Act 1795.

128 Wharam's Patent Stirrup Bill 1782 (Ingrossment: HL/PO/JO/10/2/57).

129 Hornblower's Patent Bill 1792 (Birmingham Library: MS 3147/2/36/1).

130 Kendrew and Porthouse's Bill 1794 (Ingrossment: HL/PO/JO/10/2/67).

131 James Watt's Fire Engine Patent Act 1775, recital (2).

132 See Patent No 1,306 (1781); No 1,321 (1782); No 1,432 (1784); No 1,485 (1785).

133 Letter from James Watt to Matthew Boulton, 17 January 1775 (Birmingham Library: MS 3782/12/76/6).

134 The patent being £130 and the Act being £110: see Letter from James Watt to Matthew Boulton, 31 January 1775 (Birmingham Library: MS 3782/12/76/8).

135 The geographical extension is noted by Robert Burrell and Catherine Kelly, "Parliamentary Rewards and the Evolution of the Patent System" (2015) 74 *Cam LJ* 423 at 435. However, they go on to describe an "Imperial patent" which was unique in the history of the British Empire. While it is true that before 1852 it was necessary to get a patent separately in England, Scotland and Ireland, it had been possible to get the English patent endorsed so as to extend to the colonies – indeed James Watt and John Liardet had done just that. It was also possible to have the patent extended to the Crown Dependencies (the Channel Islands and the Isle of Man) – an extension which was not included in any of the private Acts. Indeed, the change of policy was one of the things petitioned against in 1852: see Sugar Refiners of Greenock (23 June 1852): Forty-Fifth Report of the Public Petitions Committee 1852, p 620 (No 5,611). And the issues with sugar led to questions being asked as to the new law being extended to the colonies: see *The Times*, 20 May 1854; also see Moureen Coulter, *Property in Ideas: The Patent Question in Mid-Victorian Britain* (Thomas Jefferson University Press 1991), pp 65–67.

136 No 913 (1769).

private Act the invention was protected not only in England but also in Scotland[137] and the colonies.[138] While the cost of a private Bill could be large it was usually cheaper (and much cheaper) than obtaining a patent in England and then in Scotland.[139] Similarly, John Liardet's and David Hartley's English patents[140] were prolonged and extended to cover Scotland as well as England.[141] In each case, the claim was made that without the Act (and so the protection) extending to Scotland it would not be possible to recover for the expense incurred.[142] Indeed, once Watt had been successful at extending the protection for the invention both temporally and geographically it is not surprising that others sought the same thing.

What is surprising, however, is that not *every* petitioner sought to have the invention protected across the whole of Great Britain. In one case it would have been because the Act simply extended the existing patents[143] and in others it was because there was an underlying patent already applied to Scotland and so it was simply extending something that was already in existence.[144] Towards the end of the eighteenth century and until prolongation was taken over by the Privy Council, there was an increased resistance to private Acts and so this might explain why neither James Turner's Bill in 1791[145] nor his similar Act that followed in 1792[146] extended the patent beyond England and likewise nearly forty years later why James Hollingrake only extended the time and not the geography of his patent.[147] It is Edward Bancroft's failure to extend his patent to Scotland which is surprising. He sought and obtained his Act[148] while the going was good and at a time when others were seeking and obtaining geographical as well as temporal extensions. The reason for his reluctance may be no more than caution. While it is clear that private Acts which extended the geographical scope were granting protection without any underlying patent (and so were Parliamentary grants), it was the ability to extend the term which must have motivated the petitioners. So obtaining an extension of the geographical scope (often for what would only be a few years if the term was not extended) was probably little more than a bonus. From extending English patents to Scotland, the story moves to considering Scottish Parliamentary grants.

Scottish Parliament

While the English Parliament during the seventeenth century period occasionally granted some protection for inventors, the Scottish Parliament was far more active. As discussed in Chapter 2, the procedure before the Scottish Parliament was not uniform during the

---

137 This was before the unification of Ireland and Great Britain so an Act could only extend to England and Scotland (and the colonies).
138 James Watt's Fire Engines Patent Act 1775, s 1.
139 Hence the comments by Watt about it being cheaper: see p 63.
140 Liardet: Patent No 1,040 (1773); Hartley: Patent No 1,037 (1773).
141 Liardet's Cement Patent Act 1776, s 1; Hartley's Patent (Fire Prevention) Act 1776, s 1.
142 James Watt's Fire Engines Patent Act 1775, recital (5); Liardet's Cement Patent Act 1776, recital (2); Hartley's Patent (Fire Prevention) Act 1776, recital (5).
143 Elizabeth Taylor's Patent Act 1776.
144 Lord Dundonald's Patent (Tar, Pitch, etc.) Act 1785; Conway's Patent Kiln Act 1795; Cartwright's Woolcombing Machinery Act 1801 (where there was an equivalent Scottish patent in relation to one of those "extended"); Fourdriniers' Paper Making Machine Act 1807 (where the existing patents already extended to Scotland and Ireland).
145 James Turner Dye Invention Bill 1791 (Ingrossment: HL/PO/JO/10/2/65A).
146 Turner's Patent Act 1792.
147 Hollingrake Letters Patent Act 1830.
148 Bancroft's Patent Act 1785.

seventeenth century and neither was its function. Thus, when reference is made to Acts before 1640, the Scottish Parliament was usually ratifying the decisions of the Lords of the Articles. Nevertheless, the Parliament enacted various legislative monopolies during the reign of James VI of Scotland.[149] The earliest example appears to be the ratification in 1581 of a thirty-year privilege to Robert Dickson for silk-making in the Flemish or French style.[150] A few years later a seven-year grant was given to Margaret Balfour for making salt "in any other manner than the same was made in this realm before"[151] and in 1598 a twenty-one year grant was given to Gavin Smith and James Acheson for their artificial pumping engine.[152] These were a series of isolated examples of grants and it took decades later before any systematic policy was adopted.

Scottish protectionism

When the Crowns of England and Scotland united in James I (and VI of Scotland), manufacturing was still largely regulated by craft guilds.[153] Industry in Scotland was backward due largely to want of capital[154] and the Scots were so poor that James' proposal to united his realms of Scotland and England would have been no benefit to the latter.[155] Nevertheless, over the last fifty years of its existence, the old Scottish Parliament implemented a determined policy to develop local industry and so Scotland became increasingly protectionist. The real beginning of this policy was during the so-called Covenanters' Parliament. With his problems in England, Charles I was forced into agreeing to the Covenanters' wide range of constitutional changes[156] as well as to various industrial enactments. These included the Act Discharging Monopolies 1641,[157] which was much narrower in scope than its English equivalent. It invalidated certain named patents[158] and provided that all patents for invention were void, whenever granted, where they were prejudicial to the public. Thus, any patent (whether for an invention or not) could be granted provided it was not prejudicial to the public. In theory, at least, this meant that in contrast to England there was no need to resort to Parliament to get any special dispensation except during the King's enforced absence.[159]

Act for Manufactories 1641

The Act [Commission] for Manufactories 1641[160] was part of a continuing Scots policy which has been said to have been "to rival the Dutch in the fishing industry and the English

---

149 Later, James I of England.
150 Ratification of the Privilege of Silk-making to Robert Dickson 1581 [RPS: 1581/10/83]; in the same year an Act was passed to encourage Flemish weavers to come to Scotland. However this granted protection, but not exclusive rights.
151 Act in Favour of Lady Burleigh, Touching the Privilege of Refined Salt [RPS: 1587/7/123].
152 Act Regarding the Sole Making of Pumps [Smith and Acheson's Act] 1598 [RPS: 1598/10/7].
153 Theodora Keith, *Commercial Relations of England and Scotland 1603–1707* (Cambridge 1910), pp xviii–xix.
154 Theodora Keith, *Commercial Relations of England and Scotland 1603–1707* (Cambridge 1910), p xix.
155 Theodora Keith, *Commercial Relations of England and Scotland 1603–1707* (Cambridge 1910), p 11.
156 See David Stevenson *The Government of Scotland under the Covenanters* (Scottish History Society 1982), p xxvii.
157 [WPC 33] [RPS: 1641/8/192].
158 Sir Samuel Leslie and Thomas Dalmahoy (tobacco); James Erskine, Ear of Mar (leather); James Bannatyne (Pearling); Robert Buchan (Pearling); and Henry Mauld (Armoury).
159 As the Parliament would be hardly likely to grant an Act it thought prejudicial to the public.
160 Commission for Manufactories 1641 [RPS: 1641/8/194].

in the cloth trade".[161] The Act was specifically to encourage the production of fine cloth as, at the time, Scottish wool was not good enough for broadcloth and so wool had to be imported from Spain as did other raw materials.[162] Thus, the 1641 Act enabled foreign manufacturers to come to Scotland and to have the same rights and privileges as Scots, allowing foreign manufactories to incorporate and be exempt from import duties and taxation.[163] It also empowered the Privy Council (then known as the Lords of the Secret Council) to give further rights and privileges if they thought fit.

As time went by other industries sought similar privileges from the Scottish Parliament.[164] Indeed, as the Parliament was willing to grant immunities from customs and taxation it is not surprising that it was also willing to extend exclusive rights to individuals. When the Covenanters, and later the Committee of the Estates,[165] became the executive of the Scottish Government the Privy Council effectively ceased to function.[166] This meant that, as in England, there was no clear mechanism for granting patents. With a clear Scottish policy of encouraging foreigners to bring their technology to Scotland this vacuum had to be filled and so it was by the Parliament itself.

Thus, in 1646 the Scottish Parliament granted[167] Sir Robert Bruce an exclusive right for nineteen years over his invention for drying out mines.[168] Two years later, Colonel James Wemyss was granted a nineteen-year term for his inventions relating to ordnance. In contrast to Bruce, this grant was over a range of only loosely particularised technology: light ordnance (otherwise called leather ordnance), shooting ordnance from a pound bullet to a demi-cannon, with various others engines of war such as mortar pieces, petards and the like of leather.[169] Scottish industrial policy was essentially brought to an end by the impediments of war with the English Commonwealth.[170] Eventually, with the Scottish defeat at the Battle of Worcester and the uniting of Scotland and England under the Commonwealth Parliament the Scottish policy was forced into a hiatus.[171] The period of the Interregnum was not a good one for the Scots as Theodora Keith described it:[172]

---

161 See William Scott, "Fiscal Policy of Scotland" (1904) *Scottish Historical Review* 173 at 174, which is based on *John Keymor's Made upon the Dutch Fishing about the Year 1601* (Sir Edward Ford 1664) (Wing K390).

162 Cecil Carr, *Select Charters of Trading Companies 1530–1707* (Selden Society, 1913), Vol 3, p 125.

163 During the wars with the King, their employees were also exempt from conscription: Act in Favour of Manufactories, Masters, Workers Therein, Servants and Apprentices 1645 [RPS: 1645/1/163].

164 By the soap workers: see Act anent the Soap-works 1649 [RPS: 1649/1/310]; there was also a private Act to extend an already granted privilege by the Secret Council to a gold worker from a husband to wife: Act in Favour of the Silver and Gold Lace Weavers 1647 [RPS: 1646/11/479].

165 See David Stevenson, *The Government of Scotland Under the Covenanters* (Scottish History Society 1982), pp 1–3.

166 Thus, why an Act of the Privy Council was ratified by the Estates of Parliament: see Act in Favour of the Silver and Gold Lace Weavers 1647 [RPS: 1646/11/479].

167 Act [Sir Robert Bruce], laird of Clackmannan [RPS: 1646/11/547].

168 It was probably some form of hand pump which could be worked by two people (rather than many as was otherwise the case).

169 Act in Favour of Colonel James Wemyss 1648 [RPS: 1648/3/48] – there was also a prohibition on disseminating the technology: see p 113.

170 See generally, John Grainger, *Cromwell against the Scots: The Last Anglo-Scottish War 1650–52* (Tuckwell Press 1997).

171 As to Scottish representation in this Parliament see: Paul Pinckney, "The Scottish Representation in the Cromwellian Parliament of 1656" (1967) 46 *Scottish Historical Review* 95.

172 Theodora Keith, "Economic Condition of Scotland under the Commonwealth and the Protectorate" (1908) 5 *Scottish Historical Review* 273 at 284.

Poverty was great, manufactures could not be set up. Trade, both inland and foreign, had decayed, and showed little sign of recovery, and the bankruptcy of the country contributed to the bankruptcy of the whole [England and Welsh] government.

Thus, while the Acts passed by the Commonwealth Parliament extended to Scotland (as did the patents granted by Cromwell) the Protectorate did not lead to a continuation of any Scottish policy, but rather shoehorned the Scots into the English policy. This was devastating to the Scottish economy and it dislocated all its industry.[173] After the Restoration neither England nor Scotland wanted to keep the united Parliament. Furthermore, many of the new industries introduced by James VI and Charles I had died out and the traditional industries had also "considerably decayed".[174] Immediately, therefore, the revived Scots Parliament returned to its protectionist policy and its method of encouraging manufacturers to come to Scotland.

Act of Manufactories 1661

The first Parliament after the Restoration saw the enactment of the Act for Erecting Manufactories 1661.[175] This continued the Parliament's previous policy of naturalising foreigners who brought technology relating to cloth, soap or "any other kind of manufactory". The policy under the 1641 Act to favour cloth had expanded to all types of manufacture. Under the 1661 Act, manufactories could import the raw materials without paying any customs duties as well as being given nineteen years of duty free exports of their finished products. They were also exempt from all taxation and had special rights in relation to their employees. These privileges were just the starting point.

Their introduction led to a two-tier approach from those seeking to introduce a manufactory. They could seek similar immunities and privileges for their industry[176] or they could seek those things *and* exclusive rights. In any event, the measures did not achieve what they were trying to do as the new industries could not effectively compete with the long-established importers who could sell goods more cheaply.[177] Thus, when supplicants approached Parliament it was rare that they sought only the exemptions from duty. Indeed, the only clear example of such an instance was where the supplicants had previously had a patent.[178] In 1661 the Scottish Parliament granted Edward Lun the privileges of being a manufactory as well as the exclusive right to make needles for nineteen years.[179] More surprising than these grants are the extraordinary rights granted for nineteen years to Ludovic Leslie and James Scott in relation to

---

173 Theodora Keith, *Commercial Relations of England and Scotland 1603–1707* (Cambridge 1910), pp 31 and 55.
174 Theodora Keith, *Commercial Relations of England and Scotland 1603–1707* (Cambridge 1910), p 72.
175 RPS: 1661/1/344.
176 The only real instance of this is appears to be the Act in Favour of Silk Weavers, Printers etc 1663 [RPS: 1663/6/42]; although some industries obtained exemptions from duties on their raw materials without all the other privileges: Act in Favour of Printers and Stationers 1669 [RPS: 1669/10/132].
177 William Scott, *The Constitution and Finance of English, Scottish and Irish Joint-Stock Companies to 1720* (Cambridge 1911), Vol 3, p 127.
178 Act Concerning the Making of Cards 1663 [RPS: 1663/6/83] (John Aikman, James Riddell, James Currie and James Auchterlony).
179 Act for Major Lun anent the Making of Needles 1661 [RPS: 1661/1/367].

salt petre, salt upon salt, potashes, tanning of skins and hides without bark, pitch, tar, white iron, iron-thread, making of iron with coal, castlesoap, raising of water and weights out of pits, improving of ground, making of ploughs and salt pans, and for making of anything in crystal as well for ornament as use.[180]

Leslie and Scott were given three years to try and make inventions from these substances or they became free for others to use again. In other words, they were granted a three-year right to *experiment* and receive exclusive rights over anything they discovered – something quite extraordinary in the history of protecting inventions. In the same year, James Wemyss obtained another grant[181] for his invention for raising water although it was not clear to the Scottish Parliament whether it was the same as that of Leslie and Scott and so a comparison was required and if they were the same it was void.[182]

The Scottish Parliament willingly granted extensive exclusive rights to supposed inventors over above those granted by patents. However, it appears that the conventional prerogative patent system (and Acts of the Privy Council prohibiting competitors importing products[183]) become well established and understood for encouraging industry over the next two decades as there is evidence of only one other person (James Lockhart for alum[184]) seeking (but not obtaining) exclusive rights. Yet the final two decades of a separate Scotland led to extreme protectionism as rafts of legislation to protect individual inventors were enacted following the Act of Manufactories of 1681.

Act for Encouraging Trade and Manufactories of 1681

By the last quarter of the seventeenth century there had been little advance in Scottish industry.[185] So in 1681 the Scottish Parliament enacted a wide-ranging law to protect the Scottish cloths, wool and linen industry almost absolutely from foreign competition while at the same time exempting them from tax. So this meant that products made from imported gold or silver thread or silk had to be certified (or destroyed) so as to increase the consumption of Scottish woollens.[186] In addition, any material useful for a manufactory could be imported free from duty in perpetuity[187] and all exports of cloths, wool and linen were to be exported free from duty for nineteen years.[188] The owners of manufactories also continued to have protection to stop employees moving or being taken for military service.[189] In other words, a protected manufactory could trade without tariff and without foreign competition.[190]

---

180 Act in Favour of Colonels Ludovic Leslie Leslie and James Scott 1661 [RPS: 1661/1/92].
181 He also got a renewed grant for his leather ordnance the original having been lost at sea: Act in Favour of Colonel James Wemyss 1661 [RPS: 1661/1/91].
182 Act in Favour of James Wemyss, General of Artillery, and Colonels Leslie and Scott 1661 [RPS: 1661/1/200].
183 William Scott, *The Constitution and Finance of English, Scottish and Irish Joint-Stock Companies to 1720* (Cambridge 1911), Vol 3, p 127.
184 Petition of James Lockhart for Making Alum [RPS: A1672/6/37].
185 Theodora Keith, *Commercial Relations of England and Scotland 1603–1707* (Cambridge 1910), p 78.
186 Act for Encouraging Trade and Manufactories 1681 [RPS: 1681/7/36], ss 1 to 3.
187 Act for Encouraging Trade and Manufactories 1681, s 6 and similarly for those things used to make manufactories: s 8.
188 Act for Encouraging Trade and Manufactories 1681, s 7.
189 Act for Encouraging Trade and Manufactories 1681, ss 9 and 10.
190 It should be borne in mind that the protectionism was not always complete in practice: Theodora Keith, *Commercial Relations of England and Scotland 1603–1707* (Cambridge 1910), pp 75 and 80.

In the years that followed, individuals sought protection for their own manufactories whether it related to cloths or otherwise.[191] In 1681 such rights were given to Frederick Hamilton and John Coarse for their sugar manufactory in Glasgow[192] and to the Greenland fishery.[193] Similar protection was given in 1686 to John Meikle for his iron casting manufactory[194] and as the economic depression continued so did the number of industries[195] and individuals given protection. The real boom in these manufactories was in the middle of the 1690s when the Huguenot refugees had spilled over from England to Scotland bringing in a new pool of skilled labour.[196] The outcome of this protectionist policy was the ill-fated attempt by the Scots to create their own international markets and so the infamous attempt by the Scots to establish a colony[197] on the Isthmus of Panama (the so-called Darien project). The project was an attempt to boost Scottish trade and the national economy in a period of nationalism and protectionism.[198] As explained by Scott over a hundred years ago the Darien project:

> . . .was the logical outcome of the act of 1681; for once Scotland prohibited the manufactures of other countries, the retaliation of those countries had to be faced. Therefore, just when Scotland was reaching the ideal that her statesmen had aimed at -namely, the establishment of diversified manufactures under the protection of a series of prohibitions of competitive foreign products, it began to be seen that this advance had been made at the sacrifice of most foreign markets. . . .But owing to the policy of prohibitions the markets of all developed countries were closed to Scottish finished goods, and so the policy of protection must either be given up or else a new market found.[199]

191 Often through joint stock companies: see Theodora Keith, *Commercial Relations of England and Scotland 1603–1707* (Cambridge 1910), p 80.

192 Act Declaring the Sugar-work at Glasgow to Be a Manufactory 1681 [RPS: 1681/7/64].

193 Act Declaring the Greenland Fishery to Be a Manufactory 1685 [RPS: 1685/4/75]; also see William Scott, *The Constitution and Finance of English, Scottish and Irish Joint Stock Companies 1720* (Cambridge 1911), p130–132.

194 Act in Favour of John Meikle 1686 [RPS: 1686/4/60].

195 As to various industries and the companies incorporated under the Acts see William Scott, *The Constitution and Finance of English, Scottish and Irish Joint Stock Companies 1720* (Cambridge 1911), Vol 3, pp 130–198. Scott also wrote a series of article on these industries in the *Scottish Historical Review* which he incorporated into this book: William Scott, "Scottish Industrial Undertakings before the Union" (1904) 1 *Scottish Historical Review* 407; Scott, "Scottish Industrial Undertakings before the Union: II The Scots Linen Manufacture" (1904) 2 *Scottish Historical Review* 53; Scott, "Scottish Industrial Undertakings before the Union: III The Textile Group" (1905) 2 *Scottish Historical Review* 287; Scott, "Scottish Industrial Undertakings before the Union: IV The Wool-Card Manufactory at Leith" (1905) 2 *Scottish Historical Review* 406; Scott, "Scottish Industrial Undertakings before the Union: V The Society of White-Writing and Printing Paper Manufactory of Scotland" (1905) 3 *Scottish Historical Review* 71.

196 William Scott, "The Fiscal Policy of Scotland before the Union" (1904) 1 *Scottish Historical Review* 173 at 180.

197 For the story of the colonies' failure see John Drebble, *The Darien Disaster* (1968) (Pimlico 2002); also see David Armitage, *The Scottish Vision of Empire: Intellectual Origins of the Darien Venture* (Cambridge 1995).

198 Douglas Watt, *The Price of Scotland: Darien, Union and the Wealth of Nations* (Luath Press 2007), pp 17 and 20.

199 WR Scott, "The Fiscal Policy of Scotland before the Union" (1904) 1 *Scottish Historical Review* 173 at 181; also see Douglas Watt, *The Price of Scotland: Darien, Union and the Wealth of Nations* (Luath Press 2007), p 253 ("The notion that a company from a state with practically no naval power and very limited financial resources could control both sides of the isthmus of America, at a time of intense international trade rivalry, was a delusion, and reflected the loss of reality typical of a financial mania").

In addition to those seeking exemption from taxes as a manufactory others went further and also wished for exclusive rights to produce particular goods. In 1690, James Gordon attempted to secure the right to be sole maker of gunpowder within Scotland during his lifetime and for a certain number of years after his death.[200] However, less excessive monopolies were obtained by James Lyall who was granted the privileges of a manufactory and a nineteen-year monopoly on making lint, hemp and rape seed oil in 1695[201]; in the same year Alexander Hope was given a nineteen-year monopoly for making alum and gunpowder;[202] and a year later James Melville's grant of seven years for making sailcloth was ratified;[203] in 1698 David Wemyss obtain a nine-year monopoly of looking glasses for his manufactory[204] although it was shared with the Morison's Haven Glass Manufactory.[205] These monopolies like the ones that followed may not all be for new inventions,[206] although some clearly were,[207] but in contrast to the English Parliament it is clear that Scotland was very active in trying to encourage industry albeit the excessive zeal with which they pursued that policy ultimately led to its failure. The biggest difference between north and south of the border appears to have been the intervention of the Scottish Parliament without the need to first obtain a patent.[208] Whether or not William Scott was right and it was this zeal which led to Scotland commercially starving and coercing itself into the Union with England[209] it was clear that the Parliament was seen as an active participant in the development of industry through the grant of a large number of exclusive rights. Yet the problems with the policy were not apparent to all Scots, as during the Treaty of Union there was an attempt to maintain the protection for manufactories.[210] When this failed, the Scots did not return to the united Parliament to seek similar privileges as probably, and eventually, the failure of the policy appears to have been understood by all.

Parliamentary patents

It is clear that the English Parliament was occasionally content in some cases to step in and protect inventions which could not be otherwise given protection under the prerogative patent. This continued, albeit in a limited form, throughout the eighteenth century by way of the British Parliament giving protection to improvement patents and extending the geographical coverage of the "patents" to the entirety of the United Kingdom. Parliament was, therefore, quite content to reward certain inventors well beyond that which was

---

200 Gordon's Gunpowder Manufactory Bill 1690 [RPS: A1690/4/7].
201 Act in Favour of James Lyall 1695 [RPS: 1695/5/153].
202 Act in Favour of Hope of Kerse and Co-partnery for Erecting a Manufactory for Making Gunpowder and Alum [RPS 1695/5/154].
203 Ratification in Favour of Mr James Melville of Halhill 1696 [RPS: 1696/9/202].
204 Act and Ratification in Favour of the Glass Manufactory at the Wemyss 1698 [RPS: 1698/7/170].
205 Act and Ratification in Favour of the Glass Manufactory at Morison's Haven 1698 [RPS: A1698/7/171].
206 Making Salt: Act in Favour of Mr George Campbell 1705 [RPS: A1705/6/48].
207 Act in Favour of Mr Thomas Rome and Partners 1701 [RPS: A1700/10/56]; Act in Favour of William Montgomery and George Linn for a Manufactory of Lame, Purslane and Earthern Ware 1703 [RPS: 1703/5/199].
208 The only examples where there were underlying patents were Act in Favour of Mr James Smith 1700 [RPS: A1700/10/218] which was the extension of Savery's patent; and the Ratification in Favour of Mr James Melville of Halhil 1696 [RPS: 1696/9/202].
209 William Scott, "The Fiscal Policy of Scotland before the Union" (1904) 1 *Scottish Historical Review* 173 at 190.
210 Proposal to include clause in Act of Union to preserve manufactories (13 December 1706) [RPS: M1706/10/64] and [RPS: 1706/10/178].

allowed by the Statute of Monopolies.[211] In contrast to other types of private patent Act it was not something that could ever move toward public legislation unless the Statute of Monopolies were repealed or at least substantially amended. More significant than the activity of Westminster is that of the Old Scottish Parliament where it was clear that it saw its role as encouraging Scottish manufacture at all costs and, ultimately, to its own demise. It may well be that this over-zealous policy north of the border meant that many were wary of all but the exceptional instances of private Acts actually replacing the rules of the underlying granted patent.

211 Also see discussion of Parliamentary rewards: see Chapter 9.

5 The *non obstante* clause and the right to work

Introduction

The grant of a patent to dispense with a particular law enabled the patentee to avoid the penalty of a penal statute. Essentially, it allowed the patentee to bargain with the King for the right to break the law or alternatively to be excused for having done so.[1] The outright dispensing patent seems to have disappeared early in James I's reign following the judges deliberating for three days[2] and concluding they were unlawful.[3] This finding was adopted by the Book of Bounty when the King proclaimed that dispensing from penal statutes was against the law.[4] However, in parallel with the outright dispensing patent was the slightly more subtle *non obstante* clause.[5] By the beginning of the fifteenth century,[6] a gift, privilege or grant from the Crown by Letters Patent would usually include such a *non obstante* clause.[7] Its gave effect to the privilege notwithstanding any previous grants, or more significantly, any Act of Parliament. The justification of the *non obstante* clause was discussed in *Thomas v Sorrell*[8] but a simple explanation was provided much later by Herbert CJ in *Godden v Hales*.[9]

1 See William Hyde Price, *The English Patents of Monopoly* (Houghton, Mifflin & Co 1906), p 12; there is considered to be a difference between the dispensing of a penal offence in advance, and the prerogative of mercy being used to pardon it afterwards. For a history of the prerogative of mercy see: Stanley Grupp, "Some Historical Aspects of the Pardon in England" (1963) 7 *American J of Legal History* 51; and US Attorney General, *The Attorney General's Survey of Release Procedures, Pardon, Volume III* (United States Government 1939), pp 1–25.

2 See comment of Sir Edward Coke: Wallace Notestein, Frances Relf and Hartley Simpson, *Commons Debates 1621* ('CD 1621') (Yale 1935), Vol 2, X's Journal, p 228.

3 See "The Judges to Council" in State Papers Domestic (National Archive: SP 14/19A f. 9) (8 November 1604); a copy of the letter is in William Hyde Price, *The English Patents of Monopoly* (Houghton, Mifflin & Co 1906), p 167; it is also summarised by Coke, CD 1621, X's Journal, p 228. The Penal and Monopolies Bill 1606 (HL/PO/JO/10/2/1E) appears to have been to confirm that penal statutes could not be dispensed (as well as banning monopolies). It failed in the House of Lords at Second Reading (2 LJ 422; 1 May 1606) after passing the Commons.

4 Also see Wallace Notestein, Frances Relf and Hartley Simpson, *Commons Debates 1621* (Yale 1935) ('CD 1621'), Vol 2, X's Journal, p 228 (15 March 1621).

5 As to their inclusion in patents see: David Seaborne Davies, "The Early History of the Patent Specification" (1934) 50 *LQR* 260 at 262–263.

6 For the origins of the clause, by way of the Statute of Mortmain, see Charles Crump, "Eo Quod Espressa Mentio, etc" in *Essays in History Presented to Reginald Lane Poole* (Oxford 1929, Reprinted 1969), p 30 at 30.

7 Charles Crump, "Eo Quod Espressa Mentio, etc" in *Essays in History Presented to Reginald Lane Poole* (Oxford 1929, Reprinted 1969), p 30 at 35.

8 *Thomas v Sorrell* (1666) 2 Keb 245 at 246 (84 ER 152 at 153); and for a detailed discussion see: *Thomas v Sorrell* (1672) Vaug 330 (124 ER 1098).

9 (1686) 11 State Trials 1165 at 1196.

There is no law whatsoever but may be dispensed with by the supreme law-giver; as the laws of God may be dispensed with by God himself; as it appears by God's command to Abraham, to offer up his son Isaac: The law of man may be dispensed with by the legislator, for a law may either be too wide or too narrow, and there may be many cases, which may be out of the conveniences which did not induce the law to be made; for it is impossible for the wisest lawmaker to foresee all cases that may be, or are to be remedied, and therefore there must be a power somewhere, able to dispense with these laws.

Thus, in common with Clifford's explanation of private legislation,[10] the need for the *non obstante* clause was to make up for defects or limitations imposed by the general law; particularly when Parliament met infrequently and legislated little.[11] In many ways, therefore, the *non obstante* clause might be seen as a forerunner of the need for private legislation.

Statute of Monopolies

While there was an attempt to insert a proviso "fraudulently" into the Bill of Monopolies in 1621[12] specifically to allow *non obstante* clauses,[13] it appears that the final statute took quite the opposite view.[14] Section 6 of the Statute of Monopolies precludes the grant of patents which are "contrary to law", that is grants could not be made to manufacture illegal things.[15] It is difficult to know how this phrase was perceived during the seventeenth century, but by the nineteenth Hindmarch suggests:[16]

This clause of the statute seems also to mean that the excepted grants must not be for the sole making of anything which is to be used for any purpose which is illegal, or "contrary to law", such as implements for house-breaking, picking pockets, locks, &c. Such grants, however, it is clear would be void, not only on the ground of want of public utility, but also because they are contrary to the policy of the law; and indeed it would be absurd if, by one law, patents might be granted to reward persons for providing the means of violating any other law.

The absence of contemporary reported cases does not help clarify how "contrary to law" might be read.[17] But it eventually became a prohibition for granting a patent even where

---

10 See p 2.

11 Dennis Dixon, "*Godden v Hales* Revisited – James II and the Dispensing Power" (2006) 27 *J Legal History* 129 at 135; also see Carolyn Edie, "Revolution and the Rule of Law: The End of the Dispensing Power, 1689" (1977) 10 *Eighteenth-Century Studies* 434 at 437–438.

12 1 CJ 612 (8 May 1621); a committee was appointed to find who was responsible for the so-called "fraud" and the clauses were removed: CD 1621, Vol 4, Pym, p 318 (8 May 1621); Member of the House, *Proceedings and Debates of the House of Commons in 1620 and 1621* (1766) ('Nicholas'), Vol 2, p 41 (8 May 1621).

13 See CD 1621, Vol 4, Pym, p 318; Nicholas, Vol 2, pp 40–41 (8 May 1621).

14 There were also various statements during 1621 that the King's dispensing power was unaffected: CD 1621, Vol 4, Pym, p 173 (20 March 1621) and p 197 (26 March 1621).

15 This remained the law until the commencement of the Patents Act 1977; but see Paris Convention for the Protection of Industrial Property, art 4*quater* which was added to the Convention at the Lisbon Conference in 1958.

16 William Hindmarch, *Treatise on the Law Relating to the Patent Privileges for the Sole Use of Inventions* (Stevens 1846), p 142.

17 There are only two reported court cases on the exception itself, both outside our period and both relating to gaming machines and, in neither case, was the patent refused as there were legal uses of the invention: *Pessers and Moody v Haydon & Co* (1909) 26 RPC 58; *Walton v Ahrens* (1939) 56 RPC 195.

the practice was against a minor regulation.[18] Thus, an illegal patent should not be granted in the first place and, if it were, a *non obstante* clause would be dispensing with the Statute of Monopolies itself (i.e. section 6). Indeed, if the "contrary to law" provision could be dispensed with then there is no reason why the term of fourteen years could not also put aside or indeed the requirement that it was a "new method of manufacture". At first blush, therefore, the *non obstante* clauses had no place after 1624, but this does not represent the whole of the picture.

Statute of Monopolies to the Bill of Rights

Notwithstanding the clear edict in the Statute of Monopolies, the *non obstante* clause returned to Letters Patent after the Restoration. It has been suggested by Christine MacLeod that the grant of patents continuing to include a dispensing power was to allow illegal inventions to be worked. She gives the example of Joseph Bacon's[19] attempts to introduce an outlawed friezing mill[20] and Charles Howard's patent for tanning leather[21] without bark may have been granted to avoid the increasingly complex regulation.[22] Thus, MacLeod suggests these patents were granted to avoid regulation as much as to get exclusive rights. The difficulty with this proposition is not just the fact that a patent contrary to law should not have been granted, but Howard *also* pursued a number of private Bills before Parliament.[23] If he was confident that the *non obstante* clause in his patent would protect him from regulation then why would he apply for a private Act as well? As there is only evidence of isolated examples where such a clause might have been useful to an inventor, and while there may have been more, there is not enough evidence to see a pattern.

In any event, the end of the *non obstante* clause in all contexts is clear. This is because its use[24] to override statutes was one of the reasons for James II being ousted. The first of the complaints against James II in the preamble to the Bill of Rights was[25]:

> (1) By assuming and exercising a Power of dispensing with and suspending of Laws, and the Execution of Laws, without Consent of Parliament.

---

18 In *Carpmael's Application* (1928) 45 RPC 411, a grant which would have been against food regulations was said to be contrary to law. However, following a practice from an earlier (unidentified) case in 1900 and an *Official Ruling 1923 (C)* (1923) 40 RPC App iv, it was possible to disclaim any illegal use of the invention. This was effected in statute by the Patents and Designs Act 1932, s 11.

19 Christine MacLeod, *Inventing the Industrial Revolution: The English Patent System 1660–1800* (Cambridge 1988), p 82. Joseph Bacon never obtained a patent.

20 See Gig Mills Act 1551; also see Joan Thirsk and John Cooper, *Seventeenth Century Economic Documents* (Oxford 1972), p 313–314; discussed below at p 79.

21 Patent No 130 (1660) the exact wording was "and notwithstanding. . .any act, statute, ordinance, pvision, pclamacon, or restraint to the contrary thereof in any wise notwithstanding".

22 Christine MacLeod, *Inventing the Industrial Revolution: The English Patent System 1660–1800* (Cambridge 1988), p 82; Lesley A Clarkson, "English Economic Policy in the Sixteenth and Seventeenth Centuries: The Case of the Leather Industries" (1965) 38 *Historic Research* 150 at 159.

23 Leather Trade Bill 1660 (Ingrossment: HL/PO/JO/10/1/300) (defeated at First Reading in second House: 8 CJ 215 (18 December 1660) and Leather Trade Bill 1661 (did not progress pass Second Reading: 8 CJ 277 (21 June 1661)).

24 Not patents for invention, but the principle is the same.

25 Bill of Rights Act 1688, art 2.

And so from 1688, by reason of article 12 of the Bill of Rights,[26] *non obstante* clauses were not allowed and any granted were void.[27] Accordingly, Fox, Boehm and Macleod suggest that this also brought to an end the use of *non obstante* clauses in relation to patents for inventions as well.[28] While this might have brought an end to the inclusion of the clause in the patent, it is far from clear what effect it had, if any, before 1688.

The uncertain dispensing power

It is suggested that in the period after the Statute of Monopolies patentees could not be confident that a *non obstante* clause would dispense with statutory regulation. Not only was there express statutory prohibition on such dispensation in section 6, but the law on the clause itself was unclear. Before *Godden v Hales*,[29] which confirmed the King's absolute dispensing power, the law was unsettled as to its scope and extent. Contemporaries at the time of the decision of *Godden v Hales* clearly considered it wrongly decided (as the recital to the Bill of Rights demonstrates).[30] Whilst it is clear that legal historians,[31] including Holdsworth,[32] have suggested that the decision was at least technically correct[33] following the *Case of Sheriffs*,[34] others disagree.[35]

For present purposes, it is not relevant whether *Godden v Hales* was correctly decided in 1686, but it is germane that contemporaries were *not sure* that a *non obstante* clause could set aside a statute until *Godden*. This means that while a patentee might hope a patent, with its *non obstante* clause, excluded him or her from the relevant legislation, it was far from clear that this was the case and so reliance on a patent alone would have been risky, particularly when faced with the penalties of praemunire.[36] In contrast to the uncertain scope of the *non obstante* clause, a private Act could sweep any regulatory issues aside. Accordingly,

---

26 The Act was confirmed by the Crown and Parliament Recognition Act 1689.

27 They appear to have become habit and clerks continued to include them in certain types of patents for a few years thereafter: Charles Crump, "Eo Quod Espressa Mentio, etc" in *Essays in History Presented to Reginald Lane Poole* (Oxford 1929, Reprinted 1969), p 30 at 44–45 (referring to a grant to John Williams in 1692 including such a clause). However, there appear to have been no patents for inventions granted with such a clause after the Glorious Revolution.

28 Klaus Boehm with Aubrey Silberston, *The British Patent System: Part 1* (Cambridge 1967), p 18; Christine MacLeod, *Inventing the Industrial Revolution: The English Patent System 1660–1800* (Cambridge 1988), p 82; Harold Fox, *Monopolies and Patents: A Study of the History and Future of the Patent Monopoly* (Toronto 1947), p 157.

29 (1686) 11 State Trials 1165 at 1196.

30 Similarly, see Thomas Macaulay, *Macaulay's History of England* (Dent and Son 1906), Vol 2, pp 39–40; also see *Memoirs of the Earl of Ailesbury* (ed W Buckley) (Nichols & Sons 1890), Vol 1, p 150.

31 For a general discussion see: Frederick Maitland, *Constitutional History of England* (Cambridge 1919), pp 302–306; Tim Harris, "The People, the Law, and the Constitution in Scotland and England: A Comparative Approach to the Glorious Revolution" (1999) 38 *Journal of British Studies* 28 at 41–46; also see EF Churchill, "The Dispensing Power of the Crown in Ecclesiastical Affairs – Part II" (1922) 38 *LQR* 420 at 434.

32 William Holdsworth, *A History of English Law* (2nd Ed Sweet 1937), Vol 6, p 225.

33 The most comprehensive treatment is by P Birdsall, "Non Obstante: A Study of the Dispensing Power of English Kings" in *Essays in History and Political Theory in Honour of Charles Howard McIlwain Poole* (Oxford 1929, Reprinted 1969), p 30.

34 (1486) Ex Ch; YB Mic 2 Hen VII, fol 6, pl 20 (Seipp No 1486.076).

35 Paul Birdsall, "Non Obstante: A Study of the Dispensing Power of English Kings" in *Essays in History and Political Theory in Honour of Charles Howard McIlwain Poole* (Oxford 1929, Reprinted 1969), p 30; Dennis Dixon, "*Godden v Hales* Revisited – James II and the Dispensing Power" (2006) 27 *J Legal History* 129 at 135.

36 See p 42.

it is possible that some of the unsuccessful Bills sought during the seventeenth century were actually a way of overcoming regulation: Howard's case being just one example. In any case, once the Bill of Rights had outlawed *non obstante* clauses, any departure from a generally applicable Act of Parliament required private legislation.

Scotland

It is less clear that the King had a dispensing power in Scotland before the Claim of Right Act 1689.[37] It states "That all proclamations asserting an absolute power to cass, annul, and disable laws. . .are contrary to law". Accordingly, after 1689, a Scottish patent could not include a *non obstante* clause any more than it could in England. In any event, as has been already discussed in Chapter 3, the Scottish Parliament's industrial policy in the second half of the seventeenth century was to exempt manufactories, either by industry or individually, from customs and taxes; the exemptions often including the grant of exclusive rights as well. Dispensing with general regulation in individual cases was an intrinsic part of Scottish policy long before the *non obstante* clauses ceased to be lawful and so industrialists probably had already turned to Parliament for protection rather than the King.

After the Bill of Rights

With the *non obstante* clause being damned by the Bill of Rights, it would be expected that there would be a flurry of private Acts to replicate its effect, but the first Bill arrived decades later when certain manufacturers tried to avoid duty.[38] The first private Act took over a century to be enacted.

Avoiding duties

The first petition was by Alexander Fordyce in 1780 seeking to be exempted from duties in relation to the raw materials for making his patented marine acid.[39] The inevitable consequence of one patentee seeking a dispensation from duties to work his invention was that his competition followed suit. In the month after Fordyce petitioned Parliament, a series of other marine acid manufacturers requested the same exemption[40] while others said that granting the exemption to anyone would prejudice them and the Treasury.[41] Despite its opposition, Fordyce's petition was favourably reported[42] and overcame a division[43] to allow a Bill to be presented and read a first time, yet it lapsed at the end of the session soon thereafter.

---

37 The Declaration of the Estates Containing the Claim of Right and the Offer of the Crown to the King and Queen of England [RPS: 1689/3/108]; also see Tim Harris, "The People, the Law, and the Constitution in Scotland and England: A Comparative Approach to the Glorious Revolution" (1999) 38 *Journal of British Studies* 28 at 50–51.

38 It is possible that some Bills before the House of Commons, of which no record remains, may have included some form of dispensing power. But there is no evidence to support that this is the case.

39 37 CJ 865 (22 May 1780).

40 James Keir (37 CJ 891; 31 May 1780); Peter De Bruges (37 CJ 892; 31 May 1780); James Watt and Joseph Black (37 CJ 892; 31 May 1780); John Collison (37 CJ 897; 1 June 1780); Joseph Fry (37 CJ 908; 19 June 1780); and Isaac Cookson and Edward Wilson (37 CJ 916; 21 June 1780).

41 Richard Shannon (37 CJ 909; 19 June 1780) and Samuel Garbett (37 CJ 912; 21 June 1780).

42 37 CJ 893 (31 May 1780).

43 37 CJ 917 (21 June 1780).

The resistance the Bill faced even before introduction suggests that even had there been Parliamentary time it would have failed later in the process. Put simply, the unified Parliament was not willing to follow the policy that the Scottish Parliament had adopted a hundred years earlier.[44] In 1794, a similar petition to exempt an invention from duty was presented by Abraham Bosquet[45] in relation to his (at that time unpatented) invention for pumping out water from ships. The petition got no further than a reference to a committee. A related example, which was successful, is the East India Company Act 1796. This was enacted because the company was prohibited from trading with individuals[46] and wished to pay a royalty to William Sabatier[47] for his patented invention. However, this was a matter of modifying the powers of a company, rather than dispensation from more general legislation.

General Acts

In contrast to exemption from duties or taxes, where an invention actually needed to be exempted from a general statute to allow it to be worked, Parliament seemed more sympathetic. Samuel Ashton obtained a private Act in 1794[48] to allow him to work his patented invention[49] for tanning leather notwithstanding the Leather Act 1603 prohibiting it.[50] There also appears to have been some doubt regarding the validity of the Letter Patent should it be found to be contrary to the 1603 Act. This too was resolved by the Act. This suggests that by the end of the eighteenth century at the latest the view had developed that section 6 of the Statute of Monopolies should have precluded the grant such as Ashton's patent (even if Parliament was now willing to save it). Similarly, when a Bill was before Parliament to amend the Leather Act 1603 to allow different methods of tanning to be used, Edward Sealy successfully petitioned the House of Commons for a clause[51] to allow him, in particular, to work his patent.[52] The Lords removed Sealy's clause (it is not clear why, but probably because it was unnecessary as he was covered by the general case) and any event, the amendments by the Lords were never approved by the Commons and so the Bill failed.[53]

An attempt to enact private legislation to work a patent appears to have arisen on two further occasions. In 1810, Ambrose Bowden John's obtained a private Act[54] to enable him to work his patent for using tar to protect buildings[55] notwithstanding the Fire Prevention (Metropolis) Act 1774. However, in contrast to Ashton, the grant of his patent would not have been contrary to law as the prohibition under the 1774 Act only applied to London

---

44 See pp 65–70.
45 49 CJ 278 (4 March 1794).
46 East India Company Act 1793, s 105.
47 East India Company Act 1796, s 1; also see earlier Bill: Sabatier's Petition 1795 (50 CJ 118; 3 February 1796); he had to provide a specification so that the company could know what the invention was: s 2.
48 New Method of Tanning Act 1794.
49 Patent No 1,977 (1794).
50 In the recital the Act does not refer to the Act it is trying to modify for his invention. However, Aston's petition refers to the Leather Act 1603 (by its long title: An Act concerning Tanners, Curriers, Shoe-makers, and Other Artificers Occupying the Cutting of Leather): see 53 CJ 480 (23 April 1798).
51 Making it a hybrid Bill: see p 36.
52 Tanning Leather Bill 1798 (1798 HL Papers), Vol 1, cl 3.
53 In the subsequent session, the Act was passed (Tanners' Indemnity Act 1799), but there was no special provision for Sealy or any other patentee.
54 John's Patent Tessera Act 1810.
55 Patent No 2,996 (1806).

and its surrounds and so his invention could be worked elsewhere in the country. The other attempt was in 1852 when Donald Grant sought to be allowed to use his apparatus for ventilating buildings[56] notwithstanding the Metropolitan Buildings Act 1844; once more the 1844 Act did not apply nationally and so there were places where the use of Grant's invention was not contrary to law. His Bill passed the House of Lords, but stalled in the Commons.[57] It is not clear why it failed.

It is evident, therefore, that there was little need for private Acts to enable patents to be worked. Putting aside those trying to exempt themselves from duties (i.e. overcoming financial rather than legal impediments) there were only four attempts to obtain a special exception between the Bill of Rights and Grant's failed attempt in the 1850s. While some general Acts were amended to work new technology when it was made available, there was little to support any need to deal with patents more particularly. This is probably because, in general, patents were not granted where it was illegal to work the invention and the practicalities of risk, sanction and cost (not to mention the problems with novelty) meant that a private Act could not be sought in advance. The restriction on granting patents contrary to law did not end until long after the end of the period we are examining.[58]

Prohibiting the use of inventions

Before moving on it is worth looking at legislation trying to achieve the opposite objective, namely to stop a patentee working his invention. A well-known early example of an attempt to stop a new technology was the gig-mill.[59] Adoption of this mill meant that there was no need for the labour intensive practice of treading cloth and so to protect labourers Parliament enacted legislation to suppress the gig-mill.[60] The Act was not effective as Charles I had to issue a further proclamation on 16 April 1633.[61]

Similarly the Leather Act 1603 was generally considered to be so prescriptive that it was difficult if not impossible to satisfy and most tanners therefore did not try to comply[62] (except maybe Ashton and Sealy). The attempts to repress technological development continued for most of the eighteenth century culminating in the failed Woolcombers Bill in 1794 that would have prevented anyone using any machine for combing wool. The significance of the Bill is that Edward Cartwright, the owner of a patent for a woolcombing machine,[63] petitioned Parliament stating his invention was beneficial to the kingdom. In an attempt to save his business he pleaded that he was willing to limit the number of machines he sold each year[64]; and William Toplis, another owner of a woolcombing patent, similarly petitioned Parliament to be heard against the Bill.[65] The Bill failed.

---

56 Patent No 10,146 (1844).
57 Leading Grant to petition the Lords once more: 85 LJ 710 (19 July 1853).
58 Under the Patents Act 1977.
59 See William Hyde Price, *The English Patents of Monopoly* (Houghton, Mifflin & Co 1906), pp 12–13.
60 Gig Mills Act 1551.
61 See James Larkin and Paul Hughes, *Stuart Royal Proclamations: Royal Proclamations of Charles I 1625–46* (Oxford 1983), Vol 2, p 376 (No 169).
62 William Hyde Price, *The English Patents of Monopoly* (Houghton, Mifflin & Co 1906), p 13.
63 Patent Nos 1,747 (1790), 1,787 (1791) and 1,876 (1792).
64 18 March 1794 (49 CJ 347).
65 8 May 1794 (49 CJ 565).

This was followed by at least one craftsmen trying to enforce the gig-mill prohibition. In *Shearman v Cooke*,[66] a journeyman Shearman argued that a machine owned and used by Samuel Cooke was contrary to the Gig Mills Act 1551. Cooke's Counsel argued that Cooke's machine was new and that he had obtained a patent and, additionally, that the use of such machines had led to the development of the woolen industry and was an inexhaustible source of wealth for the country. The judge, in directing the jury, agreed not only that the machine was different from that prohibited by the Act, but also that the country was greatly benefited by the introduction of machinery in general. It can be seen that Parliament, and indeed the establishment more generally, had moved towards encouraging new technology and supporting the new industrialists and away from protecting the old craft workers.

Patents are subject to law

It is apparent that it would be difficult, if not impossible, to obtain patents which were contrary to law. While there was something which appeared to be a *non obstante* clause in the patents granted between the Restoration and the Bill of Rights it is doubtful what effect it would have if it had been challenged. More importantly, once the *non obstante* clause was prohibited there do not appear to be any patents granted which were contrary to the general law as well as to section 6 of the Statute of Monopolies. This meant there was no need to have specific legislation to overcome general regulation, rather it might be needed to overcome local regulation only – and here it is clear that Parliament was willing to step in.

66 *The Times,* 28 July 1796 (Salisbury Assizes).

6 The restriction and regulation of company patents

Introduction

The relationship between corporations, patents and private Bills is a long and varied one. It can be divided into three phases. In the early period, monopolies were granted to regulated companies, including guilds, to regulate entire industries. Such rights when granted to individuals, such as Sir Giles Mompesson, were outlawed by the Statute of Monopolies but in relation to corporations[1] these rights were specifically excluded from the Act.[2] It is clear that despite later criticism of these exclusive rights, Parliament welcomed them – including by enacting private legislation. The second phase began with the passage of the "Bubble Act" in 1720 when joint stock companies became pariahs and almost contemporaneously a restriction was introduced to restrict joint ownership of patents to five individuals. In this phase a handful of individuals tried, some successfully, to obtain private legislation to enable them to transfer to more than five persons. The final phase begins with the repeal of the Bubble Act in 1825 when joint stock companies became an accepted part of business – but the restriction on patent ownership remained. And so individuals were compelled to petition Parliament when they wanted to work a patent through a joint stock company until the long-antiquated eighteenth-century rule was finally abrogated in 1852.

Corporations and the Statute of Monopolies

The passage of the Statute of Monopolies can be divided into two parts. The first part is the Parliament of 1621 where debates on the general regulation of monopolies was debated alongside the Parliamentary prosecution of Mompesson[3] The second part is the Parliament of 1624 when the Statute was actually enacted. The 1621 Parliament was not only concerned with the grant of patents, but also with the privileges granted to corporations.[4] Nevertheless, the Commons made it clear that the extension of the prohibition on monopolies should not extend to corporations[5] and so a proviso for chartered corporations was inserted during

---

1 Notwithstanding Coke's dislike of these sorts of monopolies: see Stephen D White, *Sir Edward Coke and "The Grievances of the Commonwealth": 1621–1628* (North Carolina Press 1979), p 112 (he believed that certain customs are void at common law and opposed corporate charters granting monopolies) (117), but see p 119.

2 Statute of Monopolies, s 9; a distinction Sir Edward Coke did not acknowledge: Stephen White, *Sir Edward Coke and "The Grievances of the Commonwealth": 1621–1628* (North Carolina Press 1979), p 119.

3 See Chapter 3.

4 Robert Ashton, *The City and the Court 1603–1643* (Cambridge 1979), p 118.

5 Wallace Notestein, Frances Relf and Hartley Simpson, *Commons Debates 1621* (Yale 1935) ('CD 1621'), Vol 4, Pym, p 160 (15 March 1621).

committee stage.[6] The concern remained and in 1624, the Lords were worried about the abridgement of the King's power to make new corporations.[7] Coke, however, took the view that a charter for appointing a government or officers is valid, but a sole restraint is void (a "liberty of sole buying and selling")[8] and so section 9 was enacted. Accordingly, the first part of section 9 of the Statute of Monopolies was intended to preserve the privileges and rights of the City of London, and other cities, towns and boroughs where they were corporate entities.[9] These entities were a central part of local government and were usually able to regulate the trade within their boundaries. This coupled with the restriction in the Towns Corporate Act 1554 which prevented non-resident retailers from retailing[10] "Woollen Cloth, Linen Cloth, Haberdashery Wares, Grocery Wares, Mercery Wares"[11] within these towns meant the charter boroughs were able to grant many local monopolies (or at least allowed others, usually guilds, to run monopolies within the town[12]). Accordingly, the first part of the proviso was retaining the status quo and the autonomy of the towns to regulate their own markets.[13] It was not some subtle attempt at abuse.

The "abuse" of the corporation exception

It was the second part of section 9, providing that the Statute of Monopolies does not apply to trade corporations, which was the most controversial in practice. The clause was necessary if the trade guilds, livery companies and others were not to lose their privileges following the enactment of the Statute of Monopolies.[14] It was intended to protect these so-called "regulated companies" (which should be contrasted with the joint stock companies which were to follow). It is said that it provided a "loophole" for Charles I to continue granting new monopolies by setting up new companies and granting privileges to them.[15] This presents only part of the story. The relevant part reads:

> or unto any Corporations, Companies or Fellowships of any Art, Trade, Occupation or Mystery, or to any Companies or Societies of Merchants within this Realm, erected for the Maintenance, Enlargement, or ordering of any Trade of Merchandize.

6 CD 1621, Vol 5, Smyth, p 322 (26 March 1621); also see George Unwin, *The Gilds and Companies of London* (Methuen & Co 1908), p 318.

7 Stephen D White, *Sir Edward Coke and "The Grievances of the Commonwealth": 1621–1628* (North Carolina Press 1979), pp 134–135.

8 1 CJ 770 (19 April 1624): Philip Baker (ed), *Proceedings in Parliament 1624: The House of Commons* (2015), British History Online, 19 April 1624: Pym, f 71V; also see Earle, f 149v.

9 As to the early franchises and privileges under charter to boroughs see: William Holdsworth, *A History of English Law* (3rd Ed, Sweet and Maxwell 1945), Vol 4, pp 131–134.

10 Wholesale trade was unaffected: Towns Corporate Act 1554, s 3.

11 Towns Corporate Act 1554, s 2.

12 But see *Davenant v Hurdis* (1599) 11 Co Rep 86; Moor KB 576, 591 (72 ER 769); *Clothworkers of Ipswich* (1614) 1 HPC 31; 11 Co Rep 53 (77 ER 1218); Godbolt 252 (78 ER 147).

13 See Gerald E Aylmer, *The Struggle for the Constitution – England in the Seventeenth Century* (4th Ed, 1975), p 81.

14 Robert Ashton, *The City and the Court 1603–1643* (Cambridge 1979), p 119; J Cooper, "Economic Regulation and the Cloth Industry in Seventeenth Century England" (1970) 20 *Transactions of Royal Historical Society* (5th Ser) 73 at 82.

15 Robert Ashton, *The City and the Court 1603–1643* (Cambridge 1979), p 118; Christine MacLeod, *Inventing the Industrial Revolution: The English Patent System 1660–1800* (Cambridge 1988), p 17; John Baker, *An Introduction to English Legal History* (4th Ed, Butterworths 2002), pp 451–452; William Hyde Price, *The English Patents of Monopoly* (Houghton, Mifflin & Co 1906), p 35.

This provision made it possible for Charles I to grant charters to companies and as part of that charter to give the company the exclusive right to work a particular trade. Again, what is important is the fact that the *trade* was monopolised. While it may be true that during the period of fifteen years between Charles I's accession and the start of the Long Parliament in 1640 more charters were granted in absolute numbers than in any period before,[16] the number was still quite small. These charters were essential to regulate a particular trade. This was why charters gave the right to "searchers" to investigate whether members were complying with the rules of the company. In other words, trading standards within a particular industry were maintained by charter companies, often the livery companies of London. The grant of exclusive rights to companies to regulate a trade within a particular locality (such as the City of London) was ancient. Yet despite their monopolistic nature, Members of Parliament were sympathetic to regulated companies[17] often due to their close association or membership of them.[18] In the late 1620s when concerns were raised they largely related to overseas companies and even those were few and far between. For example, the Greenland Company – which had whaling rights – fell to be challenged as part of the push for free fishing[19] and there was also a challenge to the Guiana Company which no longer traded but simply licensed others to do so.[20] In short, Parliament was less concerned about the grant of rights to chartered companies than to individuals. Yet what was granted by the King seems – at this distance in time – quite extraordinary.

For example, in 1628 the Company of Playing Card Makers was chartered[21] and given the exclusive right to regulate the making and sale of playing cards in the City of London and within a ten-mile radius. So what the court took away in *Darcy v Allin*[22] when granted to an individual patentee could be granted within a more geographically restricted space to a chartered company (as permitted by section 9 of the Statute). Nevertheless, the picture is not as simple as at first appears. When the Playing Card Makers petitioned for the grant there was already an (ineffective) ban on the importation of playing cards under the Exportation, Importation, Apparel Act 1463 and all foreign patents dispensing with this law had been set aside in 1621.[23] So extending the regulation of playing cards to the domestic sphere was, at least from one point of view, entirely logical rather than an affront to the earlier landmark case.[24]

Indeed, the monopolisation of industries within particular regions became part of the industrial framework of the society. Sir Richard Brooke founded a chartered company

---

16 George Unwin, *The Gilds and Companies of London* (Methuen & Co 1908), p 319.

17 Robert Ashton, *The City and the Court 1603–1643* (Cambridge 1979), p 123.

18 George Unwin, *The Gilds and Companies of London* (Methuen & Co 1908), p 318.

19 It was heard by the Committee of Grievances in the Summer of 1628: 1 CJ 890 (28 April 1628) and 1 CJ 919 (25 June 1628); as well as before the Privy Council: RF Monger (ed), *Acts of the Privy Council 1628–1629* (HMSO 1960), Vol 44, 384–385; RF Monger (ed) *Acts of the Privy Council, 1628–1629* (HMSO 1960), Vol 45, pp 181, 188–189 and 311 (also see p 356).

20 1 CJ 931 (19 February 1629); Wallace Notestein and Frances Relf, *Commons Debates for 1629: Critically Edited* (Minnesota 1921), p 225; Robert Ashton, *The City and the Court 1603–1643* (Cambridge 1979), p 124.

21 For a short history see John Thorpe, *The Worshipful Company of Makers of Playing Cards of the City of London* (Playing Card Company 2001), Chapter 1 to 3.

22 (1601) 1 HPC 1; 11 Co Rep 84 (77 ER 1260); Noy 173 (74 ER 1131); Moore 671 (72 ER 830); 1 WPC 1.

23 James Larkin and Paul Hughes, *Stuart Royal Proclamations: Royal Proclamations of James I 1603–25* (Oxford 1973), Vol 1, p 511 (No 217).

24 For a history, see Nicholas Tosney, "The Playing Card Trade in Early Modern England" (2011) 84 *Historical Research* 637.

which controlled the making of salt between South Shields and Southampton.[25] Similarly, following patents for a new method of making soap,[26] a charter was granted to the Westminster Soap-boilers who were given a monopoly and the right of search to prevent non-members trading in soap.[27] The company vigorously pursued and prosecuted unauthorised soap boilers[28] and all soap boilers were put under its governance.[29] The company was strengthened further by a prohibition on grocers and others selling soap made by other persons.[30] Soap boilers were very unhappy, however, their resentment against the Westminster Company was not resolved by its rights being discontinued, but rather by those rights being transferred to a new more inclusive company: the London Soap Boiler Company.[31] Similar concerns arose in relation to the charter granted to the Starch Makers Company[32] and as before a new company was formed.[33]

While each of these monopolies granted to chartered companies were still granted by the Crown, there was some Parliamentary support for doing so. The approach of Charles I was not therefore one of pure monopolist greed, but was part of an accepted practice of granting exclusive rights to companies (which in turn gave rights to their members). Whilst the condemnation of section 9 of the Statute of Monopolies as prolonging the monopolisation of industries might be justified in the wider economic picture, it should not have been simplified to merely an extension of the early Stuart abuse. Indeed, the policy continued right to the end of the seventeenth century and was only questioned in the nineteenth century.[34] However, our discussion must now move on from the first half of the seventeenth century to its end and the rise of stock-jobbing.

Stock-jobbing and patents

The history of joint stock companies is quite different from that of its regulated cousin. Until the eighteenth century, there were only a small number of joint stock companies in existence, mainly concerned with overseas trade. This meant that they had little or no interaction with domestic manufacture (or patent law), rather patents may have been

25 The charter is in Cecil Carr, *Select Charters of Trading Companies 1530–1707* (Selden Society, 1913), pp 142–148; an exception was made for Nicholas Murford and Christopher Hamworth (see 147 and 148) who already held salt processing patents and this was enlarged into another company the Great Yarmouth Salt Makers (at Carr, pp 148–160). There was also an Act of the Scottish Parliament in 1599 granting rights in relation to Salt: Act Regarding Great Salt [RPS: 1599/7/5].

26 A patent was granted to Roger Johnes and Andrew Palmer: No 23 (1623).

27 The charter is in Cecil Carr, *Select Charters of Trading Companies 1530–1707* (Selden Society 1913), p 136 (in Latin).

28 *Decree in Star Chamber Concerning the Soap-boylers, in Pursuance of a Censure of that Court upon May 10 1633* in John Rushworth, *Historical Collections of Private Passages of State* (D Browne *et al* 1721), Vol 3, Appendix, p 109.

29 John Rushworth, *Historical Collections of Private Passages of State* (D Browne *et al* 1721), Vol 2, p 458; also see Cecil Carr, *Select Charters of Trading Companies 1530–1707* (Selden Society 1913), p lxxvi.

30 (1634) PR 10 Car 1, Pt 16, No 1 (National Archive: C66/2657).

31 The charter is in Cecil Carr, *Select Charters of Trading Companies 1530–1707* (Selden Society, 1913), p 160 (in English); soap boiling being restricted to members of that company by a Proclamation in 1634: James Larkin, *Stuart Royal Proclamations: Royal Proclamations of Charles I 1625–46* (Oxford 1983), Vol 2, p 395 (No 176); Cecil Carr, *Select Charters of Trading Companies 1530–1707* (Selden Society, 1913), p lxxviii.

32 The charter is in Cecil Carr, *Select Charters of Trading Companies 1530–1707* (Selden Society, 1913), p 117.

33 See Robert Ashton, *The City and the Court 1603–1643* (Cambridge 1979), pp 144–145.

34 See p 55.

granted to enable individuals to evade the regulated companies and the guilds.[35] For example, John Greene used patent law so that he could work his patent[36] for improvements to coaches without interference from the London Coachmakers Company.[37] Yet the number of patents granted during the Restoration remained low; indeed before joint stock companies became significant again in the boom of the 1690s there were only a few patent grants each year.[38]

The turning point was just before the beginning of the Nine Years War in June 1687, when Captain William Phips[39] successfully salvaged treasure from a Spanish treasure galleon ('The Almiranta') which had sunk in 1641. The haul was valued at £200,000 (at a time when the cost of running the government and royal establishment was only £700,000 per annum[40]). Phips' expedition is often seen as a marker of the beginning of a stock market boom,[41] but the boom was really the result of there being an abundance[42] of "spare" capital; as it was expressed in 1681: "There is now as much money to be let on good securities as there are securities or rather more."[43] While some of this capital was from merchants whose trade routes had been cut off or disrupted by the war,[44] it was the case that England had become a wealthy country through advances in trade and agriculture.[45] The climate was ripe for the development of investment "projects" to absorb this capital. Before the 1688 Glorious Revolution there had been only a few joint stock companies,[46] and so investment opportunities were limited.[47] Yet between 1688 and 1695 around a hundred new joint stock companies were formed[48] and while trading was not as extensive as might be expected[49] this was the birth of the English stock market.

---

35 Christine MacLeod, "The 1690s Patents Boom: Invention or Stock-Jobbing?" (1986) 39 *Economic History Review* 549 at 555; in contrast to the general law see Chapter 5.

36 Patent No 267 (1691); also see *London Gazette* 14–17 March 1692, Issue No 2749; Christine MacLeod, "The 1690s Patents Boom: Invention or Stock-Jobbing?" (1986) 39 *Economic History Review* 549 at 555 suggests the notice in the Gazette was an advertisement, but the advertisements were below it, and so rather it is the notice of grant.

37 Christine MacLeod, "The 1690s Patents Boom: Invention or Stock-Jobbing?" (1986) 39 *Economic History Review* 549 at 555; Christine MacLeod, *Inventing the Industrial Revolution: The English Patent System 1660–1800* (Cambridge 1988), p 83.

38 1688 (four patents granted: Nos 258 to 261); 1689 (one patent granted: No 262); 1690 (three patents granted: Nos 263 to 265); the boom started in 1691 (nineteen patents granted: Nos 267 to 285). These numbers ignore some which were not included in Woodcroft's list: see Christine MacLeod, "The 1690s Patents Boom: Invention or Stock-Jobbing?" (1986) 39 *Economic History Review* 549, fn 2.

39 For a history of Phips see Peter Earle, *The Wreck of the Almiranta: Sir William Phips and the Search for the Hispaniola Treasure* (Macmillan 1979).

40 The Civil List was created ten years later in 1698 and the initial annual payment was £700,000. This covered the entire expense of running a government and the Royal establishment: Taxation Act 1697, s 11.

41 See Anne L Murphy, *The Origins of the English Financial Markets* (Cambridge 2009), pp 10–11.

42 Phyllis Deane, "Capital Formation in Britain before the Railway Age" (1961) 9 *Economic Development and Cultural Change* 356; Dwyryd Jones, *War and Economy: In the Age of William II and Marlborough* (Blackwell 1988), p 301.

43 William Petyt, *Britannia languens: or, A Discourse of Trade Shewing, That the Present Management of Trade in England . . .* (London: Richard Baldwin 1689), pp 231–232 (Wing P1947).

44 Dwyryd Jones, *War and Economy: In the Age of William II and Marlborough* (Blackwell 1988), pp 249–250.

45 Anne L Murphy, *The Origins of the English Financial Markets* (Cambridge 2009), p 13.

46 E.g. The East India Company, the Hudson Bay Company and the Royal Africa Company.

47 Anne L Murphy, *The Origins of the English Financial Markets* (Cambridge 2009), p 16.

48 William Scott, *The Constitution and Finance of English, Scottish and Irish Joint-Stock Companies to 1720* (Cambridge 1911), Vol 1, p 327.

49 The transfers in the three great companies were larger and would have been over a hundred (and in the East India Company it may have been in the thousands although the records are very limited): Anne L Murphy, *The Origins*

These opportunities for investment meant that lapsed patents were re-presented and unworked patents were made ready to be put into effect.[50] There was also a rush in patents being sought and companies formed. This led to two types of company being involved in patents. The first were formed to exploit the patent and the second to exploit the selling of shares in a patent itself. In the former camp fell the Company of Glassmakers, which was formed by charter in 1691[51] shortly after the grant of the patent[52] and traded until at least 1694,[53] after which it fell into obscurity.[54] An example from the second camp is Thomas Neale who may have raised as much as £12,000 on the strength of his patent[55] albeit he struggled to work it effectively.[56] These ambitious, if not fraudulent, schemes to invest in patents led to litigation in the courts,[57] but more importantly for these purposes it led to petitions in Parliament.

White Paper Company

Three companies managed to extend their patent protection by a private Act of Parliament. The first, and most significant, is the White Paper Makers. The paper making industry dates back to Elizabethan times,[58] but manufacture of white paper in England was not attempted until much later. A patent had been granted in favour of George Hagar in 1682[59] and he formed a company to try and exploit the invention, but his enterprise failed (largely due to creditors from his pre-existing bankruptcy[60] pursing the capital he successfully raised). Three years later, in 1685, John Briscoe applied for a patent for "making, sizing and whitening writing printing and other paper".[61] He was granted his patent and on 13 June 1686 he petitioned the King again for a charter of incorporation stating capital of £100,000 would be required to start working the patent.[62] The charter was granted[63] and the Governor and Company of the White Paper Makers formed on 23 July 1686 and it was

of the English Financial Markets (Cambridge 2009), p 23. The number of transactions each year were usually well below a hundred: The ledgers of a broker – Charles Blunt – are held in the National Archive (C114/165) and they provide an insight into the work of one of the brokers (see the table in Anne L Murphy, *The Origins of the English Financial Markets* (Cambridge 2009), p 21). He traded in twenty-three companies but almost all of the trade was in seven companies.

50 Christine MacLeod, "The 1690s Patents Boom: Invention or Stock-Jobbing?" (1986) 39 *Economic History Review* 549 at 560 (example in fn 51).

51 The warrant to prepare the charter is at: State Papers Domestic (7 October 1691) (National Archive: SP 44/341 ff 197–202).

52 Patent No 268 (1691) (Granted to Robert Hookes and Christopher Dodsworth).

53 See Anne L Murphy, *The Origins of the English Financial Markets* (Cambridge 2009), p 21.

54 Christine MacLeod, "The 1690s Patents Boom: Invention or Stock-Jobbing?" (1986) 39 *Economic History Review* 549 at 566.

55 Patent No 292 (1692).

56 *George Ball Appellant, John Coggs and Other, The Appellants Case* (1710) (ETSC T040785).

57 *Dunstar v Williams* (1695) (National Archive: C6/304/39); *Clarke v Pilkington* (1692) (National Archive: C9/255/68); both discovered by Sean Bottomley, *British Patent System during the Industrial Revolution* (Cambridge 2014), p 116, fn 54.

58 For a short summary see William Scott, *The Constitution and Finance of English, Scottish and Irish Joint-Stock Companies to 1720* (Cambridge 1911), Vol 3, p 63.

59 No 220 (1682) (although it was granted to another person: Nathaniel Bladen).

60 A similar problem as Koops: see p 93.

61 No. 246 (1685); See State Papers Domestic (15 April 1685): National Archive SP 44/71 f 127.

62 State Papers Domestic (13 June 1686): National Archive: SP 31/3 f 262.

63 The charter is in Cecil Carr, *Select Charters of Trading Companies 1530–1707* (Selden Society, 1913), pp 203–207.

given the "sole power privilege and authority of making sizing and completing all sorts of writing and printing paper. . .for the term of fourteen years",[64] As was usual, the exclusive right was supported by a power of search and forcible entry by the company upon warrant granted by the Lord Chief Justice.[65] Thus, the patent was not assigned or transferred to the company, but rather a new exclusive right was granted to the company to work the invention. As mentioned above, Parliament was endorsing and continuing with the practice of creating companies (albeit now traded as joint stock) to monopolise whole industries. It was no longer necessary to rely on section 9 of the Statute of Monopolies as the companies were now relying on private legislation. The White Paper Company raised at least £20,000 from the sale of 400 shares at £50 each[66] and was actively exercising its right. So that within a year the company was petitioning for a fine of £500 to be paid to it in accordance with its charter.[67]

The Royal Lustring Company

On 23 November 1688, a patent was granted to Paul Cloudesly, William Sherrard and Peter Ducloux for the making, dressing and lustrating of silks.[68] Along with others, they were granted a charter of incorporation as the Royal Lustring Company.[69] There was extensive Parliamentary support for the company which ensured they maintained their monopoly. The Lustrings Act 1696 provided for the forfeiture of any alamodes or lustrings which did not have the mark of Custom-House or the Royal Lustring Company[70] and the following year another Act gave the company exclusive rights to produce black alamodes and lustrings for a further of fourteen years.[71] Parliament's support for the company did not cease then as a further Act was passed in 1706 giving the company further power to enforce the restriction on importing lustring and silk.[72]

Convex Light Company

The support for companies was not unquestioning. Samuel Hutchinson, through Edward Wyndus, obtained a patent for a new type of glass lamp (Convex Lights).[73] He worked out that he could charge householders an annual fee for the new lights if he could manufacture and install them.[74] He therefore needed to raise money which led to shares being issued in the patent so that it was divided into quarters and then 32 shares[75] and a sum, probably in the

---

64 See Cecil Carr, *Select Charters of Trading Companies 1530–1707* (Selden Society, 1913), p 206.

65 Cecil Carr, *Select Charters of Trading Companies 1530–1707* (Selden Society, 1913), pp 206–207.

66 See Preamble to White Paper Company Act 1690 (it was never printed: see Ingrossment: HL/PO/PB/1/1689/2W&Mn25).

67 See State Papers Domestic: National Archive: SP 16/2 f 186 (the perpetrator being Theodore Janssen).

68 Patent No 261 (1688).

69 Charter of Royal Lustring Company (1698) Wing C3725 (also see Woodcroft No. 261*).

70 Lustrings Act 1696, s 3; although those who had produced the Lustrings domestically could have them sealed without cost by the company: s 8.

71 Lustrings Act 1697, s 14.

72 Royal Lustring Company Act 1706, s 3.

73 No 232 (1684).

74 WR Scott, *The Constitution and Finance of English, Scottish and Irish Companies to 1720* (Cambridge 1911), Vol 3, p 53.

75 *The Manuscripts of the House of Lords, 1693–5* (HMSO 1964), Vol 1, p 373 (No 822(b)).

range of £5,000, was raised.[76] The Convex Lights had a direct competitor – the Light Royal – based on Edmund Hemming's invention.[77] The competition between the Light Royal and the Convex Light Companies led to what happened next. The Convex Light Company sought a private Act to give a further term to the patent in 1692:[78] this met a vigorous opposition[79] and so it did not pass.[80] However, soon after this failure, another opportunity arose from the troubles of the London Orphans Fund.

The London's Orphans Fund was about half a million pounds in deficit and the city was trying to devise schemes to remedy this shortfall.[81] In addition, the City of London required householders to hang out lights so as to light the streets during the darker months.[82] Hemming proposed to the Mayor and Common Council that his company would supply lights to the city and pay half of the profits into the Orphans Fund.[83] The Convex Lights Company made a tender somewhat later offering to pay a rent of £600 per year for a twenty-one-year contract.[84] This was the better offer[85] but Hutchinson himself did not agree to terms of the agreement between the City of London and "his" Convex Lights Company. His name was not included as a member of the company, but after petitioning Parliament he obtained a saving clause.[86] After the enactment of the London Orphans Act 1694 there was a significant falling out between Hutchinson and his allies and the rest of the company.[87] In other respects the company was a success and for some decades after the Bill the exclusive right that was granted enabled London to have a good system of lighting. However, once the twenty-one years of exclusivity expired other cheaper options were taken up.[88]

By incorporating these companies under private Acts, Parliament was purporting to encourage the introduction and development of new industries in England. It surely achieved

76 WR Scott, *The Constitution and Finance of English, Scottish and Irish Joint Stock Companies to 1720* (Cambridge 1911), Vol 3, p 53.

77 It is probably the patent of John Vematty (1 August 1683, No 227), but this is not clear, see list of patentees in Edmund Heming: *July 1. 1691. By Virtue of a Patent Granted by King Charles II. for a New Invention of Lamps with Convex Glasses* (Wing H1414A); *The Case of Edmund Heming, Who First Set Up the New Lights in the City of London* (Wing H1415).

78 Convex Light Bill 1692.

79 10 CJ 709 (22 November 1692); 10 CJ 710 (24 November 1692); 10 CJ 734 (6 December 1692); 10 CJ 747 (19 December 1692).

80 Being defeated at Third Reading in the Commons: 10 CJ 765 (30 December 1692).

81 Reginald Sharpe, *London and the Kingdom* (Longmans 1894), Vol 2, p 545; as to the various unsuccessful private bills see Frederick Clifford, *A History of Private Legislation* (1887) (Frank Cass 1969), Vol 2, pp 375–388.

82 John Beckmann (Trans William Johnston), *History of Invention, Discoveries, and Origins* (Bell & Son 1880), Vol 2, pp 178–179.

83 "Proposals Humbley Offered for the Better Lighting of All Street, Lanes, Allies and Public Courts within the City of London", *Journals of the Common Council* (1689–1694), Vol 51, Meeting of Common Council, 6 September 1662 (London Metropolitan Archive: COL/CC/01/01/049).

84 Minutes of Meeting of Common Council, 6 November 1692; and Report of Committee of Improvements, *Journals of the Common Council*, 13 December 1662 (1689–1694), Vol 51 (London Metropolitan Archive: COL/CC/01/01/049).

85 In fact a second offer was made by the Royal Light and also by another company (Glass Globe Lights): see William Scott, *The Constitution and Finance of English, Scottish and Irish Joint Stock Companies to 1720* (Cambridge 1911), Vol 3, pp 55–56.

86 London, Orphans Act 1694, s 28.

87 William Scott, *The Constitution and Finance of English, Scottish and Irish Joint Stock Companies to 1720* (Cambridge 1911), Vol 3, pp 59–60.

88 William Scott, *The Constitution and Finance of English, Scottish and Irish Joint Stock Companies to 1720* (Cambridge 1911), Vol 3, p 60.

this aim as all three companies were successful for a time. But there was also undoubtedly a backward glance to the regulated companies and the use of these companies as regulators of the wider industry. In the long term, however, Parliament was creating and supporting the market in stock and with it encouraging speculation. This led to an increase in the number of joint stock companies and thereafter a bubble developing.

The Bubble Act and the corporate ban

The trading in stock continued and rose to a crescendo with the South Sea Bubble and the so-called Bubble Act (properly known as the Royal Exchange and London Assurance Corporation Act 1719). It is commonly believed the Act was a response to the collapse of the price of stock when the South Sea Bubble burst.[89] However, as Gower[90] amongst others[91] has pointed out the Bubble Act received Royal Assent on 11 June 1720[92] and came into force on 24 June 1720 while the bubble was still inflating. A more satisfactory reason for its passage is presented by Harris who attributes it to protecting the value of South Sea stock by preventing speculation in other "bubble" companies.[93] The South Sea stock represented the national debt and so supporting it was Treasury policy.[94] The extent of speculation can be seen from the price of South Sea stock[95] which rose from 128⅜ on 1 January 1720 to 735 on the day the Bubble Act received Royal Assent and peaking at 950 on 29 June and continuing to average 838 during July and August before entering a rapid decline over the autumn (the lowest point before trading ceased was 145 on 14 October).

In any event, the relevant clause in the Bubble Act was section 18 which prevented the formation of joint stock companies without the sanction of the Crown or Parliament. The whole section is very long and describes in detail the various abuses. The relevant prohibition states:

> any such Undertaking or Attempt, and more particularly the acting or presuming to act as a Corporate Body or Bodies, the raising or pretending to raise transferrable Stock or Stocks, the transferring or pretending to transfer or assign any Share or Shares in such Stock or Stocks, without legal Authority, either by Act of Parliament, or by any Charter from the Crown, to warrant such acting as a Body Corporate, or to raise such

---

89 This stems from misleading commentaries: William Blackstone, *Commentaries on the Laws of England: Book 4: Of Public Wrongs* (ed Wilfred Priest) (Oxford 2016), Book IV, p 117 (p 77–78); Frederic Maitland, "Trust and Corporations" in *The Collected Papers of Frederic William Maitland* (Cambridge 1911) Vol 3, p 390; John Plumb, *England in the Eighteenth Century* (Penguin 1968), p 26; Eric Pawson, *The Early Industrial Revolution: Britain in the Eighteenth Century* (Basford 1979), p 89.

90 LCB Gower, "A South Sea Heresy?" (1952) 68 *LQR* 214 at 218.

91 Also see Ron Harris, "The Bubble Act: Its Passage and its Effects on Business Organization" (1994) 54(3) *Journal of Economic History* 610 at 618–619 (and Ron Harris, *Industrializing English Law: Entrepreneurship and Business Organization 1720–1844* (Cambridge 2000), pp 73–74); Colin Cooke, *Corporation, Trust and Company: An Essay in Legal History* (Manchester 1950), pp 84–85.

92 Publicity was granted to the new Act by a Notice published in the *London Gazette*, 11 June 1720 (Issue 5859, p 1).

93 See generally, Ron Harris, "The Bubble Act: Its Passage and its Effects on Business Organization" (1994) 54(3) *Journal of Economic History* 610 at 618–619; and Ron Harris, *Industrializing English Law: Entrepreneurship and Business Organization 1720–1844* (Cambridge 2000), pp 64–68.

94 But they should not be treated as the same: see LCB Gower, "A South Sea Heresy?" (1952) 68 *LQR* 214 at 221–222.

95 The figures are based on Rik Frehen, William N. Goetzmann and K. Geert Rouwenhorst, "New Evidence on the First Financial Bubble" (2013) 108 *Journal of Financial Economics* 585.

transferrable Stock or Stocks, or to transfer Shares therein, and all acting or pretending to act under any Charter, formerly granted from the Crown, for particular or special Purposes therein expressed, by Persons who do or shall use or endeavour to use the same Charters, for raising a Capital Stock, or for making Transfers or Assignments, or pretended Transfers or Assignments of such Stock, not intended or designed by such Charter to be raised or transferred, and all acting or pretending to act under any obsolete Charter become void or voidable by Nonuser or Abuser, or for want of making lawful Elections, which were necessary to continue the Corporation thereby intended, shall (as to all or any such Acts, Matters and Things, as shall be acted, done, attempted, endeavoured or proceeded upon, after the said four and twentieth Day of June one thousand seven hundred and twenty) for ever be deemed to be illegal and void, and shall not be practised or in any wise put in execution.

The drafting of the provision is somewhat opaque and it might have been arguable that the grant of a patent for invention could be seen as "lawful authority" under section 18 as it is a charter from the Crown. In any event, without specifically addressing this issue, on 5 July 1720, the Lord Justices, acting as Regents while the King was away in Hanover, ordered the law officers to consider adding a proviso into all future Letters Patent for invention to restrict multiple ownership[96] and moreover a week later (12 July) they agreed to dismiss all pending petitions[97] and an Order in Council was enacted to achieve this end.[98] Accordingly, the proviso[99] in the patent grant which precluded the patent being owned by more than five people was introduced *before* the bursting of the South Sea Bubble,[100] a typical example reading:[101]

> . . . provided. . .that if the said Jean Jacques Saint Mare, his executors or administrators, or any person or persons who should or might, at any time or times thereafter during the continuance of that grant, have or claim any right, title, or interest in law or equity of, in, or to the power, privilege, and authority of the sole use and benefit of the said invention thereby granted, should make any transfer or assignment, or any pretended transfer or assignment of the said liberty and privilege, or any share or shares of the benefit or profit thereof, or should declare any trust thereof to or for any number of persons exceeding the number of five, or should open, or cause to be opened, any book or books for public subscription to be made by any number of persons exceeding the number of five, in order to the raising any sum or sums of money under pretence of carrying on the said liberty or privilege thereby granted, or should by him or themselves, or his or their agents or servants, receive any sum or sums of money whatsoever, of any number of persons exceeding in the whole the number of five, for such or the like intents and purposes, or should presume to act as a corporate body, or should divide the benefit of the said last-mentioned letters patent

---

96 State Papers Domestic (5 July 1720): National Archive: SP 44/283, f 15.

97 State Papers Domestic (12 July 1720): National Archive: SP 44/283, f 19.

98 *London Gazette*, 12 July 1720 (Issue No 5868, p 3): there were eighteen petitions dismissed: most were various forms of incorporation but one – that of Joseph Galendo – was for an invention.

99 It was first included in Rowe's Patent (Patent No 431) (granted 12 October 1720).

100 Bottomley wrongly suggests that it was in the aftermath: Sean Bottomley, *The British Patent System during the Industrial Revolution 1700–1852* (Cambridge 2014), p 267.

101 Based on Patent No 4,928 (1824) which was litigated in *Duvergier v Fellowes* (1828) 1 HPC 943; 5 Bingham 248 at 252–253 (130 ER 1056, 1058).

or the liberties and privileges thereby granted, unto any number of shares exceeding the number of five, or should commit or do, or procure to be committed or done any act, matter, or thing whatsoever, during such time as such person or persons should have any right or title, either in law or equity, in or to the same premises, which would be contrary to the true intent and meaning of a certain act of parliament made in the sixth year of the reign of the late King George the first, intituled "An act for better securing certain powers and privileges intended to be granted by his Majesty by two charters for assurance of ships and merchandizes at sea, and for lending money upon bottomry, and for restraining several extravagant and unwarrantable practices therein mentioned,"[102] or in case the said power, privilege, or authority should at any time thereafter become vested in, or in trust for more than the number of five persons or their representatives at any one time, reckoning executors or administrators as and for the single person whom they represent as to such interest as they were or should be entitled to in right of such their testator or intestate, that then and in any of the said cases those letters patent, and all liberties and advantages whatsoever thereby granted, should utterly cease and become void, any thing therein before contained to the contrary thereof in anywise notwithstanding;

It became standard in all English and Scottish patents[103] for a hundred and thirty years.[104] Yet even if the proviso added to the patent grant was to direct investment towards official enterprises then, like the Bubble Act itself, its purpose changed as stock-jobbing became an evil in itself, as Scott put it:

> No words were too strong to condemn what was then considered to be a malign perversion of industry, destruction of commercial probity, of a well-ordered social life, even of religion and virtue. In fact the joint-stock type of organisation received only a little less abuse than the directors of the South Sea company.[105]

'Restricted to five persons'

This meant, at least initially, the Bubble Act was vigorously enforced[106] as one would expect of any law intended to protect virtue. This applied equally to the proviso in the patent and the law officers were "intractable" in requiring this clause even when a request was made to lift it.[107] A valiant attempt was made by James Christopher Le Blon who asked the Crown to incorporate notwithstanding the proviso[108] and it seemed he met with

---

102 Royal Exchange and London Assurance Corporation Act 1719 (the "Bubble Act").

103 It did not always appear in Irish patents. The patent roll for Ireland was destroyed during the Irish Civil War on 30 June 1922 when the Four Courts was bombarded to destruction (but we do know that it was not in Matthias Koops' Irish patent – see *Report on Mr Koops' Petition: Respecting his Invention for Making Paper from Various Refuse Materials* (1801 HC Papers 55), Vol 3, p 127 at p. 4).

104 Although it was increased from five to twelve persons as discussed below.

105 WR Scott, *The Constitution and Finance of English, Scottish and Irish Joint Stock Companies to 1720* (Cambridge 1911), Vol 1, p 437.

106 WR Scott, *The Constitution and Finance of English, Scottish and Irish Joint Stock Companies to 1720* (Cambridge 1911), Vol 1, p 437.

107 Christine MacLeod, *Inventing the Industrial Revolution: The English Patent System 1660–1800* (Cambridge 1988), p 55.

108 Le Blon's Petition to Incorporate: State Papers Domestic (25 August 1725): National Archive: SP 35/57/2 f 89.

some willingness within government: yet the patent finally granted included the usual five person restriction.[109] He then went on to unsuccessfully petition Parliament in 1734 to incorporate him and his partners to work the patent.[110] It is possible that the failure of this petition was inevitable in light of the increasing regulation of the selling of stock with general Acts restricting stock jobbing in 1733[111] and again in 1736.[112] The general prohibition in the Bubble Act did not prevent the development of joint stock companies entirely and in certain areas, such as mining and ship-owning and canal building, it continued.[113] It is important to remember that the restriction in the proviso was against multiple persons holding a patent. It did not prevent a body corporate from holding a patent as it would be a single legal person (and not the collection of its members)[114] – accordingly the patent would be held by one person and not more than five (as prohibited by the proviso).

However, the grant of private Acts or Royal Charters for incorporation was restricted; a reason for this is explained in a report to the Privy Council by the Attorney General in 1761: "trade seldom requires the aid of [incorporation], and stock".[115] The proviso in the patent should not therefore be seen as an attack on corporate status as such, but a restriction on the number of partners who could own a patent (i.e. those who could hold "joint stock"). Such a restriction was not unknown to the law. Although the common law provided no restriction[116] on the number of people who could form a partnership,[117] numerous statutes did: coal merchants could not be in partnership with more than five others;[118] and bankers were restricted to partnerships of six,[119] and partnerships in marine insurance were banned altogether.[120] Each of these restrictions was adopted for separate and distinct policy reason. Thus, it was not simply unincorporated joint stock companies which were precluded from holding a patent, but partnerships of over five people.

While incorporation itself remained rare in the eighteenth century, towards the end of that period an increasing number of unincorporated companies were formed. The nature

---

109 No 492 (1727); see Christine MacLeod, *Inventing the Industrial Revolution: The English Patent System 1660–1800* (Cambridge 1988), pp 55–56.

110 Le Blon's Petition 1734 (22 CJ 259; 27 February 1734)).

111 Stock Jobbing Act 1733.

112 Stock Jobbing Act 1736.

113 Ron Harris, *Industrializing English Law: Entrepreneurship and Business Organization 1720–1844* (Cambridge 2000), Ch 7; Bishop Hunt, *The Development of the Business Corporation in England 1800–1867* (Harvard 1936), p 10.

114 *Case of Sutton's Hospital* (1612) 10 Co Rep 23a (77 ER 960).

115 Report in 1761 of the Attorney and Solicitor-General on the Petition for a Charter for the Equitable Life Assurance Company (14 July 1761) included in *The Assurance Magazine* (WSD Pateman 1851), No 2 at p 89.

116 It was introduced at twenty partners by Joint Stock Companies Act 1856, s 4 (replaced a year later by the Joint Stock Companies Act 1857); a rule only finally abolished by the Regulatory Reform (Removal of 20 Member Limit in Partnership, etc) Order 2002 (SI 2002/3203).

117 Nathaniel Lindley, *A Treatise on the Law of Partnership* (William Maxwell 1860), Vol 1, p 71.

118 Coal Trade Act 1788, s 2 (repealed by the Coal Trade Act 1836).

119 The Bank of England Act 1800 meant that more than six persons could not "borrow, owe, or take up, any Sum or Sums of Money on their Bills or Notes, payable at Demand, or at any less Time than six Months from the borrowing thereof" (e.g. any banking); relaxed outside London by the Country Bankers Act 1826; and more generally by the Joint Stock Banks Act 1844 (which was in turn replaced by Joint Stock Banking Company Act 1857).

120 Royal Exchange and London Assurance Corporation Act 1719 (the Act gave the rights in relation to marine insurance to the two companies only; repealed Marine Assurance Act 1824).

and form of these companies remains contentious. Maitland, for example, took the view that by a combination of trust and partnership law it was possible to form an unincorporated joint stock company with limited liability.[121] While the development, legality and significance of the joint stock company before the repeal of the Bubble Act is uncertain[122] it is clear that it did not have a legal personality separate from its members.[123] So when members left, died or sold stock, a new partnership (or trust) needed to be formed. The absence of a separate legal personality meant that joint stock companies could not be used as a mechanism to manage the working of patents because they could not hold the patent itself.[124] Yet while the number of unincorporated companies grew in the second half of the eighteenth century,[125] the status quo was maintained in relation to patents. Once more this trend can largely be seen from the various private Acts which were passed to prolong patents.[126]

The preservation of the status quo in private Acts

The importance of the restriction can be seen from private Acts during the eighteenth century. While the early extensions of patent term, such as that for John Elwick[127] and Michael Meinzies[128] and even later with the Porcelain Patent Act 1775 and Elizabeth Taylor's Patent Act 1776, simply extended the original patent grant (which included the restriction to five) this was not uniform. When in 1749, Israel Pownoll's patent was extended (or more precisely resurrected, as it expired in 1726[129]) so that his children could work the invention, the original Queen Anne grant (without the restriction to five) was extended and so express mention was made of the restriction.[130] Furthermore, where the Act was expressly stated to protect the invention (rather than a mere extension) it continued to provide for the restriction to five. The practice began with James Watt's Fire Engine Patent Act 1775[131] and continued in subsequent enactments.[132] The policy in the second half of the eighteenth century was clearly restricting the management of patents to small groups of people.

121 Frederic Maitland, "The Unincorporate Body" in *The Collected Papers of Frederic William Maitland*, Vol 3 (Cambridge 1911), pp 278–279; also see Colin Cooke, *Corporation, Trust and Company: An Essay in Legal History* (Manchester 1950), pp 85–88.

122 See generally, Ron Harris, *Industrializing English Law: Entrepreneurship and Business Organization 1720–1844* (Cambridge 2000), Chapter 6.

123 This was not the case is Scotland where a partnership developed a legal personality: finally confirmed by the Partnership Act 1890, s 4(2).

124 It may have been possible by licence to such a company however although this left the licensee at the whim of the patent proprietor: see evidence of John Duncan (Solicitor and Law Clerk to the Eastern Counties Rail Company): *First Report of the Select Committee on Joint Stock Companies; Together with the Minutes of Evidence* (1844 HC Papers 119), Vol 7, p 1 at Q2097 (p 177).

125 See Ron Harris, *Industrializing English Law: Entrepreneurship and Business Organization 1720–1844* (Cambridge 2000), pp 194–198.

126 See p 126.

127 Elwick's Patent Act 1742.

128 Meinzies' Patent Act 1750.

129 It was granted in 1712 (No 312).

130 Pownoll's Patent Act 1749, s 1.

131 James Watt's Fire Engine Patent Act 1775, s 4.

132 Liardet's Cement Patent Act 1776, s 5; Hartley's Patent (Fire Prevention) Act 1776, s 3; Bancroft's Patent Act 1785, s 3; Turner's Patent Act 1792, s 5; Conway's Patent Kiln Act 1795, s 3; Cartwright's Woolcombing Machinery Act 1801, s. 4; Fourdriniers' Paper Making Machine Act 1807, s 7; Hollingrake's Letters Patent Act 1830, s 4.

The exception before the boom – Matthias Koops

There was one notable exception to this general trend. Matthias Koops was interested in making paper from materials other than linen and cotton. By 1800 he had produced such paper at Neckinger Mill in Bermondsey[133] but wished to expand his factory to apply his ideas more widely. He obtained a patent[134] for his invention for making paper from straw, hay, thistles, wastes, and reuse of hemp and flax[135] and it contained[136] the usual proviso that it could not be assigned to more than five persons.

Koops obtained a lease over some land to build his paper factory which would, according to experts, cost at least £50,000 and would employ at least 500 people. It was also apparent that up to £100,000 was available from various investors, but to raise this sum it was necessary to have the proviso lifted to allow joint stock to be issued.[137] Accordingly, he petitioned Parliament[138] to form the Regenerating Paper Company[139] (eventually, the Straw Paper Company), which on the second attempt[140] led to enactment of the Koops Papermaking Patent Act 1801. The Act permitted the patent to be held by up to sixty different people[141] and so enable Koops to sell stock and build a factory in Millbank in 1801.[142] Unfortunately, Koops had been an undischarged bankrupt back in 1790 and when he tried to discharge himself from bankruptcy in 1802 he failed[143] and with it so did the business.[144] This Act, however, created a precedent for others to follow.

Joint stock companies in early nineteenth century

The joint stock company had been growing in significance since the end of the eighteenth century[145] and by the first decade of the nineteenth their numbers were growing substantially. There was still a view, however, that they were not a good thing as Thomas Mortimer's description of a joint stock company shows:[146]

> A number of merchants uniting and applying to the Government for an exclusive charter, to prevent others from engaging in the sane commerce, and for a power to raise money by an open subscription in order to form their stock or capital are generally dominated companies.

---

133 RJ Goulden, "Koops, Matthias (fl. 1789–1805)" in *Oxford Dictionary of National Biography*, Vol 32 (Oxford 2004), pp 80–81.

134 It is sometimes reported as three patents because he held an English, Scottish and Irish patent.

135 No. 2481 (1801).

136 The Irish patent did not contain the proviso: *Report on Mr Koops' Petition* (1801 HC Papers 55), Vol 3, p 127 at p. 4.

137 55 CJ 647 (13 June 1801) (evidence of Elias Carpenter).

138 The original petition also tried to keep the specification secret, but this was unsuccessful: see pp 114–5.

139 55 CJ 635 (11 June 1801).

140 The Bill had a First Reading, but never a Second Reading.

141 56 CJ 174 (16 March 1801).

142 RJ Goulden, "Koops, Matthias (fl. 1789–1805)" in *Oxford Dictionary of National Biography*, Vol 32 (Oxford 2004), pp 80–81.

143 The facts are explained in *Hesse v Stevenson* (1803) 1 HP 455; 3 Bos & P 565 (127 ER 305).

144 RJ Goulden, "Koops, Matthias (fl. 1789–1805)" in *Oxford Dictionary of National Biography*, Vol 32 (Oxford 2004), pp 80–81.

145 Ron Harris, *Industrializing English Law: Entrepreneurship and Business Organization 1720–1844* (Cambridge 2000), p 216.

146 Thomas Mortimer, *Every Man His Own Broker or a Guide to the Stock Exchange* (13th Ed, WJ and J Richardson 1801), p 7 (this book was first published in 1761 and ran over fourteen editions).

Nevertheless, the number listed on the stock exchange doubled between 1803 and 1811[147] and in a 'boom' year of 1807, at least forty-two new joint stock companies were formed[148] (although, many schemes only existed on paper[149] – in other words they were schemes or projects looking for funders rather than investors in existing or viable businesses). It appeared that the enforcement of the Bubble Act had fallen into abeyance. As the number of unincorporated joint stock companies grew, the memories of the 1720s were re-awakened[150] and with it attempts to defend the companies.[151] The Bubble Act became a subject before the courts for the first time in nearly a hundred years[152] with Lord Ellenborough CJ in *R v Dodd*[153] telling the parties and others:

> [It is] recommended . . . as a matter of prudence to the parties concerned, that they should forbear to carry into execution this mischievous project, or any other specula-tive project of the like nature, founded on joint stock and transferrable shares: and we hope that this intimation will prevent others from engaging in the like mischievous and illegal projects.[154]

The court continued to be sceptical about joint stock companies more generally and their legality remained somewhat in doubt.[155] In *R v Webb*[156] Lord Ellenborough, while holding a particular issue of joint stock was lawful, did so on the basis the transfer was limited and "it was not the object of the undertaking to raise stock for the purposes of transfer, nor to make such stock a subject of commercial speculation or adventure"[157] and, it appears, some later cases read the decision to mean that only joint stock companies which lead to the "common grievance, prejudice and inconvenience" are within the Bubble Act.[158] These decisions were welcomed in many quarters. A series of correspondence in the *Morning Chronicle* suggested

---

147 Charles Dugid, *The Story of the Stock Exchange: Its History and Position* (Grant Richards 1901), p 96.
148 Ron Harris, *Industrializing English Law: Entrepreneurship and Business Organization 1720–1844* (Cambridge 2000), p 202.
149 Bishop Hunt, *The Development of the Business Corporation in England 1800–1867* (Harvard 1936), pp 15–16.
150 See David Macpherson, *Annals of Commerce: Manufactures, Fishing and Navigation* (WJ and J Richardson 1805), Vol 3, pp 76–103; and Anon, *An Account of the South Sea Scheme and a Number of Other Bubbles* (J Cawthorne 1806).
151 See Philopatris, *Observations on Public Institutions, Monopolies, Joint-Stock Companies and Deeds of Trust* (JM Richardson 1807); Henry Day, *A Defense of Joint-Stock Companies; Being an Attempt to Shew their Legality, Expediency, and Public Benefit* (Longman 1808).
152 Based on the absence of law reports of any such decision. This does not mean there were no decisions which went unreported.
153 (1808) 9 East 516 (103 ER 670).
154 (1808) 9 East 516 at 528 (103 ER 670 at 674).
155 *Buck v Buck* (1808) 1 Camp 547 (170 ER 1502) (also see footnote to that case where *R v Statton* (1809) is mentioned).
156 (1811) 14 East 406 (104 ER 658).
157 While some comments on the purpose of the Bubble Act were made in *Webb* and this phrase used, it does not appear to be the basis upon which the case was decided. However, this seems to have been taken to be the intent of the *Webb* decision in *Pratt v Hutchinson* (1812) 15 East 511 (104 ER 936) and *Brown v Holt* (1812) 4 Taunton 587 (128 ER 460).
158 *Nockels v Crosby* (1825) 3 B & C 814 at 821 (107 ER 935 at 938); also see Counsel's comment: *Josephs v Pebrer* (1825) 3 B & C 639 at 641 (107 ER 870 at 871).

that restricting joint stock companies was in accord with common sense.[159] The companies continued and some examples were found to be lawful.[160] While they grew in number, it appears that companies working patents were still rare. The wording of the grant meant that patents could be assigned to a small number of partners long before the rise of joint stock companies, but it was rare that the capital required to work an invention[161] could not be raised by an individual. In contrast to the view that the Bubble Act no longer had bite, it is probable that patentees believed that the restriction to five persons was still applicable.[162] Nevertheless, throughout the boom in joint stock companies in the early part of the nineteenth century, working patents had not been a major concern. In the period between Koops and the repeal of the Bubble Act in 1825 there were a few parties[163] who sought to incorporate to work patents albeit none with success: Fredrick Winsor in 1812[164] who got no further than a petition; James Lee[165] in 1816 whose Bill was defeated on Third Reading in the Lords largely due to his desire to keep his specification secret[166]; and the Antimephitic Company in 1819 and 1821.[167] The last of these was lost on a vote at second reading although it is not clear why so many Members of Parliament were against it.[168]

The repeal of the Bubble Act

The mid 1820s saw a "veritable avalanche of extravagant promotions"[169] with 1824 seeing a huge number of private Bills seeking incorporation.[170] There were no petitions to incorporate a company to work an invention.[171] The avalanche was followed by a number of court decisions making investing in joint stock companies more risky. A few years earlier, in *Ellison v Bignold*, Lord Eldon made it clear how few joint stock companies might be legal:[172]

159 A Plain Dealer, *Morning Chronicle*, 5 November 1807, p 3; An Old Fashioned Fellow, *Morning Chronicle*, 9 November 1807, p 3; A Looker, *Morning Chronicle*, 20 November 1807. The newspaper also published the provision prohibiting joint stock companies on its front page: *Morning Chronicle*, 12 November 1807.

160 *Brown v Holt* (1812) 4 Taunton 587 (128 ER 460) (a question for the jury whether the company beneficial and if so it was lawful); *Pratt v Hutchinson* (1813) 15 East 510 (104 ER 936)12 (restricted transfer of shares means that not within the Bubble Act).

161 For some figures see Harry Dutton, *The Patent System and Inventive Activity during the Industrial Revolution 1750–1852* (Manchester 1984), pp 157–158.

162 Indeed, this must have been why Koops sought a private Act, see p 62.

163 In addition, there was Isaac Reddell who sought to incorporate the Good Hope Company to exploit his invention, but there was no patent: see Good Hope Company Petition 1816 (71 CJ 53; 16 February 1816).

164 Fredrick Albert Winsor's Petition 1812 (68 CJ 97; 18 December 1812).

165 Lee's Patent Bill 1816 (Ingrossment: HL/PO/JO/10/2/90B).

166 See pp 115–7.

167 Antimephitic Company Bill 1819 and Antimephitic Company Bill 1821 (the texts of both Bill are lost).

168 The only report is in *The Times*, 20 March 1821 and it simply says a few names opposing but without any reasons ascribed.

169 Bishop Hunt, *The Development of the Business Corporation in England 1800–1867* (Harvard 1936), p 30.

170 The numbers vary. Hunt suggests there were 250 private bills before the House of Commons by April: Bishop Hunt, *The Development of the Business Corporation in England 1800–1867* (Harvard 1936), p 32; but this appears an exaggeration. A search of the index to Volume 97 of the Commons Journal (1824 session) suggests that about 10 per cent of that figure is closer to the mark based on the number of entries for petitions to incorporate.

171 The next was a few years later: Joseph Tilt's Bill 1827 (the preamble was found not to be proven: 82 CJ 585; 20 June 1827).

172 (1821) 2 Jac & W 503 (37 ER 720).

Now, as I have understood the law (I will not say that I am correct, but I believe that I am), when a number of persons undertake to insure each other, if the shares and interests in the money that is laid up, be not assignable and transferable to any persons who are not members, the society is not illegal; but if there may be assignments and transfers of the shares, I have understood that that made it illegal.[173]

This was followed by the Equitable Loan Bank Company being declared illegal under the Bubble Act by the Court of Kings Bench[174] and *Kinder v Taylor*[175] where Lord Eldon suggested that unincorporated companies were contrary not only to the Bubble Act, but also that they were contrary to the common law.[176] He also spoke against these companies in Parliament and considered them a nuisance and a source of fraud used to avoid debts.[177] So he proposed to bring in legislation[178] to further regulate large partnerships.[179] Additionally, Lord Lauderdale proposed new Standing Orders to preclude Bills getting to Second Reading without three-quarters of the capital having been deposited with trustees.[180] Neither Eldon's Bill nor the new Standing Orders progressed. The fever pitch continued throughout the year and eventually the government was forced to take action to clear up the uncertainty in the law. The course it adopted was to repeal the Bubble Act in June 1825.[181] Yet this did not end the challenges in the court and Lord Eldon, in particular, continued to condemn companies.[182]

The judgment in *Duvergier v Fellowes*[183] is central to what was to follow. Aimé Duvergier set up a joint stock company with 9,000 shares. The stated purpose of the company was to purchase and work certain patents relating to distilling potatoes.[184] Best CJ held that any transfer from the patentee to the joint stock company would instantly invalidate the patent.[185] Further, he held that any attempt to get money for this purpose would be a fraud and so the contracts to subscribers were not enforceable.[186] In the same year, the proviso was described by John Taylor, a manufacturer, in his evidence to the 1829 Select Committee as "inconvenient" but it got little other attention.[187] In any event, in 1832, at the suggestion of leading patent agent William Carpmael,[188] the restriction was changed from five persons to twelve.

---

173 (1821) 2 Jac & W 503 at 510 (37 ER 720 at 723).
174 *Josephs v Pebrer* (1825) 3 B & C 639 (107 ER 870); it does not seem to have been argued that it was contrary to the Bank of England Act 1800 however.
175 (1825) 3 Law Journal Reports 68.
176 *Kinder v Taylor* (1825) 3 Law Journal Reports 68 at 81.
177 HL Deb, 21 May 1824, Vol 11 (2nd), col 791.
178 This never happened as his judicial role intervened.
179 HL Deb, 18 June 1824, Vol 11 (2nd), cols 1456–1457.
180 HL Deb, 25 May 1824, Vol 11 (2nd), cols 856–857; HL Deb, 2 June 1824, Vol 11 (2nd), cols 1076–1077.
181 Bubble Companies, etc Act 1825.
182 See Bishop Hunt, *The Development of the Business Corporation in England 1800–1867* (Harvard 1936), pp 38–41.
183 (1828) 1 HPC 943; 5 Bingham 248 (130 ER 1056).
184 No 5,197 (1824) (Jean Jaques Stainmarc).
185 (1828) 1 HPC 943; 5 Bingham 248 at 263–264 (130 ER 1056 at 162).
186 (1828) 1 HPC 943; 5 Bingham 248 at 264 (130 ER 1056 at 162).
187 *Report from the Select Committee on the Law Relative to Patents for Invention* (1829 HC Papers 332), Vol 3, p 415, Evidence of John Taylor, p 12.
188 At least he claims the credit: William Carpmael, *The Law of Patents for Inventions, Familiarly Explained* (London 1832), p 41.

While there have been suggestions that the restriction could be overcome by licensing[189] it was never entirely clear during the life of the original proviso whether a licence to more than five persons would void the patent[190] (not to mention the licensee was at the mercy of the patentee in many ways[191]). Indeed, one of the reasons the restriction was changed in 1832 appears to be to clarify that the granting of any type of licences to more than (then) twelve people would not avoid the patent. Accordingly, any patent granted before 1832 was potentially thought to be at risk by licensing to more than five persons.[192] Indeed, as will be seen, private Acts often gave an express right to license. More problematic was the fact that leading lawyers took the view that the grant of an exclusive licence which purports to give the entire right could still have been treated as an assignment after that time[193] and so would still fall within the proviso.[194] The only authority on the point was *Protheroe v May*[195] where it was held that granting an exclusive licence was not contrary to the proviso. However, in that case there was a royalty paid to the inventor and so he received the profits directly derived from the patent. So the view of the leading patent lawyer of the day remained that an irrevocable profit share from the patent to a company would still have been inside the proviso and voided the patent.[196] More important than the actual legal position in the 1830s and 1840s as to whether an exclusive licence fell within the proviso was that many promoters of joint stock companies would be aware that there was a *risk* it might and it is for this reason that they turned to Parliament.

1830s–1852

After the repeal of the Bubble Act, the stigma of joint stock companies began to wane. In 1834 Parliament enacted legislation[197] which, in theory, would have made it easier for companies to be formed.[198] Nevertheless, registration was still seen as a privilege rather than a right and so many company promoters still petitioned Parliament, rather than the Crown. Eventually, however, corporate privileges (although not limited liability) became generally available under the Joint Stock Companies Act 1844.[199]

When the view of joint stock companies improved it appears that the rationale for the proviso changed: it was no longer to prevent fraud on speculators or the public but "to

---

189 It also clearly appears to be reflected in practice: *Report from the Select Committee on the Law Relative to Patents for Invention* (1829 HC Papers 332), Vol 3, p 415 at p 92; and see Evidence of John Taylor, p 12.

190 See William Hindmarch, *Treatise on the Law Relating to the Patent Privileges for the Sole Use of Inventions* (Stevens 1846), p 239.

191 Also see *First Report of the Select Committee on Joint Stock Companies; Together with the Minutes of Evidence* (1844 HC Papers 119), Vol 7, p 1 at Q2097 (p 177).

192 As the proviso related to five persons.

193 See William Hindmarch, *Treatise on the Law Relating to the Patent Privileges for the Sole Use of Inventions* (Stevens 1846), p 241.

194 Sean Bottomley, *The British Patent System during the Industrial Revolution 1700–1852* (Cambridge 2014) takes a different view: pp 268–269.

195 (1839) 3 HPC 495; 5 M & W 675 (151 ER 286).

196 WM Hindmarch, *Treatise on the Law Relating to the Patent Privileges for the Sole Use of Inventions* (Stevens 1846), p 242.

197 Grants of Privileges to Companies Act 1834.

198 It was short lived as the standard was made more difficult under the Chartered Companies Act 1837 a few years later. Notwithstanding, Parliament sometimes took the view that private bills were not appropriate where incorporation by charter was possible in 1834: see debate on the Birmingham Plate and Crown Glass Company Bill 1837: *Mirror of Parliament*, 25 April 1837, Vol 2, p 1204.

199 It came into effect for registration on 1 November 1844: see Joint Stock Companies Act 1844, s 1.

prevent the combination of a number of persons to crush any one individual".[200] This may explain the long path to the proviso's repeal. The first attempt to remove the proviso was in Godson's Letters Patent Bill 1833; it provided that the right in patents were unnecessarily limited without any advantage to the public, and so it should be possible to assign a patent to any number of persons.[201] The Act was poorly received and many of the controversial provisions were omitted during committee stage,[202] but the provision allowing assignment to an unlimited number of persons remained.[203] In the end, the whole Bill was rejected by the Lords as it was felt more time was needed to consider it.[204]

The original version of Lord Brougham's Bill (which became the Letters Patent for Inventions Act 1835) similarly provided that it should be lawful to transfer a patent to any number of persons.[205] All three witnesses before the House of Lords Select Committee considering the Bill did not see the value of the provision. The most favourable view was taken by John Farey who thought the provision "doubtful".[206] Both Alexander (Archibald) Rosser[207] and John Heathcoat[208] thought that the provision might lead to large numbers of people being thrown out of work and so should not be pursued (demonstrating its new anti-competition justification). Heathcoat further thought that licensing was more appropriate than allowing joint stock companies to obtain patents. The Select Committee, accordingly, removed the provision. When the Bill went to the House of Common the failure to lift the proviso was described as one of "missing reforms"[209] due to the hardship it caused[210]; but there was no move to reintroduce the clause.

Soon thereafter a small flood of private Bills went before Parliament to incorporate companies to work patents during the company promotion boom of the mid-1830s. The first enacted was the Anti-Dry Rot Company (Letters Patent) Act 1836.[211] It had a similar form to many that followed. It set out the purpose of the company as being to work the patent,[212] that John Kyan could assign his patent[213] and that the company could buy it without it being voided,[214] that the patent would vest in the company,[215] and thereafter the company

200 *Re Claridge's Patent* (1851) 6 HPC 277; 7 Moo PCC 394 at 397 (13 ER 932 at 933).

201 Letters Patent Bill 1833 (1833 HC Papers 34), Vol 3, p 169, cl 22.

202 But the Bill was split into two: Letters Patent Bill (As Amended in Committee) 1833 (1833 HC Papers 496), Vol 3, p 177 and the Letters Patent Expenses Bill 1833 (1833 HC Papers 497) Vol 3, p 183.

203 Letters Patent Bill (As Amended in Committee) 1833 (1833 HC Papers 496), Vol 3, p 177, cl 9.

204 HL Deb, 9 August 1833, Vol 20 (2nd), cols 440–441.

205 Letters Patent for Inventions Bill 1835 (As introduced) (1835 HL Papers 68), Vol 1, p 197, cl 8 (it was clause 7 by the time it was before the Select Committee). The Bill is also included in Sir John Eardley-Wilmot (ed), *Lord Brougham's Acts and Bills, From 1811 to the Present Time* (Longman 1857), pp 145–148.

206 Phillip Johnson, "Minutes of Evidence of the Select Committee on the Letters Patent for Inventions Act 1835" (2017) 7 *Queen Mary Journal of Intellectual Property* 99 at 109 (Q58).

207 Phillip Johnson, "Minutes of Evidence of the Select Committee on the Letters Patent for Inventions Act 1835" (2017) 7 *Queen Mary Journal of Intellectual Property* 99 at Statement of Archibald Rosser, Clause 7 (p 118).

208 Phillip Johnson, "Minutes of Evidence of the Select Committee on the Letters Patent for Inventions Act 1835" (2017) 7 *Queen Mary Journal of Intellectual Property* 99 at 112 (Q72).

209 Although, it would not have required Parliamentary sanction to change the proviso in relation to future patents, only to those which existed; but this never seems to have been taken up.

210 Thomas Barrett-Lennard, HC Deb, 13 August 1835, Vol 30 (3rd), col 469.

211 It was followed soon after by Bernhardt's Warming and Ventilation Building Companies Act 1836.

212 Anti-Dry Rot Company Act 1836, s 2.

213 Anti-Dry Rot Company Act 1836, s 3.

214 Anti-Dry Rot Company Act 1836, s 4.

215 Anti-Dry Rot Company Act 1836, s 5; this appeared whether or not the patent was granted after 1832 (e.g. Patent Dry Meter Company Act 1837, s 5 which took Miles Berry's patent of 19 March 1833 (No 6,398)). This may be, in part, because companies only have the powers given to them (as statutory creatures) or it may be that there remained doubt as to its ability to license to more than twelve persons or, of course, both

could licence[216] the patent to any number of people.[217] Similar Acts appeared notwithstanding the market crash in 1837,[218] but the public perception of incorporation remained poor. Charles Dickens had a character Tigg Montague[219] of the Anglo-Bengalee Disinterested Loan and Life Assurance Company who started a scam insurance company to take investors money.[220] Thomas Tooke, the economist, stated during the review of partnership law in 1837 that companies were rarely, if ever, as well managed as private business.[221] The *Circular to Bankers*, while generally favourable to reform, suggested that "joint stock associations for mercantile objects which are properly within the compass of individual exertion are bad" and only those companies which were fit and proper to carry out the particular purpose should be granted incorporation.[222] These views were shared by those involved in the law, with courts said to favour individuals over joint stock companies.[223] This view appears to have been shared by patent lawyers such as William Hindmarch, the leading patent barrister of his day, who stated in his 1844 treatise[224]:

> It is clear indeed that public companies cannot conduct manufacturing or trading business so efficiently as private persons or ordinary co-partnerships and the machinery necessary for the management and regulation of such companies swallows up all the profit made by their trade or manufacture.

Nevertheless, the issue of incorporation more generally was considered by an aborted Select Committee in 1841[225] and then taken up with vigour by William Gladstone as the newly appointed President of the Board of Trade. His committee reported in 1843,[226] and this directly led to the Joint Stock Companies Act 1844. So incorporation was generally available, but this did not assist patentees. The proviso remained and so did the need for private legislation. In the period between the Anti-Dry Rot Company (Letters Patent) Act 1836 (Kyan's Patent Act) and the last such Act in 1852[227] there were thirty-three private Acts

---

216 See earlier discussion of licensing at p 97; a company could only do what it had been given power to do and so a licensing power was necessary to license irrespective of the patent law issues that might also be involved.

217 Anti-Dry Rot Company Act 1836, s 5; evidencing that after 1832 (the patent was granted in 1835 (No 6726)) there was still a concern about licensing more than 12 people.

218 The crash in England was related to the Panic of 1837 in the United States: see Jessica M Lepler, *The Many Panics of 1837: People, Politics, and the Creation of a Transatlantic Financial Crisis* (Cambridge 2014).

219 Charles Dickens, *Martin Chuzzlewit* (1844) (Penguin 1999).

220 It is what would now be called a Ponzi scheme.

221 *Report on the Law of Partnership* (1837 HC Papers 530), Vol 44, p 399 (the Ker Report) – Communication from Thomas Tooker, p 33 (par 4).

222 *The Circular to Bankers*, 17 August 1838 (No 527), p 51.

223 *The Circular to Bankers*, 14 February 1840 (No 605), p 275; an example might be *Blundell v Winsor* (1837) 8 Sim 601 at 613 (59 ER 238, 243) where the court considered a mining operation to be "a wild project, entered into by speculating persons for the purpose of deluding the weak portion of the public".

224 William Hindmarch, *A Treatise on the Law Relating to Patent Privileges for the Sole Use of Inventions: And the Practice of Obtaining Letters Patents for Inventions* (London 1846), p 68.

225 It was appointed on 3 April 1841 (96 CJ 196), but not progressed much further.

226 *Report from the Select Committee on Joint Stock Companies* (1843 HC Papers 523), Vol 11, p 215 which is just the minutes of the committee; the proper report was published in the following session: *First report of the Select Committee on Joint Stock Companies; Together with the Minutes of Evidence* (1844 HC Papers 119), Vol 7, p 1.

227 There were in fact two connected bills: Claussen's Patent Flax Company Act 1852 (to work the patent in England) and the North British Flax Company's Act 1852 (to work it in Scotland) both received Royal Assent on 30 August 1852.

Table 6.1 Acts, Bills and notices seeking to allow the assignment of patents, 1836–1852

Year	Acts	Petitions/Bills	Notices
1836	2	0	–
1837	2	4	–
1838	2	2	–
1839	3	2	2
1840	4	3	4
1841	2	1	2
1842	1	2	5
1843	0	2	1
1844	0	1	1
Enactment of Joint Stock Companies Act 1844			
1845	0	0	1
1846	1	1	2
1847	2	0	0
1848	4	0	0
1849	0	0	0
1850	2	0	2
1851	4	1	1
1852	3	4	2
Total	33	24	22

passed to form companies to work patents or assign patents to existing companies.[228] There were many other aborted or unsuccessful attempts some which got as far as a Bill or petition to Parliament and others which got no further than a notice in the *Gazette*. The above table sets out these figures.

The number of joint stock companies working patents during this period is a matter of controversy. Dutton lists twenty-seven such companies (and seven in the period 1844–1852).[229] His list appears to be based on those companies which obtained private Acts to incorporate.[230] In contrast, Bottomley produces a list of thirty companies between 1844 and 1852 whose stated purpose was working patents.[231] His work is based on those obtaining complete registration from the Registrar of Joint Stock Companies.[232]

---

228 In 1854, the Royal Conical Flour Mill Company's Act 1854 was passed to incorporate the company and to work patents (s 3) and to license them (s 30), but there was no need to deal with the proviso by that time and so it is not provided for; although it was mentioned in the Gazette Notice: see *London Gazette*, 22 November 1853 (Issue 21496, p 3283). The Electric Telegraph Company of Ireland Act 1853 also allowed for assignment of patents with forfeiture (s 51), but no patents were particularised in relation to the Act.

229 Harry Dutton, *The Patent System and Inventive Activity during the Industrial Revolution 1750–1852* (Manchester 1984), p 164.

230 The only exception is the Siever and Westhead Co 1849. Its inclusion might be an error. They were the partners who earlier had obtained the London Caoutchouc Company Act 1837 to incorporate a company of that name to work their patents. Further, Westhead obtained a private Act to validate his patent after failing to file a specification in 1849 (Westhead's Patent Act 1849) (see Ch 7). This is supported by the fact it is not on Bottomley's list: Sean Bottomley, *The British Patent System during the Industrial Revolution 1700–1852* (Cambridge 2014), pp 279–283.

231 Sean Bottomley, *The British Patent System during the Industrial Revolution 1700–1852* (Cambridge 2014), p 270–271.

232 Under the Joint Stock Companies Act 1844.

Bottomley's list, however, should not be taken to suggest that the company in question ever *worked* the patent. It may be a company was set up with the intention of working the patent, but never actually did so as it could not, for example, raise the funds for a private Act to permit the transfer (and so the company dissolved). Indeed, Bottomley's list only includes sixteen companies who had not dissolved within five years and eight of these sixteen appear to be linked to a private Act being passed. It is unclear whether the other eight were exclusive licensees, simple licensees or indeed what relationship they had to the working of the patent in question.

The numbers of companies working patents and the basis upon which they were doing so therefore remains opaque. It is clear that petitioners were approaching Parliament for more than simple incorporation and there was value seen, by them at least, in obtaining a private Act to allow the patent to be transferred. It is also clear that these rights were not being granted as a matter of routine. Over the period from 1836 to 1852 there was a 59 per cent success rate for patentees who petitioned Parliament obtaining an Act.[233] It is clear, however, that Parliament was willing to grant corporate privileges (and the assignment of patents) to those it thought deserving.[234] The proviso remained however.

The end of the proviso

Since the original version of Lord Brougham's Bill, no other patent legislation – Act or Bill – considered ending the restrictions on assignment. The feeling of the industry probably remained as expressed in evidence before the 1835 Select Committee and, later, as expressed by Hindmarch. Indeed, when the leading patent lawyer Thomas Webster QC gave evidence to a Parliamentary committee in 1849 there remained support for retaining it:[235]

> [the] proviso which I should not be disposed to omit, for this reason, it is got over easily by granting a licence to a Company. . . I think it is good in principle. It not unfrequently happens that a patent is worth nothing, excepting to have legal proceeding upon, and to harass parties, for as you facilitate the introduction of capital, and a larger number of parties become interested in patents, you give rise to litigation.

The matter was raised by only one witness before the 1851 Select Committee.[236] Matthew Hill QC suggested that the restriction should be lifted.[237] One of his reasons was that

---

233 In the period 1840–1844 the overall success rate for private bills of incorporation was 67 per cent: James Taylor, *Creating Capitalism: Joint-Stock Enterprise in British Politics and Culture, 1800–1870* (Royal Historical Society 2006), p 136. As the figures above suggest, it was much lower for patent companies during this period at 41 per cent – although this figure includes petitions as well as bills (whereas the 6 per cent is bills only).

234 James Taylor, *Creating Capitalism: Joint-Stock Enterprise in British Politics and Culture, 1800–1870* (Royal Historical Society 2006), p 137.

235 *Report of the Committee on the Signet and Privy Seal Office: With Minutes of Evidence and Appendix* (1849 C 1099), Vol 22, p 453, Q837 (p 45); Webster also stated himself as not an advocate of general legislation being enacted to replace private legislation (Q840). Hardly surprising as a member of the Parliamentary bar and the potential for lost work.

236 *Select Committee of House of Lords to Consider Bills for Amendment of Law Touching Letters Patent for Inventions. Report, Minutes of Evidence* (1851 HC Papers 486), Vol 18, p 223.

237 *Select Committee of House of Lords to Consider Bills for Amendment of Law Touching Letters Patent for Inventions. Report, Minutes of Evidence* (1851 HC Papers 486), Vol 18, p 223, (Q2670–2673) (pp 353–354).

Parliament is "in the habit of passing private Acts" for the purpose of setting aside the restrictions.[238] Nevertheless, the final version of the Bill still included prohibition.[239] In the same year, Hindmarch and Webster in their observations on the defects in the patent system did not raise it as a particular problem[240]; although Turner in his pamphlet did suggest it should be removed.[241] Indeed, throughout most of the passage of what was to become the Patent Law Amendment Act 1852 the assignment proviso remained.[242] It was only during Select Committee in the House of Commons that it was finally removed[243] – very much at the eleventh hour. There is no explanation why this occurred as there was no reporting of what happened in the committee in respect of this amendment, but nobody sought to challenge the proviso being lifted as the Bill finished its passage. It may even have gone unnoticed as nearly three years later Lord Redesdale, the Lord Chairman, stated during the passage of the Limited Liability Act 1855 that removing the requirement would be a mistake.[244]

Conclusion

The company began its role in the history of patents by playing a role somewhere between regulator and monopolist. As time went on and regulation ceased to be privatised by the Crown, the company became a vehicle for investment and then fraud. In one of the periodic spikes in speculation, which became a bubble, the joint stock company was outlawed and soon after so was the sub-division of patents. Even when the joint stock company returned to prominence in the nineteenth century and ultimately the law was relaxed, the restriction in so far as it applied to patents continued. Its purpose mutated to the regulation of competition and private Acts were sought, often controversially, to allow more than five and then twelve persons to own the patent. Eventually, almost in passing, the general law was relaxed and the restriction lifted. Private Acts had shown a need and a path and the Patents Amendment Act 1852 followed it.

238 *Select Committee of House of Lords to Consider Bills for Amendment of Law Touching Letters Patent for Inventions. Report, Minutes of Evidence* (1851 HC Papers 486), Vol 18, p 223, Q2673 (p 354).

239 See Patent Law Amendment Bill 1852 (Marked Up to Show Amendments of House of Commons) (1851 HL Papers 3160, Vol 5, p 439), Schedule.

240 William Hindmarch, *Observations on the Defects of the Patent Laws of This country: With Suggestions for the Reform of Them* (London 1851); Thomas Webster, *On the Amendment of the Law and Practice of Letters Patent for Inventions* (2nd Ed, Chapman and Hall 1852) (the first edition had been published at the end of 1851). It was also not addressed in William Spence, *Patentable Invention and Scientific Evidence: With an Introductory Preface* (London 1851) but his reforms were of a very specific nature; and it was not mentioned in the earlier Charles Drewry, *Observations on Points Relating to the Amendment of the Law of Patents* (John Richards 1839).

241 Thomas Turner, *Remarks on the Amendment of The Law of Patents for Inventions* (Frederic Elsworth 1851), p 22.

242 Patent Law Amendment Bill 1852 (Brought from HL) (1852 HC Papers 299), Vol 4, p 1, Schedule.

243 Strangely, the Bill as amended in Committee (see Patent Law Amendment Bill 1852 (As Amended in Committee) (1852 HC Papers 486), Vol 4, p 33) did not include the clause or indeed any clause beyond new clause C (it was new Clause E – 84 LJ 368 (28 June 1852)). However, Thomas Webster, *The New Patent Law: Its History, Objects and Provisions* (Elsworth 1853), p 39 indicated this was when the change was made.

244 HC Deb, 22 March 1855, Vol 137 (3rd), col 947.

7 The specification and its concealment

Introduction

The rise of the specification is one of the totems of patent history. Its origins and development, and the identification of the "first" specification, are something which has been considered and reviewed in the literature. The role of private Acts in this development is acknowledged, but usually only in passing in a wider story.[1] It is not suggested that Parliament, and private Acts, were central to the development of the specification, but that the part they play needs to be given greater weight. While the traditional history[2] remains persistent, namely that a specification was first required in 1712 as a requirement of John Nasmith's grant,[3] it is an idea which in its simple form has to a great extent been debunked for a least a century.

The reason why the watershed of the Nasmith grant remains persistent is, in part, because the nature and role of the specification evolved. Indeed, the history of the "specification" is usually taken to be synonymous with history of what is currently called the "description". There were eventually two specifications[4]: the provisional specification which described the invention only and the complete specification which described the invention, the best mode of performing it and included the claims.[5] The role of the provisional specification changed little after its introduction in 1852,[6] but at that time the complete specification was largely at the same time a requirement to explain how the invention is performed.[7] Yet it was some time before specifications required what is currently considered to be an adequate disclosure.[8]

1 Christine Macleod, *Inventing the Industrial Revolution* (Cambridge 1988), p 49; David Seaborne Davies, "The Early History of the Patent Specification" (1934) 50 *LQR* 86 and 260 at 271–272.

2 It seems to originate with Webster's Reports: Thomas Webster, *Notes on Cases on Letters Patent for Inventions* (Thomas Blenkarn 1844), p 8; also see Sean Bottomley, *The British Patent System During the Industrial Revolution 1700–1852* (Cambridge 2014), p 46 which in turn relies on Christine Macleod, *Inventing the Industrial Revolution* (Cambridge 1988), p 49 where she suggests it became common from that time.

3 Patent No 387.

4 Under the Patents Act 1949 (the provisional specification became the date of filing under the Patents Act 1977).

5 Patents Act 1949, s 4.

6 Patent Law Amendment Act 1852, s 6.

7 Patent Law Amendment Act 1852, s 9.

8 *Report of the Committee Appointed to Inquire into the Working of the Law Relating to Patents for Inventions* (1864 C 3419), Vol 29, p 321 at p x; there was an additional problem in that finding the specification might take a long time and cost a lot of money: Anon, "Article V – Publications of the Commissioners of Patents" (January 1859) 105 *Quarterly Review* 136 at 140.

Any history of specification, including this one, is usually confined to the elements required when it was first changed from being a requirement of grant to a statutory requirement under the Patent Law Amendment Act 1852. The specification therefore has at least the following elements: (a) a disclosure requirement; (b) a writing requirement; (c) a filing requirement; and (d) a sanction. As will be seen Parliament has had a role in many of these requirements and it has affected the approach taken in practice.

The disclosure requirement: "the apprenticeship clause"[9]

The original disclosure requirement was not one of writing, but rather it was a general obligation to teach the art or science. The benefit of teaching others has a very early antecedence. In 1552 Henry Smyth's patent[10] included a reason for the grant as the benefits arising from the new type of glass making,[11] and it was the case that in some grants a condition was included that the patentee employed a certain number of Englishmen to every foreigner.[12] Similarity, an obligation to take or keep apprentices was included in numerous patents granted by Elizabeth,[13] James I,[14] Charles I[15] and Charles II.[16] It is this last clause which has the closest antecedent to a written description.

Before considering the teaching of apprentices as a step in the path towards disclosure it is worth looking at the other link between patents and apprentices: the term of the patent. While it is undeniable that the term of a new patent for invention under the Statute of Monopolies was fourteen years[17] and that the term of apprenticeship was seven years,[18]

---

9 A term coined by David Seaborne Davies, "The Early History of the Patent Specification" (1934) 50 *LQR* 86 and 260 at 104.

10 One of the contenders for the earliest English patent grants: see David Seaborne Davies, "Further Light on the Case of Monopolies" (1932) 49 *LQR* 394 at 396.

11 It reads "a benefite to our subiectes And besides that dyvers of theym maye be sett to worke and get theyr lyvyng and in tyme learne and be hable to make the said glasse them selfe and so frome tyme to tyme thene to instructe thothers in that science and feate": (1552) PR 6 Edw VI, Pt 5, m 26 (Cal Edw VI, Vol 4, p 323).

12 See Roger Heuxtenbury and Bartholomew Verberick (1565) 7 PR Eliz, Pt 5, m 11 (Eliz Pat Cal, Vol 3, No 1199) (No XII) (National Archive: C66/1013) "for every stranger workman they shall keep one person born in the realm as an apprentice").

13 Anthony Becku and John Carre (1567) 9 PR Eliz, Pt 11, m 33 (Eliz Pat Cal, Vol 4, No 929) (Grant XIX) (National Archive: C66/1040) "to instruct fully in the art a convenient number of Englishmen apprenticed to them": also see Edward Wyndham Hulme "On the Consideration of the Patent Grant, Past and Present" (1897) 13 *LQR* 313 at 314.

14 Charles Thynne (1614), PR 12 Jac 1, Pt 2, No 3 (National Archive: C66/2018) ("have voluntarily offered unto us teach and instruct and to permit any the craftmasters. . .in our said Realms").

15 Goyvarts and Le Ferrue's Patent: No 62 (1633) ("keepe one apprentise or servant borne in England"); Bull's Patent: No 63 (1633) ("shall keepe and instructe an apprentice or servant"); Williames and Van Wolfen: Patent No 65 (1633) ("keepe one servant att the least borne in England"); Rotispen's Patent: No 71 (1634) ("keepe an Englishe apprentice or servant").

16 Dupin, De Cardonels and De Gruchy's Patent: No 249 (1686) (teach partners); Clowdesley, Sherrard and Duclen's Patent: No 261 (1688) ("teach an instruct the present wife of him, the said Peter Duclen, being an English woman" and teach his partners).

17 Statute of Monopolies, s 6.

18 Artificers and Apprentices Act 1562 (Statute of Artificers).

the link between these two is only to be presumed.[19] It is clear that Sir Edward Coke[20] was concerned about apprentices in relation to patents[21]:

> It was thought that the times limited by [the Statute of Monopolies] were too long for the private, before the Common wealth should be partaker thereof, and such as served such privileged persons by the space of seven years in making or working the new manufacture (which is the time limited by law of Apprenticehood) must be Apprentices or servant still during the residue of the privilege, by means whereof such numbers of men would not apply themselves thereunto, as should be requisite for the common wealth, after the privilege ended.

This difficulty with disclosure may explain the approach taken in Buck's Patent Act 1651, passed during the Interregnum, which included a specific obligation on Buck to take apprentices during the last seven years of the term:

> **Buck, after seven years, to take Apprentices**
> Provided also, That the said Jeremy Buck and his Assigns, after seven years of the term hereby granted, do and shall take Apprentices, and teach them the Knowledge and Mystery of the said New Invention.

As with many private Acts of this time and later, the Parliamentary record is sparse and it is not clear whether this proviso was offered up by Buck in the original Bill or required by the House of Commons as an amendment.[22] Indeed, even if it were an amendment it might have been championed by Buck himself. What this provision does demonstrate, however, is that the link between the fourteen-year term and apprenticeships may not be as direct as is claimed.

In any event, there was not a clear pattern: other enactments during the Interregnum granted protection over inventions, namely Delicques and Fancault's Ordinance 1643[23] and George Manby's Act 1650, and neither contained provision for apprentices.[24] The former granted exclusivity for only seven years and so the issue of blocking does not arise; but Manby's Act passed only the month before Buck's Bill was introduced and had the same term, but without the apprenticeship requirement. The most likely reason for the difference is that Manby had apprentices at the time and Buck did not. It is apparent Buck's method was still untested when his Act was passed and it never turned out to work.

---

19 MacLeod suggests the period was "not chosen at random" and attributes certain thoughts to Coke: Christine MacLeod, *Inventing the Industrial Revolution: The English Patent System 1660–1800* (Cambridge 1988), p 18; Stephen D White, *Sir Edward Coke and "The Grievances of the Commonwealth": 1621–1628* (North Carolina Press 1979) suggests that Coke may have been against patents of longer than seven years as it would block apprentices (at p 140).

20 Wallace Notestein, Frances Relf and Hartley Simpson, *Commons Debates 1621* (Yale 1935) ('CD 1621'), Vol 2: X's Diary, p 175–176 (7 March 1621).

21 Sir Edward Coke, *The Third Part of the Institutes of the Laws of England* (Flesher 1644), p 184; also see comments of William Noye during the passage of the Bill: CD 1621, Vol 2, X's Diary, p 176 (7 March 1621).

22 Amendments were made: 6 CJ 543 (27 February 1651).

23 Delicques and Fancault's Ordinance 1643.

24 Neither did any of the Scottish Acts of this period: Act in Favour of Colonels Ludovic Leslie and James Scott 1661 [RPS: 1661/1/92] and Act in Favour of James Wemyss, General of Artillery, and Colonels Leslie and Scott 1661 [RPS: 1661/1/200]. However, these two grants conflicted and Leslie and Scott had to disclose the invention within three months and unless it was the same as Wemyss they were entitled to the Parliamentary grant.

Thus, a contemporary account of his (failed) workings refers to numerous partners but never to anyone learning the art.[25] Indeed, this might be said to support the hypothesis as the working was not happening at the time of the Act of Parliament and so there would be a need for some form of compulsion later; although, as Buck never got his invention working, no apprentices would ever have been indentured. In any event, passing on the art to apprentices was not the only method of disclosure as there was also the possibility of providing models.

Whilst patents were granted by Parliament during this period, later there were patents[26] granted by Oliver Cromwell, Lord Protector, in a similar fashion to Royal grants.[27] They did not include apprenticeship clauses however. Following the Restoration, as already mentioned, Charles II continued to grant the occasional patents with clauses requiring some form of apprenticeship. Thus, while Jeremy Buck's patent shows that the disclosure requirement might have been important to Parliament, and further than Parliament *may* have been aware of the blocking problem for newly trained apprentices; it did not lead to any change in practice.

Disclosure requirement: "models"

The patent of Simon Sturtevant, along with his *A Treatise of Metallica*,[28] is widely discussed in the history of the specification.[29] In summary, the indenture[30] which accompanied his patent[31] states that his invention was contained in the Treatise and the annexed Schedules. While this is an attempt to describe an invention it appears, as Hyde Price suggests, to be a prospectus[32] rather than anything like an invention. There were, however, other grants of a similar antiquity which provided that "models or descriptions" had to be produced[33]: Joseph Usher (1612),[34] Richard Barnswell (1612),[35] Edmund Brunt (1614),[36] Charles Thynne and Others (1614)[37]and additionally Edmund Sheffield[38] and

---

25 Dud Dudley, *Mettallum Martis* (London 1665), pp 21–25.

26 The Patent Rolls appear not to exist for much of the Interregnum Commonwealth: see generally: Ralph B Pugh, "The Patent Rolls of the Interregnum" (1950) 23 *Historical Research* 178 (who suggests the Patent Roll may never have actually be enrolled in the first place when the backlog was addressed following the Restoration).

27 Rhys Jenkins, "The Protection of Inventions during the Commonwealth and the Protectorate" (1913) 7 *Notes and Queries* 162.

28 (1612) (STC: 23411); the text is also in William Hyde Price, *The English Patents of Monopoly* (Houghton, Mifflin & Co 1906), p 176 (Appendix S).

29 Edward Wyndham Hulme, "On the Consideration of the Patent Grant Past and Present" (1897) 13 *LQR* 313; David Seaborne Davies, "The Early History of the Patent Specification" (1934) 50 *LQR* 86 and 260 at 271–272; William Hyde Price, *The English Patents of Monopoly* (Houghton, Mifflin & Co 1906), p 108.

30 An indenture was an agreement between the Monarch and the patentee which imposed obligations on the patentee. This could include obligations to take apprentices and so forth.

31 A patent which does not appear on the Patent Roll for some reason.

32 William Hyde Price, *The English Patents of Monopoly* (Houghton, Mifflin & Co 1906), p 108.

33 See David Seaborne Davies, "The Early History of the Patent Specification" (1934) 50 *LQR* 86 and 260 at 268.

34 (1612) PR 10 Jac I, Pt 7, No 10 (National Archive: C66/1949)(which recited "to deliver to our Chauncellor of Englande a perfecte moddell or descripcon").

35 (1612) PR 10 Jac I, Pt 23, No 9 (National Archive: C66/1965) ("Provided alawyes. . .that the said Richard Barnewell doe bring a modell of the said Ingne of pumpes. . .to remayne in some place to be appoynted by the Chauncellor of our Exchequer").

36 (1614) PR 11 Jac I, Pt 11, No 7 (National Archive: C66/1988) ("said Edmund Brunt hath undertaken within one yerye next after the date of these Letters Patent to deliver to our Attorney General a pfett modell or descripcion").

37 (1614) PR 12 Jac I, Pt 2, No 3 (National Archive: C66/2018) ("according to a description thereof left in the hand of Sir Francis Bacon knight our Attorney general").

38 1st Earl of Mulgrave, 3rd Baron Sheffield,

Others (1614).[39] Importantly, "models or descriptions" in this instance is possibly tautologous as models did not at this time necessarily mean three-dimensional representations in miniature, but rather a set of instructions.

In two of the five cases where models were required, there were disputes anticipated between the new patentees and existing patentees. This means that it may have been necessary to distinguish between them in some way[40] and so a model needed to be provided.[41] The models were for identification rather than describing. Importantly, there was no explicit sanction for failing to produce a model and where models intermittently re-appear in Charles I's reign it is still something presented at or before grant by the petitioner rather than a requirement imposed on grant.[42]

A filing requirement for a model appears in only one private Act, namely the Marquis of Worcester's Act 1663, which granted[43] exclusive rights in his water-commanding engine. For the purposes of the current discussion what is important is the proviso:

> And that a Model thereof be delivered by the said Marquess, or his Assignees, to the Lord Treasurer or Commissioners for the Treasury for the time being, at or before the Nine and Twentieth day of September, One thousand six hundred and sixty three; And be by him or them put into the Exchequer, and kept there.

There were amendments made to the Bill, and the obligation to deposit a model was introduced on re-commitment in the House of Commons[44] to ensure that there was a time limit for reducing the invention to perfection and ensuring there was no prejudice to existing inventions.[45] This obligation was similar to Barnswell's grant and other grants. Its purpose was, therefore, similar to that of the earlier period – and it was not related to disclosure as such.

It has been suggested[46] that Worcester never put his invention into effect and so (like Buck) his private Act was a damp squib. Yet some form of "water-commanding engine" existed in Vauxhall from 1663 to 1670[47] during which time it was viewed by a Monsieur de Monconis in 1665[48] and by Cosmo de Medici in 1669.[49] The engine was also described,

39 (1614) PR 12 Jac I, Pt 8, No 29 (National Archive: C66/2024) ("set down in writing and delivered to our Attorney General within the space of one year").

40 David Seaborne Davies, "The Early History of the Patent Specification" (1934) 50 *LQR* 86 and 260 at 269.

41 In this regard compare, Act in Favour of Colonels Ludovic Leslie and James Scott 1661 [RPS: 1661/1/92] and Act in favour of Colonel James Wemyss 1661 [RPS: 1661/1/91].

42 Evans' Patent: No 110 (1637) "to make declaracon and descripcon of the said invencons and benefits thereof".

43 There was no earlier patent and so it was not a confirmation: cf Christine MacLeod, *Inventing the Industrial Revolution: The English Patent System 1660–1800* (Cambridge 1988), p 49. His earlier patent (Patent No 131 (1661)) related to a number of other things: a fast firing pistol, mechanism for the quick release of horses from a carriage, a long-running watch and a method of steering a boat.

44 The proviso was a rider to the Ingrossment. While the text of the proviso is not mentioned in the Parliamentary record, there is mention of a rider being added on re-commitment: 8 CJ 475 (5 May 1663).

45 See order for re-commitment: 8 CJ 470 (13 April 1663).

46 There was a debate about whether it was made in the 1820s: see Anon, "The Steam Engine Actually Constructed and Applied to Practical Purposes" (1827) 6 *Mechanics Magazine* 515.

47 Henry Dicks, *The Life, Times and Scientific Labours of the Second Marquis of Worcester* (London: Bernard Quaritch 1865), p 305.

48 Henry Dicks, *The Life, Times and Scientific Labours of the Second Marquis of Worcester* (London: Bernard Quaritch 1865), pp 263–264; Mons de Sorbiere, *A Voyage to England, containing many things relating to the state of learning, religion, and other curiosities* (trans J Spratt) (London 1709), p 29.

49 Henry Dicks, *The Life, Times and Scientific Labours of the Second Marquis of Worcester* (London: Bernard Quaritch 1865), p 302 (citing Count Lorenzo Magolotti).

albeit in outline, in a short pamphlet[50] and in Worcester's *A Century of Invention*.[51] It has also been suggested that the deposit required by the Act was made[52] but there is no record of this having happened in the official records. Furthermore, his widow tried to make money from the engine demonstrating reliance on the Act.[53] In any event, what is lacking is a consequence should Worcester failed to provide the model, that is a sanction. The only other instance of a petitioner being required to provide a model during this period is Samuel Moreland[54] who had to deposit a model of his original invention within three months (albeit there was unlimited time for lodging any improvement models).[55] As the text of this Bill is lost, it is not clear if there was a sanction for not filing the model.

The sanction

Sir Philip Howard and Francis Watson begin the next chapter in the history of both specifications and private Acts. In 1668[56] they were granted a patent for sheathing hulls with lead.[57] The Company of Painters challenged the patent before the Privy Council[58] and subsequently Howard and Watson petitioned for a private Act. The Act did not extend the original patent (indeed, it did not mention it at all), rather it granted a term of twenty-five years for a described invention.[59] What is significant about this enactment is that during its passage through the House of Commons one of the objections recorded was:

> it does not appear what the invention is, and that it may be said if anyone hereafter does find out any other new invention relating to the better dressing of ships, that this is Sir Philip Howard's invention.[60]

50 This pamphlet was included Henry Dicks, *The Life, Times and Scientific Labours of the Second Marquis of Worcester* (London: Bernard Quaritch 1865), p 559 (Appendix C).

51 It has been republished in numerous forms, one being: John Phin, *An Exact Reprint of the Famous Century of Invention of the Marquis of Worcester* (New York: Industrial Publication Co 1887), Ch 68. A extensively explained version of this short extract is included in Henry Dicks, *The Life, Times and Scientific Labours of the Second Marquis of Worcester* (London: Bernard Quaritch 1865), pp 475–499 (the work is very favourable towards Worcester at every point and so the full explanation may be generous as to what was actually described).

52 Henry Dicks, *The Life, Times and Scientific Labours of the Second Marquis of Worcester* (London: Bernard Quaritch 1865), p 306.

53 Henry Dicks, *The Life, Times and Scientific Labours of the Second Marquis of Worcester* (London: Bernard Quaritch 1865), p 306.

54 Moreland's Pump Bill 1677 (no copy remains).

55 The existence of this obligation is evidenced from Anon [James Ward], *Reasons Offered against Passing Sir Samuel Moreland's Bill* (1677) (Wing R576), paragraph 5.

56 Patent No 158 (1668).

57 It was apparently used widely by the Royal Navy: see John Bulteel, "A Letter Written to the Publisher Concerning a New Way, by an English Manfacture to Preserve the Hull of Ships from the Worm &c" (1673) 8 *Philosophical Transactions* 6192.

58 See Privy Council Register (National Archive: PC2/61, ff 126, 138 and 160–161); mentioned in *Samuel Pepys' Diary*, 23 April 1669; See Howard and Watson's Patent (1667) 11 HPC App. The report is based on Edward Wyndham Hulme, "Privy Council Law and Practice of Letters Patent for Inventions from the Restoration to 1794" (1917) 33 *LQR* 63 at 68.

59 Sometimes misreported as thirty-one years: Basil Henning (Ed), *History of Parliament: The House of Commons 1660–1690* (Secker and Warburg 1983), Vol 2, Entry Philip Howard (1631–1686), p 592 at 593.

60 Basil Henning (Ed), *Parliamentary Diary of Sir Edward Dering Diary* 1670–1673 (Yale 1940), pp 12–13 (the entry also suggests the disclosure is the solution).

Thus, there was a specific concern in the House of Commons regarding the adequate disclosure of Howard's invention which led to the following proviso being included in Howard and Watson's Act 1670:[61]

> Provided alsoe, and bee itt Enacted, that the said S Phillip Howard and Francis Watson shall enter or cause to bee entered in His Maties Court of Excheq^r^ the said Manufacture, Art, or Invention, for the purpose aforesaid, within three moneths to bee accompted from the first day of February, One Thousand Six Hundred and Seventy.[[62]] And in default of such entry to bee made as aforesaid, this Art and everything conteyned to be utterly voyd:

Significantly, there was a requirement on Howard and Watson to file a description (in the Exchequer, rather than Chancery as was later the case) and there is a *sanction* if this is not done.[63] This sets out two of the elements of what was to become the specification requirement. Indeed, when comparing this description to later ones it was quite short, but still longer than that provided by Nasmith over thirty years later[64]:

Nasmith	Howard and Watson
That whereas the common way of fermenting of wash from sugar, molasses, or grain, is and has been by yest gott from the brewers of ale or beer, the said John Naismith ferments the wash from the above subjects by a yest, or what is equivalent to it, gott from the fermented wash it selfe with very little cost, and to as greate if not greater perfection then when done by the common way of fermenting by yest from ale or beer.	they drawe a liquor from any sorte of graine or vegetable of the growth of His Majesties Dominions yeilding spiritt, in which liquor they dissolve bees-waxe, frankincense, turpentine, and seedlack, and call this their lacker, which, togeather with a mixture of linseed oyle, redd lead, white lead, and whyting, they prepare and pay the seames and planks of shipping; over which, for the more certaine securing the sides from the worme, with nailes made of brasse, copper, or tinne, they naile on sheetes or plates of lead or other mettall of the product of his Majesties Dominions, made thinne by a certaine engine or rollers not hitherto vsed for workes of this kind; over all which they lay on their lacker aforesaid, which closeth the seames of the lead or other mettall and preserves the sides of the vessell from fowling, as by the way hitherto vsed shipps have been always lyable to.

Figure 7.1 Comparison of Nasmith's and Howard and Watson's specifications.

61 Note that Christine MacLeod, *Inventing the Industrial Revolution: The English Patent System 1660–1800* (Cambridge 1988) incorrectly states they had six weeks to file the written description (at p 51). As Royal Assent was on 6 March 1671 there were 55 days left to file the description after this date and so it is not clear from what date the six weeks (42 days) is calculated.

62 This was based on the old calendar so it was 1 February 1671 in the modern calendar: see p 31.

63 This contrasts with the Clowdesly, Sherard and Duclen's Patent 1688 (No 261) where there was an obligation to "deliver unto us an account in writing of the whole mistrey of lustrating or dressing the said sile, so that a master weaver may on pusall of the said account be able effectively to dress and lustrate any the silke afore-mentioned yet not to do the same during the continuance in force of this our grant contrary to purport or effect thereof") (at 5) and the patent would continue in force notwithstanding that it was not deposited (p 8) (in other words it only had to be deposited afterwards where there was no detriment for failing to do so).

64 A further complication about fixing the obligation is there was an increasing number of patents with some form of description over this period, albeit not a specification. Bennet Woodcroft in his *Appendix to the Reference Index of Patents of Invention* (London 1855) abstracts those patents from 1617 to 1745 (i.e. the last such patent) which have some description of the invention. While the quality of the description varies greatly some are better than Nasmith's,

In many respects, therefore, the first requirement to file a description with an attendant consequence for failing to do so was provided, by way of proviso, to Howard and Watson's Act 1670. The description is still wholly inadequate and does not properly disclose the invention (in particular what was the "certaine engine"), but it was no worse than many that followed in the first half of the eighteenth century. In contrast to earlier examples, such as the five early patents requiring models to be deposited and the Marquis of Worcester's Act 1663, there was a *sanction* for not filing the description so as to make the grant void. Indeed, Nasmith's 1711 patent did not include a sanction of this sort and one did not appear for another dozen years.[65] While it is not possible to suggest that Howard and Watson's Act required the "original" specification – as the debate over what that this requires is controversial and it clearly was not enabling – it contains more of the necessary elements than the much later Nasmith's patent and it *may* have "paved the way" to a more regular call for specifications later.[66]

What is probably more surprising is that the requirement to file a detailed description did not continue when other patentees obtained subsequent private Acts. Thus, neither William Walcot or Thomas Savery, both of whom obtained Acts to extend their patents,[67] needed to provide a description[68] of the invention despite the fact that Savery was said to have "greatly Improved the said Invention"[69] and Walcot's Act allowed him exclusive rights over the "Improvements"[70] as well as that granted by the original patent.[71]

Lombe's Silk Engines Act 1731

A further significant development in the requirement to file a specification is attributed to the Act obtained by Sir Thomas Lombe.[72] In 1732, he petitioned Parliament requesting an additional fourteen years of protection for his patented invention as much of that term had

---

others worse. It can be broken down as follows: the first patent included to Howard and Watsons (No 154) so 1617 to 1667 (36 patents of 154 have some form of description); until Nasmith's so 1667 to 1711 (No 387) (35 of 233 patents); Nasmith's Patent until 1733 (No 543) (55 of 156 patents) and from 1733 to the last one in 1745 (No 613) (6 of 70). During the latter two periods, the requirement to file a specification started to appear in patent grants.

65 No 454 (1723). Indeed, it having this effect appears not to have been confirmed by the courts until *Ex Parte Koops' Patent* 1 HPC 423; 6 Ves J 598 (31 ER 1215); 1 Ves J Supp 630 (34 ER 954).

66 In some way as Garill's dispute did in 1664: see David Seaborne Davies, "The Early History of the Patent Specification" (1934) 50 *LQR* 86 and 260 at 274.

67 Walcot's Patent Act 1694; Thomas Savery's Act 1698. Some Scottish legislation extended the patent but did not refer to improvements: Act in Favour of Mr Thomas Rome and Partners 1701 [RPS: A1700/10/56] others simply gave the exclusive right without a pre-existing patent: Act in Favour of Mr George Campbell 1705 [RPS: A1705/6/48].

68 Thomas Savery did print a description however: see Thomas Savery, "An Account of Mr. Tho. Savery's Engine for Raising Water by the Help of Fire" (1699) 21 *Philosophical Transactions* 228.

69 Thomas Savery's Act 1698; the improvements are more expressly claimed in the Scottish Act: Act in Favour of Mr. James Smith 1700 [RPS: A1700/10/218].

70 Walcot's Patent Act 1694.

71 As to improvements see pp 59–63.

72 Christine MacLeod, *Inventing the Industrial Revolution: The English Patent System 1660–1800* (Cambridge 1988), p 49 suggests that the "immediate precedent. . .perhaps" for standardising the practice of filing a specification might have been Lombe's Silk Engines Act 1731.

lapsed before his invention was perfected.[73] Unusually there was a vigorous debate on the petition[74] and it was eventually referred to committee[75] who agreed to the extension of the term being granted.[76] The Bill[77] then faced opposition from silk manufacturers,[78] which led to the King recommending that the Bill be changed from extending the patent to a prize.[79] Thus, Lombe did not get his patent extended but rather a prize and, further, he was required to enable two persons to make a perfect model of the engine "to secure and perpetuate the art of making the like engines for the advantage of the kingdom".[80] This proposal to disclose the invention to certain persons appointed by Parliament[81] was in the original Bill[82] and so it is reasonable to assume that it was included by the petitioner and not added by Parliament.

It appears, therefore, that by this stage there was a realisation by patentees that some form of disclosure might be required. Lombe's original proposal was quite different to that which had been adopted in prerogative patents (albeit infrequently) over the previous decade.[83] He offered an inspection of the machine and for the inspectors to make the model[84] rather than a deposit of a description by the prospective patentee. Nevertheless, the Bill was controversial enough to encourage the King to resolve the matter. It may have been the need for some form of disclosure was discussed with the law officers by those opposing the Bill, but there is nothing in the records supporting this position. The change in the time of disclosure results from it becoming a prize rather than an exclusive right, as the money arrived up front rather than during the patent's term. It is therefore difficult to see how the requirement in the Act could be seen as a tipping point towards an obligation to file a specification.[85] The obligation

---

73 The petition is summarised at: 11 February 1732 (21 CJ 782) and John Torbuck, *Collection of Parliamentary Debates* (London 1741), Vol 10, pp 101–102. *A Brief Statement of the Case of the Machine Erected at Derby* (i.e. the Case in Support) is included in *Harper Collection of Private Bills*, Vol 9, Bill No 31.

74 John Torbuck, *Collection of Parliamentary Debates* (London 1741), Vol 10, pp 101–109.

75 Where witnesses were heard: 21 CJ 795 (11 February 1732) (summarises the witnesses' evidence).

76 21 CJ 798 (14 February 1732).

77 For the original Bill (for the extension of term) see *Harper's Collection of Private Bills*, Vol 9, Bill No 31.

78 21 CJ 840 (9 March 1732) and 21 CJ 842 (10 March 1732). *The Case of the Silk Throwers* and *The Case of the Manufacturers of Woollen, Linnen, Mohair and Cotton Yarn* are both included in *Harper's Collection of Private Bills*, Vol 9, Bill No 31.

79 21 CJ 846 (14 March 1732).

80 Thomas Lombe's Act 1731, s 2.

81 Albeit in its original form it was not to be disclosed until after the expiry of the extended term.

82 *Harper's Collection of Private Bills*, Vol 9, Bill No 31.

83 The number of times a specification was required is, surprisingly, open to different interpretations. David Seaborne Davies, "The Early History of the Patent Specification" (1934) 50 *LQR* 86 and 260, 89 n 10 and 11, lists twenty-four patents with the requirement (Patent Nos 387, 393, 404, 408, 409, 411, 416, 417, 418, 454, 484, 488, 490, 495, 497, 503, 505, 513, 514, 517, 518, 526, 528, 539 (24 of 156 patents (387 to 543)). Different figures were produced by Sean Bottomley, *The British Patent System During the Industrial Revolution 1700–1852* (Cambridge 2014), p 46 (27 of 156; differences being, Patent Nos 401, 422, 531 and 543, but not 454). His figures were based on those patents with something being filed between Patent 387 and 543 (i.e. end of 1733) as listed in Bennett Woodcroft, *Reference Index of Patents of Invention 1617–1852* (London 1862), p 3 and 4. However, it could be complicated further as during this period there were 55 patents with some form of description often very inadequate, but sometimes better than that in Nasmith (as included in the Bennett Woodcroft, *Appendix to the Reference Index of Patents of Invention* (London: Great Seal Patent Office 1855)). Thus, over the period there were 82 of 156 patents with some form of description.

84 The model still exists. It has been removed from the Tower of London and is now held by the Science Museum: Science Museum, SCM – Textiles Machinery Ob No: 1857–290/3.

85 Indeed, over the following decade 37 specifications were ordered for 51 patents: Sean Bottomley, *The British Patent System during the Industrial Revolution 1700–1852* (Cambridge 2014), p 46.

in Lombe's Act was different from that required by the law officers as it retained some form of secrecy. It could be no more than a reminder of Parliamentary concerns.

The quality of disclosures remained very poor throughout the eighteenth century despite their purpose becoming clearer as the century progressed towards *Liardet v Johnson*.[86] Importantly for our purposes, Liardet's patent was extended by an Act of Parliament, Liardet's Cement Patent Act 1776, which included a requirement to file a specification[87] as were other Acts which encompassed improvements.[88] Strangely, despite such a provision, the House of Commons remained ambivalent as to the need to disclose inventions. When Henry Phillips sought a prize for his insect powder in 1781 it was, unusually, dealt with as an individual Bill rather than as part of the general appropriation.[89] The Bill provided Phillips with payment of £500 without disclosing the invention at all, but he was entitled to a further £3,000 when the invention was disclosed *and* certified as working.[90] This Bill was defeated in the House of Lords and the second Bill four years later[91] had only a payment of £1,000 upon certification.[92] It too was defeated in the Lords. The limited records of the first Bill do not indicate any concern about paying £500 for an *undisclosed* invention. While the second payment explicitly requires disclosure, the payment itself is for showing it to work – utility a requirement which had an chequered history in patent law.[93]

Even though there was clearly a requirement to file a specification after the grant of a prerogative patent, the extent of the obligation remained unclear for many years, despite decisions of the court in *Arkwright v Mordaunt* and *Arkwright and Nightingale*,[94] *Boulton & Watt v Bull*[95] and *Turner v Winter*.[96] Even into the nineteenth century, while the notional standard might be stated, the application of that standard was far from clear.[97] Yet the improvement in the standards of disclosure, so it became an enabling disclosure, may have become clearer when later private Acts tried to excuse proprietors from the obligation to file a specification in the first place – as it was only worth concealing a useful disclosure.

---

86   (1778) 1 HPC 195; Carp PC 35, 1 WPC 52; (1780) 1 Y&C 527 (62 ER 1000); even if that was not the turning point it was once thought to be: Sean Bottomley, *The British Patent System During the Industrial Revolution 1700–1852* (Cambridge 2014), pp 89–92; John Adams and Gwen Averley, "The Patent Specification: The Role of Liardet v Johnson" (1986) 7 *J Legal History* 156; also see Frank Kelsall, "Liardet versus Adam" (1984) 27 *Architectural History* 118.

87   Liardet's Cement Patent Act 1776, s 6.

88   See pp 61–3.

89   See Chapter 8.

90   Ingrossment: HL/PO/JO/10/2/56.

91   Ingrossment: HL/PO/JO/10/2/59B.

92   The experiments had been disclosed to Parliament by this stage: HL/PO/JO/10/7/660.

93   There are many clear statements of the courts requiring utility, but some where it is not required: see *Lewis v Marling* (1829) 2 HPC 81; 4 C & P 52 (172 ER 604) (Parke J stated "the question of [the patent's] utility has been sometimes left to the jury, I think the condition imposed by the statute has been complied with when it has been proved to be new").

94   *Arkwright v Mordaunt* (1781) 1 HPC 215; 1 WPC 59 and *Arkwright v Nightingale* (1785) 1 HPC 221; 1 WPC 60.

95   (1795) 1 HPC 369; ; 2 Blackstone (H) 488 (126 ER 664; 3 Ves J 140 (30 ER 937).

96   (1787) 1 HPC 321; 1 TR 602.

97   William Carpmael, *The Law of Patents for Inventions familiarly explained, for the use of inventors and. Patentees* (London: J Wrightman 1832), p 23; John Adams and Gwen Averley, "The Patent Specification: The Role of Liardet v Johnson" (1986) 7 *J Legal History* 156, 167–171. The 1829 Committee even asked numerous witnesses whether specifications were drafted to conceal the invention: *Report from the Select Committee on the Law Relative to Patents for Invention* (1829 HC Papers 332), Vol 3, p 415, see for instance, evidence of John Taylor (p 9) and John Farey (p 28).

Patent specifications are not what they seem

The need to keep certain inventions secret for reasons of national security remains part of British patent law[98] and the concealment of such inventions dates back to the nineteenth century.[99] There are, however, earlier examples. The Scottish Parliament enacted James Wemyss' Act 1648 to protect his war inventions and to preserve their secrecy.[100] The current discussion is not concerned with war inventions, but the protection of industrial secrets from disclosure to foreigners *using the patent system*. There are some instances of early[101] patents including provisos to stop the invention being disclosed to foreigners and the Lustring Company's original patent restricted disclosure until after the expiry of the patent.[102] However, it was not until the late eighteenth century, when the requirement to file a specification was routine, that Parliament became involved.

It appears that Joseph Booth was the first inventor who tried to protect his invention from "foreigners" by restricting its disclosure. He invented a machine and a chemical composition used in the process of making cloth.[103] He petitioned Parliament on the basis that if he was obliged to file a specification, as required by his patent, his invention would become available to foreigners and this would mean he would not be able to supply products to those foreign countries, which would disadvantage the trade into the kingdom.[104] When the committee examined the petition, witnesses came forward explaining how specifications were copied and taken to foreign parts to work the invention, with one witness saying that most specifications were copied by foreigners.[105] This meant that the allegations in the preamble that the description if enrolled would be obtained by "foreign agents and emissaries" transmitted to "foreign countries" so that foreigners could make the invention before British subjects were proved.[106] Thus, his private Act (Booth's Patent Act 1792) permitted him to file his specification, but directed that it would be sealed from view only accessible by order of the Lord Chancellor.[107] While it is clearly true that foreigners could obtain patent specifications once they were enrolled, there does not appear to be anything special about Joseph Booth's invention which made it more susceptible to "foreign agents". The comments and concerns could equally have applied to any other invention.

The first attempt at a general law

Soon after Booth's Act reached the statute book, a public Bill[108] was proposed by Scope Bernard MP,[109] who had also presented Booth's private Bill in the previous year.[110] The Rights

---

98 Patents Act 1977, ss 22 and 23.
99 Patents for Inventions Act 1859; see more generally, Thomas O'Dell, *Inventions and Secrecy: A History of Secret Patents in the United Kingdom* (Clarendon 1994).
100 Act in Favour of Colonel James Wemyss 1661 [RPS: 1661/1/91]
101 Beale's Patent: No 32 (1625); also see David Seaborne Davies, "The Early History of the Patent Specification" (1934) 50 *LQR* 86 and 260 at 105.
102 See p 109 fn 63.
103 Patent No 1,888 (1792).
104 A summary of the petition is at: 47 CJ 499 (5 March 1792).
105 A summary of the evidence is at: 47 CJ 559 (16 March 1792).
106 Booth's Patent Act 1792, recital (2); confirmation of proof: Committee Report: 47 CJ 721 (23 April 1792).
107 Booth's Patent Act 1792, ss 1 and 2.
108 Rights of Patentees Bill 1793 (House of Lords Sessional Papers, Vol 1).
109 With John Pitt and Sir John Ingilby.
110 As to requiring MP's to present private Bills see pp 12–13.

of Patentee's Bill 1793 would have enabled any person to include in their petition a request to keep the specification closed until the expiry of the patent; provided the petitioner could demonstrate that enrolling a specification would be injurious to the patentee and to the trade of the kingdom. While the proposal ultimately failed, it was not (unlike the later 1820 Bill) something which was out of keeping with prevailing thinking in Parliament. It did not fail because it was contrary to the "entire jurisprudential basis of the British patent system".[111] The Bill was passed by the House of Commons and got past a Second Reading in the House of Lords, but was dismissed during committee stage.[112] As there is no reporting of debates, this may even have been no more than managing Parliamentary business[113] as Parliament's prorogation was within a fortnight of the order.[114] It would have been strange, but not unprecedented, for it to be dismissed from committee because of an objection to the policy; it would have been more appropriate to dismiss it at Second Reading or wait to challenge it on Third Reading.[115] Put simply it is probable that the Bill was simply not considered important enough to warrant Parliamentary time in the dying days of Parliament and nothing more.

Furthermore, if the Bill had been enacted it would not have changed the fundamental nature of patent law rather its emphasis. A specification would still be required, all that would have changed was the time of disclosure. Thus, inventions would be disclosed at the end of the patent term rather than close to the beginning: something obtained by the Lustring Company in their patent and proposed by Lombe in his Bill. Indeed, Booth's single private Act, if it had been made general at that stage, might have delayed many inventions by a generation as improvements and follow-on inventions would have to wait: a delay which could even have continued to this day.

Koops' Petition

When Matthias Koops petitioned Parliament in 1801[116] he used very similar language to Booth noting how filing a specification would enable foreigners to use the invention whereas British subjects (other than himself) could not. He made particular mention of France, with whom Britain was at war, exporting his products to America. The petition was referred to a committee whose report was printed[117] and, once more, a number of witnesses explained how the enrolling of specifications led to them being copied and the inventions being worked abroad to the detriment of British industry. Indeed, particular mention was made of the *Repertory of Arts and Manufactures* which had started publishing

---

111 See suggestion of Sean Bottomley, *The British Patent System during the Industrial Revolution 1700–1852* (Cambridge 2014), p 187.

112 39 LJ 739 (10 June 1793); committee was postponed three months (after expected prorogation).

113 Delaying Second Reading or committee to after prorogation was by the eighteenth and century the usual way of rejecting a Bill: Thomas Erskine May, *A Treatise upon the Law Privileges, Proceedings and Usage of Parliament* (1st Ed, Charles Knight & Co 1844), pp 277–278.

114 It was prorogued on 21 June 1793.

115 See p 15.

116 A summary of the petition is at: 56 CJ 173 (16 March 1801); also see *Parliamentary Register*, 16 March 1801, Vol 14, pp 394–395; a petition to incorporate was made a few days later 56 CJ 204–205 (20 March 1801); there was earlier similar incorporation petition from Koops presented: 55 CJ 635–636 (11 June 1800); Favourable Report 55 CJ 647 (13 June 1800); a Bill received First Reading: Koops Papermaking Patent Bill 1800.

117 *Report on Mr Koops' Petition: Respecting His Invention for Making Paper from Various Refuse Materials* (1801 HC Papers 55) Vol 3, p 127.

specifications in 1794.[118] The report was favourable, suggesting a Bill be introduced including the secrecy clause.[119] When that Bill was in committee it was amended[120]; however it is not clear whether the provisions on secrecy were removed or if they were even included in the Bill as introduced.[121] In any event, in *ex parte Koops*,[122] when Koops subsequently tried to persuade the court to waive the requirement to file a specification mention was made by Eldon LC of the refusal by Parliament to sanction it a year earlier.[123]

Keeping it quiet

It was a little under a decade before the next patentees petitioned Parliament to try to keep their specification secret from foreigners.[124] Two further petitions were lodged for the same purpose during the 1812–1813 Session. The first was James Lee who expressed similar concerns to those of Koops stating that if he had to enrol a petition it would enable foreign manufacturers to increase their advantage and damage British subjects. The evidence before the committee once more turned on the *Repertory of Arts and Manufactures*. James Poole, who worked for the Attorney General at the Patent Office, agreed that the publication enabled a "very early and general knowledge of our inventions abroad"[125] and John Pensam, a conveyancer, gave evidence that the publication was "considerably circulated" on the Continent and it was used to provide foreigners with early information about inventions[126] and finally the committee was referred to Joseph Booth's earlier petition (but not that of Koops).[127] The Bill was criticised on Second Reading, including by Sir Robert Peel,[128] but it still passed the Commons. Thus, once more, the publication of specifications was not seen by Parliament as a social good, but the converse, a way of transmitting knowledge away from Britain to foreigners (and worst of all the French with whom Britain was at war).

The Bill was resisted on Second Reading in the House of Lords by Lord Lauderdale who objected in principle to secret specifications.[129] Yet two leading lawyers, Lord Redesdale[130] and Lord Eldon LC, took the view that while there were difficulties with the Bill, it was wrong to penalise an individual who had worked so hard. Accordingly, the Bill passed

---

118 *Report on Mr Koops' Petition: Respecting His Invention for Making Paper from Various Refuse Materials* (1801 HC Papers 55) Vol 3, p 127 at p 1.

119 *Parliamentary Register*, 12 May 1801, Vol 14, p 260; 56 CJ 347(4 May 1801).

120 56 CJ 482 (1 June 1801).

121 There were amendments made in the Commons Committee Report: 56 CJ 482 (1 June 1801), but not in the Lords: Committee, Counsel Heard and Reported without Amendment: 43 LJ 338 (23 June 1801).

122 (1802) 6 Ves J 599 (31 ER 1215).

123 Barbara Henry, *The Development of the Patent System in Britain, 1829–51* (Unpublished Ph.D., Queen's University 2012), p 74 n 26 suggests that it is a reference to the Treason Indemnity Bill. Her reference is to a comment in a debate on 19 June 1801 (*Parliamentary Register*, 19 June 1801, Vol 15, p 680 (comment of Lord Thurlow). It is clear from the Journal (43 LJ 302) that the Bill being debated is the Indemnity Bill 1801 (1801 HC Papers 87), Vol, p 231. The Bill relates to the release of traitors and had nothing to do with specifications and so it must have been referring to Koops own Bill or Act.

124 Petition of James Browell, James Jack and Thomas Lermitte: 64 CJ 15 (31 January 1809).

125 *Report in Petition of James Lee* (1813 HC Paper 67), Vol 3, p 393 at p. 7.

126 *Report in Petition of James Lee* (1813 HC Paper 67), Vol 3, p 393 at p. 7.

127 *Report in Petition of James Lee* (1813 HC Paper 67), Vol 3, p 393 at p. 7.

128 *Morning Post*, 23 March 1813, p 2 (the newspaper report mentions who objected to the Bill but not why).

129 *The Times*, 16 May 1813, p 3.

130 Lord Redesdale had been the Lord Chancellor of Ireland between 1802 and 1806 (and he was the father of the later, Lord Chairman).

Second Reading and, whilst it was extensively amended in the Lords,[131] the most significant amendment was that the secrecy was only to last for seven years (rather than the full fourteen). Accordingly, James Lee eventually obtained his Act enabling him to deliver the specification to the Lord Chancellor and for it to be kept under seal for seven years after the passing of the Act.[132] The second petitioner, John Vancouver, raised similar concerns about improper uses of his specification in his petition[133] and, unfortunately there is little other evidence about the arguments he raised. Nevertheless, his Bill was passed by the Commons[134] but it did not progress in the Lords[135] probably due to the shortage of Parliamentary time.

There were two further private Bills seeking to maintain the secrecy of an invention. James Lee petitioned for a second Bill to incorporate *and* to keep a specification secret in 1816.[136] Once more this passed the House of Commons, but was defeated on Third Reading in the House of Lords. It was Lord Lauderdale opposing the Bill once more, but this time both on the grounds of the secret specification and on the Bill being contrary to the Bubble Act,[137] and he won the division.[138] Nevertheless, Eldon LC was again in favour of the Bill.[139] Strangely, the political support of the Lord Chancellor seems at odds with statements he made in court.[140] In *Re Lacy's Patent* decided in 1816, Eldon LC stated:[141]

> Mr Lee's case was a very peculiar one: it was for securing to the State, in a time of war, the benefit of a most important discovery. If Mr Lacy could make out that the State was to be benefited by his invention in any peculiar way, as in the case of preparing hemp and flax, it might be doubtful whether he might not have a secret specification. His lordship was of the opinion, however, that the Legislature would pause a long time before they passed such an act in the future; and he thought he might venture to say, that if Mr Lacy were to apply for such an act he would not procure it.

Thus, it appears that Lord Eldon was firmly of the view that it was not the court's role to grant secrecy and Parliament had proved reluctant to do so. The final attempt to get private legislation to keep a specification secret was by John Bradbury in 1818. His invention was an anti-forgery device and so there was some logic in trying to keep the specification secret

---

131 The amendments are set out at: 49 LJ 471–472 (2 June 1813); 68 CJ 614–615 (28 June 1813).

132 Lee's Hemp and Flax Preparation Act 1813, ss 1 and 5.

133 Petition: 68 CJ 308 (26 May 1814); see Ingrossment: HL/PO/JO/10/2/88C.

134 69 CJ 405 (29 June 1814).

135 Its first reading: 49 LJ 1023 (29 June 1814); Parliament prorogued on 30 July 1816.

136 Lee's Patent Bill 1816 (Ingrossment: HL/PO/JO/10/2/90B).

137 *The Times*, 29 June 1816, p 2; the numbers of the division were not included in the Lords Journal. However, *The Times* reports it as 4 peers in favour and 4 against.

138 But only because on an equal division the motion is carried under the ancient rule ("Semper praefumitur pro Negante": 51 LJ 798 (28 June 1816); also see Thomas Erskine May, *A Treatise upon the Law Privileges, Proceedings and Usage of Parliament* (1st Ed, Charles Knight & Co 1844), p 215.

139 *The Times*, 29 June 1816, p 2.

140 Apparently applications to keep the specification secret were frequently made, but usually unsuccessfully, according to Thomas Webster, *Notes on Cases on Letters Patent for Inventions* (Thomas Blenkarn 1844), p 27.

141 (1816) 1 HPC 681; 29 *Repertory of Arts & Manufactures* (2d) 250; (1843) Carpmael's PC 353; in the same judgment he suggests that about 20,000 patents had been granted and an eighteen-month filing time had only been allowed two or three times. This was a gross exaggeration: during George III's reign (started 1761) to the date of the judgment (1816) there were a little over 3,000 patents granted; and it had been allowed twice (Booth's Patent Act 1792 and Lee's Hemp and Flax Preparation Invention Act 1813).

to ensure that it could not be "cracked".[142] Once more, in the Lords, after passing the Commons, Lord Lauderdale opposed the principle of the Bill on Second Reading[143] and the Bill did not pass.[144]

Thus it seems that keeping specifications secret was something with which the House of Commons was content. Vancouver's Bill, Lee's Second Bill and Bradbury's Bill all passing the House of Commons albeit with some dissent. However, it was Lord Lauderdale in the House of Lords who was central to the opposition to any Bill of this nature. He was successful in opposing the Bills in all but one case, namely Lee's Hemp and Flax Preparation Invention Act 1813. What is clear is that it was far from a generally accepted view in Parliament that disclosure was central to patent law, rather there was a general rule from which there could be exceptions.

Secrecy goes public

In any event, the idea of keeping specifications secret moved, albeit unsuccessfully, from private Bills to general public legislation. In June 1820 two Bills were introduced to reform patents: the first by John Curwen and Thomas Creevy[145]; and the second by Henry Wrottesley.[146] The Curwen and Creevy Bill was intended to provide a system of examination by technical men, called Commissioners, who would provide a warrant to inventors to perfect their invention before having to file the patent (a sort of priority system). While the Bill still required the enrolment of a specification there was to be a strict rule prohibiting it being copied. Such copies could only be made following a judicial order. The Wrottesley Bill was more explicit in that it appears to have followed the model of Lee's Hemp and Flax Preparation Invention Act 1813 and its successor. It directed that the specification be enrolled in the High Court of Chancery and closed with access only being granted after the patent has expired. There were to be some limited exceptions, such as a judicial order and the law officers granting access where infringement is alleged.

These were, therefore, developments of the Lee's model to ensure and prevent piracy, particularly by foreigners. Strong objection was raised to the proposal from those involved in the patent system[147] on the grounds it would hinder the progress of science as third parties might spend time repeating the (sealed and secret) work of the patentee.[148] Indeed, these concerns were sufficient to lead Curwen and Creevy to remove the restriction on copying when a similar Bill was introduced in the following session.[149] While patentees still considered

142 The utility of the invention was questioned in the House of Commons, but not the idea of keeping it secret: *The Times*, 27 May 1818, p 2; further, the evidence before the committee was largely about the utility of the invention: *Report from the Committee on Mr. Bradbury's Petition Relative to Machinery for Engraving and Etching* (1818 HC Papers 328), Vol 3, p 361.
143 *The Times*, 6 June 1818, p 2.
144 It was however printed: John Bradbury's Bill 1818 (1818 HL Papers 100), Vol 188, p 485.
145 Patents Bill 1820 (1820 HC Papers 181), Vol 1, p 277.
146 Letters Patent Specification Bill 1820 (1820 HC Papers 184), Vol 1, p. 285.
147 See Anon, "On the Proposed Alteration in the Laws Relative to Patents" (1820) 1 *London Journal of Arts and Science* 358; this view appears to have continued among the profession see Anon, "Should Specifications be Concealed?" (1840) 2 *Inventors' Advocate* (No 22) 1
148 See "On the Proposed Alteration in the Laws Relative to Patents" (1820) 1 *London Journal of Arts and Science* 358 at 363 and 365.
149 Patentees Protection Bill 1821 (1821 HC Papers 17), Vol 1, p 21.

seeking private legislation to keep their specification secret,[150] never again did any get as far as petitioning Parliament[151] for a private Bill.[152] Nevertheless, the idea of following the French law[153] and allowing specifications to be kept secret in certain cases during the term of the patent was repeatedly mooted with witnesses before the 1829 committee[154] with a somewhat mixed response. The idea was not resurrected in any of the Bills in the 1830s.

It appears that private legislation might, potentially, have led to the disclosure of the invention coming at the end of the patent term, rather than at the beginning. Had Lord Lauderdale not opposed these sorts of private Bills so successfully then more would have been enacted (and other patentees encouraged to apply). This in turn might have led to one of the 1820 Bills progressing and secrecy becoming more usual and, eventually, the disclosure moving until after the patent had expired. Indeed, it could have changed the very nature of the disclosure made. While this may seem fanciful now, there was support in principle for these sorts of private Bills from Lord Redesdale and Lord Eldon, two leading judicial figures of their age. It was the economist, Lauderdale, who persuaded a largely uninterested House of their evil.[155] Once the nature of the specification and its public nature was confirmed there was one final role of private Acts, namely saving patentees who missed the deadline.

Late specifications

The obligation to file the specification was routine from the 1730s and universal from the 1740s. It was confirmed in *ex parte Koops*[156] that the time for filing the specification could not be extended and if a longer time were needed it was proper to ask the law officers in advance of the grant. This hard and fast rule meant that where a specification was not filed on time the patent was void. Accordingly, if a patentee was late filing the specification the only remedy was to seek assistance from Parliament. There are two instances of private Acts being used to extend the time for filing a specification. The first was in 1849 when Joshua Westhead enrolled his specification five days after the deadline due to "inadvertence and wrong information"[157] and the second was in 1851 when John Laird filed the specification a day late which was due to the inadvertence of an employee.[158] In both cases, it appears that Parliament was sympathetic to their problems and granted them a private Act to allow

---

150 See John Badams' Notice 1825: *London Gazette*, 6 September 1825 (Issue 18173, p 1635).

151 Some petitions requesting law reform included the suggestion for a provision to restrict the disclosure of specifications: Thomas Morton: 81 CJ 309 (1 May 1826) and Appendix to Votes and Proceedings, 1826, pp 498–499 (No 761); John Birkinshaw: 84 CJ 187 (31 March 1829); Appendix to Votes and Proceedings, 1829, pp 1213–1214 (No 2,839).

152 Eventually, the Patents for Inventions Act 1859 enabled patents relating to munitions of war to be secretly enrolled but that was on the direction of the Secretary of State.

153 Law Relative to Useful Discoveries, and to the Means of Ensuring the Property Thereof, to Those Who Are Acknowledged to Be Authors of the Same (Law of 7 January 1791, No 308)), art 11 (a translation was included in the report: see *Report from the Select Committee on the Law Relative to Patents for Invention* (1829 HC Papers 332), Vol 3, p 415 at p 223).

154 See *Report from the Select Committee on the Law Relative to Patents for Invention* (1829 HC Papers 332), Vol 3, p 415, evidence of Mark Brunel (p 40); John Taylor (p 10); Arthur Aikin (p 44); Francis Abbott (p 65); William Newton (p 69); Samuel Morton (p 91); Samuel Clegg (p 96); John Millington (p 99); Holdsworth (p 124 and 125); Hawkins (p 130).

155 On the basis that only eight peers voted in relation to Lee's Patent Bill 1816 (his second Bill).

156 (1802) 6 Ves J 599 (31 ER 1215).

157 Westhead's Patent Act 1849, recital (3).

158 Laird's Patent Act 1851, recital (2).

them to file their specification late without invalidating the patent. Indeed, this presents an instance of Parliament addressing the problem soon after it was identified. The Patent Law Amendment Act 1852 fixed the deadline for filing the complete specification at six months,[159] but contrary to the earlier practice it was held by the courts that extensions were possible.[160] Indeed, soon afterwards the general law was amended once more by the Patent Law Act 1853[161] to allow the Lord Chancellor to grant a one-month extension where the default "has arisen from Accident, and not from the Neglect or wilful Default of the Patentee". It took less than four years for Parliament to address the problem identified by private Acts.[162]

The role of disclosure

The idea that the grant of patent, at least sometimes, involved some requirement to teach the invention is old. It is also something in respect of which Parliament played a role in normalising – when private Acts were granted in the seventeenth century (and later), requirements were imposed to describe the invention. Indeed, the first time a description was *required* by Parliament there was a more substantial[163] disclosure provided than when it was later requested by the law officers. What has been shown, however, is that while eventually by the 1830s the requirement for a disclosure of the invention was central[164] there was no central progressive movement in Parliament towards requiring disclosure.[165] The reality is far less Whiggish, as it is clear that Parliament, or at least the House of Commons, seems to have been quite willing to restrict – or at least postpone – the disclosure entirely. Parliament played a mixed role in the history of the specification – but its role should be given far greater emphasis than it has ever been given to date.

---

159 Patent Law Amendment Act 1852, s 9.
160 *Simpson and Isaac's Patent* (1853) 6 HPC 899; 21 LT 81.
161 Patent Law Act 1853 (c. 115), s 6.
162 The allowance for the late filing of specifications became of relevance when patentees sought to pay renewal fees late.
163 Yet still inadequate.
164 As suggested by Robert Burrell and Catherine Kelly, "Parliamentary Rewards and the Evolution of the Patent System" (2015) 74 *Cam LJ* 423 at 445.
165 Contrary to the hypothesis put forward by Robert Burrell and Catherine Kelly, "Parliamentary Rewards and the Evolution of the Patent System" (2015) 74 *Cam LJ* 423 at 432–435.

8 The prolongation of patents

Introduction

The early patent system was not constrained by a specific term. In the sixteenth century, Queen Elizabeth routinely granted licences or patents over inventions or technology for a period of twenty years or more[1] and, on occasion, a patent would be renewed or even reissued to someone new. The classic example is the monopoly over playing cards, which was the basis of *The Case of Monopolies (Darcy v Allin)*.[2] The patent was first granted to Ralph Bowes and Thomas Bedingfield in July 1576[3] and reissued to them again in 1578[4] and then to Ralph Bowes alone in 1588.[5] Bowes died before his patent expired and so it was reissued by Elizabeth to Edward Darcy in consideration of his service to the Crown[6] for a further twenty-one years. Thus, the monopoly would have lasted well over forty years had it run its course. Well into the seventeenth century the Stuart Monarchs were continuing to issue patents lasting twenty one years or longer[7] and, by the time of the Statute of Monopolies, this appears to have become the standard. The perceived wisdom was that the Monarch could grant a patent for a reasonable time,[8] rather for a certain period.

---

1 See William Kendall for twenty years (1562) PR 5 Eliz, Pt 1, m 8 (No IV) (Eliz Pat Cal, Vol 2 p 465) (National Archive: C66/987); Cornelius de Vos for 21 years (1564) PR 6 Eliz, Pt 8, m 38 (No VIII) (Eliz Pat Cal, Vol 3, No 486) (National Archive: C66/1003); William Waade and Henry Mekyns for 30 years (1577) PR 19 Eliz, Pt 8, m 6 (No XXXIV) (Eliz Pat Cal, Vol 7, No 2,257) (National Archive: C66/1058).

2 (1601) 1 HPC 1; 11 Co Rep 84 (77 ER 1260); Noy 173 (74 ER 1131); Moore 671 (72 ER 830); 1 WPC 1; also see Jacob Corré, "The Argument, Decision, and Reports of Darcy v. Allen" (1996) 45 *Emory Law Journal* 1261; David Seaborne Davies, "Further Light on the Case of Monopolies" (1932) 48 *LQR* 394; Matthew Fisher, "The Case That Launched a Thousand writs, or All That is Dross? Re-conceiving Darcy v Allen: the Case of Monopolies" [2010] *IPQ* 356.

3 Ralph Bowes and Thomas Bedingfield (1576) PR 18 Eliz, Pt 1, m 32 (Eliz Pat Cal, Vol 7, No 60) (National Archive: C66/1137).

4 Ralph Bowes and Thomas Bedingfield (1578) PR 20 Eliz, Pt 7, m 33 (Eliz Pat Cal, Vol 7, No 3,409) (National Archive: C66/1170).

5 Ralph Bowes (1588) PR 30 Eliz, Pt 12, m 17 (Eliz Pat Cal No 718) (National Archive: C66/1315).

6 Edward Darcy (1598) PR 40 Eliz, Pt 9, m 37 (No LIV) (Eliz Pat Cal, No 735) (National Archive: C66/15485).

7 Indeed, 21 years was the usual term and patents of this duration were granted as late as 1623: see for example Jones and Palmer's Patent: No 23 (1623); this explains Statute of Monopolies, s 5.

8 Sir Edward Coke, *The third part of the Institutes of the laws of England* (Flesher 1644), p 184 (a "convenient" time); Matthew Bacon, *A New Abridgement of the Law* (Ed Henry Gwillim) (5th Ed, Strahan 1798), Prerogative (F4) (p 591); William Hawkins, *A Treatise of the Pleas of the Crown* (Elizabeth Nutt 1716), Chapter 79, s 6. (p 231).

The Statute of Monopolies

The Statute of Monopolies saved existing patents for inventions and capped the length of any such patent at twenty-one years.[9] It further imposed a cap of fourteen years on any new patent for invention granted after that date.[10] The cap did not apply to monopolies granted to corporations (see Chapter 6), but otherwise it made void any grant for a longer period. The underlying common law rule remained and so a patent should still only have been granted for a reasonable period, but if a period of greater than fourteen years was reasonable then it was capped at that length.[11] In practice, however, patents granted after 1624 lasted fourteen years.[12] The question therefore would eventually arise as to whether and how a patentee could obtain protection for longer than fourteen years, particularly where the benefit of an invention, or the cost of its implementation, could not be fully recovered within the original term. This is where term extension came in, but first it is worth examining the term of grants by the Parliaments (both English and Scottish).

Seventeenth-century Parliamentary grants

In contrast to prerogative grants, the term of Parliamentary grants varied significantly at least in England. Delicques and Fancault's Ordinance 1643 received a limited exclusivity for seven years whereas George Manby's Act 1650 and Jeremy Buck's Act 1651 both received the standard fourteen years. More extraordinary was the grant of ninety-nine years in the Marquis of Worcester's Act 1663; albeit the deal was sweetened with one-tenth of the profits going to the Crown. The reason for the long period of this grant was to pay back the debts the Marquis had incurred during the Civil War.[13] The only other successful Parliamentary grant in the latter part of the seventeenth century, to Howard and Watson in 1680, was for a period of twenty years. It was not, as sometimes described, extending the earlier 1678 patent, but it clearly related to essentially the same subject matter.

In Scotland, without the Statute of Monopolies, matters were different. Accordingly, as late as 1648, the Scottish Parliament was content to enact monopolies of three consecutive terms of nineteen years to Colonel Wemyss in relation to certain ordinances[14] and when he lost the extract of the grant due to the calamity of the time[15] (the Civil War) he was granted a further three nineteen-year terms in 1661.[16] In the same year, it granted him and two others a separate nineteen-year term in relation to an invention for draining mines.[17] The practice of the Scottish Parliament continued throughout the century, with Marmaduke Hudson obtaining a grant of nineteen years in 1693[18] and one of twenty-one years being

---

9 Statute of Monopolies, s 5.

10 Statute of Monopolies, s 6; see the debate: Wallace Notestein, Frances Relf and Hartley Simpson, *Commons Debates 1621* (Yale 1935) ('CD 1621'), Vol 2: X's Diary, pp 175–176 (7 March 1621).

11 Sir Edward Coke, The Third Part of the Institutes of the laws of England (Flesher 1644), p 184.

12 Although where inventions were protected by Acts of Parliament different lengths might have been granted.

13 See Chapter 4.

14 Act in Favour of Colonel James Wemyss 1648 [RPS: 1648/3/48]; with the added condition of secrecy.

15 Report by the Commissioners for Bills and Trade Concerning James Wemyss [RPS: A1661/1/29].

16 Act in Favour of James Wemyss, General of Artillery, and Colonels Leslie and Scott 1661 [RPS: 1661/1/200].

17 Act in favour of James Wemyss, General of Artillery, and Colonels Leslie and Scott 1661 [RPS: 1661/1/200].

18 The Act is listed, but the text appears lost. Records of the supplication however continue to exist: RPS A1693/4/19.

granted to Thomas Rome in 1701.[19] The situation in Scotland, and the problems of its economic policy, are discussed in Chapter 4; accordingly, it is to the English Parliament that the story returns.

The first attempts to extend a patent's term

In the literature on patent history, one of the most commonly described reasons for obtaining a private Act was to extend the term of a patent.[20] However, as will become clear, it was incredibly rare that a patentee would seek, let alone be granted, an extension by Parliament. It may be that Sir Samuel Moreland was the first to try to extend a patent's term through legislation[21] but as the text of the Bill and the papers relating to it are so patchy it is impossible to know. The first successful claim related to William Walcot's patent which was granted in 1675[22] for his method of distilling water and making it drinkable. Soon thereafter, in 1678, he petitioned for a private Act to extend its term.[23] This did not proceed as he was asked to demonstrate that his invention worked at sea[24] which he could not do. In any event, he was soon facing different problems as Robert Fitzgerald obtained a rival patent in 1683 for a different method[25] of desalinating water.[26] He also managed to persuade the Privy Council to revoke Walcot's patent in 1685 for not yet putting the invention into effect (i.e. non-working).[27] Fitzgerald followed this up with a petition to Parliament in 1685[28] which appears to have been seeking longer protection. This was aborted as it transpired that it was Walcot, and not Fitzgerald, whose invention worked; and so the initiative returned to Walcot. This led to Walcot petitioning the Commons in 1690, 1692, 1694 and 1695 for a revival and extension of his patent (which had expired in 1689).[29] His 1692 Bill[30] made it as far as Third Reading in the Lords (after beginning in the Commons), but it was rejected after debate.[31] It is probable that it failed by reason of a case published by Fitzgerald.[32]

---

19 Draft Act in Favour of Mr Thomas Rome and Partners 1701 [RPS: A1700/10/56].

20 See p 4.

21 Moreland's Pump Bill 1674.

22 Patent No. 184 (1675) (it may never have been granted as this was the Signet Bill).

23 Walcot's Salt-Water Patent Bill 1678 (HL/PO/JO/10/1/375).

24 See *The Case of Mr Walcot, Concerning the Making of His Sea Water, Fresh, Clear and Wholesome* (1694) (Wing W285A and W285B).

25 He published various pamphlets promoting it: Robert Fitzgerald, *Salt-water sweetned, or, A True Account of the Great Advantages of the Invention Both by Sea and by Land* (1684) (Wing F1087) along with a publication which gave "farther additions" (Wing F1082) and a supplement (Wing F1090) (both 1684).

26 In relation to the dispute between the two see: Stephen Hales, *Philosophical Experiments* (Innys and Manby: London 1739), 1–66; Robert Forbes, *A Short History of the Art of Distillation* (Brill 1942), Chapter 6; Humphrey Walcot, *Sea Water Made Fresh and Wholesome* (London: Parker 1702); Robert Maddison, "Studies in the Life of R Boyle, FRS: Part II Salt Water Freshened" (1952) *Notes and Records of Royal Society* 196.

27 Walcot's Patent (1683) 11 HPC App; Privy Council Register (National Archive: PC 2/70, f 56; Edward Wyndham Hulme, "Privy Council Law and Practice of Letters Patent for Inventions from the Restoration to 1794" (1917) 33 *LQR* 63, 70–71.

28 Fitzgerald's Salt-Water Patent Bill 1685; again there is very little material on this petition.

29 Walcot's Salt-Water Bill 1690; [Walcot's] Salt-Water Bill 1692; [Walcot's] Salt Water, Making into Fresh Bill 1694.

30 *The Case of Mr Walcot, Concerning the Making of His Sea Water, Fresh, Clear and Wholesome* (1694) (Wing W285B).

31 15 LJ 284 (10 March 1693).

32 A copy is included in Walcot's *An Answer to Mr Fitz-gerald's State of the Case Concerning the Patent of Making Salt Water Fresh* (January 1695) (Wing W285A). It is undated, but must relate to 1692 as it refers to Fitzgerald's patent having five years unexpired (and his patent was granted on 9 June 1683 (No 226)).

As the Bill had died at the last stage, Walcot tried once again to obtain a private Bill in 1695[33] when he published a detailed response to Fitzgerald's case.[34] This proved enough and an Act was passed granting him a further thirty-one years of protection. This was arguably[35] the first time that a patent had been extended by private Act. It was a precedent based on an unusual case.

However, the next person who successfully sought an extension[36] was more conventional. Thomas Savery was one of the early inventors of a steam-powered engine for raising water for which he obtained a patent in 1698.[37] The following year he sought, and obtained, a private Act.[38] The passage of his Act was uneventful and James Smith, to whom Savery had licensed the right to use the invention in Scotland, obtained a similar exclusive right for that extended period in Scotland.[39] In both Walcot's and Savery's case, one of the grounds for obtaining the Acts was the improvements made since the original grant (or assignment).

This linking of extending patents to improvements continued for the next few years. In 1702, Thomas Ferrers petitioned to extend his patent[40] on the grounds he made certain improvements and would need additional time to reap the benefits.[41] It was roundly opposed[42] as it passed through the House of Commons and did not make it out of committee. Similarly, a couple of years later, in 1704, Nicholas Facio and his partners petitioned Parliament[43] to extend a patent for using precious stones in watch making which had been granted a year earlier. The basis of the petition was that improvements had been made and the cost of putting them into effect was too great without a revived (or longer term). This petition faced fierce opposition from the Clockmakers Company and Jewellers[44] on the grounds that the patent was not new – thus it was an objection to the patent itself rather than its extension.[45] The Clockmakers Company also brought in allegations of the patent being used to stock-job, which – after the fashion of the 1690s[46] – had fallen out of favour

---

33 The 1694 Bill was lodged only a few weeks before Parliament was dissolved and so it did not progress far.

34 *Walcot's An Answer to Mr Fitz-gerald's State of the Case Concerning the Patent of Making Salt Water Fresh* (January 1695) (Wing W285A).

35 It could be argued that Howard and Watson's Act 1670 was a patent term extension (and Woodcroft treated it such as the Act was included in his index immediately after the patent with a star). However, it did not mention the patent itself in the preamble.

36 There were two attempts for Bills from Robert Ledginham one in 1698 (Robert Ledgingham's Invention for Ship Pumps Bill 1698) and one the following year (Robert Ledgingham's Fire Engine Petition 1699). It is not clear if these relates to the same invention or not but it appears they might. The first died in Bill committee and the second did not get out of petition committee.

37 Thomas Savery, *The Miner's Friend: Or, an Engine to Raise Water by Fire* (1702) (Reprinted 1827, ed S. Crouch).

38 Walcot's Patent Act 1694.

39 Act in Favour of Mr James Smith 1700 [RPS: A1700/10/218].

40 No 346 (1704).

41 13 CJ 756 (23 February 1702); the Damasking Stuffs Bill 1702.

42 With four petitions against: Woollen Drapers (13 CJ 780; 7 March 1702); Robert Parker (13 CJ 785; 10 March 1702); Thomas Freeman (13 CJ 817; 23 March 1702); Levant Company (13 CJ 821; 27 March 1702).

43 14 CJ 445(6 December 1704); Watches, Inventions and Extension of Patent Bill 1704.

44 *Reasons of the English Watch and Clockmakers against the Bill to Confirm the Pretended New Invention of Using Precious and Common Stones about Watches, Clocks, and Other Engines* (1704) (ETSC T046472); *Reasons Humbly Offer'd by the Jewellers, Diamond-cutters, Lapidaries, Engravers in Stone, &c. against the Bill for Jewel-Watches* (1704) (EEBO).

45 17 CJ 233 (22 May 1712).

46 Christine MacLeod, "The 1690s Patents Boom: Invention or Stock-Jobbing?" (1986) 39 Economic History Review 549.

at least temporarily. The challenge was successful in that during committee the opponent's Counsel managed to get the Bill so heavily amended that all the operative clauses were struck out and so it was futile to continue with it.[47] After Nicholas Facio's Bill was killed, there were no further attempts to extend patents for nearly thirty years.

It is unclear why nobody else tried to extent his or her patent for so long. Walcot and Savery had set a precedent; it was clearly something Parliament might grant. So why didn't other patentees try? It was expensive to petition Parliament; but a patentee would already have invested significant sums in their patent and so it is difficult to imagine expense alone would have discouraged all patentees. One possible reason is that patents were under a cloud in the wider economy and their economic value was questioned.[48] This coupled with the small number of patents granted means that there were simply not enough patents granted during this period (149 between 1700 and 1730[49]) with proprietors who had the necessary criteria for an extension, namely a successful invention, a case of under-exploitation, money for a private Bill, and sufficient influence in Parliament to realistically get a Bill passed.

Thomas Lombe

In 1731 Sir Thomas Lombe picked up the torch and petitioned Parliament to extend his (now nearly expired) patent.[50] His original Bill[51] was for a term extension, albeit with a blank for the term to be granted.[52] There was principled opposition to the Bill with Members of Parliament stating during the debate on his petition that it would be a dangerous precedent for Parliament to prolong the term of the patent and that Lombe had made enough money already.[53] Others took the view that the term was set at fourteen years due to prevent "bubbles" and Lombe's was no such thing.[54] Yet Lombe's support in Parliament was sufficient to get his petition referred to a committee.[55] He continued to face substantial opposition during committee,[56] which eventually led to an impasse, ultimately forcing the King to intervene to suggest that the extension be changed into the payment of a substantial reward.[57] This must have suggested to patentees that extensions were unlikely to be forthcoming and it took another decade for anyone else to try again.

---

47 Edward Wood, *Curiosities of Clocks and Watches: From the Earliest Times* (Richard Bently 1866), p 307–8.
48 Christine MacLeod, "The 1690s Patents Boom: Invention or Stock-Jobbing?" (1986) 39 *Economic History Review* 549 at 569.
49 Based on Bennet Woodcroft, *Title of Patents of Invention: Chronologically Arranged 1617–1852* (Eyre and Spottiswoode 1854) as the first patent granted in 1700 was No 365 and the first in 1730 was No 514).
50 No 422 (1718).
51 It was drafted by Robert Harper (and the only patent-related Bill which appears to have been): see Sheila Lambert, *Bills and Acts: Legislative Procedure in Eighteenth-Century England* (Cambridge 1971), p 201.
52 See Lombe's Bill as drafted by Robert Harper and also see the *A Brief Statement of the Case of the Machine Erected at Derby* (i.e. the Case in Support) (1731) (i.e. Lombe's case): *Harper's Collection of Private Bills*, Vol 9, Bill No 31.
53 Sir Thomas Aston, *Collection of Parliamentary Debates from the Year MDC XVIII to the Present Time* (John Torbuck 1741), Vol 10, pp 102–103.
54 James Oglethorpe, *Collection of Parliamentary Debates from the Year MDC XVIII to the Present Time* (John Torbuck 1741), Vol 10, p 107.
55 *Collection of Parliamentary Debates from the Year MDC XVIII to the Present Time* (John Torbuck 1741), Vol 10, p 109.
56 *The Case of the Silk Throwers Company* (1732); *Case of the Manfacturers of Woollen, Linnen, Mohair and Cotton Yarn in Manchester & c* (1732): Harper's Collection of Private Bills, Vol 9. Bill No 31.
57 21 CJ 846 (14 March 1732).

A short run

The 1740s saw a spate of successful attempts to extend the term of a patent. Two petitions were made to extend a patent in 1742. Both stem from inventions by John Tuite. One for a water engine,[58] and another, held by his successor John Elwick was for stone pipes.[59] Tuite's own petition was lodged before his patent was even granted[60] yet it raced through the House of Commons with a twenty-year extension being granted.[61] It died in committee in the House of Lords and it is not clear why; it may have been the fact that the patent was not granted until after the end of the session. Tuite petitioned the House of Commons for an extension again in the following session of Parliament[62] without it progressing further. It was, ironically maybe,[63] his assignee John Elwick who secured the private Act to extend his patent by fourteen years.[64]

This success was followed by a handful of other attempts over the next thirty years. Issac Pownoll's patent[65] was revived and an additional fourteen years granted to his children on the grounds he had never been able to work the invention during his life[66] and there was no way to meet the cost of bringing the invention to completion.[67] Michael Meinzies' patent was extended for fourteen years within months of the patent being granted.[68] This was on the basis that he had spent great sums and that the term of the original patent was not going to be sufficient to recover the expense.[69] This clearly shows that where there was no opposition, Parliament could be quite lax. Put simply, how would Meinzies know what money he would make from his patent within months of it being granted; accordingly, how could Parliament have known that fourteen years would not be enough to recoup the investment? It appears that it was opposition, rather than anti-monopoly sentiment,[70] that led to patent extension Bills failing.

Indeed, when William Champion[71] petitioned in 1751[72] for an extension he withdrew it when an opposition petition was lodged between the report on his petition and First Reading.[73] Similarly, Richard Lydell's 1755 petition to extend his patent[74] faced strong opposition – ten petitions against – and so the committee found against him.[75] It concluded not only that Lydell had not made out the allegations entitling him to extend his patent, but also that his method might be dangerous to some harbours and it would occasion

---

58 No. 585 (1742).
59 No. 549 (1734).
60 Petition: 24 CJ 123 (14 March 1742); Grant: 30 July 1742.
61 See Tuite's Water Engine Bill 1742, Cl 1 (Ingrossment: HL/PO/JO/10/2/41).
62 24 CJ 374 (11 January 1743).
63 As later as an assignee he would not be able to apply.
64 Elwick's Patent Act 1742.
65 Which had expired in 1726.
66 See Report on the Petition, 25 CJ 970 (31 January 1750); also see Pownoll's Patent Act 1749, recital (2) and (3).
67 See Petition: 25 CJ 938 (18 January 1749).
68 Meinzies' Patent Act 1750.
69 Meinzies' Patent Act 1750, recital (2).
70 As suggested by Christine MacLeod, *Inventing the Industrial Revolution: The English Patent System 1660–1800* (Cambridge 1988), p 73.
71 The father of Richard Champion (who secured the Porcelain Patent Act 1775).
72 William Champion's Petition: 26 CJ 54 (21 February 1751).
73 Indeed, the next successful private Act for extending a patent was sought by Champion's son in 1775.
74 No 682 (1753).
75 There is a seven-page summary of the evidence in the Commons Journal: 27 CJ 235–242 (17 March 1755).

frauds. It is not clear why Edward Cox never introduced a Bill to extend his patent[76] after his petition received a favourable report.[77] As any established industry would oppose an useful patent it was clear that a petition would inevitably face opposition.

A glorious return

It took until 1775, twenty-five years later, before another private Act was enacted to extend a patent, and in the space of a few years five were passed. The first petition was lodged by Richard Champion, a leading Bristol Whig,[78] and a few days later the second was lodged by James Watt to extend his steam engine patent.[79] Champion's Bill faced numerous petitions against and three divisions.[80] The limited record[81] of the Parliamentary debates shows that there were general rumblings against patents (or monopolies) being extended. Lord Clare, during the debate on Watt's Bill, cautioned against unduly extending monopolies without strong evidence,[82] others simply saw the Bill as a necessary way to encourage invention.[83] These sorts of comments, as will be seen, turned out to be more common in the House of Lords.

Form of Act

There were two approaches to the extension of patents which were demonstrated by the first two patents to be extended in this period: James Watt's Fire Engine patent and Richard Champion's Porcelain patent.[84] The Acts themselves included obligations on Champion to enrol a more precise specification[85] and a strange provision saying the Act did not prevent other potters from mixing raw materials in proportions different from those specified by Champion.[86] This second provision is particularly odd, but was a common feature in extension Acts. In essence, a patent was said to protect a particular thing (as described in the specification) and nothing outside it, and this provision was to confirm this position. Thus, the legislation contained both a positive (only this is prohibited) and a negative (nothing else is prohibited except that which is prohibited). This strange form of double legislating was probably a result of the uncertainty and dissatisfaction with the scope of protection that patents were perceived to get. A variation of this provision was included in James Watt's Fire Engine Patent Act 1775 along with prior user protection[87] and also a restatement that anything which could be used to challenge the patent could be used against the Act.[88]

---

76 Patent No 712 (1757); see report: 27 CJ 859 (28 April 1757).

77 Cox's Unloading Machine Petition 1757: 27 CJ 693 (10 February 1757); Report (27 CJ 859; 28 April 1757).

78 See Peter T Underdown, "Burke's Bristol Friends" (1958) 77 *Transactions of the Bristol and Gloucestershire Archaeological Society* 127 at 128–135.

79 Sampson Swain petitioned for a term extension for his furnace invention, but it never got beyond the lodging of the petition in the House of Commons: 35 CJ 155 (27 February 1775).

80 Divisions being rare, particularly on private legislation.

81 The record of these debates in the newspapers is actually some of the best for private Bills, but it is still very poor.

82 *Middlesex Journal and Evening Advertiser*, 6–8 April 1775.

83 See comments of Sir William Bagot and General Conway (who sought "balance"): *Middlesex Journal and Evening Advertiser*, 6–8 April 1775.

84 For a more detailed history of these two Bills see: Phillip Johnson, "The Myth of Mr Burke and Mr Watt: For Want of a Champion!" (2016) 6 *Queen Mary Journal of Intellectual Property* 370.

85 Porcelain Patent Act 1775, s 2.

86 Porcelain Patent Act 1775, s 3.

87 James Watt's Fire Engine Patent Act 1775, s 2.

88 James Watt's Fire Engine Patent Act 1775, s 3 (there was also the prohibition on assignments to more than five people: s 4).

It may seem strange that Watt's Act contained a provision suggesting that the invention could be challenged on the same grounds as before, but no similar provision was included in Champion's Bill. Both faced opposition based on their lack of novelty. This difference may relate to the fact that Champion's Bill was extending a patent simplicter[89] whereas Watt's was protecting his invention by way of Act for a further twenty-five years (i.e. replacing the underlying patent).[90] Wedgwood alleged that Champion's invention was not new[91] but the Solicitor-General (Alexander Wedderburn) stated during a debate on the floor of the House that the extended patent could be challenged for want of novelty in the same way as before; accordingly he suggested there was no need for the House to consider the validity of the underlying patent.[92] Watt, however, was not extending a patent as such but it was an Act for protecting his invention and, accordingly, the Bill was recommitted and the novelty of the invention considered.[93] This meant a clause was needed to void the Act if the invention lacked novelty. In the Acts that followed it was, generally,[94] the approach in Watt's Act that prevailed and so the Act would protect the invention itself, rather than simply extending the rights granted by the patent, so it became necessary to have a clause to invalidate the Act if the underlying invention was not valid.[95]

Further successes. . .and failures

In the year following Champion's and Watt's success, there were two other private Acts. The first was to extend a patent granted to Walter Taylor, later to his widow Elizabeth,[96] which had a straightforward passage through Parliament lasting only six weeks. It passage was probably eased by an amendment made during committee whereby a compulsory licence[97] was granted so that when dealing with the navy Taylor was faced with a maximum royalty of 3 per cent.[98] This Act was shortly followed by Liardet's Cement Patent Act 1776 which included a similar compulsory licence setting the maximum price that the cement could be sold at,[99] as well as a double legislative provision similar to that in James Watt's Fire Engine Act 1775.[100] While the Act passed, there were some concerns expressed in the Lords regarding the principle. The Duke of Chandos suggested that such Bill should only pass where the inventor has proved "in the most satisfactory manner, that a common patent is quite inadequate to his expense, and to the originality and the merit of the invention",[101] with

89 Porcelain Patent Act 1775, s 1.

90 James Watt's Fire Engine Patent Act 1775, s 1.

91 The various papers and cases are reproduced in Llewellynn Jewitt, *The Wedgwoods: Being a Life of Josiah Wedgwood* (London: Virtue Bros 1865), Ch 13; Petitions lodged in Commons (35 CJ 364; 10 May 1775) and Lords (34 LJ 464; 19 May 1775).

92 See *Morning Post*, 12 May 1775.

93 The Minutes of this examination are in Eric Robinson and Albert Musson (ed), *James Watt and the Steam Revolution (A Documentary History)* (Adam & Dart 1969), pp 69–76 (Document 16).

94 Save in relation to Elizabeth Taylor's Patent Act 1776.

95 See comments of the Lord Chancellor (Earl Bathurst) *Middlesex Journal and Evening Advertiser*, 30 March to 2 April 1776; *Morning Post and Daily Advertiser*, 2 April 1776.

96 Patent No 782 (1762).

97 Elizabeth Taylor's Patent Act 1775, s 3; additionally it was necessary to file a specification setting out all the improvements: s 2.

98 "three pounds for every one hundred Pounds".

99 Liardet's Cement Patent Act 1776, s 2; the amendments were added by the House of Lords Committee.

100 Liardet's Cement Patent Act 1776, s 3.

101 *Middlesex Journal and Evening Advertiser*, 30 March to 2 April 1776; *Morning Post and Daily Advertiser*, 2 April 1776.

similar comments being made by the Earl of Cathcart, who generally supported the Bill, and so emphasised that the claim for the Bill was as much on the basis of the fresh novelty of the improvements as the original Bill.[102]

These successes were followed by another when David Hartley obtained an extension to his patent by the enactment of Hartley's Patent (Fire Prevention) Act 1776 despite the fact he had already been awarded a Parliamentary prize for the use of his invention to prevent fire in shipping.[103] He was a Member of Parliament,[104] which may explain how he managed to have his invention considered before Parliament twice. Nevertheless, the extension of his patent was very unusual in that it extended the patent in relation to preventing fire in buildings only[105] (as the prize was for preventing fire in shipping). The extension also provided[106] an exception for uses by Her Majesty's docklands provided the work was approved by the Admiralty.[107] In relation to the use of the invention in buildings there was, once more, a compulsory licence of sorts.[108]

Two of the Act also provided that any objection against the underlying patent could be raised against the Act.[109] This meant that at the subsequent trial on Liardet's inventions challenges could be made as to its novelty.[110] The same case raised issues regarding the adequacy of the specification, which related not to the original specification for the grant of the patent, but to that filed under the Act.

These successes were followed by a series of failures. In 1782, Anne Wharam sought to extend her patent for stirrups; it passed the House of Commons[111] without incident but never reached First Reading in the Lords.[112] After Richard Arkwright lost his infringement case on the grounds the patent was insufficient,[113] he petitioned Parliament a few days after Wharam[114] to consolidate the term of his two patents (so his 1769 patent[115] was extended so as to expire at the same time as his 1775 patent[116]). He faced substantial opposition on the

---

102 *Middlesex Journal and Evening Advertiser*, 30 March to 2 April 1776; *Morning Post and Daily Advertiser*, 2 April 1776.
103 See p 151 and 158.
104 He was the MP for Kingston-upon-Hull: 1774–1780 and 1782–1784.
105 Hartley's Patent (Fire Prevention) Act 1776, s 1 ("except as to Ships within the Kingdom of Great Britain, and his Majesty's Colonies and Plantations abroad").
106 It also includes provision restricting assignment to more than five people: Hartley's Patent (Fire Prevention) Act 1776, s 3.
107 Hartley's Patent (Fire Prevention) Act 1776, s 2.
108 Hartley's Patent (Fire Prevention) Act 1776, s 5.
109 Liardet's Cement Patent Act 1776, s 4; Hartley's Patent (Fire Prevention) Act 1776, s 4.
110 For the reports of the various stages of the case: see generally, John Adams and Gwen Averley, "The Patent Specification: The Role of Liadert v Johnson" (1986) 7 *J Legal History* 156; Sean Bottomley, *The British Patent System during the Industrial Revolution 1700–1852* (Cambridge 2014), pp 88–91. For what they are worth, the citations are: *Liardet v Johnson* (1778) Carp PC 35, 1 WPC 52; the actual result can be seen from *Liardet v Johnson* (1780) 1 Y & CC 527 (62 ER 1000); also see James Oldham, *The Mansfield Manuscripts and the Growth of English Law in the Eighteenth Century* (North Carolina Press 1992), Vol 1, pp 749–750.
111 The Ingrossment and Breviate exists: HL/PO/JO/10/2/57.
112 She petitioned Parliament in the following session, but it got no further than her petition being referred to Committee: 39 CJ 151 (5 February 1783).
113 *Arkwright v Mordaunt* (1781) 1 HPC 215; 1 WPC 59.
114 38 CJ 687 (6 February 1782); there was a case published by Richard Arkwright: *Mr Richard Arkwright & Co, in Relation to Mr Arkwright's Invention of an Engine for Spinning Yarn* (1782) (ESTC: T188828), but it is not clear whether it was ever presented to Parliament.
115 Patent No 931 (1769).
116 Patent No 1,111 (1775).

grounds that he had already obtained a substantial benefit and the extension was a detriment to industry.[117] He did not proceed with his Bill and his subsequent petition[118] in the next session faced opposition and did not proceed.[119] His patent was revoked in 1785.[120]

The extension of Edward Bancroft's patent,[121] at his first attempt, is little documented but he managed to secure a fourteen-year extension for his invention. While it can be only speculation, it is probable that his spying activities during the American War of Independence[122] curried favour with the government and eased the passage of his Bill but the record is very slight to support this. The passage of the Earl of Dundonald's[123] Bill, on the other hand, was widely reported in the press. It also sees the beginning of the tide turning against the prolonging of patents. The detailed record of the Second Reading debate[124] and that on report[125] shows that the general feeling of the House of Commons was much as it had been a decade earlier, sceptical of the principle, requiring a tightly drafted Bill, but not totally adverse.[126] There were dissenting voices however. Sir Herbert Mackworth MP suggested that instead of extending the patent a reward should be paid and, as will be seen in Chapter 9, the payment of Parliamentary prizes was in the ascendency at this time. There was a further challenge on report, with Lord Surrey unsuccessfully trying to defeat the Bill by having it recommitted.[127]

A few years later after two further failed petitions,[128] in 1791 James Turner sought to extend his patent.[129] Brook Watson MP spoke against the Bill on the grounds that he had already received all the benefit he should receive.[130] In the Lords, the Bill was opposed by Lord Loughborough, and Lord Lauderdale who called for evidence that the patentee had actually lost out from his patent.[131] The Bill did not progress.[132] The following session his Bill once more passed the House of Commons, but in the Lords it faced opposition again. Lord Thurlow LC, near the end of his tenure as Lord Chancellor, was strongly opposed to the entire principle of such a Bill; he saw it "as a monopoly beyond the meaning of patents" and he was supported by Lord Hawksbury.[133] Yet this time the Bill passed. Similarly, when

---

117 There were eight petitions against: 38 CJ 865 (four petitions) (4 March 1782); 38 CJ 882–883 (2 petitions) (11 March 1782); 38 CJ 897 (18 March 1782); and 38 CJ 938 (20 April 1782).

118 39 CJ 147 (5 February 1783).

119 There were two petitions: 39 CJ 269 (4 March 1783) and 39 CJ 313 (21 March 1783).

120 *R v Arkwright* (1785) 1 HPC 245; 1 WPC 64 and 73; 1 Carp PC 53 and 101; a transcript was published: The Trial of Richard Pepper Arden; Attorney-General v Richard Arkwright (Hughes and Walsh 1785) (ETSC: 142878)

121 Bancroft's Patent Act 1785.

122 Thomas Schaeper, *Edward Bancroft: Scientist, Author and Spy* (Yale 2011), pp 252–253; Arthur MacNaulty, "Edward Bancroft, MD FRS and the War of American Independence" (1944) 38 *Proceeding of Royal Society of Medicine* 7 at 11.

123 Lord Dundonald's Patent (Tar, Pitch, etc.) Act 1785; for a general background see: Archibald Clow and Nan L Clow, "Lord Dundonald" (1942) 12 *Economic History Review* 47.

124 *The Times*, 30 April 1785.

125 *The Times*, 24 May 1785.

126 *The Times*, 30 April 1785.

127 *The Times*, 24 May 1785.

128 Legh Master's Petition 1788: 43 CJ 199 (8 February 1788); Anthony Bourboulon de Boneuil's Petition 1788: 43 CJ 202 (8 February 1788).

129 Patent No 1,281 (1781).

130 *Evening Mail*, 4–6 May 1791.

131 *Evening Mail*, 3–6 June 1791.

132 The Ingrossment is: HL/PO/JO/10/2/65A.

133 *The Times*, 8 June 1792.

Conway's Patent Kiln Act 1795 was before the Lords, Lord Loughborough LC, supported by Lord Hawksbury and Lord Auckland, spoke against the principle of such Bills, pointing out that foreign manufacturers could obtain the specification and make the invention at the expense of British manufacturers; accordingly, a reward of some sort would be more appropriate than an extension,[134] once more showing a preference by some Parliamentarians for grants.[135] There was also a concern that the floodgates would be opened to other patentees seeking extensions.[136] Yet these three significant voices were not enough to quash the Bill of such a significant figure as Field Marshall Conway.[137]

In 1792, Jonathan Hornblower petitioned to extend his steam engine patent.[138] The papers relating to this opposition are some of the best on record, as James Watt, his opponent, retained them and they are now held in the Boulton and Watt Archive.[139] His Bill failed on Second Reading after witnesses were heard at the bar of the House of Commons.[140] The thrust of Watt's case was that Hornblower had plagiarised Watt's engine[141] and that evidence should be heard in respect of the differences of his engine from Watt's.[142] Further, that the Hornblower engine was superior to that of Watt. This last allegation, he claimed, would be injurious to Watt as his product would have been said by the legislature to be inferior to Hornblower's engine.[143] Hornblower's reply was essentially that his patent, if extended, could not interfere with their rights; if it was invalid then so too would be the extension.[144] Thus, unlike other Bills at this time, it was defeated not because Members of Parliament or their Lordships objected to the policy of granting the extension, but rather that Hornblower could not prove his preamble in the face of robust opposition.

Standing Orders introduced

The number of private Acts sought to extend patents remained very low in comparison with other areas of private legislation. Yet in 1798, the House of Commons introduced Standing Orders[145] requiring any petition for the extending and confirming of a patent to be preceded by three advertisements in the *London Gazette*.[146] This was part of a trend of requiring notice to be given of an intention to introduce a private Bill.[147] The cause of it seems to have been

---

134 See Chapter 9.

135 There were those who took the polar opposite view when prizes were being considered: see p 156.

136 See *Whitehall Evening Post*, 12–14 May 1795; *Oracle and Public Advertiser*, 13 May 1795.

137 In fact, the division was 3 Not Content and 31 Content (so they persuaded nobody): 40 LJ 433 (12 May 1795).

138 No 1,298 (1781).

139 In Birmingham Library: MS/3147/2/35 and 36.

140 The Minutes of this cross-examination are in the Birmingham Archive: MS 3147/2/35/23.

141 Observations on the Part of Messrs Boulton and Watt concerning Mr Hornblower's Steam Engine Bill: Birmingham Library: MS 3147/2/36/2.

142 As Watt had had to show how his engine differed from Newcomen's, Savery's and Blakey's.

143 Observations on the Part of Messrs Boulton and Watt concerning Mr Hornblower's Steam Engine Bill: Birmingham Library: MS 3147/2/36/2.

144 Mr Hornblower's Case Relative to a Petition to Parliament for the Extension of the Term of His Patent (Birmingham Library: MS3147/2/36/3); he also produced postcards with that simple point printed on it which he gave out to members of the House.

145 53 CJ 524 (1 May 1798); proposed by Rowland Burdon MP: *Parliamentary Debates*, 1 May 1798, Vol 6, p 84. There had long been Standing Orders requiring a patent to appended to the Bill: 10 CJ 412 (13 May 1690).

146 Where the patent extended to Scotland or Ireland then it was necessary to advertise as well.

147 The first relating to draining land and turnpikes in 1774 (see Orlo Williams, *The Historical Development of Private Bill Procedure and Standing Orders in the House of Commons* (HMSO 1948), Vol 2, p 17) although

issues with Bramah's Bill 1798 to extended his patent right. An attempt had been made by Rowland Burdon MP to delay Second Reading of this Bill on the basis that an opponent wanted Counsel to appear against the Bill and more time was needed to instruct.[148] It was Burdon who introduced the Standing Order a little over a month later.[149]

The requirement of the publication of notices means that it becomes possible to find patentees who considered extending their patent and so gave notice, but did not pursue the matter as far as petitioning Parliament. The reasons such patentees gave up could of course vary. First, in many cases it can be assumed that potential opponents contacted the patentee upon seeing a notice, providing the patentee with an indication of the opposition that he or she would face in Parliament and with it the escalated cost of pursuing the petition: a cost which might outweigh the potential benefit of extending the term. Secondly, there may be cases where a person was advised by the Parliamentary clerk that the petition had no chance of success or, following specialist advice,[150] became aware of the real cost of obtaining a private Act. At this stage, it would be the solicitor who posted the notices in the *Gazette* and he would subsequently approach either an outdoor or indoor Parliamentary agent[151] who would then give them more advice. Thirdly, there will be those patentees who decide to wait a little longer before incurring the expense associated with extending a patent. In other words, they wanted to see if the invention was valuable enough to be worth the cost and risk of petitioning Parliament. One such case might be that of Richard Willcox[152] who gave notice in August 1802 to extend a patent he had only been granted in January that year.[153]

The first Bill introduced after advertising by notice was required was the (second) Bill of Bancroft. He said he needed the Bill as he had not been given rights against importation[154] and his business strategy had been to sell the product to everyone, rather than only a few, reducing his potential profit. Further, he argued that the original Act just restored the original fourteen-year term he lost due to the war, so the (second) Bill would be his first extension.[155] Finally, he stated he had a loss of £6,000[156] (in 2016 money, £579,600).[157] The Bill passed through the Commons with little comment, but on Second Reading in the Lords it was roundly rejected. Earl Derby was "decidedly hostile"[158] to the Bill as Bancroft

notices were given in relation to particular Bills before that time: see Fredrick Clifford, *A History of Private Bill Legislation* (1885) (Frank Cass 1968), Vol 2, p 762–763.

148 *The Star,* 28 March 1798.

149 There is no evidence on record, but the little on record is demonstrated by the account in *The Sun,* 2 May 1798 which simply states that Rowland Burdon, "after a short Preface" moved the orders (then sets out in summary the effect of the orders) and then indicates they were agreed.

150 At this time, most Parliamentary agents were also Parliamentary clerks.

151 As to the difference see p 10.

152 At this time there was no rule to this effect and a generation earlier such Acts had been granted.

153 Patent No 2,574 (1802); *London Gazette*: 1 September 1801 (Issue: 15403, p 1077).

154 Edward Bancroft, *Facts and Observations, Briefly Stated in Support of an Intended Application to Parliament* (London: 1798), p 6.

155 Edward Bancroft, *Facts and Observations, Briefly Stated in Support of an Intended Application to Parliament* (London: 1798), p 17.

156 Edward Bancroft, *Facts and Observations, Briefly Stated in Support of an Intended Application to Parliament* (London: 1798), p 20.

157 Based on retail price comparison: Lawrence H Officer and Samuel H Williamson, "Five Ways to Compute the Relative Value of a UK Pound Amount, 1270 to Present," MeasuringWorth, 2017.

158 He also complained about the lack of notice for opponents, despite Bancroft's being one of the first Bills to comply with House of Commons Standing Orders: see *The Sun,* 24–27 May 1799.

had already had an extension of his patent which was felt adequate to reimburse him for the losses suffered. The Lord Chancellor was the most critical as there were,

> many Bills of a similar description. . .[but] he hardly knew but one which deserved to pass their Lordship's House. . .Notwithstanding the peculiar pretensions of Mr Watt to the indulgence of Parliament. . .it would have been to the advantage of the Public, if Mr Watt had been paid 100,000l for his suggestions.

He went on to challenge all the specific allegations made by Bancroft in his Bill[159] and so it failed at Second Reading.

The first Bill enacted after the introduction of Standing Orders was that of Edmund Cartwright[160] in 1801[161] to extend his patent by fourteen years. There were two aborted notices[162] but the next major change followed the claim of the Fourdrinier brothers. Their petition was to extend certain patents relating to paper-making; the English patents had been granted in 1801[163] and 1803[164] to John Gamble. They had been assigned to Henry and Sealy Fourdrinier in 1804[165] who petitioned to extend both patents and to claim for improvements in February 1807.[166] The basis of the petition to Parliament was that they had incurred great expense and the remainder of the patent terms would not enable them to recover "any reward at all adequate to such expense".[167] The House of Commons had been inclined to give the Fourdrinier brothers a fourteen-year extension, but the House of Lords agreed to seven years, but with liberty to return if that extension was not adequate.[168] The reduction of years was pushed for by Lord Lauderdale and, it appears, he was the only one who took objection to the Bill.[169] The Act received Royal Assent on the last day of the session in 1807.

Early in the new session in March 1808, Lord Lauderdale proposed[170] that three new Standing Orders[171] be introduced in the House of Lords. The first of these was a notice requirement which was the essentially the same[172] as that in the Commons. It introduced two other rules which were of more significance. The second rule was that the patent had to expire within two years of the commencement of the session of Parliament in which the application for the Bill was made. This brought to an end the practice of applying for

---

159 The most detailed account of the debate is in *The Sun*, 24–27 May 1799 (with an identical account in *True Briton*, 25 May 1799).

160 He had resisted the Woolcombers Bill 1794 (see 49 CJ 349; 18 March 1794) a few years earlier.

161 Cartwright's Woolcombing Machinery Act 1801.

162 John Garnett's Notice 1801: *London Gazette*, 1 September 1801 (Issue: 15403, p 1077); Richard Wilcox's Notice 1802: *London Gazette*, 28 August 2002 (Issue: 15510, p 920).

163 Patent No 2,487 (1801).

164 Patent No 2,708 (1803).

165 Fourdriniers' Paper Making Machine Act 1807.

166 62 CJ 169 (26 February 1807).

167 62 CJ 587 (29 June 1807); this was the re-presentation of a similar earlier petition (62 CJ 169) as it expired when the previous session of Parliament ended (on 29 April 1807).

168 See Evidence of William Harrison KC (Counsel in 1807) in *Report from the Select Committee on Fourdriniers' Patent; With the Minutes of Evidence* (1837 HC Papers 351), Vol 20, p 35 at p 6.

169 Evidence of William Harrison KC (Counsel in 1807) in *Report from the Select Committee on Fourdriniers' Patent; With the Minutes of Evidence* (1837 HC Papers 351), Vol 20, p 35 at p 6.

170 HL Deb, 25 March 1808, Vol 10 (1st), cols 1253–1254.

171 46 LJ 512 (25 March 1808).

172 It precluded the Third Reading without the notices, rather than the original petition as in the Commons.

a private Bill early in the life of the patent as had been common practice.[173] The third and final rule required two things: (a) that the application for the extension was to be made by the inventor or his representative (and so precluded assignees obtaining a prolongation of the patent)[174]; and (b) that "the inventor" was not someone who had acquired the invention from abroad[175]: in other words, the person had to be the real first inventor and not that deemed to be such in law. This too was a major change in practice as numerous earlier grantees had been assignees – including the Fourdrinier brothers.

The reasons Lord Lauderdale introduced these Standing Orders is almost certainly[176] related to concerns he had about Fourdriner's patent;[177] although it is not entirely clear what they were precisely. It had been suggested that it might relate to the idea that an assignee who paid too much for an invention should not be able to get it extended due to their over-estimation of its worth or that only the inventor should get some benefit from the invention.[178] Another view is that the Standing Orders were to prevent the Fourdrinier brothers in particular from returning to Parliament to get their extension; but this is not supported by any evidence.[179] Lord Lauderdale's famous economic writings, *An Inquiry into the Nature and Origin of Public Wealth*,[180] discusses patents and the effect they might have where workers are substituted by machines[181] but he does not engage with any economic analysis of the advantages or disadvantages of the system. It might be reasonably assumed that if Lord Lauderdale were strongly against the patent system as a whole he would have expressed this view in his book. More likely, therefore, is that Lord Lauderdale was unhappy with aspects of the system of patent term extension. In any case, the Standing Orders he introduced seem to have more or less killed that system.

The difficulty was increased when the House of Lords adopted a further Standing Order in 1819 requiring a Select Committee to inquire into the expediency of Bills of this class before First Reading.[182] While this did not change the standard of expediency a Bill had to

---

173 See for example Richard Wilcox's Notice 1802: *London Gazette*, 28 August 1802 (Issue: 15510, p 920); when his patent was granted on 23 January 1802 (No 2,574).

174 Thus, an assignee could not apply: see Evidence of William Harrison KC (Counsel in 1807) at *Report from the Select Committee on Fourdriniers' Patent; With the Minutes of Evidence* (1837 HC Papers 351), Vol 20, p 35 at p 7 (as to advice he had given in relation to Kyan's Patent, which was extended by Privy Council).

175 It was the case that a person who brought an invention from abroad was the first inventor in English law: *Edgeberry v Stephens* (1691) 1 HPC 117; 1 WPC 35.

176 Only the intention to speak to the Orders is reported in the newspapers or Hansard on a subsequent day. However, nothing is reported on the day the Standing Orders were introduced to explain their purpose or reason.

177 Robert Burrell and Catherine Kelly, "Parliamentary Rewards and the Evolution of the Patent System" (2015) 74 *Cam LJ* 423 at 443.

178 Robert Burrell and Catherine Kelly, "Parliamentary Rewards and the Evolution of the Patent System" (2015) 74 Cam LJ 423 at 443; in relation to the second rule they put forward the existence of the reversion in copyright law.

179 Andrew Ure, *A Dictionary of Arts, Manufactures and Mines* (New York 1842), pp 935–936 (this is based on the evidence before the 1837 Select Committee (*Report from the Select Committee on Fourdriniers' Patent; With the Minutes of Evidence* (1837 HC Papers 351), Vol 20, p 35) and so is not actually supported by any evidence other than the same person objecting and making the Standing Orders); the view was also put forward by RH Clapperton, *The Paper Making Machine: Its Invention, Evolution and Development* (Pergamon Press 1967), p 47.

180 (Longman 1804).

181 Lord Lauderdale, *An Inquiry into the Nature and Origin of Public Wealth* (Longman 1804), pp 168–171.

182 52 LJ 879 (7 July 1819); its proposal was explained the day before: *The Times*, 7 July 1819; a similar order was unsuccessfully proposed for the House of Commons: *The Times*, 5 July 1820.

meet, it made obtaining a private Act more expensive and procedurally more complicated. There are only a couple examples of these Select Committees being formed. In considering Langton's Invention Bill, the committee was largely concerned that the invention worked, and how it worked: they went as far as to have experiments undertaken. The need for expediency was concerned, therefore, with the benefit from the invention.[183] The committee considering what became Hollingrake's Letters Patent Act 1830 similarly discussed how the invention worked and whether it was superior to everything else. Thus, most witnesses testified as to the quality of the invention, but Hollingrake himself discussed the expenditure on the invention and he claimed he was still out of pocket from investing in the invention (and that he made no profit in the first seven years).[184]

The Standing Orders that killed the Bill

In the years between the House of Lords introducing its requirements through Standing Orders in 1808 and the Judicial Committee of the Privy Council being given power to extend patents under the Letters Patent for Inventions Act 1835 there were at least[185] seventeen patentees[186] who started the process for prolonging their patent by Act of Parliament by publishing notices in the *London Gazette*,[187] only one or two[188] of which led to a private Act.

This failure rate appears to be catastrophic, particularly, when the one Act which passed was twenty-two years after the Standing Orders were made. This picture, however, is misleading. While sixteen patentees started the process only seven petitioned Parliament: it was clear one of those petitions did not comply with Standing Orders for numerous reasons[189]: one was for reviving Fourdriniers' patents which had been revoked[190] since their 1807 Act (which had already been extended in any event),[191] one led to an award of money

183 See *Minutes of Evidence Taken before Lords Committee to Whom Langton's Bill Was Referred* (1829 HL Papers 82), Vol 162, p 223.

184 See Hollingrake's Bill, Minutes of Evidence, 12 May 1830 (HL/PO/JO/10/8/913).

185 There were some who posted notices in one year, but then delayed it to the next – possibly because of the Standing Orders: Robert Barber's Notice 1810: *London Gazette*, 8 August 1809 (Issue: 16284, p 1260); Robert Barber's Bill 1811 (ended at Second Reading: 66 CJ 157 (8 March 1811).

186 See Phillip Johnson, *Parliament, Inventions and Patents: A Research Guide and Bibliography* (Routledge 2017), Part 5.

187 This includes Frederick Alfred Winsor who it appears did not actually post a notice, rather he petitioned Parliament directly (68 CJ 97; 18 December 1812). His petition did not get beyond being referred to committee. This is probably because he became aware that his application did not comply with any of the Standing Orders (it was filed too early, the patent was owned by a company – incorporated by an earlier Act of Parliament – and not by him, and he did not publish notices).

188 John Langton's Wood Seasoning Invention led to an extension, but the approach of this Act was somewhat unusual: Langton's Profits (Wood Seasoning Invention) Act 1829 and an amending Act Langton's Profits Act 1831; see pp 57–8.

189 Frederick Alfred Winsor's Petition 1812 (68 CJ 97; 18 December 1812); although it was never found by the House authorities not to comply).

190 It was suggested that the court was wrong: Evidence of William Harrison KC (Counsel in 1807) in *Report from the Select Committee on Fourdriniers' Patent; With the Minutes of Evidence, and Appendix* (1837 HC Papers 351), Vol 20, p 35, p 6–7 and Evidence of Richard Godson (ibid), p 40.

191 Fourdriniers' Patent Petition 1822 (55 LJ 70; 14 March 1822); it had been revoked and the appeal was unsuccessful: *Bloxam v Elsee* (1827) 1 HPC 879, 6 B &C 169 (108 ER 415).

instead,[192] two were strongly opposed,[193] two never got beyond the initial petitions[194] and one was passed.[195]

Why did so many patentees post notices, but not proceed? Three of the remaining patentees[196] would have been doomed to fail as they would have been petitioning too early; indeed, these earlier comers applied to Parliament in the session immediately following that when their patent was granted. It is only possible to speculate why the remaining seven patentees[197] did not proceed. The reasons are probably the same as for the earlier era, potential cost and potential opposition.[198]

One case where substantial opposition was faced was Crossley's (Gas Lights) Bill 1829. Samuel Clegg had assigned his Letters Patent for a Gas Meter to Samuel Crossley.[199] He in turn petitioned Parliament to extend the term of the patent, but he failed to post the notices required by Standing Orders[200]; however, the Standing Order Committee allowed him to proceed if he posted the notices as required.[201] The notices led to nine petitions against the Bill,[202] some arguing that seeking an extension of a patent was "unknown",[203] others that it was not a private Bill at all as it was continuing a monopoly in relation to gas apparatus.[204] When a petition from the Liver Gas-Light Company was presented William Huskisson MP stated that "it has been the uniform practice, of late years, for Parliament not to interpose its authority, to the aid the extension of the exclusive right enjoyed by patentees".[205] Crossley was the assignee and this was seen as a ground of preventing the passage of the Bill[206]; it was

---

192 Morton's Patent Slip Bill 1832; he was given £5000 instead of an extension; see Chapter 9.

193 Crossley's Petition (Gas Lights) Bill 1829 died in Committee and Robert Barber's Bill 1811 earlier in the process. Barber also posted notices in 1809 (which would have been within time) and petitioned Parliament in 1811 (publishing more notices thereafter) and faced three petitions against his and so it did not get pass Second Reading. Both failed due to the petitioner being an assignee of the patent: in relation to Barber's patent (see *The Globe*, 9 March 1811); in relation to Crossley's Petition (Gas Lights) Bill 1829 (see *Mirror of Parliament*, 1 May 1829, Vol 2, pp 1359–1360),

194 Parker's Cement Petition 1810: 65 CJ 48 (7 February 1810); and Simeon Thompson's Petition 1823: 78 CJ 59 (21 February 1823).

195 Hollingrake's Patent Act 1830.

196 John Heathcoat Notice 1822: *London Gazette*, 27 August 1822 (Issue: 17847, p 1412); Richard Williams Notice 1831: *London Gazette*, 17 September 1830 (Issue: 18727, p 1973); Peter Young Notice 1832: *London Gazette*, 15 November 1831 (Issue: 18872, p 2357); also Frederick Alfred Winsor (1812) was too early, but he actually petitioned Parliament: 68 CJ 97 (18 December 1812).

197 In fact, two of the seven patentees were actually the same person (so it was really six). Arthur Woolf published notices about two different patents (1817 and 1818) (*London Gazette*, 13 September 1817 (Issue: 17285, p 1936) and *London Gazette*, 25 August 1818 (Issue: 17391, p 1516)), but proceeded with neither application.

198 See p 131.

199 Patent No 3,968 (1815).

200 *Standing Orders*, Part XVI, Ords 1–3 (see 66 CJ 681).

201 84 CJ 108 (6 March 1829).

202 See 84 CJ 206 (7 April 1829); 84 CJ 210 (8 April 1829); 84 CJ 211 (9 April 1829); 84 CJ 217 (10 April 1829); 84 CJ 226 (14 April 1829); 84 CJ 242 (28 April 1829); 84 CJ 248 (1 May 1829); 84 CJ 275 (8 May 1829); 84 CJ 366 (3 June 1829).

203 See John Marshall, *Mirror of Parliament*, 7 April 1829, Vol 2, p 1142 (speaking on behalf of Leeds Gas-Light Company).

204 Joseph Hume, *Mirror of Parliament*, 7 April 1829, Vol 2, p 1142.

205 William Huskinsson, *Mirror of Parliament*, 28 April 1829, Vol 2, p 1345; although he conceded that there may be cases where Parliament should extend a patent.

206 It did not matter that he might have failed in the Lords in any event as the non-compliance with Standing Orders in the Lords was not relevant to the considerations of the Commons: Charles Manners-Sutton (Speaker), *Mirror of Parliament*, 1 May 1829, Vol 2, pp 1359–1360.

felt that as he was not the "original inventor" he should not benefit.[207] He had made money during his time of ownership and that was seen as enough.[208] The valiant defence of the Bill was that he had not got the full benefit because of his need to bring infringement proceedings.[209] Whether Crossley's Bill demonstrates a general antipathy towards extending patents or simply a well-organised and significant opposition from the gas companies is difficult to know. Despite the grand rhetoric, objection on principle seems unlikely as Hollingrake had his patent extended only a year later.[210] It may be little more than principle needs to be roused by objection and the members of the Commons

Letters Patent for Inventions Act 1835

What is more extraordinary with such limited activity and success is the Privy Council being granted the power to extend patents. Before the 1829 Select Committee, while there were concerns with the difficulty in extending the term of patents, the evidence was against the power being transferred to a body outside Parliament.[211] John Farey, an engineer-cum-patent agent, was expressly against Parliament losing its role in extending patents. He was concerned that transferring the power to extend patents from Parliament to the Crown might lead to the sorts of abuses which the Statute of Monopolies had been enacted to prevent.[212] Samuel Morton, who later sought to extend his own patent, believed the power should be transferred to a commission.[213] Mr Dyer, who had a letter read out to the Committee, criticised the rule that only the inventor could obtain an extension as it was usually an assignee who had made the investment. He did not, however, suggest the power should be vested elsewhere.[214] While there were numerous petitions to Parliament in the early 1830s relating to patent reform,[215] the prime concern of petitioners was the high fees: none expressed concern about the difficulty in prolonging a patent, rather the concerns lay in getting it in the first place.

The Letters Patent Bill 1833[216] included provision for patentees to extend the term of their patent if they had not obtained adequate profit.[217] The Bill was widely criticised both

---

207 Sir Thomas Wilson, *Mirror of Parliament*, 1 May 1829, Vol 2, p 1359.

208 Sir Thomas Wilson, *Mirror of Parliament*, 1 May 1829, Vol 2, p 1340.

209 Matthew Wood, *Mirror of Parliament*, 1 May 1829, Vol 2, p 1359.

210 Hollingrake's Patent Act 1830.

211 Samuel Clegg was asked about the matter but had no opinion: *Report from the Select Committee on the Law Relative to Patents for Invention* (1829 HC Papers 332), Vol 3, p 415 at p 95.

212 *Report from the Select Committee on the Law Relative to Patents for Invention* (1829 HC Papers 332), Vol 3, p 415 at p 33; he also mentions some of the extension Acts at p 141.

213 *Report from the Select Committee on the Law Relative to Patents for Invention* (1829 HC Papers 332), Vol 3, p 415 at p 92.

214 *Report from the Select Committee on the Law Relative to Patents for Invention* (1829 HC Papers 332), Vol 3, p 415 at p 133.

215 Petition of Thomas Richard Yare: 88 CJ 132 (28 February 1833); Second Report of the Public Petitions Committee, 1833, p 48; Petition of Richard Roberts: 88 CJ 179 (18 March 1833); Seventh Report of the Public Petitions Committee, 1833, p 176; Petition of John Kitchen: 88 CJ 231 (28 March 1833): Tenth Report of the Public Petitions Committee, 1833, p 294 (No 2,140); Petition of Joseph Holiday: 88 CJ 505 (20 June 1833); Thirteenth Report of Public Petitions Committee, 1833 p 1150; Petition of Julius Schroder: 88 CJ 535 (1 July 1833): Thirty-Third Report of the Public Petitions Committee, 1833, p 1268 (No 9559); Petition of Edward Moxhay: 89 CJ 117 (13 March 1834); Eighth Report of Public Petitions Committee, 1834, p 91 (No 1,292); Petition of William Ivory: 89 CJ 227 (28 April 1834); Sixteenth Report of Public Petitions Committee, 1834, p 198 (No 3,186).

216 (1833 HC Papers 34), Vol 3, p 169.

217 Letters Patent Bill 1833, cl 22. The process was to be for His Majesty to grant a new patent in the same way as before, but for advice to be sought from the Attorney-General as to whether it was appropriate for the extension.

inside and outside the House. The *Mechanics Magazine,* which had been campaigning for patent reform, described the Bill in general as "excessively careless and slovenly. . .[and] faulty" and so it should be abandoned soon.[218] Later in the year, the Magazine said it was "faulty – we had almost said villanous"[219] while a meeting in Leeds put forward substantial amendments (or a complete re-write) to the Bill.[220] Indeed, the criticism had been such that the 1833 Bill had been divided on report in the Commons[221] to save that which was thought uncontroversial[222] from that which would not pass.[223] The provision on extending patents did not make the cut as it was not thought to be important enough or it was too controversial. In any event, the Lords eventually rejected the 1833 Bill due to lack of time for its proper consideration.[224] So it is surprising that the next attempt at legislation, what became the 1835 Act, was so restricted in what it attempted.

Indeed, when the 1835 Act was making its way through Parliament it was widely criticised as not reforming enough. The *Mechanics Magazine* was similarly unimpressed with the Bill's ambitions describing it as "a very crude and ill-digested affair" which does not deal "with the actual defects of the law".[225] In any event, the evidence heard before the House of Lords Select Committee considered patent term extensions in a very rudimentary way. There was a discussion of Watt's extension and the reasons his patent extension was granted[226] and the particular problem caused by the Standing Orders requiring the original inventor to own the patent for it to be extended.[227] Indeed, there was support from all the witnesses (including Farey), but very little real discussion of the merit of the Privy Council being able to extend patents.[228]

However, the provision faced a robust challenge in the House of Commons who felt that it was inappropriate for the power to prolong patents to be moved from Parliament to the Privy Council. The issue was first raised by Richard Potter MP at Second Reading who thought "the cases are rare when patents ought to be renewed. . .The power of renewing patents is with Parliament, and I doubt the policy of transferring it to the Privy Council."[229] When the Bill reached committee, the relevant provision (clause 4) was strongly condemned, Henry Warburton MP arguing that as "Parliament views, with a jealous eye, all monopolies, they. . .should be the only judges as to the propriety of conferring them".[230] There were also concerns that the cost before the Privy Council may be too high for the extension to

218 Anon, "Mr Godson's Bill for the Improvement of the Patent Laws, with Remark" (1833) 19 *Mechanics Magazine* 26 (setting out Bill) and 43, the comment is at 48.

219 Anon, "The Patent Laws" (1833) 19 *Mechanics Magazine* 271.

220 Set out in (1833) 2 *Newton's London Journal and Repertory of Patent Inventions* 237.

221 88 CJ 559 (9 July 1833).

222 Letters Patent for Inventions Bill (As Amended in Committee) 1833 (1833 HC Papers 496), Vol 3, p 177.

223 Letters Patent Expenses Bill 1833 (1833 HC Papers 497), Vol 3, p 183.

224 HL Deb, 9 August 1833, Vol 20 (2nd), cols 440–441.

225 Comment following Letter from Archibald Rosser (1835) 23 *Mechanics Magazine* 170 at 171.

226 Evidence of John Farey: Phillip Johnson, "Minutes of Evidence of the Select Committee on the Letters Patent for Inventions Act 1835" (2017) 7 *Queen Mary Journal of Intellectual Property* 99 at 105–6 (Q 31 to Q33).

227 Evidence of John Farey: Phillip Johnson, "Minutes of Evidence of the Select Committee on the Letters Patent for Inventions Act 1835" (2017) 7 *Queen Mary Journal of Intellectual Property* 99 at 109 (Q58) and Archibald Rosser at p 104 (Clause 4).

228 See Witness Statement of Archibald Rosser: Phillip Johnson, "Minutes of Evidence of the Select Committee on the Letters Patent for Inventions Act 1835" (2017) 7 *Queen Mary Journal of Intellectual Property* 99 at 102 (Q4) and 105.

229 *Mirror of Parliament,* 13 August 1835, Vol 3, p 2481.

230 *Mirror of Parliament,* 18 August 1835, Vol 3, p 2594.

be challenged.[231] This view was supported by other members as well as the Solicitor General, and, accordingly, the clause was removed from the Bill by the House of Commons.[232]

When the Bill returned to the Lords with the clause struck out, Lord Brougham took the contrary view as to the cost of prolonging patents. He suggested that the Privy Council would be a far cheaper forum than pursuing a private Bill (£30–£40 instead of £700–£800)[233]; and, if the Commons was right and it was cheaper, nothing prevented anyone petitioning Parliament for a Bill if they so chose.[234] Yet as the *Mechanics Magazine* points out:

> When a patent. . . .has become of such value as to make it worth while to apply for an extension of it, a few hundreds, one way or the other, count but for little. It is seldom in that stage of an inventor's history that expense is of any consequence.[235]

When the Commons considered the Lords' insistence on the clause it still faced opposition, Warburton continuing in his belief that the nature of patent term extension was not a judicial matter, but a legislative one.[236] He even preferred the idea of the matter being determined by the Attorney-General, rather than judges. His fear was that the trickle of extensions would become a flood as almost all patents would be entitled to extension, which, as will be seen below, proved not entirely baseless.[237] Section 4 was eventually carried after a division,[238] the relevant extracts of that very long clause being as follows:

> . . .That if any Person who now hath or shall hereafter obtain any Letters Patent as aforesaid shall advertise in the London Gazette Three Times [and various other places] that he intends to apply to His Majesty in Council for a Prolongation [who may petition the Privy Council who will hears the petition and any opponent]. . .the Judicial Committee may report to His Majesty that a further Extension of the Term in the said Letters Patent should be granted, not exceeding Seven Years. . . Provided that no such Extension shall be granted if the Application by Petition shall not be made and prosecuted with Effect before the Expiration of the Term originally granted in such Letters Patent.

Section 4 did not provide any "test" whatsoever for when an extension of the patent should be granted. It merely set out the procedure. Accordingly, it fell to the Privy Council to determine when a patent should be extended. In *Kay's Patent*[239] the Opponent argued that "The Prolongation of a patent ought not to be recommended. . .unless the Houses of Parliament. . .would have seen it right to grant a prolongation." The test being based on

231 *Mirror of Parliament*, 18 August 1835, Vol 3, p 2594.

232 *Mirror of Parliament*, 18 August 1835, Vol 3, p 2594.

233 This figure was much higher than the £400–500 suggested by Samuel Morton to the 1829 Committee: *Report from the Select Committee on the Law Relative to Patents for Invention* (1829 HC Papers 332), Vol 3, p 415 at p 92.

234 *Mirror of Parliament*, 1 September 1835, Vol 3, p 2849; HL Deb, 1 September 1835, Vol 30 (3rd), col 1187.

235 Anon, "Lord Brougham's Patent Law Amendment Bill" (135) 23 *Mechanics Magazine* 310 at 311; however, elsewhere in the Magazine it was suggested that the power to extend was the only good bit of the Bill: Anon, "Patent Law Amendment Act" (1835) 23 *Mechanics Magazine* 524 at 526.

236 Henry Warburton, *Mirror of Parliament*, 7 September 1835, Vol 3, p 2976.

237 Henry Warburton, *Mirror of Parliament*, 7 September 1835, Vol 3, pp 2976–2967.

238 90 CJ 654 (7 September 1835).

239 (1839) 2 HPC 957; 1 WPC 568 at 569.

whether Parliament would have granted the extension was one put forward in a number of the text books. Hindmarch suggests that the Privy Council "seems to have considered themselves. . .merely acting in the place of Parliament. . .[and] have granted extensions of terms in patents in such cases only as Parliament would have granted them",[240] and Webster that "[t]he privy council, in the exercise of their discretion. . .have adopted the same principles for their guidance, as to the special circumstances, as the legislature followed."[241] The former view at least was based on the mistaken belief that Acts to extend patents were "a frequent occurrence".[242] The treatise writers' view was not adopted by the Privy Council however. In *Soames' Patent*[243] Lord Brougham made it clear that the test applied by the Privy Council was not whether Parliament would have granted the extension, but a more liberal test. A view he reiterated in *Morgan's Patent*[244] when he said the Privy Council could extend a patent where Parliament would not.

In any event, the suggestion that the Privy Council could follow Parliament's precedent as to when to grant an extension was close to absurd. There had only been one patent extended by Parliament since Lord Brougham's had been elected to the House of Commons[245] or even since his call to the bar.[246] There were only five examples of extensions being granted by private Act of Parliament in the fifty years preceding the jurisdiction being given to the Privy Council. The test applied by the Privy Council was essentially that which the House of Lords Select Committee[247] adopted and which Parliament seemed to apply as stated in the preambles to the most recent private Act:[248] Hollingrake's Letters Patent Act 1830.

The preambles for patent extensions would explain how the petitioner had gone to great expense and how the term of the patent left would not adequately remunerate him (or her) for the expense so far. In the last such Act, Parliament expressed this concept simply. Thus, Parliament had given an extension to Hollingrake because he "expended large sums of money" and "had not hitherto obtain any Rewards adequate to the Expence, Time and Labour" he spent on the invention and so the extension was to "obtain reasonable Remuneration".[249] Thus, the only indication of how Parliament made its decision was based on whether the patentee had obtained a reasonable return for the work of developing the invention. Indeed, this test was the test the court applied and it was codified[250] in the

---

240 William Hindmarch, *A Treatise on the Law Relating to the Patent Privileges for the Sole Use of Inventions: And the Practice of Obtaining Letters Patents for Inventions* (London: Stevens 1846), p 150.

241 Thomas Webster, *The Law and Practice of Letters Patent for Inventions: Statutes, Practical Forms, and Digest of Reported Cases* (Crofts and Blenkard 1841), p 20.

242 William Hindmarch, *A Treatise on the Law Relating to the Patent Privileges for the Sole Use of Inventions: And the Practice of Obtaining Letters Patents for Inventions* (London: Stevens 1846), p 556.

243 (1843) 1 WPC 729, 733–734

244 (1843) 1 WPC 737, 739.

245 He was originally elected to the House of Commons for Camelford in 1810.

246 He was called by Lincoln's Inn in 1808 (although he had been admitted to the Faculty of Advocates in Scotland in 1800).

247 Meeting under SO No 198: see 52 LJ 879 (7 July 1819) as amended by 55 LJ 826 (30 June 1823).

248 It is doubtful that the views of Select Committees would be relevant at the time as Parliamentary debate was not relevant to statutory interpretation: *Miller v Taylor* (1769) 4 Burr 2303 at 2332 (98 ER 201 at 217), Willes J (although as there was no real Parliamentary record this is hardly surprising).

249 Hollingrake's Patent Act 1830, recital (5).

250 The Patents, Designs and Trade Marks Act 1883 codified some of the basic principles of the case law as no principles had been expressed in the Letters Patent for Inventions Act 1835; cf Robert Burrell and Catherine Kelly, "Parliamentary Rewards and the Evolution of the Patent System" (2015) 74 *Cam LJ 423* at 446 (suggesting a link between the Parliamentary system and the new Privy Council system).

Patents, Designs and Trade Marks Act 1883, which required the Privy Council to consider whether the patentee had been "inadequately remunerated"[251] having regard to the "nature and merits" of the invention and "profits made by the patentee".[252] At the most superficial level, by way of the Privy Council, it appears that the rules from one private Act at least were adopted in the general law.

The old Standing Orders

While it is clear that the substantive rules for obtaining a prolongation could not be those based on "established" Parliamentary practice, the House of Lords Standing Orders did play a role.[253] The Standing Order requiring notice to be posted was more or less adopted in the text of section 4 of the Letters Patent for Inventions Act 1835 itself. The second requirement that the Bill will not be considered unless the patent has less than two years to run was not included on the face of the Act. However, in *Macintosh's Patent*[254] the Privy Council refused to hear a petition eighteen months before the expiry of the patent because the income earned during that period might affect the outcome of the application.[255] The Patents Act 1839 imposed a new requirement that the petition be presented more than six months before the expiry of the patent to minimise the chances of a gap in protection.[256] It also allowed for cases to continue where the patent expires before the end of the application.[257] In other words, the effect of the Standing Orders appears to have been reflected, albeit in modified form, through the cases and subsequent enactments. The practice became to petition the Privy Council six to twelve months before the expiry of the patent.[258] As the Standing Orders required the patent to expire within two years of the commencement of the session by the time the Bill was passed, in effect, it would be only a little longer than the period expected by the Privy Council; and allowing for the uncertainties attached to Parliamentary proceedings it is possible that the effect was the same.

The final Standing Order had two limbs: first, to precluded assignees from obtaining an extension of letters patent and, secondly, prohibiting inventors who purchased their inventions from abroad getting an extended patent. In relation to the first limb, the 1835 Act did not on its face appear to restrict the right to petition to the original inventor. Indeed, the Privy Council granted a patent to assignees on a number of occasions.[259] Nevertheless, a

251 Patents, Designs and Trade Marks Act 1883, s 25(5).
252 Patents, Designs and Trade Marks Act 1883, s 25(4).
253 The relevant Standing Orders were only omitted in 1889 (that on notice was merged with general notice provisions in 1837).
254 (1837) 2 HPC 1017; 1 WPC 739 (the very limited reporting of this case does not refer to the Standing Orders).
255 *Kyan's Application* (No 2 of 1838) was dismissed for being premature (made six years after grant): see *Commissioner of Patents Journal* (1859), 8 April 1859, Issue 549: 449.
256 Patents Act 1839, s 2.
257 This was to address the issue that occurred in *Bodmer's Case* (1839) 3 HPC 261; 2 Moo PC 471 (12 ER 1085) (where the patent expired by the time the Privy Council could hear the case and so no extension was possible); see Patents Act 1839, s 2. The issue was also mentioned in evidence before the 1844 Select Committee on the Judicial Committee: *Report of Select Committee of House of Lords to Consider an Act for Amending [the Judicial Committee Act 1833] with Minutes of Evidence* (1844 HL Papers 34), Vol 19, p 323 at Henry Reeve (Clerk to Privy Council) Q598 (p 52) and Lord Brougham Q916 (p 82–3).
258 William Hindmarch, *A Treatise on the Law Relating to the Patent Privileges for the Sole Use of Inventions: And the Practice of Obtaining Letters Patents for Inventions* (London: Stevens 1846), p 561.
259 *Whitehouse's Patent* (1838) 3 HPC 743n; 1 WPC 473; *Russell's Patent* (1838) 2 HPC 323; 2 Moo PCC 496 (12 ER 1095); *Southworth's Patent* (1837) 3 HPC 213; 1 WPC 486; *Wright's Patent* (1837) 3 HPC 227; 1

view developed in the profession that an extension should not be granted to an assignee.[260] This view was acted upon in *Spilsbury v Clough*[261] where the court pointed out that the 1835 Act refers to the person who "hath or shall hereafter obtain any Letters Patent" which, the Court said, must mean the person who obtained the Letters Patent from the Crown (and so not an assignee).[262] While it is unlikely that Lord Brougham, the proponent of the 1835 Act, had intended to use the words with that intention[263] as the previous cases before the Privy Council suggest,[264] it became clear that the effect of the old no assignee rule from Standing Orders might be felt even if not intended. Accordingly, Parliament stepped in once more in the Judicial Committee Act 1844 and confirmed that a prolongation could be granted to an assignee.[265]

The second limb, which prohibited extensions from those who obtained the patent from abroad, was not adopted by the Privy Council. In *Soames' Patent*[266] Lord Brougham stated that the fact that the invention was imported and not invented did "take away the merit, but it makes it much smaller" and later after the jurisdiction was well established it was clear that something well known abroad would struggle to get an extension.[267] It was a factual, rather than legal, difficulty.

A remaining role for Parliament?

Lord Brougham's suggestion that a petitioner could still return to Parliament came true. In 1837, the Fourdrinier brothers petitioned Parliament once more in an attempt to revive their lost patent[268] and obtain a further term of protection.[269] The Bill had only had a First Reading before it became clear that it was thought that some form of reward was more appropriate.[270] In 1844, the Earl of Dundonald (the famous sailor and son of the petitioner in 1785) petitioned Parliament complaining that a seven-year extension was not adequate for him to recover a just reward from the patents for the steam engines

WPC 561; *Jones' Patent* (1840) 2 HPC 177; 1 WPC 577; *Galloway's Patent* (1843) 2 HPC 821; 1 WPC 724; *Soames' Patent* (1843) 4 HPC 715; 1 WPC 729, 4 HPC 715; as well as to an administratix: *Dowton's Patent* (1839) 1 WPC 565.

260 See Richard Godson, *A Practical Treatise on the Law for Patents for Inventions and Copyright* (2nd Ed, London: Saunders and Benning 1840); referred to after the event in William Hindmarch, *A Treatise on the Law Relating to the Patent Privileges for the Sole Use of Inventions: And the Practice of Obtaining Letters Patents for Inventions* (London: Stevens 1846), p 561.

261 (1842) 4 HPC 633; 2 QB 466 (114 ER 184); this was a confirmation case under s 1 of the 1835 Act, but the relevant text is the same in s 1 and s 4.

262 (1842) 4 HPC 633; 2 QB 466 (114 ER 184 at 187).

263 William Hindmarch, *A Treatise on the Law Relating to the Patent Privileges for the Sole Use of Inventions: And the Practice of Obtaining Letters Patents for Inventions* (London: Stevens 1846), p 561, n (u)) points to some observations by Lord Brougham in *Galloway's Patent* (1843) 2 HPC 821; 1 WPC 724 at 725–726. However, as this was an assignee case and an extension was granted, it is difficult to see how this supports the view.

264 *Morgan's Patent* (1843) 4 HPC 707; 1 WPC 737 at 738 (if the assignee is not remunerated at all, the chance of the patentee making an advantageous conveyance materially diminished).

265 Judicial Committee Act 1844, s 4 (and s 7 saved those to assignees already extended).

266 *Soames' Patent* (1843) 4 HPC 715; 1 WPC 717 at 733.

267 See *Claridge's Patent* (1851) 6 HPC 277; 7 Moo PCC 394 (13 ER 932).

268 I.e. which were the subject of the earlier Fourdriniers' Paper Making Machine Act 1807 and Fourdriniers' Patent Petition 1822.

269 Fourdriniers' Patent Bill 1837.

270 See Chapter 9.

he had invented.[271] This petition directly led to the Letters Patent Amendment Bill 1844[272] being introduced which would give the Privy Council power to grant a fourteen-year extension.[273] That Bill did not progress beyond First Reading, but it was soon followed by what became the Judicial Committee Act 1844, which also provided for extensions of up to fourteen years.[274] So the role of Parliament was entirely overtaken by the Privy Council. The evidence for allowing extensions of fourteen years rested largely on the evidence of the Earl of Dundonald, who reiterated the issues he had set out in his petition by describing the delays and problems he faced in exploiting his own steam engine and the problems faced by his father.[275] Thus, it might be argued that the failure of a private Act was used as a reason to extend the Privy Council's jurisdiction. The new jurisdiction also affected the number of extensions granted.

Prolongation before the Privy Council

Indeed, the fears of Warburton were well founded, the Privy Council proving to be far more generous in granting extensions than Parliament ever was. In the period between 1835 and 1858[276] the following shows the success rate:

Table 8.1 Applications for patent prolongation before the Privy Council, 1835–1859

Year	Number of petitions	Granted	Refused	Withdrawn/abandoned
1835	3	1	1	1
1836	5	3	0	2
1837	3	1	0	2
1838	5	3	2	0
1839	5	5	0	0
1840	3	1	2	0
1841	1	0	0	1
1842	1	0	1	0
1843	5	3	1	1
1844	3	3	0	0
1845	4	2	0	2
1846	5	1	2	2

271 See Earl of Dundonald, Third Report of Select Committee on Public Petitions 1844 at p, 19 (No 147) and Appendix at p 18 (No 32); a similar petition was lodged in the House of Lords: 76 LJ 32 (16 February 1844).
272 Letters Patent Amendment Bill 1844 (1844 HL Papers 17), Vol 4, p 565.
273 This is clear from the newspaper reporting: see for example, *The Times*, 20 February 1844.
274 Judicial Committee Act 1844, s 2.
275 *Report of Select Committee of House of Lords to Consider an Act for Amending [Judicial Committee Act 1833] with Minutes of Evidence* (1844 HL Papers 34), Vol 19, p 323, Q740 to Q74 and Q91 to Q93 (it appears that his father still made no money despite the Act extending his patent).
276 A list of all the applications for prolongation (and confirmation) were included in the Patent Office, *Commissioner of Patents Journal* (1859), 8 April 1859, Issue 549: 449, at 449–472 and extended by Patent Office, *Commissioner of Patents Journal* (1860), 13 November 1960, Issue 716, p 1361; this list was extended further by Patent Office, *Commissioner of Patents Journal* (1861), 17 May 1861, Issue 769, p 631; Patent Office, *Commissioner of Patents Journal* (1867), 9 August 1867, Issue 1419, p 1387; there was a complete list, in a different form in Patent Office, *Official Journal of the Patent Office* (1884), 23 December 1884, Issue 102, p 1427; an earlier shorter list was presented to Parliament in 1840: *Return of Cases in Which Judicial Committee of Privy Council Have Reported on Person Having Letters Patent; Application for Prolongation of Patents* (1840 HC Paper 155), Vol 29, p 559). The number of prolongations was also reported (until the end of the power in 1977) in the Commissioner's and then Comptroller's annual reports.

Year	Number of petitions	Granted	Refused	Withdrawn/abandoned
1847	4	1	3	0
1848	1	1	0	0
1849	8	5	1	2
1850	8	3	4	1
1851	8	4	3	1
1852	6	4	1	1
1853	10	4	4	2
1854	9	4	2	3
1855	3	2	1	0
1856	6	1	5	0
1857	5	1	3	1
1858	3	0	2	1
1859	1	1	0	0
Total	115	54	38	23

Accordingly, in the twenty-five years following the power to extend patents being granted to the Judicial Committee fifty-three applications were successful. In the twenty-five years prior there were two successful applications before Parliament. This simple comparison, however, ignores external factors. The number of patents granted annually started to increase significantly from the early 1830s and so there were simply more patents which *could* be extended. Yet if we contrast the failure rate before the Privy Council with that before Parliament it is clear that 47 per cent of patents were extended whereas before Parliament on one reading only 12 per cent of those who started the procedure before Parliament actually received an Act. The granting of this power to the Privy Council really did make a difference.

A chequered history?

It is the role of private Acts to extend patents which has been mentioned most frequently in the literature. However, aside from a few flurries of activity, such as in the last quarter of the eighteenth century, it was actually an incredibly rare thing. More telling still is the fact that when the power to extend patents was transferred from Parliament to the Privy Council it was not due to any great demand. Indeed, most patent reformers thought it was a relatively unimportant reform – yet it was one of the first. Once the Privy Council started considering patent term extensions not only did the numbers increase substantially, but the standard was lowered. The idea of patent term extension was clearly adopted from private legislation, but not the practice.

9 The grant of Parliamentary rewards
An alternative

Introduction

A patent was not the only award for an invention. It was also possible for Parliament to vote to supply an inventor with a reward.[1] These sometimes went to inventors who had petitioned the House of Commons[2] and sometimes inventors were given it without a petition. The rewards formed a small but established role for inventors during the eighteenth and nineteenth centuries.[3] Indeed, these payments by Parliament have received more attention than other aspects of Parliament's role in encouraging invention. Some patent historians have seen the rewards as Parliament stepping in to remedy defaults otherwise existent in the patent system.[4] However, the scope of these rewards is somewhat in the eye of the beholder. The discussion of Parliamentary rewards is framed very much by the awards in question. In many respects, the rationale for giving the reward is individualised. Thus, a list of rewards is very important. The most well-known list of awards is that of Patrick Colquhoun,[5] which was included in the evidence before the 1829 Select Committee.[6] This list was improved upon in the 1830s[7] and, more recently, by the work of Burrell and Kelly.[8] It has been developed further by the author.[9]

Parliamentary rewards

It is important to clarify what is meant here by a Parliamentary reward for the purposes of this story. Since 1688, it has been a basic principle of the British constitution that

---

1 They were not prizes as such as the reward was sought and paid after the event.
2 There were some which were awarded on the motion of a member.
3 Robert Burrell and Catherine Kelly, "Public Rewards and Innovation Policy: Lessons from the Eighteenth and Nineteenth Centuries" (2014) 77 *MLR* 858 at 859.
4 Klaus Boehm with Aubrey Silberston, *The British Patent System: I. Administration* (Cambridge 1967), pp 25–26; Christine MacLeod, *Inventing the Industrial Revolution: The English Patent System 1660–1800* (Cambridge 1988), p 193.
5 Patrick Colquhoun, *A Treatise on the Wealth, Power, and Resources of the British Empire* (London: Joseph Mawman 1815), pp 231–232.
6 *Report from the Select Committee on the Law Relative to Patents for Invention* (1829 HC Papers 332), Vol 3, p 415 at p 181.
7 "List of Parliamentary Reward Granted for Useful Discoveries, Inventions and Improvements" (1832) 13 *Mechanics Magazine* 61.
8 Robert Burrell and Catherine Kelly, "Public Rewards and Innovation Policy: Lessons from the Eighteenth and Nineteenth Centuries" (2014) 77 *MLR* 858.
9 See Phillip Johnson, *Parliament, Inventions and Patents: A Research Guide and Bibliography* (Routledge 2018), Part 5.

the government[10] can only spend the money it has been given[11] by Parliament.[12] This means that any payment made by the government is ultimately authorised by Parliament. In one sense, therefore, any government payment to an inventor is a reward from Parliament and so it would be perfectly legitimate to consider any government award to be indirectly a Parliamentary reward. A narrower definition is used here so that a payment is only treated as a Parliamentary reward where there is a specific resolution of Parliament authorising payment to a named individual as a reward for an invention. Using this narrow definition means that Parliament specifically and individually considered and then voted as to whether to make the reward.

For example, the Admiralty and Army routinely paid rewards to inventors during the nineteenth century, such payments being mentioned in the annual estimates.[13] The payment to the inventor was not, however, specifically authorised by a resolution of Parliament. There was also funding to the Longitude Board, set up under the Longitude Acts,[14] to give prizes and payments to those who made progress towards a method of finding longitude.[15] Derek Howe has identified £52,535 having been paid in this way.[16] These payments were made under a general power[17] and not by specific resolution.[18] Except in a few cases, there was no direct involvement of Parliament[19] in determining whether a reward should be paid to the individual inventor and so it is suggested that these general cases should not be seen Parliamentary rewards.

Similarly, the government sometimes paid someone to design (or invent) something. The most well-known example of this is probably the payment of £15,287 4s 10d[20] over nearly 15 years to Charles Babbage to enable him to perfect his machine for the construction of numerical tables.[21] These payments, while authorised by Parliament as part of the Civil

---

10 I.e. the Crown.

11 There are some government entities which "trade", such as the Intellectual Property Office, but the basis for this – the Government Trading Funds Act 1973 – does not need to be explored here as it is not relevant to our discussion.

12 The position was more complicated before the Bill of Rights, art 4, as the King could levy certain duties but not taxation. Thus, where the King could raise enough money from these duties there was no need to summon Parliament to raise taxation: see Thomas Erskine May, *A Treatise upon the Law Privileges, Proceedings and Usage of Parliament* (1st Ed, Charles Knight & Co 1844), p 319.

13 These rewards seem to be a regular inclusion from the 1860s (see for example, *Estimates of Effective and Non-effective Army Services: 1864–65* (1864 HC Papers 50), Vol 35, p 1 at p 64 where £3,000 was allocated for rewards to inventors). In some years, additional information was published relating to the rewards paid: *Reports and Correspondence Explanatory of Item C (Rewards to Inventors) in Army Estimates, 1870–71* (1870 HC Papers 266), Vol 42, p 375; *Supplementary Army Estimate, 1871–72 (Rewards to Inventors)* (1871 HC Papers 426 and 451), Vol 38, p 365 and 367.

14 It was constituted under the Discovery of Longitude at Sea Act 1713, s 1.

15 There was also a prize scheme to find the so-called North West Passage around the top of North America: see Discovery of North-West Passage Act 1744.

16 Derek Howe, "Britain's Board of Longitude the Finances 1714–1828" (1998) 84 (4) *The Mariner's Mirror* 400.

17 This was originally in the Discovery of Longitude at Sea Act 1713, s 5 and extended by later longitude enactments.

18 Some payments were made by Parliament in relation to longitude: see p 150.

19 But there was by particular Members of Parliament, see below.

20 This is usually rounded up £17,000: see Anthony Hyman, *Charles Babbage: Pioneer of the Computer* (Princeton 1982), p 169; Bruce Collier and James MacLachlan, *Charles Babbage: And the Engine of Perfection* (Oxford 1998), p 61; also see Charles Babbage, *Passages from the Life of a Philosopher* (Longman 1864), Chapters 5 and 6 where the figures are also somewhat imprecise.

21 Account of the sum expended under *Civil Contingencies: For the Year 1823* (1824 HC Papers 40), Vol 16, p 275 at p 6 (£1,547); *For the Year 1829* (1830 HC Papers 127), Vol 18, p 535 at p 13 (£1,500); *For the Year 1830*

Contingencies, were not a Parliamentary reward as there was no specific resolution.[22] There are also instances where the government has paid damages (or a licence) to an inventor to use the inventions; such as the £20,000[23] paid to Francis Petit Smith and others for the use of the screw propeller.[24] Once more this is not a Parliamentary reward in the sense used here. Similarly, John Palmer was paid £50,000 in relation to setting up a coach system to carry the mail.[25] This could be said to be a "reward"[26] whereas in fact it is suggested that it is better seen as the settlement of a long-running dispute between Palmer and the government relating to a share of the profits agreed in the original contract for setting up the postal service.

There are difficult cases where it is unclear whether something is a reward or not. Sir William Congreve[27] and Henry Shrapnel were given a pension[28] by the Master of Ordnance in 1814, but after a specific debate in the House of Commons[29] it was held to be lawful[30] despite being a Crown pension. Thus, Parliament specifically authorised its continued payment (and made allowances in the estimates[31]) but did not originally authorise the pension. There are also awards to the likes of Sir William Adams who pursued a reward relating to his treatment of ophthalmia,[32] but he actually received an award of £4,000 for his superintendence and foundation of the eye hospital.[33] There are also payments to Thomas Chapman who petitioned Parliament for a reward[34] and was given a reward of £218 2s 6d out of the Civil Contingency Fund.[35] Chapman's payment was not specifically voted by Parliament and so is not treated as a reward by Parliament for these purposes.

(1831 HC Papers 25), Vol 13, p 355 at 10 (£3,600); *For the Year 1831* (1832 HC Papers 114), Vol 13, p 355 at p 12 (£2,000); *For the Year 1832* (1833 HC Papers 172), Vol 14, p 509 at p 11 (£3,657 16s 6d); *For the Year 1833* (1834 HC Papers 186), Vol 42, p 483 at p 11 (£1,782 11s 4d); and *For the Year 1834* (1835 HC Papers 148), Vol 38, p 553 at 9 (£1,200).

22 The payment was specifically stated to be a payment for the machine not the invention: HC Deb, 13 February 1832, Vol 10(3rd), cols 302, 303 and 306.

23 Sometimes mistakenly stated to be a reward to inventors: also see Leader in *Naval and Military Gazette*, 19 May 1855 at p 314 extracted as a Letter in *On the Introduction and Progress of the Screw Propeller* (Longman, Brown and Green 1856), p 45; and *Vance v Bond*, The Times, 1 February 1858.

24 *Screw Propeller: Navy Estimates* (1853–4 HC Papers 100), Vol 58, p 135 p 45; see HC Deb, 15 May 1855, Vol 138 (3rd), cols 639–660.

25 Grant of John Palmer, Esquire (Post Office Services) Act 1813 (also see the earlier John Palmer Bill 1808 (1808 HL Papers 105), Vol 15, p 765).

26 See Robert Burrell and Catherine Kelly, "Public Rewards and Innovation Policy: Lessons from the Eighteenth and Nineteenth Centuries" (2014) 77 *MLR* 858 at 863.

27 A payment of £316 was made to Congreve in relation to his method of impeding the forgery of bank notes (see Accounts 1819, Appendix 12 (75 CJ 860)) but this was not paid by any specific resolution and so is not a reward: cf Robert Burrell and Catherine Kelly, "Public Rewards and Innovation Policy: Lessons from the Eighteenth and Nineteenth Centuries" (2014) 77 *MLR* 858 at 864.

28 See *Notification of Grant to Colonel Congreve for His Invention of Rockets* (1814–15 HC Papers 329), Vol 9, p 459.

29 HC Deb, 20 June 1815, Vol 31 (1st), cols 901–905.

30 On whether it violated the Civil List and Secret Money Act 1782, s 32 (described as Burke's Act in the debate) and the Succession to the Crown Act 1707, s 25 (described as Anne's Act).

31 See for instance, *Return of Pensions in Artillery Service, and Ordnance Military Corps, 1820* (1821 HC Papers 234), Vol 15, p 379.

32 See *Report of the Ophthalmic Committee Presented to the House of Commons* (William Clowes: London 1821), p 6–7.

33 77 CJ 460 (25 July 1822). Robert Burrell and Catherine Kelly, "Public Rewards and Innovation Policy: Lessons from the Eighteenth and Nineteenth Centuries" (2014) 77 *MLR* 858 at 864 take the view that the payment was for the treatment. However, the resolution of the Commons makes it clear that it was for superintendence of the hospital.

34 74 CJ 94 (4 February 1819).

35 Appendix No 3, 76 CJ 574 (76 CJ 80; 16 February 1821).

Procedure and rewards

A grant of money from the Commons[36] of any type is not effectual in law without the assent of the Crown and the House of Lords.[37] The statutory authority[38] for such a grant is usually a Supply or Appropriation Act which goes through the same Parliamentary procedure as other enactments.[39] There were, however, a handful of individual Bills passed to grant a reward to an individual.

The process of obtaining a reward was usually started by a petition[40] from the inventor or his or her representative being presented to the House of Commons. Standing Orders required that such a petition must be recommended by the Crown before a resolution could be passed.[41] Accordingly, where a petition did not have Crown approval it had to be re-presented[42] for it to proceed. This requirement greatly restricted the availability of rewards to inventors as Parliament could not side-step this requirement. So when the petition for a private Bill by the Fourdrinier brothers to restore and extend their patents was considered by a Select Committee and a payment (without Crown approval) proposed as an alternative to the Bill, it was recommitted to remove this irregularity.[43]

Once a petition (or motion) had been received it would usually be referred to a Select Committee to consider its worth and make a recommendation to the House as to an appropriate sum. The report would be referred to the Committee of Supply[44] who would pass a resolution usually in the form: "That a sum not exceeding £X, be granted to His Majesty, to be paid to Y for Z," and so, by way of example, Charles Irving was awarded five thousand pounds for making sea water fresh and so the resolution read:[45]

> . . .That a Sum, not exceeding Five thousand Pounds, be granted to His Majesty, to be paid to Charles Irving, for the Discovery of an easy and practicable Method of making Sea Water fresh and wholesome

These resolutions are then referred to the Committee of Ways and Means. The Committee of Supply therefore controls the public expenditure and that of Ways and Means provides for the application of money to the purpose. Thus, Ways and Means votes for the money out of the Consolidated Fund to pay for the grants awarded.[46] Once both Committees have

---

36 The House of Lords could not make such a grant during the relevant period as the supply was entirely the privilege of the House of Commons.

37 Thomas Erskine May, *A Treatise upon the Law Privileges, Proceedings and Usage of Parliament* (1st Ed, Charles Knight & Co 1844), p 319.

38 Burrell and Kelly suggests that grants were made without specific legislative authority: Robert Burrell and Catherine Kelly, "Public Rewards and Innovation Policy: Lessons from the Eighteenth and Nineteenth Centuries" (2014) 77 *MLR* 858 at 862. It may be they are distinguishing between the general Appropriation Acts and a specific Act of Parliament for a reward.

39 Three readings in both Houses and then Royal Assent.

40 In contrast to private Bills, rewards could still start by motion.

41 15 CJ 211 (11 December 1706).

42 For example, John Harrison's petition in 1773 was presented on 2 April 1773 (34 CJ 244), withdrawn 6 May 1773 (34 CJ 302) and re-presented with Crown consent the same day (34 CJ 302).

43 92 CJ 478 (15 June 1837).

44 E.g David Hartley's petition: 13 May 1774 (34 CJ 746); the Committee of Supply had to be held on a different day: Order 18 February 1668 (9 CJ 52).

45 33 CJ 745 (11 May 1772).

46 See Thomas Erskine May, *A Treatise upon the Law Privileges, Proceedings and Usage of Parliament* (1st Ed, Charles Knight & Co 1844), pp 329–331.

passed the relevant resolutions they are implemented by a Supply (or later Appropriation) Act which, amongst other things, includes a long list of the resolutions turned into statutory form.[47] The legal power to pay the reward therefore comes from the Appropriation Act and not the resolution itself.[48] The Appropriation Act had to be introduced in the House of Commons and it would go through the normal three readings and committee stage before being passed to the House of Lords to go through the same (often truncated) stages. It then become law upon being given Royal Assent.

The rights and privileges of the House of Commons in relation to money Bills have their origins in the fifteenth century[49] and from the end of the seventeenth century the Commons increasingly took objection to the Lords amending money Bills.[50] By the eighteenth century the claims of the House of Commons in matters of supply were "seldom or but faintly controverted by the Lords".[51] It appears that by the late eighteenth century, the period when most rewards were given, it was accepted that the only amendments that could be made to the supply Bills by the Lords were literal mistakes.[52] Thus, the supply granted by the Commons should not have been challenged in the Lords. Indeed, except in relation to Henry Phillips' claim,[53] this privilege was observed in relation to rewards.

Where the payment was made through a special Act of Parliament (e.g. Joanna Stephens' Reward (Cure of Stone) Act 1738), a resolution would still be passed for the money to be paid[54] but that resolution would be implemented through a particular Act and not in the general Appropriation Act. This approach to paying a reward occurred only twice[55]: to Joanna Stephens and Thomas Lombe,[56] although there were also various payments to individuals through the Longitude Acts 1753–1765 following a resolution.

Deductions and fees

In addition to Parliamentary fees,[57] costs paid up front as it were, there were also deductions made to any Parliamentary award. The officers of the Exchequer were entitled to take

---

47 Rewards to inventors have also been made in a slightly different fashion. This involved a resolution of the Committee of Supply and then an Address being made by the Commons to the Crown asking for payment to be made. The Crown would then make the payment and, in the subsequent session, present an account to Parliament of payments made pursuant to Addresses of the House of Commons. The Appropriation Act would then authorise the payment of the sum to reimburse the money.

48 However, Appropriation Acts usually included a power to authorise payments already made pursuant to resolutions: Thomas Erskine May, *A Treatise upon the Law Privileges, Proceedings and Usage of Parliament* (1st Ed, Charles Knight & Co 1844), p 320.

49 John Hatsell, *Precedents and Proceedings in the House of Commons* (Hansard 1818), Vol 3, p 147.

50 The first express exception taken by the Commons was in 1690: see John Hatsell, *Precedents and Proceedings in the House of Commons* (Hansard 1818), Vol 3, p 152 (also see p 125, No 41).

51 John Hatsell, *Precedents and Proceedings in the House of Commons* (Hansard 1818), Vol 3, p 153.

52 John Hatsell, *Precedents and Proceedings in the House of Commons* (Hansard 1818), Vol 3, p 154.

53 See pp 155–6.

54 23 CJ 325 (10 April 1739).

55 Henry Phillips' attempt to get a reward was tried through this method, but both times it was rejected by the House of Lords. Further, John Palmer's payment was by a personalised Act: Grant of John Palmer, Esquire (Post Office Services) Act 1813.

56 Lombe's Silk Engines Act 1731.

57 These were similar to private Bills: see pp 27–9.

certain fees for paying a grantee money. The fees were usually based on a percentage of the amount of money granted, although like much eighteenth- and early nineteenth-century administration the matter was complicated.[58] During the latter part of the eighteenth century and until the mid-nineteenth century the positions at the Exchequer were slowly regulated (i.e. capped) or eventually phased out as the office holder died.[59] But during the relevant period fees were routinely paid. As it was not based on simple percentages it is difficult to estimate how much would have been paid. Dr Jenner, for example, paid £725 10s 6d[60] on a receipt of £10,000.[61] While some of these fees paid by Jenner *may* have been Parliamentary fees[62] most would have been made up by these Exchequer fees. When Henry Phillips' unsuccessful Bill was before Parliament it was suggested that the Exchequer fees for £4,000 would be around £400.[63]

However, Parliament could exempt a grantee from these Exchequer fees by stating the money be "issued and paid without any Fee or other Deduction whatsoever". In such a case, no Exchequer fees were payable and the entire grant would be paid to the inventor. Indeed, Jenner's second grant of £20,000[64] was made with this stipulation and so he received the entirety of the sum.

Rewards paid

The payment of rewards began with Thomas Lombe in 1732 and continued until the award to Captain Scott in 1872. The following table sets out the rewards paid by Parliament, showing the payee, what the reward related to and the amount awarded, and to enable comparisons of the "value" of the reward the rewards have been put into 2016 money.[65] There are some rewards included on the list which are not actually rewards within the meaning used here (in italics). They are included as earlier commentators included them in their list.[66] For these purposes, the inflation value has been worked out by reference to labour earnings (the relative wealth compared to average wage), which have been used as it views inventing as a job, but other measures could be used. Finally, so that the relative value of the rewards can be given there is a rank assigned so that it is possible to see where the award is in terms of other rewards paid:

---

58 The Taxation Act 1692, s 9 required the Barons of the Exchequer to provide a Table of Fees of ancient usage. From that point onwards, these were the only fees that could be charged. A copy of this table of usage is at Appendix No 34 of the Sixth Report of the Commissioners into the Public Account of the Kingdom 1782 printed as William Molleson, *The Reports of the Commissioners Appointed to Examine, Take, and State the Public Accounts of the Kingdom* (Caddell 1783), pp 353–360.
59 For a discussion of this see Philip Harling, *The Waning of 'Old Corruption': The Politics of Economical Reform in Britain, 1779–1846* (Clarendon 1996).
60 Parliament had not intended for any deduction to be made so the fees were refunded: see Appropriation Act 1803, s 18.
61 See Appropriation Act 1802, s 18.
62 See pp 27–9.
63 *Morning Chronicle and London Advertiser*, 7 June 1781.
64 Appropriation Act 1807, s 20.
65 All figures are based on Lawrence H Officer and Samuel H Williamson, "Five Ways to Compute the Relative Value of a UK Pound Amount, 1270 to Present," MeasuringWorth, 2017.
66 See p 144.

Table 9.1 Parliamentary rewards for inventions, 1732–1872

Year	Inventor	Invention	Value	2016 Value	Rank
1732	Thomas Lombe	Silk machine	£14,000	£26,470,000	2
1739	Joanna Stephens	Cure for stone	£5,000	£9,434,000	7
1753	John Harrison	Longitude/Timekeeper	£1,250	£2,302,000	26
1753	William Whiston	Longitude/Survey	£500	£920,900	36
1755	Thomas Stephens	Making potash	£3,000	£5,434,000	13
1759	Thomas Lowndes	Improve brine salt	£1,280	£2,317,000	25
1762	John Harrison	Longitude/Timekeeper	£5,000 (not claimed)	£8,866,000	8
1764	John Blake	Transporting fish	£2,500	£4,457,000	16
1765	John Harrison	Longitude/Timekeeper	£10,000	£17,530,000	4
1765	Tobias Mayer	*Lunar tables*	£3,000	£5,259,000	14
1765	Leonhard Euler	Longitude/Calculations	£300	£525,900	40
1769	Charles Dingley	*Repairing windmill*	£2,000	£3,446,000	22
1772	Charles Irving	Making sea water fresh	£5,000	£8,109,000	10
1773	John Harrison	Longitude	£8,750	£14,500,000	5
1773	Richard Williams	Yellow dye	£2,000	£3,313,000	23
1774	David Hartley	Fire prevention	£2,500	£4,065,000	18
1779	James Berkenhout and Thomas Clark	Scarlet dye	£5,000	£7,856,000	11
1786	Louis Borrell	Turkey red dye	£2,500	£3,763,000	20
1790	Cuthbert Gordon	Dyes	£200	£273,300	43
1791	William Forsyth	Curing defects in trees	£1,500	£1,991,000	28
1793	Cuthbert Gordon	Cultivating plants	£100 (+£18 12s expenses)	£128,900 (+£23,980)	44
1795	Thomas Mudge	Time keepers	£2,500	£3,234,000	24
1799	Joseph Elkington	Draining system	£1,000	£1,162,000	33
1800	John Davis	Improving wheat affected by smut	£1,000	£1,111,000	34
1801	Arthur Young	Agriculture essays	£800	£859,600	37
1801	Thomas Foden	Wheat flour substitute	£500	£537,300	39
1802	Edward Jenner	Vaccination	£10,000 (+ £725 expenses)	£10,380,000 (+£752,800)	6
1802	Henry Greathead	Lifeboat	£1,200	£1,246,000	32
1803	James Carmichael Smith	Nitrous fumigation	£5,000 (+ £258 17s expenses)	£4,998,000 (+£258,700)	15
1807	Edward Jenner	Vaccination	£20,000	£17,710,000	3
1809	Edmund Cartwright	Cotton (wearing) manufactures	£10,000	£8,476,000	9
1810	George Manby	Communicating with stranded ships	£2,000	£1,651,000	30
1812	Samuel Crompton	The Mule (spinning)	£5,000	£3,824,000	19
1812	George Manby	Saving shipwrecked mariners	£1,250 (+expenses)	£955,900	35
1812	Henry Greathead	Life boat	£650	£497,100	41
1813	John Palmer	*Post Office*	£50,000	£36,450,000	1
1814	George Manby	Communicating with stranded ships	£2,000	£1,479,000	31

Year	Inventor	Invention	Value	2016 Value	Rank
1815	John Bell (by daught Elizabeth Whitfield)	Saving shipwrecked mariners	£500	£374,200	42
1823	George Manby	Communicating with stranded ships	£2,000	£1,744,000	29
1833	Thomas Morton	Patent slip	£2,500	£2,023,000	27
1840	Henry and Sealy Fourdrinier	Paper making	£7,000	£5,567,000	12
1853	William Snow Harris	Electrical conductors on ships	£5,000	£3,716,000	21
1860	Professor Hansen	Lunar tables	£1,000	£680,000	38
1872	Captain Scott	Gunnery inventions	£8,000	£4,340,000	17

Why rewards?

In comparison with the number of patents awarded during this period, the number of rewards is miniscule. During the height of Parliament's practice of giving rewards, 1750–1815, only about 1.5 per cent of "rewards" given were payments by Parliament with a little under 99 per cent being patents granted (the percentage of rewards then plummets as the number of patents granted increase substantially).[67] It is therefore important to consider why the 1 per cent chose Parliament over patents. While the reasons in an individual case may vary, the most likely reasons are availability of patents for the invention, the cost, and the potential money available. Each of these will be explored in turn.

Availability of patents

If a patent was not available to protect the "invention" then an inventor would clearly have to look elsewhere if he or she wishes to refund any expenses incurred (or to cover future expenses) and to get any profit from an invention. This may be Boehm's and Macleod's "defects" in the patent system spurring rewards.[68] Such an inventor might petition Parliament for a reward payment. There are at least three classes of rewarded inventions which clearly were not patentable. In the first class are those things which had been already been patented; as any second patent would lack novelty. Thomas Lombe's reward stems from his failure to extend his patent[69]; David Hartley's patent[70] was extended[71] but not in relation to ships where he was paid a reward to fund his future research; Thomas Morton's patent[72] was not extended but he was given a reward instead; and similarly, the Fourdrinier brothers' (second[73]) attempt to resuscitate and extend their patent by private Act[74] was instead dealt with by a reward. In each case, it is clear from the history of the grants that while the invention had been patentable (in the past) it was no longer novel and so was no longer patentable

---

67 There were about 2,500 patents granted over the period and 34 rewards given.
68 Klaus Boehm and Aubrey Silberston, *The British Patent System: I. Administration* (Cambridge 1967), pp 25–26; Christine MacLeod, *Inventing the Industrial Revolution: The English Patent System 1660–1800* (Cambridge 1988), p 193.
69 Patent No 422 (1718).
70 Patent No 1,037 (1773).
71 Hartley's Patent (Fire Prevention) Act 1776.
72 Morton's Patent Slip Bill 1832.
73 See Fourdriniers' Patent Petition 1822.
74 Fourdriniers' Patent Bill 1837.

at the time of the reward. Accordingly, the patent system was simply not available to these inventors – they were trying to get a greater reward than the patent system offered.

Similarly in the case of Edmund Cartwright, who had patented a number of textile inventions[75] and had had one of those patents extended by a private Act.[76] Well aware of this the Parliamentary committee gave him a reward largely to enable him to invest money to work the invention following various mill burnings by Luddites.[77] The payment to Charles Dingley 1769 was similarly to rebuild an innovative windmill after it had been destroyed in a riot.[78]

Finally, the £200 granted to Cuthbert Gordon was a "further" reward[79] as he had already received a patent for his cudbear dye.[80] Indeed, the small payment given to him compared to other dyers may be because of his earlier patent. Thus, once more, the rewards were not an alternative to granting a patent but rather the only option to the petitioner as patent rights were no longer available.

In contrast to these inventors, who had had patents, there was a second class of rewards to inventors for things which were clearly not patentable at any time: William Whiston's survey, Leonhard Euler's lunar theory,[81] Tobias Mayer's[82] and Professor Hansen's lunar tables, and Arthur Young's agricultural essays suggesting how to farm fenland.[83] None of these rewards could have been compensated by a patent as they would never have been seen as a method of manufacture.[84] In addition, it is unlikely that Dr Jenner's method of vaccination or Joseph Elkington's method of drainage would have been patentable at the time. Accordingly, this group of inventors would only had the option of a reward from Parliament.

A third class of rewards which would be ineligible for patents would be the repeat reward seeker. Accordingly, while George Manby may have been able[85] to get a patent for his Manby Mortar[86] when he first got a reward in 1810,[87] he would not have been able to do so in 1812, 1814 or 1823. The subsequent rewards were after the invention had been disclosed and so the patent system would no longer been available. The same would apply to Henry

---

75 Patent Nos 1,747 (1790); 1,787 (1791) and 1,876 (1792).

76 Cartwright's Woolcombing Machinery Act 1801; as to the burning see: *Report from the Committee on Dr. Cartwright's Petition Respecting His Weaving Machine* (1808 HC Papers 179), Vol 2, p 135 at pp 4–6.

77 See generally, *Report from the Committee on Dr. Cartwright's Petition Respecting His Weaving Machine* (1808 HC Papers 179), Vol 2, p 135.

78 See J Appleby, "Charles Dingley's Sawmill, or Public Spirit at a Premium" (1995) 143 *RSA Journal* 54.

79 44 CJ 411 (28 May 1789).

80 Patent No 727 (1758).

81 Emil A Fellmann, *Leonhard Euler* (Springer 2007), p 123 (it was theory used to produce Mayer's tables).

82 For details of his claim before the Longitude Board, see Eric Forbes, "Tobias Mayer's Claim for the Longitude Prize: A Study in 18th Century Anglo-German Relations" (1975) 28 *Journal of Navigation* 77.

83 These essays were published much earlier as Arthur Young, *Political Essays Concerning the Present State of the British Empire* (Stahan and Caddell 1772).

84 Statute of Monopolies, s 6.

85 Notwithstanding Manby's own workings of the invention before he petitioned Parliament, it is unlikely the idea of firing a rope to a stranded ship was novel, as John Bell, an artillery sergeant (later officer) seems to have devised something similar in 1792 and was awarded 50 guineas for his invention: see "LXXVI – On Saving the Lives of Mariners" (1811) 37 (Issue 158) *Philosophical Magazine* Series 1, p 455. His daughter was subsequently awarded another £500 in 1815.

86 The mortar worked by firing a thin rope from shore into the rigging of a ship in distress. This small rope would have a strong one attached which could then be pulled onto the ship and used to pull the ship to safety. For a detailed description see Robert Forbes, *Life-boats, Projectiles and Other Means for Saving Life* (Boston 1872), pp 19 et seq.

87 Had he patented it immediately in the early nineteenth century.

Greathead's reward for his development of the first lifeboat. In 1802 his lifeboat might have been novel, but this would not have been the case in relation to his subsequent application in 1812.

Accordingly, if one further excludes the payments to John Harrison for his timekeepers to work out longitude which were granted when his work still did not qualify for the prize under the Discovery of Longitude at Sea Act 1713,[88] it can be seen that many inventors who obtained rewards had no other choice. They were applying to Parliament because the patent system would simply not have been available to them (and in most cases would not even be today).

Cost

The cost of obtaining patents was notoriously high; the issue is dealt with in more detail in Chapter 10 but a figure of £100 for a patent extending to England is indicative. This figure only includes the fees and not the expenses that would have been incurred by having to live in London, hire clerks and agents and so forth. Thus, the full cost of getting a patent would be much higher. While the cost of a private Bill would usually have been higher still, as discussed in Chapter 2, a petition for a public grant would probably have had a lower cost.

It is difficult to provide precise figures as to how much it would *actually* cost to obtain a Parliamentary grant as there would be costs associated with visiting London and writing to MPs and others for support. However, the Parliamentary fees would be quite low.[89] Using the fees at the end of the period as a guide,[90] it would cost 6s 8d for a clerk to take charge of a petition and then a fee of £2 per day for a clerk sitting on a committee and a further £1 for writing the report of the committee. Assuming the committee sat for three days (which would be a long committee session at the time) it would cost £7 6s 8d plus general costs for witnesses attending and so forth. This means fees of £20–30 would be the most that would be expected. Accordingly, Cuthbert Gordon was given £18 12s in refunds of fees (which may have also included Exchequer fees). It was suggested in relation to Henry Phillips' reward that the Parliamentary fees would be about £80, but this was to be by way of a Bill and so the fees would be much higher (in particular there would be an ingrossment fee).[91] The two other recipients of Parliamentary rewards where fees are dealt with separately were James Carmichael Smyth who was given £258 17s to cover expenses and Dr Jenner an astronomical £725 10s 6d. However, as already explained, these fees are likely to be substantially made up of Exchequer fees in any event as their rewards were more significant.

Accordingly, it is suggested[92] that one of the incentives for inventors to petition Parliament for a grant was the relative low cost and low risks involved. If the petition was not picked

88 For a detailed history of Harrison's timekeeper see: Rupert Gould, "John Harrison and His Timekeepers" (1935) 31 *The Mariner's Mirror* 2; there is also the popular history: Dava Sobel, *Longitude* (Harper 2005).

89 The Table of Fees did not include grants of public money; but analogies seem to have been made as it was separately listed in the Anon, *Key to Both Houses of Parliament* (Longman 1832), p 497.

90 They were rationalised in 1830 so as to attribute a fee to doing something rather than to a person.

91 See debate: Sir Gilbert Elliot in *Morning Chronicle*, 7 June 1781.

92 Contrary to the suggestion in Robert Burrell and Catherine Kelly, "Public Reward and Innovation Policy: Lessons from the Eighteenth and Early Nineteenth Century" (2014) 77 *MLR* 858 at 880; they refer to the costs Adams faced for printing the evidence of committees (*The Times*, 11 July 1821). However, this cost was paid to commercially print the evidence and he was not ordered to print the evidence by Parliament.

up and the matter did not proceed to committee the cost would be less than one pound; and even if it went all the way to a resolution or refusal it would still be less than a fifth of the cost of a patent. Indeed, if successful the person *would* receive money and not simply a patent which may (or may not) make them sufficient revenue to cover the cost of obtaining that exclusive right in the first place.

Money available

As with many things, once one person has sought a Parliamentary reward other people will consider whether they think they might be eligible for a similar award. While this might apply across technologies it is much more likely to apply where the person works in the same field. It can be seen that Parliament paid rewards to a number of dye inventors. The first such reward was paid to Richard Williams for seven years of work and development and, with £2,000 being awarded, the Select Committee finding that Williams' yellow and green dyes had helped restore the reputation of British textiles in Spain.[93] Three other dyers[94] received payments over the next fifteen years totalling another £7,700. Accordingly, it may appear that many dyers,[95] although not all, went to Parliament for payment, rather than to the Crown for the grant of a patent. In respect of those who did not seek payment, James Turner who had patented his colour yellow[96] and Edward Bancroft who patented tree-based dyes (he called them quercitron),[97] may have thought that Parliament was sympathetic to dyers and that is why they sought to extend their patents,[98] in Bancroft's case twice.

Similarly, the payment of a reward to Greathead for his lifeboat could have encouraged Manby to petition. Furthermore, it is clear that Manby's success led to the successful claim by John Bell's daughter (Elizabeth Whitfield) for a reward of £500 and a series of unsuccessful petitions from William Mallison in 1811,[99] 1814,[100] 1816,[101] 1819[102] and 1820[103] for a reward for his life preservers. Mallison's case also shows that a favourable report from a Commons committee[104] is not enough. As other members of the Commons were reluctant to give him a reward, often pouring scorn on the utility of the invention.[105]

93 34 CJ 371 (14 June 1773).

94 James Berkenhout and Thomas Clark received £5,000 for scarlet and crimson (1779); Louis Borell received £2,500 for Turkey red (1786) and Cuthbert Gordon received £200 for cudbear (petitioned 1786, received 1789).

95 In addition, Anthony Bourboulon de Boneuil petitioned to extend his patent for bleaching clothes: 43 CJ 202 (8 February 1788).

96 Patent No 1,281 (1781).

97 Patent No 1,103 (1775).

98 Unsuccessfully in 1791 (James Turner Dye Invention Bill 1791: see Ingrossment: HL/PO/JO/10/2/65A), but in 1792 he was granted eleven years from the end of the session: Turner's Patent Act 1792, s 1.

99 66 CJ 357 (21 May 1811).

100 69 CJ 264 (13 May 1814).

101 71 CJ 485 (19 June 1816).

102 74 CJ 456 (18 May 1819) and 75 CJ 30 (7 December 1819).

103 75 CJ 446 (13 July 1820).

104 *Report of Committee on Mr Mallison's Petition* (1810–11 HC Papers 206), Vol 2, p 375.

105 See for example, the comments of Sir Joseph Yorke: HC Deb, 28 June 1815 vol 31(1st) cc1020 ("the plan to be wholly destitute of that practical utility. . .The great and only merit of Mr. Mallison's invention appeared to be, to have proved that cork was of a light and floating nature").

Public support

The Fourdrinier brothers originally obtained patents[106] related to paper-making which they managed to get extended by a private Act.[107] Their extended patent was revoked by the court and so they originally sought a private Act to restore the patent[108] and subsequently they sought a patent to restore and extend the patent.[109] A Select Committee was appointed by the House of Commons to consider the Bill and it concluded that it would be more appropriate for a Parliamentary reward to be given.[110] When this reward was not paid, many users and sellers of paper petitioned Parliament in support of the brothers arguing that they deserved the reward for the advantages they brought to the industry.[111] Indeed, there was a sustained campaign of support and a larger number of public petitions lodged the following year.[112] While this public support may not have been the original cause of the reward of £7,000 being proposed[113] such support probably ensured that payment was eventually made. This brings us to the final consideration, how many unsuccessful applications there were.

Unsuccessful applications

The lists of rewards rarely indicate the failed attempts to get rewards.[114] As most failures ended in petitions it is difficult to know why Parliament rejected the petition, or it may be the petitioner simply did not find a Parliamentary champion. These failed petitioners can be found in 1747 (Wadsworth's Cartridge Petition[115]), 1754 (Henry Delamaine[116]) and 1780 (William Storer[117]). The unsuccessful applicant whose petition went the furthest was Henry Phillips; in his case there is significant evidence of why it was refused and so it will be looked at in detail.

Henry Phillips invented a powder that he said to be particularly useful at killing insects on board ships. In contrast to most rewards, he had a Bill dedicated to his payment; it provided a payment of £500 immediately after the passage of the Act and a further £3,000 when the Admiralty indicated its efficacy.[118] When the Committee of Supply was considering giving a reward, Lord Nugent took the view that it was not appropriate "to vote away public money for private purposes",[119] but after a division[120] the Commons agreed with the

106 Patent Nos 2,487 (1801), 2,708 (1803) and 3,068 (1807).

107 Fourdriniers' Paper Making Machine Act 1807.

108 Fourdriniers' Patent Petition 1822: 55 LJ 70 (143 March 1822).

109 Fourdriniers' Patent Bill 1837.

110 *Report from the Select Committee on Fourdriniers' Patent; With the Minutes of Evidence, and Appendix* (1837 HC Papers 351), Vol 20, p 35.

111 See Public Petitions Committee: 4 July 1838, Thirty-Fifth Report, p 570 (Nos 8,623–8625); 10 July 1838, Thirty-Sixth Report, p 583 (No 8,732); 16–18 July 1838, Thirty-Seventh Report, p 603 (Nos 8,960–8,962).

112 See Public Petitions Committee: 24–25 April 1839, Twentieth Report, p 350–1 (No 6,495 to 6,510); 1 May 1839, Twenty-Second Report, p 386 (No 6,987 and 6,989).

113 See Henry and Sealy Fourdrinier 1840: Appropriation Act 1840, s 16.

114 See Robert Burrell and Catherine Kelly, "Public Reward and Innovation Policy: Lessons from the Eighteenth and Early Nineteenth Century" (2014) 77 *MLR* 858 at 861; but see Phillip Johnson, *Parliament, Inventions and Patents: A Research Guide and Bibliography* (Routledge 2018), Pt 4.2.

115 25 CJ 276 (6 February 1747).

116 26 CJ 913 (21 January 1754). This petition was referred to a committee, but it appears to have never sat.

117 37 CJ 579 (8 February 1780).

118 Henry Phillips' Bill 1781, Cl 1 (Ingrossment: HL/PO/JO/10/2/56).

119 *Morning Chronicle and London Advertiser*, 7 June 1781.

120 38 CJ 506 (7 June 1781).

reward being paid. In the Lords, there was some support for the reward although there was opposition from those, like Lord Ferrars, who were against the principle that public money should be applied for this purpose.[121] When debate resumed, Lord Abingdon spoke at length calling the Bill "shameful" as he said Phillips' powder was not a secret at all, but the same method that young boys used at school and, more troubling, he said the evidence Phillips had presented elsewhere suggested that the application of his powder to land would cost more than the value of the underlying land itself.[122] It was, therefore, useless and he said no reward should be given and the House of Lords essentially rejected the Bill.[123]

Henry Phillips was persistent. Further petitions were presented (and reported upon) in 1783[124] and 1784[125] and a Bill made it through the House of Commons again in 1785.[126] The House of Lords rejected it at Second Reading largely on the grounds that there was no better evidence that the powder worked than there had been in 1781. However, importantly, there was a suggestion, by the Lord Chancellor, that a patent was the proper way to reward such inventors and not these sorts of reward.[127]

What is most significant about this Bill is that it was, essentially, the House of Lords' only opportunity to comment on these sorts of rewards. Usually, as they were included in Appropriation Bills, the Lords would not interfere with the Commons prerogative over the supply.[128] It can be seen that there were concerns expressed about the efficacy of the invention, and that the evidence presented was not satisfactory, and also suggestions that patents, and not rewards, were the appropriate way of rewarding such inventors. An about-turn from the statements made when patents were not extended.[129]

Parliament, prizes and policy making

Robert Burrell and Catherine Kelly suggest that the rewards given by Parliament have had an "[i]mportant influence on the development of the patent system".[130] They suggest that the reward system demonstrates the growth of the social contract between patentee and state, and more particularly, they argue that the reward system solidified the function of the specification and the requirement of public disclosure. It is the second proposition which will be examined here.

Specification

Burrell and Kelly argue that Parliament "took a leading role in promoting the need for public disclosure of the invention as a precondition for assistance from the state"[131] and so, in other words, Parliament played a significant role in the development of the role of

---

121 House of Lords Debate on 4 July 1781 in *Morning Chronicle and London Advertiser*, 4 July 1781.
122 See House of Lords Debate on 10 July 1781 in *Dublin Evening Post*, 17 July 1781.
123 By adjourning out of the session: see 36 LJ 354 (10 July 1781).
124 Henry Phillips' Petition 1783: 39 CJ 488 (17 June 1783).
125 Henry Phillips Petition 1784: 40 CJ 31 (27 May 1784).
126 Henry Phillips' Bill 1785.
127 See House of Lords Debate on 20 July 1785 in *Saunder's News Letter*, 27 July 1785.
128 See pp 148; although strictly speaking this could equally apply to this Bill as it is also part of the supply.
129 See p 130.
130 Robert Burrell and Catherine Kelly, "Parliamentary Rewards and the Evolution of the Patent System" (2015) *Cam LJ* 423 at 424.
131 Robert Burrell and Catherine Kelly, "Parliamentary Rewards and the Evolution of the Patent System" (2015) *Cam LJ* 423 at 427.

the specification through the grant of Parliamentary rewards. At the outset, this hypothesis presents a problem in that it ignores the two Houses of Parliament. In the case of most of the awards the payment was made in the general supply and so, in accordance the Commons privilege, would not be considered by the House of Lords in any significant way.

In any event, their hypothesis begins with the reward granted to Thomas Lombe who had obtained a patent for his silk loom in 1718.[132] In 1732, he sought an Act for extending his patent but, instead was awarded a fortune of £14,000. Significantly, the Act awarding him the reward also required that a model be made of the machine. This requirement, they suggest, meant that Parliament clearly felt that more was needed than the specification itself.[133] While this might at first glance seem a compelling argument, it faces one significant problem. The original patent extension Bill[134] which was introduced in the House of Commons includes the requirement for the model to be created and deposited. The date of the Bill[135] suggests that this was drafted before the petition was even lodged. This means that Lombe was offering up a model before it ever reached Parliament. Once offered by Lombe in his original Bill, it would have been implausible to suggest that Parliament would have removed the requirement. At best Lombe may have taken soundings from some Members of Parliament as to what is required in the private Act; but it is going too far to suggest that it was Parliament requiring it.[136]

Burrell and Kelly next point to the second prize awarded by its own dedicated Bill, that of Joanna Stephens who was awarded £5,000 on condition she disclose her cure for the stone.[137] There is no record of whether she originally proposed the disclosure condition although her petition refers to her trying to "sell" her discovery for £5,000[138] rather than seeking some reward. Accordingly, it is plausible that she was offering to disclose her invention to the public for money from Parliament, rather than being offered money by Parliament on the condition that she disclosed her invention. In other words, like Lombe before, it is possible that the disclosure obligation was included in her original Bill and not insisted upon by Parliament.

The next example they present is the Discovery of Longitude at Sea Act 1762 where a £5,000 payment was offered to John Harrison for the disclosure of the principles associated with his new watch.[139] This is a clear indication of Parliament offering a reward for disclosure of the invention. The problem is that John Harrison *never* made the disclosure as he would not accept £5,000 when he believed he was entitled to the full £20,000 prize under the Longitude Acts.[140] Payment was therefore being used by Parliament as a way to encourage him to make a disclosure he apparently did not want to otherwise make.

It is suggested, therefore, that Burrell and Kelly's hypothesis is too optimistic. While it is true that some petitioners mention the communication of their invention to some

---

132 Patent No 422 (1718).

133 Robert Burrell and Catherine Kelly, "Parliamentary Rewards and the Evolution of the Patent System" (2015) *Cam LJ* 423 at 432.

134 Found among the papers of Robert Harper: see Sheila Lambert, *Bills and Acts: Legislative Procedure in Eighteenth-Century England* (Cambridge 1971).

135 It is dated 11 June 1831 in the Harper papers and said to be read on 7 March 1832.

136 Also see pp 110–12.

137 She published it in the *London Gazette*, Issue 7815, 16 June 1739.

138 26 March 1739 (23 CJ 302).

139 Discovery of Longitude at Sea Act 1762, s 1.

140 See J Donald Fernie, "Harrison-Maskelyne Affair" (2003) 91 *American Scientist* 403.

government body or other person in their request for money,[141] there were a number of rewards given without any suggestion of disclosure. Charles Dingley was given £2,000 in 1769 for a rebuilding his sawmill, which was of a new type without any idea of disclosure.[142] There were also payments made to fund (or reimburse) the cost of experiments: such as the £2,500 reward to David Hartley.[143]

The final reason their hypothesis is weak is that the House of Commons passed a number of Bills to *restrict* the disclosure of inventions.[144] One public Bill and five private Bills passed the House of Commons between 1792 and 1818 to restrict the disclosure of inventions.[145] Only two of the private Bills made it through the House of Lords. However, as mentioned above, the supply was the remit of the Commons and while, on the one hand, it was granting rewards, on the other it was restricting access to inventions. Accordingly, it is reasonable to suggest that disclosure was not a prerequisite of getting a reward for an invention it was simply something which might assist a person seeking public funds.[146] Assuming this is correct, the granting of rewards by Parliament did little to steer the requirement to disclose the invention, but rather it was part of a wider understanding of society that the dissemination of knowledge was of value.

It is impossible to disagree with their conclusion that "the reward system also played an important role in avoiding or side-lining the question of the proper basis on which the state should provide support to inventors".[147] But the importance rewards should not be overstated: rewards played a small role, where patents were not available for reasons of subject matter, cost or otherwise. It is not suggested that those seeking rewards were making conscious choices between patents and seeking Parliamentary rewards, but rather that they usually had no choice as patents were not available. Indeed, the petitioners seeking rewards were often following earlier successes, either their own or those with similar inventions, and this might have attracted them to Parliament where otherwise they would have received little or no compensation at all.

The end of rewards

The grant of rewards to inventors by specific vote slowly petered out after the end of the first quarter of the nineteenth century. While there were a few rewards thereafter[148] and

---

141 E.g. Thomas Stephens (Resolution of Committee of Supply: 27 CJ 281; 12 April 1755: "introducing that Manufacture into the British Plantations") (also see Supply, etc Act 1755, s 19); and Edward Jenner (Resolution of Committee of Supply: 57 CJ 544; 3 June 1802: "promulgating his Discoveries" (also see Appropriation Act 1802, s 18).

142 See J Appleby, "Charles Dingley's Sawmill, or Public Spirit at a Premium" (1995) 143 *RSA Journal* 54.

143 He also received a patent extension, see Hartley's Patent (Fire Prevention) Act 1776; also see p 128.

144 See Chapter 7.

145 See p 113–8.

146 The best example supporting their view is William Forsyth, who would only get paid upon disclosing the invention (44 CJ 643; 30 July 1789), which he did, see Forsyth, "In Consequence of an Address of the House of Commons to His Majesty and of an Examination Made Respecting the Efficacy of a Composition, Discovered by Mr William Forsyth, for Curing Injuries and Defects in Trees" (1791; 1824 Reprint) 33 *Annual Register* 351. However, this demand came from the government (in the reply to the Royal Address) and not from Parliament itself.

147 Robert Burrell and Catherine Kelly, "Parliamentary Rewards and the Evolution of the Patent System" (2015) *Cam LJ* 423 at 442.

148 Robert Burrell and Catherine Kelly, "Public Reward and Innovation Policy: Lessons from the Eighteenth and Early Nineteenth Century" (2014) 77 *MLR* 858 at 865 refer to Henry Needham Shrapnel who petitioned Parliament on 7 May 1847 and 14 May 1847 (102 CJ 492 and 526), but his petition related to the general

specific votes as late as 1872 for Captain Scott's gunnery invention (albeit this did not follow a petition to Parliament but was a separate resolution on the Navy vote),[149] inventors slowly stopped turning to Parliament to petition for rewards, rather they were approaching the government directly.[150] Whether a particular government department should give a reward to inventors could create enough interest to have it discussed in the House of Commons,[151] particularly where the people getting the rewards were sometimes on government procurement committees.[152] In any event, where particular inventors sought support from Parliament they did it through individual Members of Parliament asking questions of the government. For example in 1871, Henry Scott MP asked the First Lord of the Admiralty why no reward had been paid to Henry Cunningham in relation to his invention for working heavy guns[153] and a little over a decade later questions were asked for payments to be made to John Clare for his invention for building iron ships, a matter he had been pursuing for over twenty years.[154] There were protracted debates in the 1890s over the magazine rifle and the payments given to inventors (mainly by this stage patentees) in relation to it.[155] Later, after the First and Second World War, committees were set up to give rewards to inventors although these were largely seen to be a method of determining Crown use[156] payments.[157] The idea of rewards for innovation, paid by the government, still continues.[158] But the time when Parliament made an individual decision to give a reward to a particular inventor largely ended with the rise of a more modern government structure.[159] At the same time, the patent system was moving towards modernity.

mistreatment of his father, which included not only the absence of a reward for various inventions, but also the failure of the East India Company to pay its debts and the inadequacy of the pension, and the second petition was for an enquiry rather than just consideration (there were petitions in support, Bradford: 102 CJ 719 (22 June 1847) and Southampton: 102 CJ 841 (9 July 1847).

149 Captain Scott 1872 (£2,000 and £6,000 rewards).

150 There was a continuing trickle of petitions lodged and recorded by the Select Committee on Public Petitions until well into the second half of the century: see Phillip Johnson, *Parliament, Inventions and Patents: A Research Guide and Bibliography* (Routledge 2018), Part 7; Robert Macfie suggested that the patent system could be replaced by awards to inventors: HC Deb, 25 March 1872, Vol 210 (3rd), col 651.

151 For example, over Colonel Boxer's invention of a fuse when he was on the relevant committee which approved the procurement, and so there was a motion for a Select Committee to investigate: HC Deb, 29 April 1870, Vol 200 (3rd), cols 2062–2089; also see *Correspondence between War Office and Colonel Boxer Relating to his Patent for Fuses* (1870 HC Papers 161), Vol 42, p 501; and see HC Deb, 5 May 1870, Vol 201 (3rd), cols 277–279.

152 Eventually, the Treasury sent a letter to the War Office suggesting that inventors elect between owning the patent and holding the incompatible office: see HC Deb, 26 March 1872, Vol 210 (3rd), cols 690–691 and further explained: HC Deb, 14 July 1893, Vol 14 (4th), col 1565.

153 HC Deb, 13 July 1871, Vol 207 (3rd), cols 1626–1627.

154 HC Deb, 16 July 1883, Vol 218 (3rd), cols 1644–1645; he petitioned Parliament repeatedly over the period: e.g. Twentieth Report of Public Petitions Committee, 5 May 1863, p 467 (No 6,631) his claim was essentially one of patent infringement/Crown use; however see *Clare v The Queen*, The Times, 3, 4, 5, 6 and 7 February 1863 (detailed summary of the proceedings), but not otherwise reported. However, see Anon, "Inventors and the Crown" (1865) 13 *Mechanics Magazine* 70.

155 HC Deb, 3 February 1891, Vol 349 (3rd), cols 1643–1684.

156 I.e. the compulsory licence introduced by the Patents, Designs and Trade Marks Act 1883, s 27 which enables the government to work inventions without permission provided remuneration was paid to the patentee.

157 See question regarding terms of references of Royal Commission: HC Deb, 22 May 1919, Vol 116 (5th), cols 586-588W.

158 Health Act 2009, s 14 (not yet brought into force).

159 The competitive, and meritorious, civil service, based on examination introduced following the *Northcote-Trevelyan Report, Report on the Organisation of the Permanent Civil Service* (1854 C 1713), Vol 27, p 1; for a summary see: Rodney Lowe, *The Official History of the British Civil Service: Reforming the Civil Service, Volume 1: The Fulton Years 1966–81* (Routledge 2011), pp 18–29.

10 Restoration and renewal fees

Introduction

When patents were still predominately a way of raising revenue for the Stuart Monarch annual rents were often charged,[1] often these were similar to the old customs farms. This approach eventually faded out and it became the usual case that once a patent was granted it would last fourteen years without any payment of annual fees. The fees to obtain the patent were very high and became the source of great disquiet and the calls for reform. The beginning of the modern system of patents under the Patent Law Amendment Act 1852 also led to a radical change of practice with the introduction of renewal fees. Once such fees were due, however, it was not long before people found their patent lapsing for failure to pay the fees and turned to Parliament to save their rights. It is important, however, to begin by considering the payment of fees more generally.

Payment of fees

The issue of patent fees was not likely to be politically contentious when the number of patents granted each year was still low. Some milestones in the number of patent grants demonstrate this well. The first year when more than 50 patents were granted was 1783, 100 patents in 1801 and 150 in 1824 and, although 250 were granted in 1825, this did not happen again until 1834. Even though the numbers gradually increased from that point there were still only three years before the revolution under the Patent Law Amendment Act 1852, in which the number of patents granted topped 500 (1845, 1849 and 1850).[2] As the number of patents, and patentees, complaints about fees came to the surface.

The campaign for patent reform was pushed forward by William Newton who published (and may have written[3]) the *Vindicator Letters* in 1829. These letters were very critical of the patent system and the first letter printed[4] specifically addressed "the *legion* of fees".[5] Further

---

1 For example, Thomas Murraye's Patent No 5 (1617) and that of David Ramey and Thomas Wildgosse: No 6 (1618) required an annual "rent" of £10; but other rents were charged: John Gilbert's Patent No 9 (1618) had a rent of £6 13s 8d; although more common was a share of the revenues: see for example Sir William St John's *et al* Patent No 15 (1620) where 5s had to be paid to the Crown for every ton of metal made according to the patent.

2 These figures are based on Woodcroft's *Index* (corrected) and were compiled as Table A1 in Richard Sullivan, "England's 'Age of Invention': The Acceleration of Patents and Patentable Invention during the Industrial Revolution" (1989) 26 *Explorations in Economic History* 424.

3 See Jeremy Phillips, *Charles Dickens and the Poor Man's Tale of a Patent* (ESC 1984), p 2.

4 Letter on the Fees Charged upon Patents for Invention (1829) 2 *London Journal of Arts and Science* 311 (reprinted in Jeremy Phillips, *Charles Dickens and the Poor Man's Tale of a Patent* (ESC 1984), p, 38).

5 Emphasis in the original.

concerns regarding fees were raised by Sir Henry Cole[6] and Charles Dickens's *A Poor Man's Tale of a Patent.*[7] There were also a plethora of petitions presented to Parliament complaining about fees. These began in 1822 with Thomas Walker's petition[8] and continued with a few during the sitting of the 1829 Select Committee[9] and the lead-up to Letters Patent Bill 1833[10] and the Letters Patent for Inventions Act 1835,[11] and once more as patent reform returned to the agenda in the early 1850s.[12]

The fees payable[13] for an unopposed[14] English patent at the end of the old system (in the late 1840s) were around £100.[15] Putting this in a modern context is difficult.[16] It is about four to five times the per capita earnings of an individual in 1850 (£20 9s 7d) although it was about three times average annual earnings (£33 19s 7d). Put into modern money is even more troubling. In terms of retail prices, the modern fee is £9,814; if wages comparison is undertaken it is now £77,130 or if per capita earnings compared it is £119,800. Notwithstanding the comparison it can be said with certainty that obtaining a patent was

---

6 See *Sir Henry Cole: Fifty Years of Public Works* (Bell 1884), Vol 2, p 276–277.

7 Charles Dickens, "A Poor Man's Tale of a Patent" (1850) 2 (3) *Household Words* 73 (also see Jeremy Phillips, *Charles Dickens and the Poor Man's Tale of a Patent* (ESC 1984)).

8 See 77 CJ 359 (20 June 1822); the text of the petition was included in the Appendix to Votes and Proceedings, 1822, p 487–488 (No 705).

9 Petition of Thomas Flannagan: 84 CJ 128 (12 March 1829); Appendix to Votes and Proceedings, 1829, p 748–749 (Nos 1,802 and 1,803); Petition of John Birkinshaw: 84 CJ 187 (31 March 1829); Appendix to Votes and Proceedings, 1829, p 1213–1214 (No 2,839).

10 Petition of Richard Roberts: 88 CJ 179 (18 March 1833); Seventh Report of the Public Petitions Committee, 1833, p 176; Petition of John Kitchen: 88 CJ 231 (28 March 1833): Tenth Report of the Public Petitions Committee, 1833, p 294 (No 2,140); Petition of Julius Schroder: 88 CJ 535 (1 July 1833): Thirty-Third Report of the Public Petitions Committee, 1833, p 1268 (No 9,559).

11 Petition of James Marsh: 90 CJ 578 (21 August 1835); Thirty-Ninth Report of the Public Petitions Committee, 1835, p (No 3,718) and Appendix, p 1331–1332 (No 1,733); Petition of Patentees & c of Birmingham: 90 CJ 584 (24 August 1835); Fortieth Report of the Public Petitions Committee, 1835, p 300 (No 3,806) and Appendix, p 1372–1373 (No 1785).

12 See for example: Petition of John Jones (13 February 1850): Fifth Report of the Public Petitions Committee, 1850, p 41 (No 484); Petition of Henry Archer: 82 LJ 62 (15 March 1850); Petition of Huddersfield Committee on Great Exhibition (17 February 1851): Sixth Report of the Public Petitions Committee, 1851, p 73 (No 1,916) and Appendix, p 81 (No 175); Petition of National Patent Law Amendment Association (18 March 1851), Seventeenth Report of the Public Petitions Committee, 1851, p 237 (No 4, 522) and Appendix, p 193 (No 426). There were many others; for a full list see Phillip Johnson, *Parliament, Inventions and Patents: A Research Guide and Bibliography* (Routledge 2018), Part 7; also see the discussion in Moureen Coulter, *Property in Ideas: The Patent Question in mid-Victorian Britain* (Thomas Jefferson University Press 1991), Ch 2.

13 The fees, which were not set out in legislation and varied slightly: see Thomas Webster, *The Law and Practice of Letters Patent for Inventions: Statutes, Practical Forms, and Digest of Reported Cases* (Crofts and Blenkard 1841), p 123; William Carpmael, *The Law of Patents for Inventions: Familiarly Explained for the Use of Inventors and Patentees* (4th Ed Simpkin, Marshall & Co 1846), p lviii; *Sir Henry Cole: Fifty Years of Public Works* (Bell 1884), Vol 2, (rate as for 1849), pp 276–277); William Hindmarch, *Treatise on the Law Relating to the Patent Privileges for the Sole use of Inventions* (Stevens 1846), pp 612–614; *Return of the Number of Letters Patent Sealed* (1849 HC Papers 23), Vol 45, p 381; the figures used here are based on Thomas Webster, *On the Amendment of the Law and Practice of Letters Patent for Inventions* (2nd Ed, Chapman and Hall 1852), pp 41–42.

14 Official fees escalated significantly if the patent was opposed before the law officers (although a successful opponent would have to repay some of the petitioners' fees: see William Hindmarch, *Treatise on the Law Relating to the Patent Privileges for the Sole Use of Inventions* (Stevens 1846), p 614).

15 The fees were as follows: £94 6s 0d of which £36 2s 0d was stamp duty; 10s for enrolling the specification in the Enrollment Office along with a further £5 0s 0d stamp duty.

16 All figures and calculations from Lawrence H Officer and Samuel H Williamson, "What Was the U.K. GDP Then?" MeasuringWorth 2017 (however, the conversion from fractions of a pound to pounds, shillings and pence are by author).

an expensive business. There could also be additional costs for extending the patent to the Channel Islands and colonies (£7 7s 6d[17]) and for adding each additional inventor to the patent (£2 13s 4d[18]). Furthermore, these fees cover England alone and additional fees would be necessary for Scotland (a little under £70[19]) and Ireland (around £125[20]). The added cost explains why many inventions were not protected in Scotland (at most a third) or Ireland (around one in ten).[21]

A substantial part of the fees was made up of stamp duties, which had been introduced (and applied to patents) by the (originally temporary) Stamps Act 1694.[22] The duty remained (or was added) to various stages of patenting.[23] By 1850 the relevant legislation was the Stamps Act 1815 which set fees[24] for the King's (or Queen's) Warrant, King's Bill, Signet Bill, Privy Seal Bill, Docquet at the Great Seal, Sealing the Patent and the Specification with additional charges for more than 2,160 words. In Scotland, the stamp duties were lower as many stages did not attract duties and the Irish stamp duties had been equalised in 1842.[25]

The cost also could increase as practices had grown up to pay "expedition fees" and other fees in certain cases,[26] which somewhat strangely included double fees where the applicant was represented by Counsel before the law officers.[27] Finally, it should be noted that the fees for England decreased following the abolition of certain stages of the process under the Great Seal Act 1851.[28]

Front-loading

The cost of obtaining a patent (whether for England or the whole of the United Kingdom) was front-loaded. Accordingly, inventors had to pay these vast sums without knowing (or at least not being sure) that the patent would actually have value. Indeed, early patent history

17 There were additional fees at each stage see: Thomas Webster, *The Law and Practice of Letters Patent for Inventions: Statutes, Practical Forms, and Digest of Reported Cases* (Crofts and Blenkard 1841), p 123.

18 Thomas Webster, *The Law and Practice of Letters Patent for Inventions: Statutes, Practical Forms, and Digest of Reported Cases* (Crofts and Blenkard 1841), p 123.

19 The fees were £63 3s 7d which included stamp duties of £1 10s 0d; and then £5 0s 0d stamp fees for enrolling the specification.

20 The fees were £119 0s 1d fees which included stamp duties of £30 0s 0d. Specifications were not always required (see p 90 fn 103) but where one was enrolled there would be a further £5 0s 0d stamp duty payable.

21 See Sean Bottomley, "Patenting in England, Scotland and Ireland during the Industrial Revolution, 1700–1852" (2014) 54 *Explorations in Economic History* 48.

22 Stamps Act 1694, s 3. The history of the Stamps Act is very complicated as various aspects of the duty were modified from its introduction: see Soloman Atkinson, *Chitty's Stamp Laws* (3rd Ed, Benning & Co 1850), Ch 1 for a summary history of stamp duties until that date.

23 They were not payable in Scotland until the nineteenth century as Scotland was exempted under the Union with Scotland Act 1706, art 10 (superseded by the Probate and Legacy Duties Act 1808, s 48).

24 In the Schedule to the Act, although various fees are found in different parts of the Schedule.

25 By the Stamp Duties (Ireland) Act 1842, s 2; the fees were lower for patents under the Stamps (Ireland) Act 1815.

26 Albeit these were limited see: *Select Committee of House of Lords to Consider Bills for Amendment of Law Touching Letters Patent for Inventions. Report, Minutes of Evidence* (1851 HC Papers 486), Vol 18, p 233, Q216 (p 40) (Evidence of William Carpmael); also see Thomas Webster, *The New Patent Law: Its History, Objects and Provisions* (Elsworth 1853), pp 39–40.

27 Thomas Webster, *The New Patent Law: It's History, Objects and Provisions* (Elsworth 1853), p 40.

28 The fees were reduced to £76 6s 0d (of which £31 12s 0d was stamp duty).

is littered with patent proprietors who did not actually exploit their invention.[29] One of the revolutions of the Patent Law Amendment Act 1852 was changing the system from front-loading to a renewal basis.[30] This meant letters patent became subject to a condition that they would be void if fees were not paid at the expiration of three years and seven years from grant.[31] The rationale for this change was stated by Earl Granville during the passage of the 1851 Bill[32] through the House of Lords:[33]

> The great advantage of this alteration would be that it would cause the inventor in the first instance: if his invention turned out useful and valuable, he could easily pay these fees at the expiration of the third and the seventh year respectively; and if not, he could dispense with their payment, whereby his letters patent would become void by the failure to pay the second and third instalments, and the injurious accumulation of a multiplication of useless patents would be entirely prevented.

The reformed system under the Patent Law Amendment Act 1852 provided for six months' provisional protection[34] from first filing for the fee attached to the leaving of a petition[35] £5 (£498.60 in 2016 money[36]). There was also a fee of £5 for filing a specification. Additional fees of £5 were payable when the applicant gave notice of intention to proceed.[37] In addition, a single payment of stamp duty of £5 was required on the warrant for the letters patent from the law officers.[38] A further £5 was payable for sealing the patent. This meant that it cost £25 to obtain a patent which had effect throughout the United Kingdom. Crucially for the purposes of this discussion a fee of £40 (and stamp duty of £10) was payable before the expiration of the third year of the patent and a further fee of £80 (and stamp duty of £20) was payable before the expiration of the seventh year.[39] This particular fees regime lasted less than a year as the Patent Law Act 1853 changed all the fees to stamp duties. The overall cost

29 See evidence of the Earl of Dundonald on his father's failure to exploit his invention even though he got his own private Act: see *Report of Select Committee of House of Lords appointed to consider of the [Judicial Committee Bill] with Minutes of Evidence* (1844 HL Papers 34), Vol 19, p 323, Q811–831 (p 71–72).

30 Even today, the UK system avoids front load so that the cost of examining a patent is not met unless the patent is renewed to its fifteenth year: Intellectual Property Office, *Proposed Changes to Statutory Patent Fees* (2017), [6].

31 Patent Law Amendment Act 1852, s 17.

32 Patent Law Amendment (No 3) Bill 1851 (1851 HL Papers 167), Vol 5, p 383, Schedule.

33 HL Deb, 1 July 1851, Vol 118 (3rd), col 9; however there were some who took the view that this approach was "robbing" inventors who forget to renew their patent: see Evidence of Alfred Newton: *Report and Minutes of Evidence Taken before the Select Committee of the House of Lords Appointed to Consider of the Bill, Intituled, "An Act Further to Amend the Law Touching Letters Patent for Inventions;" and also of the Bill, Intituled "An Act for the Further Amendment of the Law Touching Letters Patent for Inventions;" and to Report Thereon to the House* (1851 HC Papers 486), Vol 18, p 223, Q1083–1084 (p 165).

34 This was introduced for things exhibited at the Great Exhibition by the Protection of Inventions Act 1851, s 3; extended by the Protection of Inventions Act 1852.

35 Provisional protection granted what is now commonly known as a priority date – that allowing the novelty to be judged at a date earlier than the date upon which the complete specification was filed.

36 Value calculated using Lawrence H Officer and Samuel H Williamson, "Five Ways to Compute the Relative Value of a UK Pound Amount, 1270 to Present," MeasuringWorth, 2017 using retail prices.

37 Patent Law Amendment Act 1852, ss 8 and 9; fees, s 44 and Schedule.

38 Patent Law Amendment Act 1852, s 15; fees, s 44 and Schedule.

39 Patent Law Amendment Act 1852, s 17.

of each activity (including renewal) did not change however.[40] Section 2 of the 1853 Act[41] included the requirement to pay renewal fees:

> All Letters Patent for Inventions to be granted under the Provisions of the said Patent Law Amendment Act, 1852. . . shall be made subject to the Condition that the same shall be void, and that the Powers and Privileges thereby granted shall cease and determine, at the Expiration of Three Years and Seven Years respectively from the Date thereof, unless there be paid before the Expiration of the said Three Years and Seven Years respectively the Stamp Duties in the Schedule to this Act annexed expressed to be payable before the Expiration of the Third Year and of the Seventh Year respectively, and such Letters Patent, or a Duplicate thereof, shall be stamped with proper Stamps showing the Payment of such respective Stamp Duties, and shall, when stamped, be produced before the Expiration of such Three Years and Seven Years respectively at the Office of the Commissioners; and a Certificate of the Production of such Letters Patent or Duplicate so stamped, specifying the Date of such Production, shall be endorsed by the Clerk of the Commissioners on the Letters Patent or Duplicate, and a like Certificate shall be endorsed upon the Warrant for such Letters Patent filed in the said Office.

The effect of this provision meant that patents would be void and cease to have effect when the relevant payments were not made. Inevitably, this led to patentees not paying fees and losing their patent. While many would have made the intentional decision not to maintain the patent – Granville's useless patents – others wanted their patents to remain in force. However, there was no mechanism to enable fees to be paid late[42] and so patentees who wanted to save their valuable patents from their own mistakes or inadvertence had to turn to Parliament.

The lapsing of patents – before the Patents, Designs and Trade Marks Act 1883

The requirement to pay stamp duty/renewal fees applied to all patents granted from 1 October 1852[43] and, furthermore, the number of patents granted rapidly increased during the 1850s. The annual report of the Commissioners of Patents set out the number of valid patents which were allowed to lapse for want of renewal fees:[44]

---

40 A further effect of this was that the stamp duty was under the care and management of the commissioners of the Inland Revenue: Patent Law Amendment Act 1852, s 45 and Patent Law Act 1853 (c. 5), s. 5; whereas the fees had gone into the consolidated fund: Patent Law Amendment Act 1852, s 46. This change would have made management of office more straightforward; but it was made due to the poor accounts kept by the office holders: see *The Times,* 17 November 1852.

41 This replaced s 17 of the Patent Law Amendment Act 1852.

42 That fees could be paid on the last day is as far as the courts went: *Williams v Nash* (1859) 7 HPC 863; 28 Beav 93 (54 ER 301).

43 The coming into force of the Patent Law Amendment Act 1852 (see s 57).

44 The annual report of both the Commissioners (and later the Comptroller) included the figures as to the payment of renewal (stamp) duty. The system changed in relation to existing patents under the Patents, Designs and Trade Marks Act 1883 so only patents granted during 1876 would have the second renewal fee paid under the old system. The table produced is based on the Report of the Commissioners of Patents for Inventions for the Year 1883 (1884 C 4164), Vol 28, p 785 at p 4 (it should be noted subsequent reports have slightly different numbers for certain years – so there may have been marginal corrections subsequently).

Table 10.1 Patents which were not renewed, 1852–1876

Year of grant	Number of valid patents granted (inc specification filed)	Number where stamp duty at three years paid	Number where stamp duty at seven years paid
1852	891	310	102
1853	2,113	621	205
1854	1,812	513	140
1855	1,994	551	195
1856	2,047	573	214
1857	1,976	584	221
1858	1,923	540	197
1859	1,938	542	217
1860	2,016	579	194
1861	2,012	575	179
1862	2,156	646	214
1863	2,066	632	215
1864	2,002	550	178
1865	2,159	582	193
1866	2,100	574	227
1867	2,253	619	260
1868	2,456	729	272
1869	2,366	793	309
1870	2,140	738	280
1871	2,338	819	307
1872	2,734	853	291
1873	2,906	856	281
1874	3,104	953	301
1875	3,049	895	295
1876	3,367	947	347

It can be seen that during this period (1852–1876) around a third of applicants paid the stamp duty at the end of year three and about 10.5 per cent (of the original number) paid it at year seven. This indicates that the system largely achieved its aim of ensuring that useless patents would disappear quickly (after three years) and only very useful (valuable) patents would last the full fourteen years (meaning the second payment of stamp duty was made) nevertheless some said the fees were collected too early before the inventor had time to ascertain the value of the invention.[45] While the introduction of renewal fees invariably led to many useless patents lapsing it was inevitable that the stamp duty would not be paid on some useful and valuable patents.

Private legislating for late payers (1862–1885)

The loss of a patent right can clearly be a significant one and it appeared that paten-tees were not particularly good at getting themselves organised to pay the renewal fees. As we have seen in relation to the extension of patent term, holders of letters patent

---

45 *Royal Commission Appointed to Inquire into the Working of the Law Relating to Letters Patent for Inventions* (1864 C 3419), Vol 29, p 321, p x.

would do what they could to ensure that valuable[46] rights would last as long as possible. Accordingly, where stamp duties were not paid patent proprietors took the only steps they could to try and save their right – they petitioned Parliament. Indeed, Acts confirming letters patent form by far the largest class of private Act connected to patents. However, the history of this type of legislation can be divided into two periods: patents lapsing before the commencement of the Patents, Designs and Trade Marks Act 1883 and those lapsing afterwards.

The first period begins in 1855 (three years after the commencement of the Patent Law Amendment Act 1852 and when renewal fees were first due) and ended on 31 December 1883 when the 1883 Act came into force. The period is however slightly different from what would be expected. It took seven years for the first private Act (Webb and Craig's Patent Act 1862)[47] to confirm a patent lost for failure to pay renewal fees. And the last Act under the pre-1883 Act regime (Auld's Patent Act 1885) reached the statute books on 21 May 1885.[48] Over this twenty-three year period, thirty-one private Acts were passed to confirm lapsed patents and a further nine private Bills[49] unsuccessfully started the process of Parliamentary confirmation. Only one of those Bills failed after evidence was heard during an opposition.[50] On the rejection of three of those private Bills[51] in 1865, Lord Redesdale made the first suggestion that there should be a general law to address the difficulties by late payers.[52] Others, however, took the view that no remedy was appropriate as third parties suffered.[53] These failed Bills may have been the acorn that grew into the third-party protection later on. The development of these private Acts into almost a routine means that there was a consistency in their preambles that is worth examining. This begins with considering the formal aspects.

Formalities

Compliance with requirements

The private Acts usually included certain standard recitals as to what was required and the petitioner's failure. Accordingly, although not relevant to fees, it was usual to recite that the petitioner was required to file a specification describing the invention and that this was

---

46 As the previous table shows, many patents were not valuable.

47 The first private Act relating to the payment of the second (seven year) fee was Goux's Patent Act 1876.

48 The renewal fee having fallen due 11 December 1883 (a little under three weeks before the 1883 Act came into effect).

49 Shepard's Patent Bill 1865 (HL/PO/JO/10/9/585); Spencer's Patent Bill 1865 (HL/PO/JO/10/9/585); Wright's Patent Bill 1865 (HL/PO/JO/10/9/587) were all denied a second reading: HL Deb, 27 February 1865, Vol 177(3rd), col 736; for Shaw's Patent (Lining Lead Pipes) Bill 1871; Smith's Patent Bill 1876 was withdrawn on initial report: 131 CJ 28 (11 February 1876); Leigh's Patent Bill 1877 was withdrawn at Third Reading: 132 CJ 277 (15 June 1877); Taylor's Patent Notice 1882: withdrawn after notice in *Gazette*: *London Gazette*, 29 November 1881 (Issue: 25042, p 6425).

50 See Shaw's Patent (Lining Lead Pipes) Bill 1871 (House Bill: HL/PO/JO/10/9/760): see below, p 173.

51 Shepard's Patent Bill 1865; Spencer's Patent Bill 1865; Wright's Patent Bill 1865.

52 HL Deb, 24 February 1865, Vol 177 (3rd), col 635; the Lord Chancellor having a power to accept late fees was also raised before the Royal Commission a year earlier: *Royal Commission Appointed to Inquire into the Working of the Law Relating to Letters Patent for Inventions* (1864 C 3419), Vol 29, p 321, p x (based on Evidence of Albert Newton, Q1829–1833 (at p 109)).

53 Lord Chelmsford, HL Deb, 27 February 1865, Vol 177 (3rd), col 736.

duly filed.[54] Further, when the failure was to pay the second stamp duty (at seven years) it was common to recite payment of the first fee[55] but this was by no means required.[56]

Promptness

A person seeking a private Bill needed to petition Parliament promptly and the fact this was done was usually stated in the preamble such as "on making such discovery. . .without loss of time gave the requisite instructions for an application to Parliament".[57] Nevertheless, the length of delay between the patent lapsing and the petitioner placing the necessary notice[58] in the *Gazette* varied greatly from the shortest being nine days[59] to the longest at 418 days.[60] Indeed, the Standing Orders requiring the notices and petition to be lodged at certain times of the year were routinely dispensed with for confirmation patents (as waiting for the next session caused greater loss). The reciting of the promptness (or reasons for lack of it) began with Gardiner's Patent Act 1868 where it had taken William Sparks Thomson nearly a year[61] from the lapse of the patent to giving the required notice. Thomson explained his delay as ill-health and the need to be away from his place of business.[62] Promptness was in the recitals of almost[63] every subsequent private Act for confirming a patent.

There were a number of Acts where the inadvertence was stated to be short, but the delay in petitioning Parliament was much longer.[64] Where a petitioner had not acted expediently some, although not all, tried to explain why. The Universal Charcoal and Sewage Company (successors to Robey and Chantrell's Patent) had a delay of four hundred days yet simply recited their promptness upon discovery[65]; whereas the really tardy petitioners omitted to recite anything to do with their promptness (or otherwise) at all.[66] Only three other petitioners explained delays. William Harper explained his delay (eighty-four days) was because

---

54 This was included in original confirmation Act (Webb and Craig's Patent 1862, recital (2)) and every other pre-1883 private Act except Hall's Patent Act 1876 (which was a Wyatt, Hoskins and Hooker Bill) and Boult's Patent Act 1884 (which was a Sherwood & Co Bill). Further, Hunt's Patent Act 1880, recital (2) refers to the complete specification being filed along with the petition rather than the specification being filed in accordance with the proviso.

55 Goux's Patent Act 1876, recital (3); Harper's Patent Act 1877, recital (3); Copland's Patent Act 1881, recital (3); Hancock's Patent Act 1881, recital (3).

56 The payment of the first £50 fee (which must have occurred) was not recited in Greene's Patent Act 1881, Bradbury and Lomax's Patent Act 1884 or Auld's Patent Act 1885 (each with different Parliamentary Agents).

57 Wording from Mills' Patent 1873, recital (5).

58 See p 17.

59 Williamson's Patent Act 1880 (lapsed 17 May 1880; notice dated 26 May 1880): *London Gazette*, 28 May 1880, Issue 24848, p 3223.

60 Bradbury and Lomax's Patent Act 1884 (lapsed 21 October 1882; notice dated 13 December 1883): *London Gazette*, 18 December 1883, Issue 25297, p 6523.

61 344 days.

62 Gardiner's Patent Act 1868, recital (6) and (7).

63 The only case where it was not mentioned and the petitioner was prompt was Boult's Patent Act 1884 (where the delay was only 16 days).

64 E.g. Barlow's Patent Act 1874: the cheque was two days late – recital (3) – but the notice was 81 days thereafter – see *London Gazette*, 27 February 1874, Issue 24069, p 894; similarly Bousfield's Patent Act 1876, Fourth recital and *London Gazette*, 30 November 1875, Issue 24271, p 6166.

65 Robey and Chantrell's Patent Act 1877, recital (7); they discovered it seven days before the date of the notice in the *Gazette*.

66 Hunt's Patent Act 1880 (365 days), Greene's Patent Act 1881 (319 days), Auld's Patent Act 1885 (350 days).

he believed he could not apply to Parliament when it was not sitting[67]; William Chetham's was because when he inquired about obtaining an Act of Parliament he found out it was too late for the then current session[68]; and George Nash was late due to a falling-out with his business partner.[69]

Grounds for confirmation

Basic standard: inadvertence

The basic standard for confirming a lapsed patent appears to have been "inadvertence" (i.e. not deliberately failing to pay the fee). The earliest private Act, Webb and Craig's Patent Act 1862, recites "inadvertence" of an agent as the reason for the petition,[70] and "inadvertence" simpliciter was recited repeatedly in subsequent Acts.[71] This is not to suggest that some petitioners did not explain the omission, as discussed below, but it appears that Parliament did not require a good explanation of the reason for failing to pay; indeed, most petitioners simply stated the failure was "an accident and not from wilful disobedience to the law".[72] It was suggested in a near contemporary statement that from the 1882 Session to the end of the pre-1883 Acts, Lord Redesdale, the Chairman of Committees, "took a less strict view" of the private confirmation Bills.[73] While it is true that many of the last Acts did not seem to be required to meet a high standard, in reality there was a low standard throughout the period. It is still worth considering the reasons put forward.

Mistake of fact or law

Some petitioners blamed their inadvertence on a mistake of fact or law. One such was that the three-year period had been computed from the date the complete specification was filed rather than the date of the letters patent (i.e. six months later),[74] or simply that they believed the payment was due at a later date.[75]

Illness

Ill-health was repeatedly recited as a reason why petitioners had failed to pay. William Sparks Thomson recited how he did not notice the fraud of his agent until he returned from

---

67 See Harper's Patent Act 1877, recital (7).

68 Chetham's Patent Act 1883, recital (5).

69 Wright's Patent Act 1884, recital (7) and (8).

70 Webb and Craig's Patent 1862, recital (3).

71 Rammell's Patent Act 1864, recital (3); Mills' Patent Act 1873, recital (3); Campbell's Sewage Patent Act 1875, recital (3); Whitthread's Patent Act 1875, recital (5); Goux's Patent Act 1876, recital (8); Sillar's and Wigner's Patent 1876, recital (5); Harper's Patent Act 1877, recital (4); Robey and Chantrell's Patent Act 1877, recital (6); Vicars and Smith's Patent Act 1879, recital (3); Muirhead's Patent Act 1880, recital (3); Chetham's Patent Act 1883, recital (4); Law's Patent Act 1883, recital (3); Boult's Patent Act 1884, recital (3); Wright's Patent Act 1884, recital (5); Auld's Patent Act 1885, recital (4).

72 This first appeared in Mills' Patent Act 1873, recital (5) and it appeared in every pre-1883 Act after that although sometimes in the form of "wilful neglect or disobedience. . .".

73 *Report of a Select Committee on Potter's Patent Bill, Skrivanow's Patent Bill and Gilbert and Sinclair's Patent Bill* (1887 HL Papers 100), Vol 9, p 469, Appendix A, p 42.

74 Milner's Patent 1876, recital (6).

75 Copland's Patent Act 1881, recital (5); Haddan's Patent Act 1883, recital (4).

convalescing in the South of France.[76] Similarly, William Harper had "broken down from intense application to business and to the development and working" of the invention and was told to go to the sea-side to restore his health and so in his state he overlooked paying the fee.[77] George Eyre was so ill he was forced into retirement and his business partner was away and so could not make the payment.[78] And William Williamson mentions his ill-health, although it appears for sympathy and no more, as it seems to have no relationship to why the payment was not made.[79]

Misdirecting post

Some petitioners recited how their failure to pay was due to a postal mistake, such as mis-directing the letter with payment to London rather than Manchester,[80] sending the wrong letters patent to be stamped,[81] or the failure of a courier company to deliver on time.[82] Similarly, Henry Lomax relied on his agent's failure to send him the notice that payment was due in the first place.[83]

Relying on an agent

Many petitioners blamed their agents or employees for the mistakes.[84] Considering a prin-cipal or employer is generally responsible for the acts of their agent or employee this is surprising. Yet Lewis Aspinwall recited how he left his correspondence to another who inadvertently failed to pay[85] and William Williamson blames the failure on his overworked confidential clerk.[86]

Litigation and dispute

John Greene mortgaged his patent and this in due course became the subject of litigation between him and his mortgagee. This, he claimed, prevented him from paying the duty.[87] James Hancock, on the other hand, fell into dispute with his patent agent who refused to deliver up the letters patent for stamping, claiming a lien on the same for unpaid fees.[88]

Absence of general principles

It appears that Parliament was willing to allow a patent to be confirmed if the relevant private Bill fees were paid. While many petitioners set out reasons for the failure to pay

---

76 Gardiner's Patent Act 1868, recital (6).
77 Harper's Patent Act 1877, recital (6).
78 Mullings' Patent Act 1883, recital (7).
79 See Williamson's Patent Act 1880, recital (5).
80 Barlow's Patent Act 1874, recital (3).
81 Hall's Patent Act 1876, recital (4).
82 Bousfield's Patent Act 1876, recital (4); Hunt's Patent Act 1880, recital (6).
83 Bradbury and Lomax's Patent Act 1884, recital (4).
84 Indeed, the first such private Act did just this: Webb and Craig's Patent Act 1862, recital (3).
85 Aspinwall's Patent Act 1878, recital (5).
86 Williamson's Patent Act 1880, recital (5) (combined with a bank holiday).
87 Greene's Patent Act 1881, recitals (6) and (7).
88 Hancock's Patent Act 1881, recital (8).

fees – from minor mistakes and illness to blaming agents and couriers – this did not seem to be proved to a high standard. Indeed, it was not a matter that longer delays required justifications whereas shorter ones did not. William Williamson gave the quickest notice of his petition for a private Bill and he explained his inadvertence whereas William Auld, the beneficiary of the last pre-1883 Act, was nearly a year late yet he gave no explanation at all. This is quite extraordinary. Once the system was established and stating inadvertence simpliciter was enough, why did petitioners go on to recite more? Each recital needed to be proved (if challenged) so why did petitioners make things more difficult for themselves? This reason may be nothing more than an abundance of caution, but it leaves us with some indication of practice.

Hardship

It was routine to recite some hardship that would be suffered should the patent not be confirmed. Importantly, once more, not all applicants set out any hardship[89] but when it was recited it took a common form.

Expenditure of money and time

Almost all petitioners pleaded hardship by explaining they had expended time, money or both in perfecting the invention.[90] It was also common to recite how the patentee would be deprived of the advantage of the patent in the future. In some instances the plight of licensees, including their expenditure of money, might be set out as well.[91] Similarly, the fact that a petitioner had not obtained any reward from the invention to date was also sometimes used as a basis for excusing the failure to pay renewal fees.[92] In most cases, there would be little more than a bald statement that time or money had been expended. However, sometimes lengths of time or amounts of money spent would be recited. For instance, the successors of Edward Milner claimed they paid out upwards of £12,000 (about £1,036,000 in 2016 money[93]) developing the invention and their licensees spent upwards of £6,000 (£518,000).[94] William Harper stated that he spent upward of six years perfecting his invention.[95] An extreme example was William Sparks Thomson who said that he had purchased the patent from Perry Gardiner for around £14,000 (£1,156,000) and he spent at least another £3,000 (£247,700) to establish offices, machinery and works.[96]

---

89 Nothing was said in Webb and Craig's Patent Act 1862 or Rammell's Patent Act 1864.
90 Except Webb and Craig's Patent Act 1862 and Rammell's Patent Act 1864.
91 Hall's Patent Act 1876, recitals (3) and (6).
92 Goux's Patent Act 1876, recital (7) (only just becoming profitable); Milner's Patent Act 1876, recital (9); Copland's Patent Act 1881, recital (6) (considerable capital raised not hitherto remunerative).
93 Lawrence H Officer and Samuel H Williamson, "Five Ways to Compute the Relative Value of a UK Pound Amount, 1270 to Present," MeasuringWorth, 2017 (based on retail price calculations higher values could be attributed under other comparisons).
94 Milner's Patent Act 1876, recitals (5) and (7).
95 Harper's Patent Act 1877, recital (5).
96 Gardiner's Patent Act 1868, recitals (3) and (4).

Loss of foreign patents

At this time[97] it was not uncommon for a patent's term to be cut short where it was owned by a foreigner and the domestic patent lapsed or expired.[98] So the loss of a foreign patent might be recited to explain hardship.[99] Thus, Edward Milner pleaded the loss of his French[100] and American patents[101] as grounds for granting him a private Act to allow late payment.[102] It is reasonable to assume that those seeking private Acts for lapsed fees represented the more valuable patents, yet few recite the loss of foreign patent rights (four of thirty). It may be that some petitioners did not see value in reciting the loss of a foreign right, but more likely is that the vast majority of petitioners held a British patent only.

Important character

Dugald Campbell recited how scientific bodies and public bodies were highly satisfied with the process and the experiments performed.[103] Bristow Hunt pleaded that his invention was of a particularly important character and that his specification described complicated and elaborate machinery.[104] This goes back to the sort of arguments which were routinely used for prolongations (and continued before the Privy Council[105]).

The operative provisions of these private Acts

The Acts usually had three provisions. The first section would entitle the patentee to pay and stamp the patent within one month of the passing of the private Act.[106] The second section would confirm the patent as valid as if the stamp duty had been paid on time.[107] The third section would grant third party protection. Finally, some, but not all, would include

---

97 This changed with Article 5*bis* of the Paris Convention for the Protection of Industrial Property, the original version of which was agreed at the 1900 London Conference: see Samuel Ricketson, *The Paris Convention for the Protection of Industrial Property* (Oxford 2015) [10.64 to 10.69].

98 In the UK, this rule was found in Patent Law Amendment Act 1852, s 25; also see *Nordenfelt v Gardener* (1884) 1 RPC 10 (as to relevant dates); the object of the rule was suggested in *Daw v Eley* (1868) 8 HPC 709; LR 7 Eq 496 (at 510) to be to ensure that English manufactures are not fettered where foreign ones are free.

99 Many stated this without specifying which countries (the rule was not uniform): see Copland's Patent Act 1881, recital (7); Lecky and Smyth's Patent Act 1882, recital (9); Mullings' Patent Act 1883, recital (9).

100 Law of 5 July 1844, art 29: translation in Benjamin Abbott, *The Patent Laws of All Nations* (Charles Brodix, 1886), pp 187–188. A similar rule existed in Belgium, Law of 24 May 1854, art 14 (p 44) and Italy (Sardinian Law of 30 October 1859 extended by Italian Law and Regulation of 31 January 1864), art 11 (p 285); Turkey, Law of 18 February 1880, art 35 (Alfred and Edward Carpmael, *Patent Laws of the World: Collected, Edited And Indexed* (2nd Ed William Clowes 1889), p 34); Finland, Supreme Decree of 30 March 1876, s 3 (ibid, 164). No such rule existed in Germany.

101 Revised Statutes (1874), Title 40, s 4887.

102 Milner's Patent Act 1876, recital (8).

103 Campbell's Sewage Patent Act 1875, recital (4).

104 Hunt's Patent Act 1880, recital (4).

105 See for instance, *Smith (Petitt)'s Patent* (1850) 6 HPC 183; 7 Moo PCC 133 (13 ER 830); *McDougal's Patent* (1867) 9 HPC 25; 5 Moo PCC NS 1 (16 ER 415).

106 E.g. Webb and Craig's Patent Act 1862, s 1.

107 E.g. Webb and Craig's Patent Act 1862, s 2.

a provision setting out the Act's short title.[108] The first two provisions remained largely unchanged over the period[109] but that granting third party protection evolved.

Third party protection

In Webb and Craig's Patent Act 1862, limited third party protection was given by section 3:

> no Action or Suit shall be commenced or prosecuted at Law or Equity, nor any Damage recovered, for, or in respect of any Infringement of the Letters Patent which have taken place after the Expiration of the said Three Years from the date of the said Letters Patent, and before the Payment of the said Fifty Pounds and the stamping of the said Letters Patent in pursuance of this Act

This ensured that something which was lawful at the time it was done (during the renewal fee hiatus) did not become unlawful once the stamp duty was deemed to have been paid properly. It did not, however, protect third parties who used a patented article acquired from a third party during the period of the lapse. It also did not permit manufacturers to sell things legally made during that period. This was first remedied by Mills' Patent Act 1873, section 4:

> Nor shall any action or suit be commenced or prosecuted at law or in equity, nor shall any damage be recovered, in respect of the use of any machine or machinery made within the United Kingdom or any part thereof in infringement of the said letters patent between the expiration of the said period and [the date the Bill completes it passage through the first House of Parliament] such use is by the person by or for whom any such machine or machinery[110] was bona fida manufactured, or his executors, administrators or assigns.

This sort of third party protection had already been granted in relation to other procedural failures, such as when a specification was not filed.[111] While similar provisions were in most subsequent private Acts, it was far from universally adopted and it appears it became less common in the last few pre-1883 Acts.[112] Mills' Patent Act 1873 also provided that no greater royalty might be charged to use the invention in the United Kingdom, the Isle of Man or the Channel Islands than that being charged by the inventor (Richardson) for working the invention in the United States.[113] It is unclear why this restriction only appeared once; particularly as there were other patents owned by foreign inventors.[114]

---

108 Short titles were introduced in the 1840s, but did not become standard until the end of the century. Thus, some of the private Acts included short titles (e.g. Rammell's Patent Act 1864, s 4) while others did not, such as Law's Patent Act 1883.

109 Although sometimes these provisions were combined into one section: see Auld's Patent Act 1885, s 1.

110 Sometimes this was particularised more so in relation to Greene's Patent Act 1881, s 3 it referred to "logotype phrasotypes and apparatus".

111 See for instance Laird's Patent Act 1851, s 2; also see Chapter 7.

112 E.g. Campbell's Sewage Patent Act 1875, s 3; Muirhead's Patent Act 1880, s 3; Copland's Patent Act 1881, s 3; and a variant in Sillar's and Wigner's Patent Act 1876, s 3; Haddan's Patent Act 1883, s 3; Boult's Patent Act 1884, s 2; Bradbury and Lomax's Patent Act 1884, s 2; Wright's Patent Act 1884, s 2.

113 Mills' Patent Act 1873, s 3.

114 For example, Hunt's Patent Act 1880 (US inventor) and Goux's Patent Act 1876 (French inventor).

A failed case – Shaw's Patent (Lining Lead Pipes) Bill 1871

While some Bills did not make it through the Parliamentary process,[115] there was only one where there was evidence heard in opposition. The preamble of Shaw's Bill[116] alleged that the patent owner had purchased the patent for a large sum of money and then expended further money trying to develop the invention. The failure to pay the fee arose because the required stamp duty was given to a Hiram Haines. He was an employee who, it was alleged, not only failed to pay the stamp duty but went on to patent his own related invention. The owners of the patent (a certain George Campbell and Stewart Walker) claimed they had spent a substantial amount of money in purchasing or pursuing two patents; however both patents were purchased at the same time and the less valuable patent was the one in respect of which renewal fees had not been paid. Their Lordships found that the preamble was not proven. As is usually the case there was no reason given. The case clearly demonstrates that a robust opposition to a private Bill may stop it in its tracks.[117] In other respects, once again Shaw's Bill was little different from many that passed.

Private becomes general

While many of the numerous government[118] and private members' Bills[119] introduced between the passage of the Patent Law Amendment Act 1852 and the first session of Parliament in 1880 addressed the issue of fees (usually to reduce them or to change the points at which renewals were made), it was not until George Anderson introduced his fourth Bill for patent reform that any made provision for the late payment of renewal fees.[120] While that Bill, like his others, did not progress, the concept it introduced was included in all subsequent Bills[121] until a new regime was introduced in 1883. The Patents, Designs and Trade Marks Act 1883 provided two mechanisms for paying renewal fees. Patentees could either pay twice as before (now in the fourth and eighth year[122]) or they

---

115 In this period the following Bills failed: Shepard's Patent Bill 1865 (House Bill: HL/PO/JO/10/9/585); Spencer's Patent Bill 1865 (House Bill: HL/PO/JO/10/9/585);Wright's Patent Bill 1865 (House Bill: HL/PO/JO/10/9/587); Smith's Patent Bill 1876; Leigh's Patent Bill 1877.

116 House Bill: HL/PO/JO/10/9/760.

117 Indeed, the fact that no such Bill had survived an opposition at that time was raised by Counsel (Thomas Webster): see Opposed Private Bill Evidence, 1871, Vol 6, 30 March 1871, at p 21–22 (HL/PP/PB/5/37/6).

118 Patents for Inventions Bill 1875 (1875 HC Papers 133), Vol 6, p 491; Patents for Inventions Bill 1876 (1876 HC Papers 137), Vol 5, p 461; Patents for Inventions Bill 1877 (1877 HC Papers 64), Vol 4, p 359; Patents for Inventions (No 2) Bill 1879 (1878–9 HC Papers 77), Vol 5, p 75.

119 Patent Law Amendment Bill 1858 (1857–8 HC Papers 54), Vol 4, p 1; International Patent Rights Bill 1858 (1857–8 HL Papers 276), Vol 4, p 297; Patents for Inventions Bill 1871 (1871 HC Papers 65), Vol 4, p 419; Patent Law Amendment Bill 1878 (1878 HC Papers 127), Vol 5, p 387 (Anderson Bill); Patents for Inventions Bill 1879 (1878–9 HC Papers 55), Vol 5, p 71 (Anderson Bill); Patents for Inventions Bill (Session 1) 1880 (1880 Sess 1 HC Papers 92), Vol 5, p 547 (Anderson Bill).

120 Patents for Inventions Bill (Session 2) 1880 (1880 Sess 2 HC Papers 184), Vol 5, p 551, Cl 7;

121 Patents for Inventions Bill 1881 (1881 HC Papers 15), Vol 4, p 369, Cl 7 (Anderson Bill); Patents for Inventions Bill 1882, Vol 5, p 239, Cl 7 (Anderson Bill); Patent for Inventions (No 2) Bill 1882 (1882 HC Papers 104), Vol 5, p 245, Cl 22 (government Bill); Patents for Inventions (No 2) Bill 1883 (1883 HC Papers 83), Vol 8, p 417, Cl 22 (government Bill); Patents for Inventions (No 3) Bill 1883 (1883 HC Papers 99), Vol 8, p 451, Cl 7 (Anderson Bill).

122 The new law applied to existing patents: Patents, Designs and Trade Marks Act 1883, s 45. However, the period expired at the end of the seventh rather than eighth year: Patents Rules 1883, rr 42 and 43.

could pay annual fees from year four.[123] More importantly, section 17(3) of the Act created a mechanism for where a payment was missed:

> If, nevertheless, in any case, by accident mistake or inadvertence, a patentee fails to make any prescribed payment within the prescribed time, he may apply to the comptroller for an enlargement of the time for making that payment.

Thus, the test of inadvertence – the touchstone used in the private Acts – became the general test for extending the time to pay renewal fees. This test was supplemented by mistake and accident, which had routinely been recited as a ground for not paying the renewal fee. Section 17(3) created limited third party protection to those who started using the invention during that three-month period.[124] It appears, therefore, that the general law began to catch up with the petitioners for private Bills. Nevertheless, the 1883 Act only allowed extensions of time for three months – and no longer.[125] This, it was thought, would be enough to remove the need for private Acts.[126]

Potter's Patent Bill, Skrivanow's Patent Bill and Gilbert and Sinclair's Patent Bill

After 1883, there were a handful of Bills relating to patents which lapsed before the commencement of that Act. Eventually, cases started to appear where the patentee had missed the three-month period and still wanted to restore their patent. A Select Committee was formed to consider the first three such private Bills and it attempted to set the policy for all future Bills. The first Bill considered, Gilbert and Sinclair's Patent Bill,[127] was very similar to the routine Acts that had been passed during the previous 30 years. The patent agent failed to give notice to the company that fees were due and so the company missed the deadline. These grounds, the committee decided, were not sufficient to allow a private Bill to proceed. The second case related to Mr Nicholson, who was the successor to the original patentee Philipp Skrivanow.[128] In his case, the patent agent sent a notice to Skrivanow (who had poor English) but did not send a notice to Nicholson himself (who continued spending substantial sums of money developing the product)[129] Once more the committee did not think that the private Bill should proceed. Indeed, it was only Potter's Bill which was allowed to proceed.[130] Dan Rylands was a bottle manufacturer[131] who employed a Mr Potter to invent

---

123 Patents, Designs and Trade Marks Act 1883, s 17(2).
124 Patents, Designs and Trade Marks Act 1883, s 17(3)(b).
125 Patents, Designs and Trade Marks Act 1883, s 17(4)(a); interestingly any other time period under the Act could be extended on whatever terms the Comptroller thinks fit: Patents Rules 1883, r 47.
126 Appendix A of *Report of a Select Committee on Potter's Patent Bill, Skrivanow's Patent Bill and Gilbert and Sinclair's Patent Bill* (1887 HL Papers 100), Vol 9, p 469 at p 42.
127 Gilbert and Sinclair's Patent Bill 1887 (HL/PO/JO/10/9/1224); and see Statement in Explanation, Appendix C of Report of a *Select Committee on Potter's Patent Bill, Skrivanow's Patent Bill and Gilbert and Sinclair's Patent Bill* (1887 HL Papers 100), Vol 9, p 469, 47 and 48.
128 Skiranow's Patent Bill 1887 (HL/PO/JO/10/9/1229).
129 See Statement in Explanation, Appendix B of Report of a *Select Committee on Potter's Patent Bill, Skrivanow's Patent Bill and Gilbert and Sinclair's Patent Bill* (1887 HL Papers 100), Vol 9, p 469, p 46.
130 Potter's Patent Act 1887.
131 See *Report of a Select Committee on Potter's Patent Bill, Skrivanow's Patent Bill and Gilbert and Sinclair's Patent Bill* (1887 HL Papers 100), Vol 9, p 469, Thomas Johnson Q74 (p 7).

a new type of furnace. Due to overwork, Rylands was advised by his doctor that he should take complete rest.[132] This meant that when the renewal fee was due Rylands was suffering from a serious illness and was unable to pay. The committee thought that his case was one where a private Act should be granted.

The committee thereafter made some general rulings in relation to future private Bills. Such Bills would be refused: (1) whenever an application to extend the payment deadline could have been made and was not so made; (2) where such an application was refused; and (3) where the grounds for non-payment falls short of serious illness or some other cause for which the patentee could not be held responsible.[133] The committee went further, making it clear that defaults by the patentee's servants or agents would not be sufficient in themselves.[134] This was a substantial change of policy as private Bills from the earlier period had allowed the agent to be the fall-guy for the default. Finally, the committee provided a precedent for the saving third party rights. Subsections (1) and (2) of this precedent largely followed the savings that had existed in previous private Acts. An additional subsection (3) limited the third party right to use in the buildings, works and premises of the user. This presumably was intended to limit the right to what might be called home use and not to allow a person to develop a wider trade in the invention. Another new addition was a right of compensation for a person who used the invention while the patent was void and before it was restored by Act of Parliament. This provided third party protection upon restoration.

The second wave

The Select Committee appears to have set very strict rules for when a patent could be restored by private Act. Accordingly, there were a number of rejected Bills.[135] This had effects both on the form and substance of petitions.

Form

Standard recitals

The private Acts retained the recitation of the obligations imposed by the grant of the patent, and in particular the obligation to pay renewal fees[136] and the ten instalments payable.[137] It was also usual to recite that the time limit for enlarging time to pay (under section 17) had expired and when it expired.

---

132 See Statement in Explanation, Appendix D of Report of a *Select Committee on Potter's Patent Bill, Skrivanow's Patent Bill and Gilbert and Sinclair's Patent Bill* (1887 HL Papers 100), Vol 9, p 469 at p 49.
133 *Report of a Select Committee on Potter's Patent Bill, Skrivanow's Patent Bill and Gilbert and Sinclair's Patent Bill* (1887 HL Papers 100), Vol 9, p 469 at p iii.
134 *Report of a Select Committee on Potter's Patent Bill, Skrivanow's Patent Bill and Gilbert and Sinclair's Patent Bill* (1887 HL Papers 100), Vol 9, p 469 at p iii.
135 The notices where no Bill was passed were: Clark's Patent Bill 1887 reached its First Reading in the second House: 119 LJ 272 (28 June 1887); Livet's Petition 1895 and Holmes' Petition 1895 both only got as far as confirmation that Standing Orders were complied with: 150 CJ 13 (8 February 1895).
136 Under Patents, Designs and Trade Marks Act 1883, s 24; see for instance, Whithead's and Pickles' Patent Act 1892, recital (6); a different form was used in Church's Patent Act 1900, recital (3) (also see *Norwood's Patent* (1895) 12 RPC 214 and (1898) 15 RPC 99).
137 See for instance, Simpson's and Fawcett's Patent Act 1892, recitals (2) and (3).

The payment of the fee

The Select Committee had also required the outstanding fees to be deposited with the Comptroller and proof of payment to be provided to Parliament.[138] Thus, it became usual to recite that the fee had been paid.[139]

Investment and loss

The preambles of the latter petitions for private Bills retained many of the characteristics of the earlier ones. Thus, it was common to recite the lack of adequate or sufficient return from the patent[140] or the time and money devoted to the project.[141]

Grounds for restoration Acts being allowed

The grounds upon which Parliament would grant the restoration were also stricter and it was no longer enough to rely on inadvertence: rather fraud, serious illness or the mistakes of the Patent Office were blamed

Fraud

Joseph Harding, a registered patent agent, had received renewal fees from numerous clients and he absconded with the monies rather than paying the fees. This led to four private Acts being passed to restored those patents: Horsfall's Patent Act 1892, Nussey and Leachman's and Nussey's Patent Act 1892, and Whitehead's and Pickles' Patents Act 1892. There were also some other patentees who were defrauded by Harding who started, but did not finish, the process.[142]

Patents with the wrong date – fault of the Patent Office

The dating of a patent[143] being wrong or causing confusion might be a reason to permit a private Act.[144] Melvin Church faced unusual problems leading to his private Act.[145] Two patents had been granted to Romulus Norwood which were revoked by the High Court on it being found that it had been obtained in fraud of Church.[146] This led Church to obtain a patent in a special form following the entitlement dispute. Thereafter, a saga followed where the patent was given one date and the fees paid in time (in terms of section 17) for that first date, but various amendments were made to the patent and its date. According to the revised date, the fees were late and so the Comptroller returned

---

138 *Report of a Select Committee on Potter's Patent Bill, Skrivanow's Patent Bill and Gilbert and Sinclair's Patent Bill* (1887 HL Papers 100), Vol 9, p 469 at p iv; this became a requirement of the Standing Orders: SO No 8a (HL) and (HC): when it was introduced in 1889: 144 CJ 428 (15 August 1889); and 121 LJ 340 (6 August 1889).
139 Kip's Patent Act 1903, recital (14).
140 See for example, Horsfall's Patent Act 1892, recital (9).
141 See for example, Whitehead's and Pickles' Patent Act 1892, recital (12).
142 A earlier Bill went before Parliament confirming these patents and also those of John Midgley and Benjamin Preston: see Nussey and Leachman's and Other Patents Bill 1892. There was a similar case later: Crellin's Patent Act 1906, recital (13).
143 As to when term runs see *Holste v Robertson* (1876) 4 LR Ch D 9 (held to be the date of the patent and not the date it was sealed).
144 Also see Vauclain's Patent Act 1906, recital (7) (wrong advice as to date being given from patent agent to client).
145 Church's Patent Act 1900.
146 See *Norwood's Patent* (1895) 12 RPC 214 (revocation of first patent; and dismissal of petition as concession wrongly made); *Norwood's Patent* (1898) 15 RPC 99 (revocation of second patent).

the fee as it could no longer be paid.[147] Unsurprisingly, this sorry saga, which was largely the fault of the Comptroller,[148] led to a private Act being passed to enable late payment to be made.

Sickness and death

Where the patentee's family or staff were sick so causing additional stress and mental anxiety to the patentee this might be a sufficient ground to pass a restoration private Act.[149] In Whiting's case, the responsibility for payment had be delegated to a clerk of a patent agent who was suffering from domestic trouble and so became unfit to perform his job (and he had not told his employer of the same).[150] Similarly, the sickness or death[151] of the patent agent himself[152] or a secretary[153] was also considered to be good grounds for restoring the patent by way of private Act.

The standard lowers

The high standard imposed by the Select Committee was lowered somewhat around the turn of the twentieth century.[154] For example, the case of Alexander Imschenetzky is one which would appear not to meet the strict test set out by the select committee, yet a private Act was passed.[155] In his case, a notice was sent to his Russian patent agent from his British patent agent and the former did not pass the message on to Mr Imscheneztzky. This appears to be straightforward negligence on the part of the Russian agent – and fault on the part of an agent, the Select Committee said, was not enough. Similarly, Rodger's Patent Act 1901 was passed where the patentee had been granted an exclusive licence and then failed to pay the renewal fee (as agreed under the licence) due to overwork.[156] And "completely overlooking" paying the renewal fee due was acceptable for another private Act.[157] Similarly, the failure of a wife to forward mail was considered sufficient.[158] However, in contrast to the actions of courts, where Parliament passes a private Act contrary to its own precedents, guidance or Standing Order it is still a valid Act.

Patents and Designs Act 1907

The last of the private Acts, Harrison's Patent Act 1907, received Royal Assent on 4 July 1907. A little over a month later on 28 August 1907, the Patents and Designs Act 1907[159]

---

147 The dating saga is explained in the preamble of Church's Patent Act 1900.
148 This would probably allow an extraordinary extension of time under the modern law (Patents Rules 2007, r 107): *Daido Kogyo KK's Patent* [1984] RPC 97, 117–118.
149 Roe's Patent Act 1900, recital (4) (this was combined with additional work caused by moving office).
150 Whiting's Patent Act 1897, recitals (10) and (11).
151 Leven's Patent Act 1905, recital (8).
152 See Holmes' Patent Act 1898, recital (7); Kip's Patent Act 1903, recital (8) (here the agent had actually received the money).
153 Young and Bell's Patent Act 1904, recital (10).
154 See comments of Counsel, *Land's Patent* (1910) 28 RPC 481, 482.
155 Uralite Patent Act 1900.
156 A summary of his busy schedule is included in the Preamble: Rodger's Patent Act 1901.
157 Richard Jaeger's Patent Act 1904, recital (7).
158 Harrison's Patent Act 1907.
159 The Patents and Designs (Amendment) Act 1907 received Royal Assent the same day. This was the amending Act and the Patents and Designs Act 1907 was the consolidating Act.

received Royal Assent and with it section 20,[160] a general power to restore where renewal fees were not paid. This section was introduced by George Radford MP during committee in the Commons[161] and was not otherwise debated. Indeed, it appears to have been "hurriedly accepted".[162] But while there were some minor drafting amendments made there was no attempt to reverse the acceptance by the government.

Section 20 retained the need for the application to be advertised before restoration was granted, but as it was a notice by the Comptroller this moved from the *Gazettes* to the *Patents Journal* only.[163] The standard provided was such that restoration was available where the omission was unintentional and that no undue delay had occurred during the making of the application.[164] It was believed by commentators at the time that the 1907 Act had maintained the "high" standard that had been required by the Select Committee. Terrell suggested:

> A patentee will be obliged to show a clear case of hardship, and mere inadvertence will not be sufficient to justify restoration.[165]

He continued by setting out some of the preamble[166] from Vauclain's Patent Act 1906 suggesting thereby that similar extreme circumstances would be needed to restore a patent. In that case a taxing clerk had put the wrong date in the fees book and so nobody knew the fees were due. It was, like other more recent Acts, more generous than the select committee had allowed. Robert Frost had a different view of the new test[167]:

> The conditions imposed by [section 20] are very similar to the circumstances which it was necessary to establish in order to succeed in obtaining a private Act. . .Hitherto there was not much chance of obtaining a private Act of Parliament if the patentee was unable to establish that the failure was owing to some personal misfortune. . . .Mere neglect on the part of the patentee or his agent was a very unfavorable circumstance. A patentee's position in the matter of obtaining restoration is, thus, much improved by the statutory provision.

It was Frost, and not Terrell, whose view turned out to be right. In *Land's Patent*[168] submissions apparently referred to the standards imposed by Parliament for private Bills[169] and there was express acknowledgment by the judge of the fact the section replaced the role of private Acts.[170] Yet Parker J did not follow the approach which had been adopted before Parliament, as Terrell believed was intended, but rather he held that in

---

160 There was also Patents and Designs Act 1907, s 17 which replaced Patents, Designs and Trade Marks Act 1883, s 17 (save the maximum time to pay was prescribed rather than fixed at three months).

161 Supplement to Votes and Proceedings, 1907, 4 June 1907, p 908.

162 Letter to Sir FF Liddell KCB (Parliamentary Counsel) from CN Dalton (Comptroller-General) dated 10 July 1907: National Archive: AM/1/26.

163 Patents and Designs Act 1907, s 20(3).

164 Patents and Designs Act 1907, s 20(3).

165 Courtney Terrell, *The Law and Practice Relating to Letters Patent for Inventions* (5th Ed, Sweet and Maxwell 1909), p 152.

166 Vauclain's Patent Act 1906, recital (7).

167 Robert Frost, *The Patents and Designs Act 1907* (Stevens 1908), pp 34–35.

168 (1910) 28 RPC 481, Parker J; also see *Comptroller's Ruling I of 1910* (1910) 28 RPC (Supplement) xi.

169 *Land's Patent* (1910) 28 RPC 481 at 484 ("the section only provides for one a series of cases in which. . . Parliament used to give relief to patentees").

170 *Land's Patent* (1910) 28 RPC 481 at 483.

order that an omission to pay a fee should be intentional, it is only necessary that it should be present to the mind of the person who has to pay the pay, that the fee is payable, and that he should deliberately elect not to pay it. His reasons for that election are, it appears to me, absolutely immaterial.

Accordingly, it appears that the court was adopting the original practice of Parliament (before the Select Committee report in 1887), rather than the firmer line Parliament directed itself to take thereafter (which wilted around 1900). In other respects, the Select Committee's approach remained important. Fifteen years after the introduction of section 20, the role of private Acts was considered once more. In an *Official Ruling*[171] the Comptroller when asked to restore a patent ten years after it lapsed turned back to the private Acts and concluded that it had never been appropriate to have such a long delay before reinstatement.[172] Section 20 also created third party protection when the patent was restored, which was[173] exactly the same as that which had been required by the select committee.[174] In this case, it appears, the rules for private Bills had actually passed into the general law.

However, as with patent term prolongation,[175] once restoration became generally available under the 1907 Act, the number of applications increased substantially as the following table demonstrates: [176]

Table 10.2 Applications for restoration of a patent, 1908–1918

Year	Restoration applications	Restored	Withdrawn (or abandoned)	Refused	Unknown
1908	61	27	5	–	29
1909	31	21	3	–	7
1910	35	18	1	(1)	11
1911	41	28	2	–	11
1912	42	36	5	1	–
1913	46	39	7	–	–
1914	35	32	3	–	–
1915	26	25	1	–	–
1916	42	42	–	–	–
1917	15	14	1	–	–
1918	23	20	1	–	2

171 *Official Ruling 1922 (B)* (1922) 39 RPC ii; the only other ruling in the interim was *Official Ruling 1913 (D)* (1913) 30 RPC viii.
172 A formal time limit of three years was introduced by the Patents and Designs Act 1949, Sch 1 (which became Patents Act 1949, s 27).
173 The protection required was set out in the Patents Rules 1908, rr 58 and 59 (made under s 20(5) of the Patents and Designs Act 1907). Strangely, Courtney Terrell, *The Law and Practice Relating to Letters Patent for Inventions* (5th Ed, Sweet and Maxwell 1909), p 153 stated that the conditions might be those similar to Vauclain's Patent Act 1906 (which they were, although the same edition includes the Patents Rules 1908 (from p 513) with the actual rule).
174 *Report of a Select Committee on Potter's Patent Bill, Skrivanow's Patent Bill and Gilbert and Sinclair's Patent Bill* (1887 HL Papers 100), Vol 9, p 469 at p iii.
175 See pp 142–3.
176 The table is based on figures in the 26th to 37th Report of the Comptroller General of Patents, Designs and Trade Marks (for references to these reports see Phillip Johnson, *Parliament, Inventions and Patents: A Research Guide and Bibliography* (Routledge 2018), Part 6.3). The figures for 1908 to 1912 are based on end of year figures (and so the outcome of pending applications is not recorded). The figures for 1913 to 1918 are based on the final figures included in the following year's report.

As can be seen, the total number of applications in the first year was similar to the number of petitions lodged in Parliament over the previous fifty years; and by year three of the new regime a substantially greater number of patents had been restored by the Comptroller than ever had by Parliament under private Acts.

Fees become general – a concluding thought

The history of the power to restore a lapsed patent is the clearest example of where the special case became general; and private legislation led to a general power. The factors that set this class of Bill apart from the others discussed is that there were a sufficient number of private Acts passed for a jurisprudence (legiprudence) to develop and so there was something meaningful which the courts could consider following after the introduction of the general power. It is a clear example of how the private Acts led to a history of patent reform, initially, with the introduction of a three-month time extension under the Patents, Designs and Trade Marks Act 1883 and, ultimately, with a power to restore patents under section 20 of the Patents and Designs Act 1907. But as with patent prolongation the creation of a general right meant the number of cases increased and with it the need for more complex legislation.

11 Re-dating and priority fights

Introduction

The system of priority is now a well-known feature of patent law. It enables a person filing an application in one country to claim the date of its filing as a priority date, that priority date being used to judge the novelty of the invention. Thus, where an application was filed in the United States two months ago and a publication destroying novelty became available last month, it is still possible to file an application in the United Kingdom today and to have the novelty judged from the date of the United States application. This system originates from Article 4 of the Paris Convention for the Protection of Industrial Property which was agreed in 1883 and which was given effect by section 103 of the Patents, Designs and Patents Act 1883.[1] The original priority period in the Paris Convention on industrial property was six months, plus one month where the application is filed beyond the sea,[2] thus for the United Kingdom the period of priority was originally seven months.

The system of priority in the 1880s

When an application was filed under the 1883 Act it was filed on either Form A for a normal application[3] for a patent or Form A1 for an application communicated from abroad.[4] Originally, there was not a specific form for a Convention application. The question arose whether a person who filed a patent could retrospectively claim priority from an earlier filed patent. This is best explained by an example.

In *L'Oiseau and Pierrard's Application*[5] an application was filed by L'Oiseau and Pierrard in France on 18 August 1886. They subsequently filed the same application in the United Kingdom on 8 October 1886, the latter application making no reference at all the French application. A certain Everitt applied for a patent on 20 August 1886 and he applied on 28 May 1887 to oppose the 8 October application. The Law Officer held that provided the applicant had not misled the Patent Office, the 8 October application should be re-dated to 18 August notwithstanding there had been no claim of priority at the time (and the

---

1 It was amended slightly by the Patents, Designs and Trade Marks (Amendment) Act 1885, s 6.
2 Paris Convention for the Protection of Industrial Property (1883 text), Art IV.
3 Patents Rules 1883, r 6(1).
4 Patents Rules 1883, r 27.
5 (1887) Griffiths' Law Officers Cases 36; a similar result was later obtained in *Main's Patent* (1888) 7 RPC 13.

seven-month period had expired). In both this case and in *Main's Patent*[6] the re-dating was during the opposition process (i.e. before the final patent had been sealed).

Worm and Balé

Whether a patent could be re-dated after sealing was addressed in *British Tanning Company v Groth*.[7] The case related to a patent granted to Worm and Balé who had, like L'Oiseau and Pierrard, obtained a French patent and then subsequently filed a British patent. However, they had not indicated that they wished to rely on a claim of priority under section 103 of the Patents, Designs and Trade Marks Act 1883. During an infringement action by the assignees of Worm and Balé, the issue arose as to whether their French patent (which had been published in Britain before the filing of the British patent) anticipated the British patent. Romer J held that it did. He did this by finding that there were two sorts of application under the 1883 Act: ordinary applications and "restricted" applications made under section 103. Further, that Worm and Balé had applied for an ordinary application and they could not subsequently change this to a "restricted" application. Accordingly, the publication of their own French patent led to the invalidity of their British one. Importantly, when Worm and Balé's application was filed in 1887, the same form (Form A or A1) was used for an ordinary application and for a restricted application.[8] And the fact that they did not ensure the patent was dated properly was "not their fault, it was their misfortune".[9]

This sorry affair led to the enactment of Worm and Balé's Patent Act 1891[10]: one of only three attempts at getting a patent re-dated.[11] One of the justifications for passing the Act was the lack of clear rules as to applying for a "restricted" application. The promoters of the Bill pointed out that a new regulation[12] had been enacted since the application was made[13] which meant that such a mistake could not be made again (a new Form A2 and a requirement to make a declaration[14] had been introduced for applications under section 103). Parliament passed their Act and enabled the letters patent to be re-dated[15] and so confirmed the validity of the patent[16] as well as granting the same third party rights which were granted when patents were restored after failing to pay renewal fees.[17]

But no rule – Willson's Patent

The introduction of the new form, negating the difficulty faced by Worm and Balé, meant that when something similar occurred to Thomas Willson, Parliament was not

---

6 (1890) 7 RPC 13.

7 (1891) 8 RPC 113.

8 Noted in *British Tanning* (1891) 8 RPC 113 at 122, Romer J.

9 (1891) 8 RPC 113 at 122, Romer J.

10 There was an opposition on the Bill, but the petitioners (Groth the defendant in the infringement case) did not appear at the hearing and so it was treated as unopposed: Worm and Balé's Patent Bill (HL/PO/PB/5/57/17).

11 The other two being Willson's Patent Bill 1896 (House Bill: HL/PO/JO/10/9/1566) and Saloman's Patent Petition 1895 (150 CJ 12; 7 Feb 1895).

12 This was a reference to the Patents (International and Colonial Arrangements) Rules 1888.

13 Worm and Balé's Patent Act 1891, recital (13).

14 Patents (International and Colonial Arrangements) Rules 1888, r 6.

15 Worm and Balé's Patent Act 1891, s 2.

16 Worm and Balé's Patent Act 1891, s 3.

17 Worm and Balé's Patent Act 1891, s 4; see pp 172 and 174–5.

as accommodating.[18] He filed his patent in the United States on 28 February 1894. There were two applications filed in the United Kingdom. The first on 27 August 1894 was filed on Form A1 (in the name of his agent Ellis) and the second one on Form A on 1 September 1894[19] (in his own name). Accordingly, neither was using the new Form A2.[20] The two British applications were for the same invention with the latter one having a fuller and more complete description.[21] Ellis was instructed to file an ordinary application[22] and not an application under section 103. Indeed, he was not allowed to file an application under section 103 as this had to be filed by the foreigner himself.[23] Thus, as the standard form was used for the application there was no way for the Patent Office to even know a US application was in existence[24] and the required declaration had not been made (and could not be made).[25]

It was subsequently discovered by his agent that on 5 March 1894[26] an article had been published in a French journal *Couples Reudus*, which described Bullier's French patent.[27] This patent anticipated Willson's as it was apparent a copy of it had arrived in the Patent Office a fortnight later – before the filing of either of Willson's patents.[28] Accordingly when this publication was discovered by the patentee in June 1895,[29] Ellis wrote to the Comptroller asking to antedate the application and claim priority under section 103 of the Act.[30] The Comptroller refused the application because it was not made within seven months of the United States application (as required to claim priority)[31] and the law officers indicated that there was no discretion in the matter.[32]

Thus, a private Bill was sought to re-date the patent and claim priority from the US application.[33] It was in the same form as that obtained by Worm and Balé,[34] but unlike that Bill, opponents to the Bill turned up and launched a full-scale assault on it. The committee found against the petitioner with the preamble not be proven (meaning it was not expedient to grant the Bill).[35] It appears the reasoning was largely that, unlike the Worm and Balé Bill, it was clear that at the time of filing the British application what was requested, and

18 A Bill for re-dating a patent had been lodged by George Downing (Salomon's Patent). However, this did not get beyond the confirmation of Standing Orders: 150 CJ 13 (8 Feb 1895). The only information is in the notice: *London Gazette*, 27 Nov 1894, Issue 26574, p 6912.
19 Opposed Private Bill Evidence, 1896, Vol 29 (HL/PO/PB/5/62/29), Evidence of Ellis, p 34.
20 By this time found in the Patents Rules 1890, rr 6(1), 23 and 26.
21 Opposed Private Bill Evidence, 1896, Vol 29 (HL/PO/PB/5/62/29), Evidence of Ellis, p 53.
22 Opposed Private Bill Evidence, 1896, Vol 29 (HL/PO/PB/5/62/29), Evidence of Ellis, pp 48–49.
23 *Shallenberger's Application* (1889) 6 RPC 550; *Carey's Application* (1889) 6 RPC 552.
24 Opposed Private Bill Evidence, 1896, Vol 29 (HL/PO/PB/5/62/29), Evidence of Ellis, p 57.
25 Opposed Private Bill Evidence, 1896, Vol 29 (HL/PO/PB/5/62/29), Evidence of Ellis, pp 85–86.
26 Opposed Private Bill Evidence, 1896, Vol 29 (HL/PO/PB/5/62/29), Evidence of Ellis, p 45.
27 Opposed Private Bill Evidence, 1896, Vol 29 (HL/PO/PB/5/62/29), Evidence of Ellis, p 58.
28 See preamble read out in evidence: Opposed Private Bill Evidence, 1896, Vol 29 (HL/PO/PB/5/62/29), Evidence of Ellis, pp 15–16 and evidence p 45.
29 Opposed Private Bill Evidence, 1896, Vol 29 (HL/PO/PB/5/62/29), Evidence sof Ellis, p 58–59.
30 Opposed Private Bill Evidence, 1896, Vol 29 (HL/PO/PB/5/62/29), Evidence of Ellis, pp 32–33.
31 Letter from Comptroller, Opposed Private Bill Evidence, 1896, Vol 29 (HL/PO/PB/5/62/29), pp 36–37.
32 Letter from law officers on an appeal: Opposed Private Bill Evidence, 1896, Vol 29 (HL/PO/PB/5/62/29), pp 38–39.
33 Opposed Private Bill Evidence, 1896, Vol 29 (HL/PO/PB/5/62/29), Submissions, p 73–74.
34 Opposed Private Bill Evidence, 1896, Vol 29 (HL/PO/PB/5/62/29), Submissions, p 74.
35 Opposed Private Bill Evidence, 1896, Vol 29 (HL/PO/PB/5/62/29), Chairman comments, p 132.

it was after the change in the rules and so Form A2 should have been used.[36] Parliament was confirming that the rules of priority should be rigidly applied and, it appears, it would not be possible to loosen the rules of priority. The modern system had been established.[37]

Conclusion

The attempts to re-date patents is one of the few examples of a private Act, or at least the court case preceding it, identifying a problem and it being solved very quickly by a statutory change. What made the response so quick was the fact it needed just a new form to be created rather than an Act of Parliament. With the new form being introduced the courts and Parliament quickly confirmed there was nothing further to be done.

36 Opposed Private Bill Evidence, 1896, Vol 29 (HL/PO/PB/5/62/29), Pembroke-Stephens, pp 76–77.
37 It was only with the ratification of the Patent Law Treaty 2000 in 2004 by the Regulatory Reform (Patents) Order 2004 (SI 2004/2357) and Patents (Amendment) Rules 2004 (SI 2004/2358) that it became possible to claim priority at a time later than the date of filing.

12 The end of private business

The last private Act relating to patent law came into force in 1907, and since that time no patentee has sought a private Act to fix their particular problem. This was clearly not because patent law reached its perfect state with the enactment of the Patents and Designs Act 1907. There are probably a multitude of reasons why no such Acts were sought such as the general decline in private business, the increasing role of international treaties, the substantial growth in the number of patents to name but a few. This story ends, however, with that last Act in 1907. It was a story based a single principle: private Acts led to reform of the general law.

The protection of individual interests was evidenced in the great Statute of Monopolies itself. Even in those early days exceptions were made for some of the great and influential men of the day.[1] The role of private legislation throughout the rest of the seventeenth century was largely to assist inventors where a prerogative grant could not assist them either for want of a King or because what was sought went beyond the scope of the Statute of Monopolies. Yet the number of recognised inventions and the variety of interests in patents or private Acts were so small that no clear pattern could ever emerge.

The private patent Acts in the eighteenth century, in contrast, were largely concerned with extending the right of the patentee either temporally or geographically (or both).[2] It was these patent term prolongation Acts which were first addressed in the general law with a power to extend a patent being granted to the Privy Council. Yet as has been shown, in contrast to the views of Clifford,[3] the response in Letters Patent for Inventions Act 1835 was not really a response to swells of private legislation. Parliament had not been clogged up with this sort of business. Indeed, its work in relation to such Bills had been slight to non-existent for most of the previous half century. Nor was there a call for this change when reform had been on the agenda a few years earlier.[4] While it was clear that private legislation had established the most basic principle, the most likely reason that the general legislation was introduced when it was is that it could easily be isolated from other aspects of patent law and was not too controversial.[5] Or maybe Lord Brougham simply included the power in his Bill to give the Privy Council, and himself, more work.[6] When the power had been granted,

---

1 See pp 43 and 47–8.
2 See pp 63–64; as well, perhaps, as to overcome potential objections to "improvement" inventions: see pp 59–63.
3 Fredrick Clifford, *A History of Private Bill Legislation* (1885) (Frank Cass 1968), Vol 1, pp 266*–266**; for the extract see p 2.
4 See pp 136–40.
5 Although it turned out to be controversial in the House of Commons: see pp 137–8.
6 See comments on Judicial Committee Act 1844 which was suggested by a leader in *The Times* to be a Bill introduced by him, and shepherded through the Lords by him so as to give himself a new job: *The Times*, 3 July 1844.

the courts – and more particularly Lord Brougham himself – took the view it was not a mere enactment of the existing Parliamentary practice, but a more generous jurisdiction.[7]

The next "movement", to use Clifford's words, was to incorporate companies to work patents. The restriction on the number of people who could hold patents began as a mechanism to prevent patent jobbing or similar frauds[8] yet it became an early way of controlling anti-competitive behaviour. The spate of companies formed under private Acts in the second quarter of the nineteenth century included many set up to work patents – simply to avoid the restriction. These companies continued to form and seek private Bills even after company registration became more commonplace in 1844.[9] Nevertheless, early attempts to remove the restriction failed on the grounds of being too controversial[10] yet when the restriction finally went it happened with so little fanfare that the Lord Chairman, the most powerful man in relation to private Bills, did not even notice that it had happened.[11] Frustratingly, there is no record of why the amendment was made. Whether it was a response to private legislation or simply an overdue law reform but whatever the reason the general law followed a path private legislation had long trodden down.

The final reforms more closely fit Clifford's model. The late payment of renewal fees caused many an anxious patentee to seek a Parliamentary remedy. The number of such enactments grew substantially as the number of patents granted increased. Parliament took action to try and stem the flow of these private Acts in the Patents, Designs and Trade Marks Act 1883[12] and when it was found the general remedy provided was not enough it acted once more in the Patents and Designs Act 1907.[13] The courts even recognised that this was what was done and took action accordingly. The final success was soon followed by failure. The attempts to re-date patents present a very short-lived part of this story, which abruptly ended with no more than a new form being introduced. Once this simple reform had been made Parliament took a firm line on priority which, supported by the courts, remained in place for over a hundred years.[14] It appears, therefore, as we approach the end of the story, Clifford was right and the general law followed the movement of private Bills.

More important, however, may be where Parliament did not respond. The patent specification, the public disclosure of the invention, is seen as its *raison d'être*. It has been shown that not only did private legislation (and petitioners to Parliament) have a role in making the filing of the specification a requirement with a sanction but importantly they equally had a (less successful) role in trying to delay that disclosure until after the expiry of the patent. Indeed, the first public patent Bill to pass the House of Commons[15] after the Statute of Monopolies was to *restrict* disclosure of the invention. Thereafter, the Commons seemed content with the principle of restricting disclosure in individual cases (on often spurious grounds) for another two decades usntil two attempts almost simultaneously to make that

---

7 See p 139.

8 See pp 88–92.

9 Following the possibility of registration under the Joint Stock Companies Act 1844; see pp 99–101.

10 See p 98.

11 See p 102.

12 See p 173–4.

13 Or more accurately, the Patents and Designs (Amendment) Act 1907 which was the pre-consolidating reform Act.

14 It was only relaxed to give effect to the Patent Law Treaty (2000) by the Patents (Regulatory Reform) Order 2004 (SI 2004/ 2357) and the Patents (Amendment) Rules 2004 (SI 2004/2358).

15 Rights of Patentees Bill 1793 (House of Lords Sessional Papers, Vol 1); see pp 113–4.

restriction a part of the general law failed.[16] Private legislation therefore marks out the ambivalent feelings of the establishment towards the requirement for disclosure until well into the nineteenth century.

The history shows once more that the law of patents is not a story of steady evolution, but one of stops and starts; progress and regress. The reforms that came did not always address the most pressing problems of the day and when these problems were addressed it was usually after many false starts. The role of private legislation in this history is a small one, but a significant one. It highlighted particular problems which were ultimately addressed – rarely quickly; and it help set the parameters of the patent bargain. It highlighted the successes of the patent system as well as its failures. It showed how some inventors had a different patent system from everyone else – provided they went to Parliament to ask for it. Ultimately, as the private Bill system evolved and influence became less important the changes made became routine and formulaic. The ability to experiment with the boundaries of patent law through private legislation ultimately died. Yet it once lived; and how it lived.

---

16 Letters Patent Specification Bill 1820 (1820 HC Papers 184), Vol 1, p 285; Patents Bill 1820 (1820 HC Papers 181), Vol 1, p 277; see pp 117–8.

Bibliography

Newspapers

Dublin Evening Post; Evening Mail; Mechanics Magazine; Middlesex Journal and Evening Advertiser; Morning Chronicle and London Advertiser; Morning Post and Daily Advertiser; Morning Post; Naval and Military Gazette; Oracle and Public Advertiser; Repertory of Arts and Manufactures; Saunder's News Letter; The Globe; The Star; The Sun; The Times; Whitehall Evening Post.

Parliamentary Reports

Mirror of Parliament; Parliamentary Register; Hansard; Collection of Parliamentary Debates from the Year MDC XVIII to the Present Time (John Torbuck 1741).

Parliamentary Papers and Reports in Commons Journal

Bills

1793   Rights of Patentees Bill 1793 (1793 HL Papers), Vol 1.

1798   Tanning Leather Bill 1798 (1798 HL Papers), Vol 1.

1801   Indemnity Bill 1801 (1801 HC Papers 87), Vol 1, p 231.

1808   John Palmer Bill 1808 (1808 HL Papers 105), Vol 15, p 765.

1818   Bradbury's Bill 1818 (1818 HL Papers 100), Vol 88, p 485.

1820   Letters Patent Specification Bill 1820 (1820 HC Papers 184), Vol 1, p 285.
          Patents Bill 1820 (1820 HC Papers 181), Vol 1, p 277.

1821   Patentees Protection Bill 1821 (1821 HC Papers 17), Vol 1, p 21.

1833   Letters Patent Bill 1833 (As Amended in Committee) 1833 (1833 HC Papers 496), Vol 3, p 177.
          Letters Patent Bill 1833 (1833 HC Papers 34), Vol 3, p 169.
          Letters Patent Expenses Bill 1833 (1833 HC Papers 497) Vol 3, p 183.

1835   Letters Patent for Inventions Bill 1835 (As Introduced) (1835 HL Papers 68), Vol 1, p 197.

1844   Letters Patent Amendment Bill 1844 (1844 HL Papers 17), Vol 4, p 565.

1851   Patent Law Amendment Bill 1851 (Marked Up to Show Amendments of House of Commons) (1851 HL Papers 316), Vol 5, p 439.
          Patent Law Amendment Bill 1851 (No 3) (1851 HL Papers 167), Vol 5, p 383.

1852   Patent Law Amendment Bill 1852 (Brought from HL) (1852 HC Papers 299), Vol 4, p 1.
          Patent Law Amendment Bill 1852 (As Amended in Committee) (1852 HC Papers 486), Vol 4, p 33.

1858   International Patent Rights Bill 1858 (1857–8 HL Papers 276), Vol 4, p 297.
          Patent Law Amendment Bill 1858 (1857–8 HC Papers 54), Vol 4, p 1.

1871   Patents for Inventions Bill 1871 (1871 HC Papers 65), Vol 4, p 419.
1875   Patents for Inventions Bill 1875 (1875 HC Papers 133), Vol 6, p 491.
1876   Patents for Inventions Bill 1876 (1876 HC Papers 137), Vol 5, p 461.
1877   Patents for Inventions Bill 1877 (1877 HC Papers 64), Vol 4, p 359.
1878   Patent Law Amendment Bill 1878 (1878 HC Papers 127), Vol 5, p 387.
1879   Patent Law Amendment Bill 1879 (1878–9 HC Papers 55), Vol 5, p 71.
        Patents for Inventions Bill (No 2 Bill) 1879 (1878–9 HC Papers 77), Vol 5, p 75.
1880   Patents for Inventions Bill (Session 1) 1880 (1880 Sess 1 HC Papers 92), Vol 5, p 547.
        Patents for Inventions Bill (Session 2) 1880 (1880 Sess 2 HC Papers 184), Vol 5, p 551.
1881   Patents for Inventions Bill 1881 (1881 HC Papers 15), Vol 4, p 369.
1882   Patent for Inventions (No 2) Bill 1882 (1882 HC Papers 104), Vol 5, p 245.
        Patents for Inventions Bill 1882 (1882 HC Papers 72), Vol 5, p 239.
1883   Patents for Inventions (No 2) Bill 1883 (1883 HC Papers 83), Vol 8, p 417.
        Patents for Inventions (No 3) Bill 1883 (1883 HC Papers 99), Vol 8, p 451.

Papers relating to private bills generally

1826   *Report from Select Committee on Fees of Private Bills* (1826–7 HL Papers 114), Vol 219, p 1.
        Standing Orders of the House of Lords (HL Papers 1 of 1826–7), Vol 120, p 1.
1833   *Report of the Select Committee on Establishment of the House of Commons* (1833 HC Papers 648), Vol 12, p 179.
1834   *Report from Select Committee on Private Bills Fees* (1834 HC Papers 540), Vol 11, p 333.
1837   *Report from Select Committee on Private Business* (1837–8 HC Papers 679), Vol 3, p 405.
1846   *Report of Select Committee to Examine Applications for Local Acts* (1846 HC Papers 556), Vol 12, p 1.
1849   *Resolutions Relating to the Ingrossing and Inrolling of Bills* (1849 HC Papers 20), Vol 45, p 19.
1851   *Select Committee on Private Business: First Report* (1851 HC Papers 35), Vol 10, p 741.
1857   *Report from the Select Committee on Second Report of Statute Law* (1857 Sess 1 HC Papers 99), Vol 2, p 773.
1883   *Standing Orders of the House of Commons, 1883* (1883 HC Papers 345), Vol 54, p 165.
        Standing Orders of the House of Lords Relative to the Bringing in and Proceedings on Private Bills 1883 (1883 HL Papers 210), Vol 1, p 37.
1907   *Standing Orders of the House of Commons. Part I.--Public business. Part II.--Private business* (1907 HC Papers 329), Vol 66, p 307.
        Standing Orders of the House of Lords Relative to Bringing in and Proceeding on Private Bills (1907 HL Papers 28 and 194), Vol 1, p 41.

Relating to patent reform and patents generally

1829   *Report from the Select Committee on the Law Relative to Patents for Invention* (1829 HC Papers 332), Vol 3, p 415.
1840   *Return of Cases in Which Judicial Committee of Privy Council Have Reported on Persons Having Letters Patent; Application for Prolongation of Patents* (1840 HC Papers 155), Vol 29, p 559.
1844   *Report of Select Committee of House of Lords to Consider an Act for Amending [the Judicial Committee Act 1833] with Minutes of Evidence* (1844 HL Papers 34), Vol 19, p 323.
1849   *Report of the Committee on the Signet and Privy Seal Office: With Minutes of Evidence and Appendix* (1849 C 1099), Vol 22, p 453.
        Return of the Number of Letters Patent Sealed (1849 HC Papers 23), Vol 45, p 381.
1851   *Select Committee of House of Lords to Consider Bills for Amendment of Law Touching Letters Patent for Inventions. Report, Minutes of Evidence* (1851 HC Papers 486), Vol 18, p 223.

1856   *Return of Amount of Fees Charged at House of Commons on Private Bills Presented to House, 1848–55* (1856 HC Papers 266), Vol 51, p 266.

1864   *Report of the Committee Appointed to Inquire into the Working of the Law Relating to Patents for Inventions* (1864 C 3419), Vol 29, p 321.

1883   *Report of the Commissioners of Patents for Inventions for the Year 1883* (1884 C 4164), Vol 28, p 785.

Financial

1821   *Civil Contingency Fund 1821, Appendix No 3* (76 CJ 574).
       Return of Pensions in Artillery Service, and Ordnance Military Corps, 1820 (1821 HC Papers 234), Vol 15, p 379.

1824   *Civil Contingencies: For the Year 1823* (1824 HC Papers 40), Vol 16, p 275.

1830   *Civil Contingencies: For the Year 1829* (1830 HC Papers 127), Vol 18, p 535.

1831   *Civil Contingencies: For the Year 1830* (1831 HC Papers 25), Vol 13, p 355.

1832   *Civil Contingencies: For the Year 1831* (1832 HC Papers 114), Vol 13, p 355.

1833   *Civil Contingencies: For the Year 1832* (1833 HC Papers 172), Vol 14, p 509.

1834   *Civil Contingencies: For the Year 1833* (1834 HC Papers 186), Vol 42, p 483.

1835   *Civil Contingencies: For the Year 1834* (1835 HC Papers 148), Vol 38, p 553.

1853   *Screw Propeller: Navy Estimates* (1853–4 HC Papers 100), Vol 58, p 135.

1864   *Estimates of Effective and Non-effective Army Services: 1864–65* (1864 HC Papers 50), Vol 35, p 1.

1870   *Reports and Correspondence Explanatory of Item C (Rewards to Inventors) in Army Estimates, 1870–71* (1870 HC Papers 266), Vol 42, p 375.

1871   *Supplementary Army Estimate, 1871–72 (Rewards to Inventors)* (1871 HC Papers 426 and 451), Vol 38, p 365 and 367.

Relating to individual private bills or rewards

1755   *Report on Richard Lydell's Ballast Engine Petition* (27 CJ 235; 17 March 1755).

1757   *Report on Cox's Unloading Machine Petition* (27 CJ 859; 28 April 1757).

1761   *Report on John Bindley's Petition* (28 CJ 1039; 23 January 1761).

1801   *Report on Mr Koop's Petition: Respecting His Invention for Making Paper from Various Refuse Materials* (1801 HC Papers 55), Vol 3, p 127.

1808   *Report from the Committee on Dr. Cartwright's Petition Respecting His Weaving Machine* (1808 HC Papers 179), Vol 2, p 135.

1810   *Report of Committee on Mr Mallison's Petition* (1810–11 HC Papers 206), Vol 2, p 375.

1813   *Report in Petition of James Lee* (1813 HC Papers 67), Vol 3, p 393.

1814   *Notification of Grant to Colonel Congreve for His Invention of Rockets* (1814–15 HC Papers 329), Vol 9, p 459.

1818   *Report from the Committee on Mr. Bradbury's Petition Relative to Machinery for Engraving and Etching* (1818 HC Papers 328), Vol 3, p 361.

1829   *Minutes of Evidence Taken before Lords Committee to Whom Langton's Bill Was Referred* (1829 HL Papers 82), Vol 162, p 223.

1837   *Report from the Select Committee on Fourdriniers' Patent; With the Minutes of Evidence, and Appendix* (1837 HC Papers 351), Vol 20, p 35.

1870   *Correspondence between War Office and Colonel Boxer Relating to His Patent for Fuses* (1870 HC Papers 161), Vol 42, p 501.

1887   *Report of Select Committee on Potter's Patent Bill; Skrivanow's Patent Bill and Gilbert and Sinclair's Patent Bill* (1887 HL Papers 100), Vol 9, p 469.

Other

1837   *Report on the Law of Partnership* (1837 HC Papers 530), Vol 44, p 399.

1843   *Report from the Select Committee on Joint Stock Companies* (1843 HC Papers 523), Vol 11, p 215.

1844   *First Report of the Select Committee on Joint Stock Companies; Together with the Minutes of Evidence* (1844 HC Papers 119), Vol 7, p 1.

1846   *Report of Select Committee of House of Lords on Management of Railroads* (1846 HC Papers 489), Vol 13, p 217 and 411.

1854   *Northcote-Trevelyan Report, Report on the Organisation of the Permanent Civil Service* (1854 C 1713), Vol 27, p 1.

Notices of Amendment

Patents and Designs Bill, Notices of Amendments, Supplement to Votes and Proceedings, 1907, 4 June 1907, p 908.

Petitions

1822   Thomas Walker, 77 CJ 359 (20 June 1822); Appendix to Votes and Proceedings, 1822, pp 487–488 (No 705) {PET7}.

1826   Thomas Morton, 81 CJ 309 (1 May 1826); Appendix to Votes and Proceedings, 1826, pp 498–489 (No 761) {PET10}.

1829   Thomas Flannagan, 84 CJ 128 (12 March 1829); Appendix to Votes and Proceedings, 1829, pp 748–749 (Nos 1,802 and 1,803) {PET12}.

   John Birkinshaw, 84 CJ 187 (31 March 1829); Appendix to Votes and Proceedings, 1829, pp 1213–1214 (No 2,839) {PET13}.

1833   Thomas Richard Yare, 88 CJ 132 (28 February 1833); Second Report of the Public Petitions Committee, 1833, p 48 {PET15}.

   Richard Roberts, 88 CJ 179 (18 March 1833); Seventh Report of the Public Petitions Committee, 1833, p 176 {PET16}.

   John Kitchen, 88 CJ 231 (28 March 1833), Tenth Report of the Public Petitions Committee, 1833, p 294 (No 2,140) {PET17}.

   Joseph Holiday, 88 CJ 505 (20 June 1833); Thirteenth Report of Public Petitions Committee, 1833, p 1150 (No 9,382) {PET18}.

   Julius Schroder, 88 CJ 535 (1 July 1833); Thirty-Third Report of the Public Petitions Committee, 1833, p 1268 (No 9,559) {PET19}.

1834   Edward Moxhay, 89 CJ 117 (13 March 1834); Eighth Report of Public Petitions Committee, 1834, p 91 (No 1,292) {PET20}.

   William Ivory, 89 CJ 227(28 April 1834); Sixteenth Report of Public Petitions Committee, 1834, p 198 (No 3,186) {PET22}.

1835   James Marsh, 90 CJ 578 (21 August 1835); Thirty-Ninth Report of the Public Petitions Committee, 1835, p 292 (No 3,718) and Appendix, 1331–1312 (No 1733) {PET26}.

   Patentees & c of Birmingham, 90 CJ 584 (24 August 1835); Fortieth Report of the Public Petitions Committee, 1835, p 300 (No 3,806) and Appendix, pp 1372–1373 (No 1785) {PET27}.

1838   Fourdrinier, Petitions in favour of, 4 July 1838, Thirty-Fifth Report of the Public Petitions Committee, 1838, p 570 (Nos 8,623 to 8,625) {PET77 to PET79}.

   Fourdrinier, Petitions in favour of, 10 July 1838, Thirty-Sixth Report of the Public Petitions Committee, 1838, p 583 (No 8,732) {PET80}.

Fourdrinier, Petitions in favour of, 16–18 July 1838; Thirty-Seventh Report of the Public Petitions Committee, 1838, p 603 (No 8,960–8,962) {PET81 to PET83}.

1839   Fourdrinier, Petitions in favour of, Public Petitions Committee: 24–25 April 1839, Twentieth Report of the Public Petitions Committee, 1839, pp 350–1 (No 6,495 to 6,510) {PET86 to PET101}.

Fourdrinier, Petitions in favour of, 1 May 1839, Twenty-Second Report of the Public Petitions Committee, 1839, p 386 (No 6,987 and 6,989) {PET102 to PET104}.

1844   Earl of Dundonald (20 February 1844), Third Report of Select Committee on Public Petitions, 1844, p 19 (No 147) and Appendix, p 18 (No 32); 76 LJ 32 (16 February 1844) {PET131}.

1850   John Jones (13 February 1850): Fifth Report of the Public Petitions Committee, 1850, p 41 (No 484) {PET161}.

Henry Archer: 82 LJ 62 (15 March 1850) {PET162}.

1851   Huddersfield Committee on Great Exhibition (17 February 1851): Sixth Report of the Public Petitions Committee, 1851, p 73 (No 1,916) and Appendix, 81 (No 175) {PET168}.

National Patent Law Amendment Association (18 March 1851), Seventeenth Report of the Public Petitions Committee, 1851, p 237 (No 237) and Appendix, 193 (No 426) {PET170}.

1852   Sugar Refiners of Greenock (23 June 1852): Forty-Fifth Report of the Public Petitions Committee 1852, p 620 (No 5,611) {PET214}.

1863   John Clare (5 May 1863), Twentieth Report of Public Petitions Committee, p 467 (No 6,631) {PET269}.

Privately printed

William Molleson, *The Reports of the Commissioners Appointed to Examine, Take, and State the Public Accounts of the Kingdom* (Caddell 1783).

Printed collections of primary resources

Abbott, Benjamin, *The Patent Laws of All Nations* (Charles Brodix 1886).

Baker, Philip (ed), *Proceedings in Parliament 1624: The House of Commons* (2015), British History Online.

Bottomley, Sean, "Patent Cases in the Court of Chancery, 1714–58" (2014) 35 *Journal of Legal History* 27.

Calendar of State Papers, Charles I, Vol 2.

Carpmael, Alfred and Edward, *Patent Laws of the World: Collected, Edited and Indexed* (2nd Ed William Clowes 1889).

Carr, Cecil, *Select Charters of Trading Companies 1530–1707* (Selden Society 1913).

D'Ewes, Simon, *Journals of All the Parliaments during the Reign of Queen Elizabeth* (John Starkey 1682).

Eardley-Wilmot, Sir John (ed), *Lord Brougham's Acts and Bills, From 1811 to the Present Time* (Longman 1857).

Gardiner, Samuel (ed), *Notes of the Debates in the House of Lords officially taken by Henry Elsing, Clerk of the Parliaments, 1621* (1871) 103 Camden Society (Old Series).

Gardiner, Samuel (ed), *Notes on the Debates in the House of Lords: Officially Taken by Henry Elsing, 1624–1626* (1879) 24 Camden Society (New Series).

Hansard, Luke, *Reports from the Committees of the House of Commons 1715–1801* (Hansard 1802).

Henning, Basil (ed), *History of Parliament: The House of Commons 1660–1690* (Secker and Warburg 1983).

House of Lords Manuscripts 1712–1714 (HMSO 1953), Vol 10, *Roll of Standing Orders of the House of Lords* (No 2923).

Henning, Basil (ed), *Parliamentary Diary of Sir Edward Dering Diary 1670–1673* (Yale 1940).

Johnson, Phillip, "Minutes of Evidence of the Select Committee on the Letters Patent for Invention Act 1835" (2017) 7 *Queen Mary Journal of Intellectual Property* 99.

Johnson, Phillip, *Parliament, Inventions and Patents: A Research Guide and Bibliography* (Routledge 2018).

Larkin, James and Hughes, Paul, *Stuart Royal Proclamations: Royal Proclamations of Charles I 1625–46* (Oxford 1983), Vol 2.

Larkin, James and Hughes, Paul, *Stuart Royal Proclamations: Royal Proclamations of James I 1603–25* (Oxford 1973), Vol 1.

Larkin, James and Hughes, Paul, *Tudor Royal Proclamations* (New Haven 1969), Vol 3.

Lyle, JV (ed), *Acts of the Privy Council of England, 1619–1621* (HMSO 1930), Vol 37.

Manuscripts of the House of Lords, 1693–5 (HMSO 1964), Vol 1.

Member of the House (Sir Edward Nicholas), *Proceedings and Debates of the House of Commons in 1620 and 1621* (1766) Vols 1–2.

Monger, RF (ed), *Acts of the Privy Council of England, 1628–1629* (HMSO 1959), Vol 44.

Monger, RF (ed), *Acts of the Privy Council of England, 1628–1629* (HMSO 1958), Vol 45.

Notestein, Wallace and Relf, Frances, *Commons Debates for 1629: Critically Edited* (Minnesota 1921).

Notestein, Wallace, Relf, Frances and Simpson, Hartley, *Commons Debates 1621* (Yale 1935).

Relf, Frances, "Lords Debates 1621" (1929) 42 Camden Society (Third Series).

Report in 1761 of the Attorney and Solicitor-General on the Petition for a Charter for the Equitable Life Assurance Company (14 July 1761) included in *The Assurance Magazine* (WSD Pateman 1851), No 2 at 89.

Robinson, Eric and Musson, Albert (ed), *James Watt and the Steam Revolution (A Documentary History)* (Adam & Dart 1969).

Royal Commission on Historical Manuscripts, *Seventh Report of Royal Commission on Historical Manuscripts* (HMSO 1879) (C 2340), Vol 40, p 721.

Royal Commission on Historical Manuscripts, *Sixth Report of the Royal Commission on Historical Manuscripts* (HMSO 1877) (C 1745), Vol 47, p 1.

Rushworth, John, *Historical Collections of Private Passages of State* (D Browne *et al* 1721), Vol 2.

Thirsk, Joan and Cooper, John P, *Seventeenth Century Economic Documents* (Oxford 1972).

Woodcroft, Bennet, *Titles of Patents of Invention: Chronologically Arranged from 1617 to 1852* (London: Eyre and Spottiswoode 1854).

Published papers relating to private Acts

Anon [James Ward], *Reasons Offered against Passing Sir Samuel Moreland's Bill* (1677) (Wing R576).

Bancroft, Edward, *Facts and Observations, Briefly Stated in Support of an Intended Application to Parliament* (London: 1798).

Brief Statement of the Case of the Machine Erected at Derby (i.e. the Case in Support): *Harper's Collection of Private Bills*, Vol 9, Bill No 31.

By Virtue of a Patent Granted by King Charles II. for a New Invention of Lamps with Convex Glasses (1691) (Wing H1414A).

Case of the Manufacturers of Woollen, Linnen, Mohair and Cotton Yarn in Manchester & c (1732): *Harper's Collection of Private Bills*, Vol 9, Bill No 31.

Case of the Silk Throwers (1732): *Harper's Collection of Private Bills*, Vol 9, Bill No 31.

Charter of Royal Lustring Company (1698) (Wing C3725).

George Ball Appellant, John Coggs and Other, The Appellants Case (1710) (ETSC T040785).

Mr Richard Arkwright & Co, in Relation to Mr Arkwright's Invention of an Engine for Spinning Yarn (1782) (ESTC: T188828).

Reasons Humbly Offer'd by the Jewellers, Diamond-cutters, Lapidaries, Engravers in Stone, &c. against the Bill for Jewel-Watches (1704) (EEBO).

Reasons of the English Watch and Clockmakers against the Bill to Confirm the Pretended New Invention of Using Precious and Common Stones about Watches, Clocks, and Other Engines (1704) (ETSC T046472).

Report by the Commissioners for Bills and Trade concerning James Wemyss [RPS: A1661/1/29].

Report of the Ophthalmic Committee Presented to the House of Commons (London: William Clowes 1821).

The Case of Edmund Heming, Who First Set up the New Lights in the City of London (1690) (Wing H1415).

The Case of Mr Walcot, Concerning the Making of His Sea Water, Fresh, Clear and Wholesome (1694) (Wing W285A and W285B).

To the Honourable House of Commons Assembled in Parliament, the Humble Petition of Peter Chamberlen, Doctor in Physic (1649) (Wing C1908).

Walcot's An Answer to Mr Fitz-gerald's State of the Case Concerning the Patent of Making Salt Water Fresh (January 1695) (Wing W285A).

Archive material

National Archive

Patents

1552   Henry Smyth (1552) PR 6 Edw VI, Pt 5, m 26 (Cal Edw VI, Vol 4, 323) (C66/846).

1562   William Kendall (1562) PR 5 Eliz, Pt 1, m 8 (Eliz Pat Cal, Vol 2 465) (C66/987).

1564   Cornelius de Vos (1564) PR 6 Eliz, Pt 8, m 38 (Eliz Pat Cal, Vol 3, No 486) (C66/1003).

1565   Roger Heuxtenbury and Bartholomew Verberick (1565) PR 7 Eliz, Pt 5, m 11 (Eliz Pat Cal, Vol 3, No 1199) (C66/1013).

1567   Anthony Becku and John Carre (1567) PR 9 Eliz, Pt 11, m 33 (Eliz Pat Cal, Vol 4, No 929) (C66/1040).

1576   Ralph Bowes and Thomas Bedingfield (1576) PR 18 Eliz Pt 1, m 32 (Eliz Pat Cal, Vol 7, No 60) (C66/1137).

1577   William Waade and Henry Mekyns (1577) PR 19 Eliz, Pt 8, m 6 (Eliz Pat Cal, Vol 7, No 2257) (C66/1158).

1578   Ralph Bowes and Thomas Bedingfield (1578) PR 20 Eliz Pt 7, m 33 (Eliz Pat Cal, Vol 7, No 3409) (C66/1170).

1588   Ralph Bowes (1588) PR 30 Eliz Pt 12, m 17 (Eliz Pat Cal, No 718) (C66/1315).

1598   Edward Darcye (1598) PR 40 Eliz, Pt 9, m 37 (Eliz Pat Cal, No 735) (C66/1485).

1612   Joseph Usher (1612) PR 10 Jac I, Pt 7, No 10 (C66/1949).
         Richard Barnswell (1612) PR 10 Jac I, Pt 23, No 9 (C66/1965).

1614   Charles Thynne (1614) PR 12 Jac I, Pt 2, No 3 (C66/2018).
         Edmund Brunt (1614) PR 11 Jac I, Pt 11, No 7 (C66/1988).
         Edmund Sheffield (1614) PR 12 Jac I, Pt 8, No 29 (C66/2024).
         Henry Vane (1614) PR 11 Jac I, Pt 14, No 9 (C66/1981).

1618   Sir Richard Young (1618) PR 16 Jac I, Pt 12, No 8 (C66/2176).

1621   Sackville Crowe (1621) PR 18 Jac I, Pt 12, No 1 (C66/2227).

1634   Soap Making Company (1634) PR 10 Chas I, Pt 16, No 1 (C66/2657).

1661   John Colnett (1661) PR 13 Chas II, Pt 25, No 8 (C66/2980).

State Papers

State Papers Domestic (--): SP 16/2 f 186 (Warrant for Arrest).

State Papers Domestic (7 October 1691): SP 44/341 f 197–202 (Warrant for Company of Glassmakers Charter).

State Papers Domestic (7 April 1618): SP 14/141 f 120 (Warrant).

State Papers Domestic (15 April 1685): SP 44/71 f 127 (John Briscoe's Patent Warrant).

State Papers Domestic (13 June 1686): SP 31/3 f 262 (White Paper Charter Warrant).

State Papers Domestic (5 July 1720): SP 44/283 f 15 (Council of Regents).

State Papers Domestic (12 July 1720): SP 44/283 f 19 (Council of Regents).

State Papers Domestic (3 July 1686): SP 44/337 ff 57–60 (Warrant for a Charter).

State Papers Domestic (25 August 1725): SP 35/57/2 f 89 (Le Blon's Petition to Incorporate).

State Papers Domestic (8 November 1604): SP 14/19A f 9 ("The Judges to Council").

State Papers Domestic (--): SP 29/93 f 116 (Memoranda [by Williamson, Taken from the Signet Books,] of Warrant and Grants Passed during the Month).

Other

Letter to Sir FF Liddell KCB (Parliamentary Counsel) from CN Dalton (Comptroller-General) dated 10 July 1907: National Archive: AM/1/26.

National Archive: Chancery: Parliament Roll, Part 1: National Archive: C65/186.

Privy Council Register

Privy Council Register (1669): PC 2/61, ff 138 and 160–161.

Privy Council Register (1685): PC 2/70, f 56.

Houses of Lords Archive

Bills

1606   Penal and Monopolies Bill 1606 (Ingrossment: HL/PO/JO/10/2/1E).

1660   Leather Trade Bill 1660 (Ingrossment: HL/PO/JO/10/1/300).

1662   Colnett's Bill 1662 (Ingrossment: HL/PO/JO/10/1/314).

1663   Colnett's Bill 1663 (Ingrossment: HL/PO/JO/10/1/316).

1678   Walcot's Salt-Water Patent Bill 1678 (Ingrossment: HL/PO/JO/10/1/375).

1692   [Walcot's] Salt-Water Bill 1692 (Ingrossment: HL/PO/JO/10/2/22).

1742   Tuite's Water Engine Bill 1742 (Ingrossment: HL/PO/JO/10/2/41).

1781   Henry Phillips' Bill 1781 (Ingrossment: HL/PO/JO/10/2/56).

1782   Wharam's Patent Stirrup Bill 1782 (Ingrossment: HL/PO/JO/10/2/57).

1785   Henry Phillips' Bill 1785 (Ingrossment: HL/PO/JO/10/2/59B).

1791   James Turner Dye Invention Bill 1791 (Ingrossment: HL/PO/JO/10/2/65A).

1794   Kendrew and Porthouse's Bill 1794 (Ingrossment: HL/PO/JO/10/2/67).

1799   Dr Bancroft's Patent Bill 1799 (Ingrossment: HL/PO/JO/10/2/70).

1814   John Vancouver's Bill 1814 (Ingrossment: HL/PO/JO/10/2/88C).

1816   Lee's Patent Bill 1816 (Ingrossment: HL/PO/JO/10/2/90B).

1865   Shepard's Patent Bill 1865 (House Bill: HL/PO/JO/10/9/585).

       Spencer's Patent Bill 1865 (House Bill: HL/PO/JO/10/9/585).

       Wright's Patent Bill 1865 (House Bill: HL/PO/JO/10/9/587).

1871   Shaw's Patent (Lining Lead Pipes) Bill 1871 (House Bill: HL/PO/JO/10/9/760).

1887   Gilbert and Sinclair's Patent Bill 1887 (House Bill: HL/PO/JO/10/9/1224).
       Skrivanow's Patent Bill 1887 (House Bill: HL/PO/JO/10/9/1229).
1896   Willson's Patent Bill 1896 (House Bill: HL/PO/JO/10/9/1566).

Private acts not otherwise printed

1689   White Paper Company Act 1689 (Ingrossment: HL/PO/PB/1/1689/2W&Mn25).
1868   Gardiner's Patent Act 1868 (Vellum: HL/PO/PB/1/1868/31&32V1n63).
1877   Robey and Chantrell's Patent Act 1877 (Vellum: HL/PO/PB/1/1877/40&41V1n242).

Committee Books

House of Lords Committee Books (HL/PO/CO/1/1), 28 March 1663, 314–315 (Marquis of
    Worcester Act 1663).
House of Lords Committee Books (HL/PO/CO/1/12), 19 May 1742, 31 (Byrom's Shorthand
    Act 1741).
House of Lords Committee Books (HL/PO/CO/1/21), 22 March 1776, 311–315 (Elizabeth
    Taylor's Patent Act 1776).
House of Lords Committee Books (HL/CO/PO/1/84), 3 June 1829, 443 (Langton's Profits (Wood
    Seasoning Invention) Act 1829).
House of Lords Committee Books (HL/PO/CO/1/250), 14 March 1873, 44 (Mills' Patent Act 1873).
House of Commons, Unopposed Bill Committee Minutes, 1880 (HC/CL/WM/UB/1/33), 2 July
    1880, 59 (Hunt's Patent Act 1880).

Evidence Books

Minutes of Evidence, 12 May 1830 (HL/PO/JO/10/8/913) (Hollingrake's Act 1830).
Opposed Bill, Evidence, 1871, Vol 6, 30 March 1871 (HL/PP/PB/5/37/6) (Shaw's Patent (Lining
    Lead Pipes) Bill 1871).
Opposed Bill, Evidence, 1891, Vol 17 (HL/PO/PB/5/57/17) (Worm and Balé's Patent Act 1891).
Opposed Private Bill Evidence, 1896, Vol 29 (HL/PO/PB/5/62/29) (Willson's Patent Bill 1894).

Other

Experiments by Henry Phillips: HL/PO/JO/10/7/660.

London Metropolitan Archives

Petition of John Hutchinson: CLS/L/CD/E/004/MS03952.
"Proposals Humbley Offered for the Better Lighting of All Street, Lanes, Allies and Public Courts
    within the City of London", *Journals of the Common Council* (1689–1694), Vol 51, Meeting of
    Common Council, 6 September 1662 (COL/CC/01/01/049).
Minutes of Meeting of Common Council, 6 November 1692; and Report of Committee of
    Improvements, *Journals of the Common Council*, 13 December 1662 (1689–1694), Vol 51 (COL/
    CC/01/01/049).
Reasons Offered against [Mr Hutchinson's] Bill by the Clockmakers Company (CLS/L/CD/E/004/
    MS03952).
Reasons for [Mr Hutchinson's] Bill (CLS/L/CD/E/004/MS03952).
The Clockmakers father Reasons against Mr Hutchinson's Bill: CLS/L/CD/E/004/MS03952.
Further Reasons for the Bill . . . in Answer to the Clockmakers: CLS/L/CD/E/004/MS03952.

Birmingham Library

Mr Hornblower's Case Relative to a Petition to Parliament for the Extension of the Term of his Patent: MS3147/2/36/3.

Minutes of the Second Reading of Hornblower's Patent Bill 1792: Birmingham Library: MS3147/2/35/23.

Observations on the Part of Messrs Boulton and Watt concerning Mr Hornblower's Steam Engine Bill: MS 3147/2/36/2.

Hornblower's Patent Bill 1792: MS 3147/2/36/1.

Letter from James Watt to Matthew Boulton, 17 January 1775: MS 3782/12/76/6.

Letter from James Watt to Matthew Boulton, 31 January 1775: MS 3782/12/76/8.

Contemporary sources

A Looker, *Morning Chronicle,* 20 November 1807.

A Plain Dealer, *Morning Chronicle,* 5 November 1807, 3.

Ailsbury, Earl of, *Memoirs of the Earl of Ailsbury* (ed W Buckley) (Nicols & Sons 1890), Vol 1.

An Appeal to the Public on the Right of Using Oil Cement (London: J Hand 1778).

An Old Fashioned Fellow, *Morning Chronicle,* 9 November 1807, 3.

Anon, *An Account of the South Sea Scheme and a Number of Other Bubbles* (J Cawthorne 1806).

Anon, "Article V – Publications of the Commissioners of Patents" (January 1859) 105 *Quarterly Review* 136.

Anon, "Inventors and the Crown" (1865) 13 *Mechanics Magazine* 70.

Anon, *Key to Both Houses of Parliament* (Longman 1832).

Anon, "List of Parliamentary Reward Granted for Useful Discoveries, Inventions and Improvements" (1832) 13 *Mechanics Magazine* 61.

Anon, "Lord Brougham's Patent Law Amendment Bill" (1835) 23 *Mechanics Magazine* 310.

Anon, "LXXVI – On Saving the Lives of Mariners" (1811) 37 (Issue 158) *Philosophical Magazine* Series 1, 455.

Anon, "Mr Godson's Bill for the Improvement of the Patent Laws, with Remark" (1833) 19 *Mechanics Magazine* 26 and 43.

Anon, *On the Introduction and Progress of the Screw Propeller* (Longman, Brown and Green 1856).

Anon, "On the Proposed Alteration in the Laws Relative to Patents" (1820) 1 *London Journal of Arts and Science* 358.

Anon, "Patent Law Amendment Act" (1835) 23 *Mechanics Magazine* 524.

Anon, "Private Business of House of Commons" (1843) *Law Magazine, or, Quarterly Review of Jurisprudence* 129.

Anon, "Should Specifications Be Concealed?" (1840) 2 (22) *Inventors' Advocate* 1.

Anon, "The Patent Laws" (1833) 19 *Mechanics Magazine* 271.

Atkinson, Solomon, *Chitty's Stamp Laws* (3rd Ed, Benning & Co 1850).

Babbage, Charles, *Passages from the Life of a Philosopher* (Longman 1864).

Bacon, Matthew, *A New Abridgement of the Law* (ed Henry Gwillim) (5th Ed, Strahan 1798).

Balfour Browne, JH, *Forty Years at the Bar* (Herbert Jenkins 1916).

Blackstone, William, *Commentaries on the Laws of England: Book 4: Of Public Wrongs* (ed Wilfred Priest) (Oxford 2016).

Bramwell, George, *The Manner of Proceedings on Bills in the House of Commons* (Hansard 1823).

Bulteel, John, "A Letter Written to the Publisher Concerning a New Way, by an English Manufacture to Preserve the Hull of Ships from the Worm &c" (1673) 8 *Philosophical Transactions* 6192.

Byrom, John, *The Universal English Shorthand or the Way of Writing Invented by John Byrom* (Manchester: Joseph Harrop 1767).

Carpmael, William, *The Law of Patents for Inventions, Familiarly Explained: Familiarly Explained for the Use of Inventors and Patentees* (London: J Wrightman 1832).

Carpmael, William, *The Law of Patents for Inventions: Familiarly Explained for the Use of Inventors and Patentees* (4th Ed, Simpkin, Marshall & Co 1846).

Circular to Bankers, 14 February 1840 (No 605) and 17 August 1838 (No 527).

Coke, Sir Edward, *The First Part of the Institutes of the Laws of England* (Flesher 1628).

Coke, Sir Edward, *The Third Part of the Institutes of the Laws of England* (Flesher 1644).

Cole, Sir Henry, *Sir Henry Cole: Fifty Years of Public Works* (Bell 1884), Vol 2.

Colquhoun, Patrick, *A Treatise on the Wealth, Power, and Resources of the British Empire* (London: Joseph Mawman 1815).

Commissioner of Patents Journal (1859), 8 April 1859, Issue 459.

Day, Henry, *A Defense of Joint-Stock Companies; Being an Attempt to Shew Their Legality, Expediency, and Public Benefit* (Longman 1808).

Drewry, Charles, *Observations on Points Relating to the Amendment of the Law of Patents* (John Richards 1839).

Dudley, Dud, *Mettallum Martis* (London 1665).

Ellis, Charles, *Practical Remarks and Precedents of Proceedings in Parliament* (Butterworths 1802).

Ellis, Charles *The Solicitor's Instructor in Parliament Concerning Estate Bills and Inclosure Bills* (London: John Rider 1799).

Erskine May, Sir Thomas, *A Treatise upon the Law, Privileges, Proceedings and Usage of Parliament* (8th Ed, Butterworths 1883).

Erskine May, Thomas, *A Treatise upon the Law, Privileges, Proceedings and Usage of Parliament* (1st Ed, Charles Knight & Co 1844).

Fitzgerald, Robert, *Salt-water Sweetned, or, A True Account of the Great Advantages of the Invention Both by Sea and by Land* (1684) (Wing F1087) "farther additions" (Wing F1082) and a supplement (Wing F1090) (both 1684).

Forsyth, William, "In Consequence of an Address of the House of Commons to His Majesty and of an Examination Made Respecting the Efficacy of a Composition, Discovered by Mr William Forsyth, For Curing Injuries and Defects in Trees" (1791; 1824 Reprint) 33 *Annual Register* 351.

Frost, Robert, *The Patents and Designs Act 1907* (Stevens 1908).

Godson, Richard, *A Practical Treatise on the Law of Patents for Inventions and of Copyright: With an Introductory Book on Monopolies* (London 1823).

Godson, Richard, *A Practical Treatise on the Law of Patents for Inventions and Copyright* (2nd Ed, Saunders and Benning: London 1840).

Hammond, Anthony, *A Summary Treatise on the Practice and Proceedings in Parliament* (Butterworth 1825).

Hatsell, John, *Precedents and Proceedings in the House of Commons* (Hansard 1818), Vol 3.

Hawkins, William, *A Treatise of the Pleas of the Crown* (Elizabeth Nutt 1716), Ch 79, s. 6.

Hindmarch, William, *Observations on the Defects of the Patent Laws of This Country: With Suggestions for the Reform of Them* (London 1851).

Hindmarch, William, *A Treatise on the Law Relating to the Patent Privileges for the Sole Use of Inventions: And the Practice of Obtaining Letters Patents for Inventions* (London: Stevens 1846).

Intellectual Property Office, *Proposed Changes to Statutory Patent Fees* (2017).

James I, *A Declaration of His Majesties Royall Pleasure, in What Sort He Thinketh Fit to Enlarge (Book of Bounty)* (Robert Barker 1610) (Facsmile Reprint 1897).

Keymor, John, *John Keymor's Observation Made upon the Dutch Fishing about the Year 1601* (Sir Edward Ford 1664) (Wing K390).

Leeds, Meeting in Leeds (1833) 2 *Newton's London Journal and Repertory of Patent Inventions* 237.

Letter on the Fees Charged upon Patents for Invention (1829) 2 *London Journal of Arts and Science* 311.

Lindley, Nathaniel, *A Treatise on the Law of Partnership* (William Maxwell 1860), Vol 1.

Lord Lauderdale, *An Inquiry into the Nature and Origin of Public Wealth* (Longman 1804).

Macpherson, David, *Annals of Commerce: Manufactures, Fishing and Navigation* (WJ and J Richardson 1805), Vol 3.

Mons de Sorbiere, *A Voyage to England, Containing Many Things Relating to the State of Learning, Religion, and Other Curiosities* (trans J Spratt) (London 1709).

Mortimer, Thomas, *Every Man His Own Broker or a Guide to the Stock Exchange* (13th Ed, WJ and J Richardson 1801).

Parliamentary Agent, *Practical Instructions on the Passing of Private Bills through Both Houses of Parliament* (Stevens and Son 1825).

Patent Office, *Commissioner of Patents Journal* (1859), 8 April 1859, Issue 459.

Patent Office, *Commissioner of Patents Journal* (1860), 13 November 1960, Issue 716.

Patent Office, *Commissioner of Patents Journal* (1861), 17 May 1861, Issue 769.

Patent Office, *Commissioner of Patents Journal* (1867), 9 August 1867, Issue 1419.

Patent Office, *Official Journal of the Patent Office* (1884), 23 December 1884, Issue 102.

Pepys, Samuel, *The Diary of Samuel Pepys*, 23 April 1669.

Petyt, William *Jus Parliamentarium: Or the Ancient Power, Jurisdiction, Rights and Liberties or the Most High Court of Parliament* (London: John Nourse 1739), Vol 1.

Petyt, William, *Britannia languens: or, A Discourse of Trade Shewing, That the Present Management of Trade in England* . . . (London: Richard Baldwin 1689) (Wing P1947).

Philopatris, *Observations on Public Institutions, Monopolies, Joint-Stock Companies and Deeds of Trust* (JM Richardson 1807).

Phin, John, *An Exact Reprint of the Famous Century of Invention of the Marquis of Worcester* (New York: Industrial Publication Co 1887), Ch 68.

Private Acts of Parliament Selected And Approved by a Committee of the House of Lords (Stevens & Sons 1829).

Rosser, Archibald, Letter from Archibald Rosser (1835) 23 *Mechanics Magazine* 170.

Savery, Thomas, "An Account of Mr. Tho. Savery's Engine for Raising Water by the Help of Fire" (1699) 21 *Philosophical Transactions* 228.

Savery, Thomas, *The Miner's Friend: Or, an Engine to Raise Water by Fire* (1702) (Reprinted 1827, ed S. Crouch).

Scobell, Henry, *Memorials of the Method and Manner of Proceedings in Parliament on Passing Bills* (1656) (1670).

Scobell, Henry, *Remembrances of Some Methods, Orders and Proceedings of the House of Lords* (Henry Hill 1689).

Sherwood, Thomas, *A Treatise upon the Proceedings to be Adopted by Members in Conducting Private Bills* (Private 1828).

Spence, William, *Patentable Invention and Scientific Evidence: With an Introductory Preface* (London 1851).

Sturtevant, Simon, *A Treatise of Metallica* (1612) (STC: 23411).

Terrell, Courtney, *The Law and Practice Relating to Letters Patent for Inventions* (5th Ed, Sweet and Maxwell 1909).

The Trial of Richard Pepper Arden; Attorney-General v Richard Arkwright (Hughes and Walsh 1785) (ETSC: 142878).

Turner, Thomas, *Remarks on the Amendment of the Law of Patents for Inventions* (Frederic Elsworth 1851).

Walcot, Humphrey, *Sea Water Made Fresh and Wholesome* (London: Parker 1702).

Webster, Thomas, *Notes on Cases on Letters Patent for Inventions* (Thomas Blenkarn 1844).

Webster, Thomas, *On the Amendment of the Law and Practice of Letters Patent for Inventions* (2nd Ed, Chapman and Hall 1852).

Webster, Thomas, *The Law and Practice of Letters Patent for Inventions: Statutes, Practical Forms, and Digest of Reported Cases* (Crofts and Blenkard 1841).

Webster, Thomas, *The New Patent Law: Its History, Objects and Provisions* (Elsworth 1853).

Woodcroft, Bennet, *Title of Patents of Invention: Chronologically arranged 1617–1852* (London: Eyre and Spottiswoode 1854).

Young, Arthur, *Political Essays Concerning the Present State of the British Empire* (Stahan and Caddell 1772).

Books and articles

Adams, John and Averley, Gwen, "The Patent Specification: The Role of Liardet v Johnson" (1986) 7 *J Legal History* 156.

Anon, "The Steam Engine Actually Constructed and Applied to Practical Purposes" (1827) 6 *Mechanics Magazine* 515.

Appleby, John, "Charles Dingley's Sawmill, or Public Spirit at a Premium" (1995) 143 *RSA Journal* 54.

Armitage, David, *The Scottish Vision of Empire: Intellectual Origins of the Darien Venture* (Cambridge 1995).

Ashton, Robert, *The City and the Court 1603–1643* (Cambridge 1979).

Aspinall, Arthur, "The Reporting and Publishing of the House of Commons Debates 1771–1834" in Richard Areas and Taylor, Alan (AJP) (ed), *Essays Presented to Lewis Namier* (London: Macmillan 1956).

Aylmer, Gerald E, *The Struggle for the Constitution – England in the Seventeenth Century* (4th Ed, 1975).

Baker, John H, *An Introduction to English Legal History* (4th Ed, Butterworths 2002).

Beckmann, John (Trans William Johnston), *History of Invention, Discoveries, and Origins* (Bell & Son 1880), Vol 2.

Birdsall, Paul, "Non Obstante: A Study of the Dispensing Power of English Kings" in *Essays in History and Political Theory in Honour of Charles Howard McIlwain Poole* (Oxford 1929, Reprinted 1969).

Boehm, Klaus and Silberston, Aubrey, *The British Patent System: I. Administration* (Cambridge 1967).

Bottomley, Sean, "Patenting in England, Scotland and Ireland during the Industrial Revolution, 1700–1852" (2014) 54 *Explorations in Economic History* 48.

Bottomley, Sean, *The British Patent System during the Industrial Revolution 1700–1852* (Cambridge 2014).

Brown, James, "Alehouse Licensing and State Formation in Early Modern England" in *Intoxication and Society: Problematic Pleasures of Drugs and Alcohol* (ed J Herring, C Regan, D Weinberg, P Withington) (Palgrave 2012).

Burrell, Robert and Kelly, Catherine, "Parliamentary Rewards and the Evolution of the Patent System" (2015) 74 *Cam LJ* 423.

Burrell, Robert and Kelly, Catherine, "Public Rewards and Innovation Policy: Lessons from the Eighteenth and Nineteenth Centuries" (2014) 77 *MLR* 858.

Carr, Cecil, *Select Charters of Trading Companies 1530–1707* (Selden Society, 1913), Vols 1–3.

Churchill, EF, "The Dispensing Power of the Crown in Ecclesiastical Affairs – Part II" (1922) 38 *LQR* 420.

Clapperton, Robert H, *The Paper Making Machine: Its Invention, Evolution and Development* (Pergamon Press 1967).

Clarkson, Lesley A, "English Economic Policy in the Sixteenth and Seventeenth Centuries: the Case of the Leather Industries" (1965) 38 *Historic Research* 150.

Clifford, Fredrick, *A History of Private Bill Legislation* (1885) (Frank Cass 1968), Vol 1.

Clifford, Frederick, *A History of Private Legislation* (1887) (Frank Cass 1969), Vol 2.

Clow, Archibald and Clow, Nan, "Lord Dundonald" (1942) 12 *Economic History Review* 47.

Collier, Bruce and MacLachlan, James, *Charles Babbage: And the Engine of Perfection* (Oxford 1998).

Cooke, Colin, *Corporation, Trust and Company: An Essay in Legal History* (Manchester 1950).

Cooper, John P, "Economic Regulation and the Cloth Industry in Seventeenth Century England" (1970) 20 *Transactions of Royal Historical Society* (5th Ser) 73.

Corré, Jacob, "The Argument, Decision, and Reports of Darcy v. Allen" (1996) 45 *Emory Law Journal* 1261.

Coulter, Moureen, *Property in Ideas: The Patent Question in Mid-Victorian Britain* (Thomas Jefferson University Press 1991).

Crump, Charles, "Eo Quod Espressa Mentio, etc" in *Essays in History Presented to Reginald Lane Poole* (Oxford 1929, Reprinted 1969).

Deane, Phyllis, "Capital Formation in Britain before the Railway Age" (1961) 9 *Economic Development and Cultural Change* 356.

Dent, Chris, "Generally Inconvenient: The 1624 Statute of Monopolies as Political Compromise" (2009) 33 *Melbourne LR* 415.

Dickens, Charles, "A Poor Man's Tale of a Patent" (1850) 2 (3) *Household Words* 73.

Dickens, Charles, *Martin Chuzzlewit* (1844) (Penguin 1999).

Dicks, Henry, *The Life, Times and Scientific Labours of the Second Marquis of Worcester* (London: Bernard Quaritch 1865).

Digby, Roy, *The Gunpowder Plotter's Legacy* (Janus 2001).

Dixon, Dennis, "*Godden v Hales* Revisited – James II and the Dispensing Power" (2006) 27 *J Legal History* 129.

Dobbs, Betty Jo, "Studies in the Natural Philosophy of Sir Kenelm Digby: Part II: Digby and Alchemy" (1973) 20 *Ambix* 143.

Drebble, John, *The Darien Disaster* (1968) (Pimlico 2002).

Dugid, Charles, *The Story of the Stock Exchange: Its History and Position* (Grant Richards 1901).

Dutton, Harry, *The Patent System and Inventive Activity during the Industrial Revolution 1750–1852* (Manchester 1984).

Earle, Peter, *The Wreck of the Almiranta: Sir William Phips and the Search for the Hispaniola Treasure* (Macmillan 1979).

Edie, Carolyn, "Revolution and the Rule of Law: The End of the Dispensing Power, 1689" (1977) 10 *Eighteenth-Century Studies* 434.

Fellmann, Emil A, *Leonhard Euler* (Springer 2007).

Fernie, J Donald, "Harrison-Maskelyne Affair" (2003) 91 *American Scientist* 403.

Firth, Charles H and Rait, Robert S, *Acts and Ordinances of the Interregnum, 1642–1660* (London 1911).

Fisher, Matthew, "The Case That Launched a Thousand Writs, or All That Is Dross? Re-conceiving Darcy v Allen: the Case of Monopolies" [2010] *IPQ* 356.

Fisher, Matthew, *Fundamentals of Patent Law: Interpretation and Scope of Protection* (Hart 2007).

Flemion, J Stoddart, "Slow Process, Due Process and the High Court of Parliament: A Reinterpretation of the Revival of Judicature in the House of Lords 1621" (1974) 17(1) *Historical Journal* 3.

Forbes, Eric, "Tobias Mayer's Claim for the Longitude Prize: A Study in 18th Century Anglo-German Relations" (1975) 28 *Journal of Navigation* 77.

Forbes, Robert, *A Short History of the Art of Distillation* (Brill 1942).

Forbes, Robert, *Life-boats, Projectiles and Other Means for Saving Life* (Boston 1872).

Foster, Elizabeth Read, *The House of Lords 1603–1649: Structure, Procedure, and the Nature of Its Business* (North Carolina Press 1983).

Foster, Elizabeth Read, "The House of Lords and Ordinances 1641–1649" (1977) *Am J Legal History* 158.

Foster, Elizabeth Read, "The Painful Labour of Mr. Elsyng" (1972) 62 *Transactions of the American Philosophical Society* 1.

Foster, Elizabeth Read, "The Procedure of the House of Commons against Patents and Monopolies, 1621–1624" in *Conflict in Stuart England: Essays in Honour of Wallace Notestein* (ed William Appleton Aiken and Basil Duke Henning) (Jonathan Cape 1960).

Fox, Harold G, *Monopolies and Patents: A Study of the History of Future of the Patent Monopoly* (Toronto 1947).

Frehen, Rik, Goetzmann, William N and Rouwenhorst, K Geert, "New Evidence on the First Financial Bubble" (2013) 108 *Journal of Financial Economics* 585.

Gomez-Arostegui, Tomas, "Copyright at Common Law in 1774" (2014) 47 *Connecticut Law Review* 1.

Gomme, Arthur A, *Patents of Invention: Origin and Growth of the Patent System in Britain* (1946).

Gordon, John W, *Monopolies by Patents and the Statutory Remedies Available to the Public* (Stevens 1897).

Gould, Rupert, "John Harrison and His Timekeepers" (1935) 31 *The Mariner's Mirror* 2.

Goulden, RJ, "Koops, Matthias (fl. 1789–1805)" in *Oxford Dictionary of National Biography*, Vol 32 (Oxford 2004), pp 80–81.

Gower, LCB, "A South Sea Heresy?" (1952) 68 *LQR* 214.

Grainger, John, *Cromwell against the Scots: The Last Anglo-Scottish War 1650–52* (Tuckwell Press 1997).

Greenberg, Daniel (ed), *Craies on Legislation* (11th Ed, Sweet and Maxwell 2017).

Grupp, Stanley, "Some Historical Aspects of the Pardon in England" (1963) 7 *American J of Legal History* 51.

Hales, Stephen, *Philosophical Experiments* (Innys and Manby: London 1739).

Harling, Philip, *The Waning of 'Old Corruption': The Politics of Economical Reform in Britain, 1779–1846* (Clarendon 1996).

Harris, Ron, "The Bubble Act: Its Passage and Its Effects on Business Organization" (1994) 54(3) *Journal of Economic History* 610.

Harris, Ron *Industrializing English Law: Entrepreneurship and Business Organization 1720–1844* (Cambridge 2000).

Harris, Tim, "The People, the Law, and the Constitution in Scotland and England: A Comparative Approach to the Glorious Revolution" (1999) 38 *Journal of British Studies* 28.

Haselgrove, Dennis, "Steps towards English Stoneware Manufacture in the 17th Century Part 1 – 1600–1650 (1989) 6 *London Archaeologist* 132.

Henry, Barbara *The Development of the Patent System in Britain, 1829–51* (Unpublished Ph D, Queen's University 2012).

Holdsworth, William, *A History of English Law* (2nd Ed Sweet 1937), Vol 6.

Holdsworth, William, *A History of English Law* (3rd Ed, Sweet and Maxwell 1945), Vol 4.

Howe, Derek, "Britain's Board of Longitude: The Finances 1714–1828" (1998) 84(4) *The Mariner's Mirror* 400.

Hunt, Bishop, *The Development of the Business Corporation in England 1800–1867* (Harvard 1936).

Hyman, Anthony, *Charles Babbage: Pioneer of the Computer* (Princeton 1982).

Ilbert, Courtenay, "The English Statute Book" (1900) 2 *Journal of the Society of Comparative Legislation* 75.

Innes, Joanna, "The Local Acts of a National Parliament: Parliament's Role in Sanctioning Local Action in Eighteenth-Century Britain" (1998) 17 *Parliamentary History* 2.

Jack, Sir Malcolm (ed), *Erskine May's Treatise on the Law, Privileges, Proceedings and Usage of Parliament* (24th Ed, LexisNexis 2011).

Jenkins, Rhys, "The Protection of Inventions during the Commonwealth and Protectorate" (1913) 11 S-VII *Notes and Queries* 163.

Jewitt, Llewellynn, *The Wedgwoods: Being a Life of Josiah Wedgwood* (London: Virtue Bros 1865).

Johnson, Phillip, "The Myth of Mr Burke and Mr Watt: For Want of a Champion!" (2016) 6 *Queen Mary Journal of Intellectual Property* 370.

Jones, Dwyryd, *War and Economy: In the Age of William II and Marlborough* (Blackwell 1988).

Keith, Theodora, *Commercial Relations of England and Scotland 1603–1707* (Cambridge 1910).

Keith, Theodora, "Economic Condition of Scotland under the Commonwealth and the Protectorate" (1908) 5 *Scottish Historical Review* 273.

Kelly, James, "The Private Bill Legislation of the Irish Parliament 1692–1800" (2014) 33 *Parliamentary History* 73.

Kelsall, Frank, "Liardet versus Adam" (1984) 27 *Architectural History* 118.

Kyle, Chris, "But a New Button to an Old Coat: The Enactment of the Statute of Monopolies 21 James I cap 3" (1998) 19 *Journal of Legal History* 203.

Kyle, Chris, "Introduction" to *Parliament, Politics and Elections 1604–1648* (2001) 17 Camden Society (Fifth Series).

Kyle, Chris, "Prince Charles in the Parliaments of 1621 and 1624" (1998) 41 *Historical Journal* 603.

Lambert, Sheila, *Bills and Acts: Legislative Procedure in Eighteenth-Century England* (Cambridge 1971).

Lepler, Jessica M, *The Many Panics of 1837: People, Politics, and the Creation of a Transatlantic Financial Crisis* (Cambridge 2014).

Letwin, William, "The English Common Law Concerning Monopolies" (1954) 21 *U Chicago LR* 355.

Lewis, James, *An Historical Account of the Rise and Progress of Short Hand* (London 1839).

Longueville, Thomas, *The Life of Sir Kenelm Digby* (Longman 1896).

Lowe, Rodney, *The Official History of the British Civil Service: Reforming the Civil Service, Volume 1: The Fulton Years 1966–81* (Routledge 2011).

Lowe, William, "Peers and Printers: The Beginnings of Sustained Press Coverage of the House of Lords in the 1770s" (1988) 7 *Parliamentary History* 241.

Macaulay, Thomas, *Macaulay's History of England* (Dent and Son 1906), Vol 2.

MacDonald, Alan R, "Deliberative Processes in Parliament, c.1567–1639: Multicameralism and the Lords of the Articles" (2002) 81 *Scottish Historical Review* 23.

Machlup, Fritz and Penrose, Edith, "The Patent Controversy in the Nineteenth Century" (1950) 10 *Journal of Economic History* 1.

McIlwain, Charles, *The High Court of Parliament and its Supremacy* (Yale 1910).

MacLeod, Christine, *Heroes of Invention: Technology, Liberalism and British Identity, 1750–1914* (Cambridge 2007).

MacLeod, Christine, *Inventing the Industrial Revolution: The English Patent System 1660–1800* (Cambridge 1988).

MacLeod, Christine, "The 1690s Patents Boom: Invention or Stock-Jobbing?" (1986) 39 *Economic History Review* 549.

MacNaulty, Arthur, "Edward Bancroft, MD FRS and the War of American Independence" (1944) 38 *Proceeding of Royal Society of Medicine* 7.

Maddison, Robert, "Studies in the Life of R Boyle, FRS: Part II Salt Water Freshened" (1952) *Notes and Records of Royal Society* 196.

Maitland, Frederic, *Constitutional History of England* (Cambridge 1919).

Maitland, Frederic, "The Unincorporate Body" *The Collected Papers of Frederic William Maitland*, Vol 3 (Cambridge 1911).

Maitland, Frederic, "Trust and Corporations" in *The Collected Papers of Frederic William Maitland* Vol 3 (Cambridge 1911).

Maxwell-Lyte, Sir Henry, *Historical Notes on the Use of the Great Seal of England* (HMSO 1926).

Mendle, Michael, "The Great Council of Parliament and the First Ordinances: The Constitutional Theory of the Civil War" (1992) 31 *Journal of British Studies* 133.

Mostoff, Adam, "Rethinking the Development of Patents: An Intellectual History, 1550–1800" (2001) 52 *Hastings LJ* 1255.

Murphy, Anne L, *The Origins of the English Financial Markets* (Cambridge 2009).

Neale, Sir John, *The Elizabethan House of Commons* (Penguin 1949).

Newton, AP, "The Establishment of the Great Farm of the English Customs" (1918) 1 *Transactions of Royal Historical Society* 129.

O'Dell, Thomas, *Inventions and Secrecy: A History of Secret Patents in the United Kingdom* (Clarendon 1994).

Officer, Lawrence and Williamson, Samuel, "Five Ways to Compute the Relative Value of a UK Pound Amount, 1270 to Present," MeasuringWorth 2017.

Oldham, James, *English Common Law in the Age of Mansfield* (North Carolina Press 2004).

Oldham, James, *The Mansfield Manuscripts and the Growth of English Law in the Eighteenth Century* (North Carolina Press 1992), Vol 1.

Owen, Hugh, *Two Centuries of Ceramic Art in Bristol* (Bell and Daldy 1873).

Partington, Charles, *A Century of Invention from the Original MS* (John Murray, 1825).

Pawson, Eric, *The Early Industrial Revolution: Britain in the Eighteenth Century* (Basford 1979).

Perceval, Robert W, "Chapter Six, VI, vi, 6 or 6: The Classification and Recording of Acts" (1949) 13 *Parliamentary Affairs* 506.

Phillips, Jeremy, *Charles Dickens and the Poor Man's Tale of a Patent* (ESC 1984).

Pinckney, Paul, "The Scottish Representation in the Cromwellian Parliament of 1656" (1967) 46 *Scottish Historical Review* 95.

Plumb, John, *England in the Eighteenth Century* (Penguin 1968).

Pollard, Albert F, *The Evolution of Parliament* (Longmans 1920).

Price, William Hyde, *The English Patents of Monopoly* (Houghton, Mifflin & Co 1906).

Pugh, Ralph B, "The Patent Rolls of the Interregnum (1950) 23 *Historical Research* 178.

Redlich, Josef (trans Ernest Steinhal), *The Procedure of the House of Commons: A Study of Its History and Present Form* (Archibald & Constable 1903).

Ricketson, Samuel, *The Paris Convention for the Protection of Industrial Property* (Oxford 2015).

Rix, Kathryn, "'Whatever Passed in Parliament Ought to Be Communicated to the Public': Reporting the Proceedings of the Reformed Commons, 1833–1850" (2014) 33 *Parliamentary History* 453.

Robinson, Eric, "Matthew Boulton and the Art of Parliamentary Lobbying" (1964) 7 *Historical Journal* 209.

Rydz, David L, *The Parliamentary Agents: A History* (Royal Historical Society 1979).

Schaeper, Thomas, *Edward Bancroft: Scientist, Author and Spy* (Yale 2011).

Scott, William, "Scottish Industrial Undertakings before the Union" (1904) 1 *Scottish Historical Review* 407.

Scott, William, "Scottish Industrial Undertakings before the Union: II The Scots Linen Manufacture" (1904) 2 *Scottish Historical Review* 53.

Scott, William, "Scottish Industrial Undertakings before the Union: III The Textile Group" (1905) 2 *Scottish Historical Review* 287.

Scott, William, "Scottish Industrial Undertakings before the Union: IV The Wool-Card Manufactory at Leith" (1905) 2 *Scottish Historical Review* 406.

Scott, William, "Scottish Industrial Undertakings before the Union: V The Society of White-Writing and Printing Paper Manufactory of Scotland" (1905) 3 *Scottish Historical Review* 71.

Scott, William, *The Constitution and Finance of English, Scottish and Irish Joint Stock Companies* (Cambridge 1911), Vols 1–3.

Scott, William, "The Fiscal Policy of Scotland before the Union" (1904) 1 *Scottish Historical Review* 173.

Seaborne Davies, David, "Further Light on the Case of Monopolies" (1932) 48 *LQR* 394.

Seaborne Davies, David, "The Early History of the Patent Specification" (1934) 50 *LQR* 86 and 260.

Sharpe, Reginald, *London and the Kingdom* (Longmans 1894), Vol 2.

Sherman, Brad, "Towards a History of Patent Law" in *Intellectual Property in Common Law and Civil Law* (ed Toshiko Takenaka) (Edward Elgar 2013).

Sherman, Brad and Bently, Lionel, *Making of Modern Intellectual Property Law* (Cambridge 1999).

Sobel, Dava, *Longitude* (Harper 2005).

Spencer, Frederick, *Municipal Origins: An Account of English Private Bill Legislation Relating to Local Government 1740–1835* (Constable & Co 1911).

Stevenson, David (ed), *The Government of Scotland under the Covenanter 1637–1651* (Scottish History Society 1982).

Strateman, Catherine (ed), *The Liverpool Tractate: An Eighteenth Century Manual on the Procedure of the House of Commons* (Columbia 1937).

Sullivan, Richard, "England's 'Age of Invention': The Acceleration of Patents and Patentable Invention during the Industrial Revolution" (1989) 26 *Explorations in Economic History* 424.

Tanner, Roland, "The Lords of the Articles before 1540: A Reassessment" (2000) 79 *Scottish Historical Review* 189.

Taylor, James, *Creating Capitalism: Joint-Stock Enterprise in British Politics and Culture, 1800–1870* (Royal Historical Society 2006).

Terry, Charles, *The Scottish Parliament: Its Constitution and Procedure 1603–1707* (James MacLehose: Glasgow 1905).

Thomas, Peter, "The Beginning of Parliamentary Reporting in Newspapers 1768–1774" (1959) 74 *English Historical Review* 623.

Thorpe, John, *The Worshipful Company of Makers of Playing Cards of the City of London* (Playing Card Company 2001).

Tite, Colin, *Impeachment and Parliamentary Judicature in Early Stuart England* (Athlone Press 1974).

Tosney, Nicholas, "The Playing Card Trade in Early Modern England" (2011) 84 *Historical Research* 637.

Trewin, John C and King, Evelyn M, *Printer to the House: The Story of Hansard* (Methuen & Co 1952).

Trollope, Anthony, *The Three Clerks* (1858) (Penguin 1993).

Underdown Peter T, "Burke's Bristol Friends" (1958) 77 *Transactions of the Bristol and Gloucestershire Archaeological Society* 127.

Unwin, George, *The Gilds and Companies of London* (Methuen & Co 1908).

Ure, Andrew, *A Dictionary of Arts, Manufactures and Mines* (New York 1842).

US Attorney General, *The Attorney General's Survey of Release Procedures, Pardon, Volume III* (United States Government 1939).

Walterscheid, Edward C, "The Early Evolution of the United States Patent Law: Antecedents" (Part 3) (1995) 77 *J Patent and Trademark Office Society* 847.

Watt, Douglas, *The Price of Scotland: Darien, Union and the Wealth of Nations* (Luath Press 2007).

White, Stephen D, *Sir Edward Coke and "The Grievances of the Commonwealth": 1621–1628* (North Carolina Press 1979).

Wilkinson, JJ, "Historical Account of Wood Sheathing for Ships" (1842) 36 *Mechanics Magazine* 403.

Williams, Orlo, *The Clerical Organization of the House of Commons* (Oxford 1954).

Williams, Orlo, *The Historical Development of Private Bill Procedure and Standing Orders in the House of Commons* (HMSO 1948), Vols 1 and 2.

Wood, Edward, *Curiosities of Clocks and Watches: From the Earliest Times* (Richard Bently 1866).

Wyndham Hulme, Edward, "On the Consideration of the Patent Grant Past and Present" (1897) 13 *LQR* 313.

Wyndham Hulme, Edward, "Privy Council Law and Practice of Letters Patent for Invention from the Restoration to 1794" (1917) 33 *LQR* 63.

Wyndham Hulme, Edward, "The History of the Patent System under the Prerogative and at Common Law" (1896) 12 *LQR* 141.

Index

For Product Safety Concerns and Information please contact our EU
representative GPSR@taylorandfrancis.com
Taylor & Francis Verlag GmbH, Kaufingerstraße 24, 80331 München, Germany

www.ingramcontent.com/pod-product-compliance
Ingram Content Group UK Ltd.
Pitfield, Milton Keynes, MK11 3LW, UK
UKHW051832180425
457613UK00022B/1213